LETTERS ON YOGA

Volume I

Sri Aurobindo

Letters on Yoga

Volume I

Sri Aurobindo Ashram
Pondicherry

First edition 1958
Fourth edition (revised and enlarged) 2012
Third impression 2020

Rs 320
ISBN 978-81-7058-953-2

© Sri Aurobindo Ashram Trust 1958, 2012
Published by Sri Aurobindo Ashram Publication Department
Pondicherry 605 002
Web https://www.sabda.in

Printed at Sri Aurobindo Ashram Press, Pondicherry
PRINTED IN INDIA

Publisher's Note

Letters on Yoga — I comprises letters written by Sri Aurobindo on the philosophical and psychological foundations of the Integral Yoga. It is the first of four volumes of *Letters on Yoga*, arranged by the editors as follows:
 I. Foundations of the Integral Yoga
 II. Practice of the Integral Yoga
 III. Experiences and Realisations in the Integral Yoga
 IV. Transformation of Human Nature in the Integral Yoga

The letters in these volumes have been selected from the large body of letters that Sri Aurobindo wrote to disciples and others between 1927 and 1950. Other letters from this period are published in *Letters on Poetry and Art* and *Letters on Himself and the Ashram*, volumes 27 and 35 of THE COMPLETE WORKS OF SRI AUROBINDO. Letters written before 1927 are reproduced in *Autobiographical Notes and Other Writings of Historical Interest*, volume 36 of THE COMPLETE WORKS.

During Sri Aurobindo's lifetime, relatively few of his letters were published. Three small books of letters on Yoga were brought out in the 1930s. A more substantial collection came out between 1947 and 1951 in a four-volume series entitled *Letters of Sri Aurobindo* (including one volume of letters on poetry and literature). In 1958, many more letters were included in the two large tomes of *On Yoga — II*. A further expanded collection in three volumes entitled *Letters on Yoga* was published in 1970 as part of the Sri Aurobindo Birth Centenary Library. The present collection, also entitled *Letters on Yoga*, constitutes volumes 28 – 31 of THE COMPLETE WORKS. These volumes incorporate previously published letters and contain many new ones as well. About one-third of the letters in the present volume were not published in the Centenary Library.

The present volume is arranged by subject in five parts:
1. The Divine, the Cosmos and the Individual
2. The Parts of the Being and the Planes of Consciousness
3. The Evolutionary Process and the Supermind
4. Problems of Philosophy, Science, Religion and Society
5. Questions of Spiritual and Occult Knowledge

The texts of all letters have been checked against the available manuscripts, typescripts and printed versions.

CONTENTS

PART ONE
THE DIVINE, THE COSMOS AND THE INDIVIDUAL

Section One
The Divine, Sachchidananda, Brahman and Atman

The Divine and Its Aspects
The Divine	5
The Divine Consciousness	5
The Divine: One in All	6
Aspects of the Divine	7
The Transcendent, Cosmic and Individual Divine	7
Personal and Impersonal Sides of the Divine	11
The Divine and the Atman	12
The Divine and the Supermind	12

Sachchidananda: Existence, Consciousness-Force and Bliss
Sachchidananda	13
Sat or Pure Existence	14
Chit or Consciousness	14
Outer Consciousness and Inner Consciousness	19
Consciousness and Force or Energy	24
Force, Energy, Power, Shakti	25
Ananda	27

Brahman
The Impersonal Brahman	28
The Inactive Brahman and the Active Brahman	28
Spirit and Life	29

The Self or Atman
The Self	30
The Cosmic Spirit or Self	30
The Atman, the Soul and the Psychic Being	31
The Self and Nature or Prakriti	32

CONTENTS

Section Two
The Cosmos: Terms from Indian Systems

The Upanishadic and Puranic Systems
Virat	37
Visva or Virat, Hiranyagarbha or Taijasa, Prajna or Ishwara	37
Vaisvanara, Taijasa, Prajna, Kutastha	38
Karana, Hiranyagarbha, Virat	38
The Seven Worlds	38
The Worlds of the Lower Hemisphere	39
Tapoloka and the Worlds of Tapas	39

The Sankhya-Yoga System
Purusha	40
Purusha and Prakriti	41
Prakriti	43
Prakriti and Shakti or Chit-Shakti	44
Purusha, Prakriti and Action	45
The Gunas or Qualities of Nature	46
Transformation of the Gunas	47
Sattwa and Liberation	48
Transformation of Rajas and Tamas	48
Transformation of Tamas into *Sama*	49
Mahat	50
Tanmatra	51

Section Three
The Jivatman and the Psychic Being

The Jivatman in the Integral Yoga
The Jivatman or Individual Self	55
The Jivatman, the Psychic Being and Prakriti	56
The Central Being and the Psychic Being	60
The Surrender of the Central Being	61
The Central Being after Liberation	62
The Karana Purusha	62
The Jivatman and the *Caitya Puruṣa*	62

CONTENTS

The Jivatman and the Mental Purusha	62
The Jivatman, Spark-Soul and Psychic Being	64
The Jivatman in a Supramental Creation	66

The Jivatman in Other Indian Systems
The Jivatman in Other Schools	68
The Jivatman and the Pure "I" of the Adwaita	68

PART TWO
THE PARTS OF THE BEING AND THE PLANES OF CONSCIOUSNESS

Section One
The Organisation of the Being

The Parts of the Being
Men Do Not Know Themselves	79
Many Parts, Many Personalities	80

Classification of the Parts of the Being
Different Categories in Different Systems	82
The Concentric and Vertical Systems	82

Section Two
The Concentric System: Outer to Inner

The Outer Being and the Inner Being
The Outer and the Inner Being and Consciousness	89
The Inner, the Outer and the Process of Yoga	91
The Inner Being	93
The Inner Being, the Antaratma and the Atman	93
The Inner Being and the Psychic Being	93
The Outer Being and Consciousness	95

The True Being and the True Consciousness
The True Being	97
The True Consciousness	99

CONTENTS

The Psychic Being
- The Psychic and the Divine — 102
- The Self or Spirit and the Psychic or Soul — 105
- The Atman, the Jivatman and the Psychic — 106
- The Words "Soul" and "Psychic" — 109
- The Psychic or Soul and Traditional Indian Systems — 110
- The Soul and the Psychic Being — 114
- The Form of the Psychic Being — 119
- The Psychic Being and the Intuitive Consciousness — 120
- The Psychic Being and the External Being — 120
- The Psychic or Soul and the Lower Nature — 121
- The Psychic Being or Soul and the Vital or Life — 123
- The Psychic Being and the Ego — 124
- The Psychic World or Plane — 124

Section Three
The Vertical System: Supermind to Subconscient

The Planes or Worlds of Consciousness
- The System of Planes or Worlds — 127
- The Planes and the Body — 132

The Supermind or Supramental
- Supermind and the Purushottama — 133
- Supermind and Sachchidananda — 133
- The Supracosmic, the Supramental, the Overmind and Nirvana — 137
- Supermind and Other Planes — 144
- Supermind and Overmind — 146
- Knowledge and Will in the Supermind — 151

The Overmind
- Overmind and the Cosmic Consciousness — 152
- Planes of the Overmind — 153
- The Overmind, the Intuition and Below — 154
- The Overmind and the Supermind Descent — 155
- The Overmind and the *Kāraṇa Deha* — 155
- The Dividing Aspect of the Overmind — 155

CONTENTS

    The Overmind and the World   156

The Higher Planes of Mind
    The Higher Planes and Higher Consciousness   158
    The Plane of Intuition   159
    The Plane of Intuition and the Intuitive Mind   161
    Yogic Intuition and Ordinary Intuitions   162
    Powers of the Intuitive Consciousness   163
    The Illumined Mind   164
    The Higher Mind   164

The Lower Nature or Lower Hemisphere
    The Higher Nature and the Lower Nature   166
    The Three Planes of the Lower Hemisphere
        and Their Energies   166
    The Adhara   167

The Mind
    Mind in the Integral Yoga and in Other
        Indian Systems   168
    Manas and Buddhi   169
    Chitta   170
    Western Ideas of Mind and Spirit   173
    The Psychic Mind   177
    The Mind Proper   177
    The Thinking Mind and the Vital Mind   178
    The Thinking Mind and the Physical Mind   179
    The Vital Mind   179
    The Physical Mind   181
    The Physical Mental or Physical Mind and
        the Mental Physical or Mechanical Mind   182
    The Mental World of the Individual   184

The Vital Being and Vital Consciousness
    The Vital   185
    The True Vital Being and Consciousness   185
    Parts of the Vital Being   187
    The Mental Vital or Vital Mind   189

CONTENTS

The Emotional Being or Heart	193
The Central Vital or Vital Proper	193
The Lower Vital, the Physical Vital and the Material Vital	195
A Strong Vital	196
The Vital Body	197
The Vital Nature	197
The Vital Plane and the Physical Plane	197
The Life Heavens	198

The Physical Consciousness

The Physical Consciousness and Its Parts	200
Living in the Physical Consciousness	206
The Opening of the Physical Consciousness	206
The True Activity of the Senses	207
The Physical Parts of the Mind and Emotional Being	207
The Mental Physical or Mechanical Mind	207
The Vital Physical	208
The Material Consciousness or Body Consciousness	209
The Gross Physical and the Subtle Physical	210
The Physical Nerves and the Subtle Nerves	211
The Sheaths of the Indian Tradition	212

The Environmental Consciousness

The Environmental Consciousness around the Individual	213
The Environmental Consciousness and the Movements of the Lower Nature	214
The Environmental Consciousness and the Subconscient	215

The Subconscient and the Inconscient

The Subconscient in the Integral Yoga	216
The Subconscient in Traditional Indian Terminology	222
The Subconscient and the Superconscient	223
The Subconscient and the Subliminal	223
The Subconscient Memory and Conscious Memory	223

CONTENTS

    The Subconscient and the Inconscient   225

Section Four
The Chakras or Centres of Consciousness

The System of the Chakras
    The Functions of the Chakras or Centres   229
    The Chakras in Reference to Yoga   231
    The Centres and the Planes   233
    The Mind Centres   234
    The Sahasradala or Sahasrara or Crown Centre   235
    The Ajnachakra or Forehead Centre   237
    The Throat Centre   239
    The Throat Centre and the Lower Centres   240
    The Heart Centre   241
    The Navel and Abdominal Centres   242
    The Muladhara   242
    No Subconscient Centre   244

The Parts of the Body and the Centres
    The Parts of the Body in Yoga   245
    The Cerebellum   245
    The Ear, Nose, Face and Throat   245
    The Chest, Stomach and Abdomen   246
    The Legs and Feet   247
    The Sides of the Body   247

PART THREE
THE EVOLUTIONARY PROCESS AND THE SUPERMIND

Section One
The Supramental Evolution

The Problem of Suffering and Evil
    The Riddle of This World   253
    The Disharmonies of Earth   262

CONTENTS

Spiritual Evolution and the Supramental
Human History and Spiritual Evolution — 265
Spiritual and Supramental — 273
The Overmind and the Supramental — 274
Involution and Evolution — 275
The Supermind and the Lower Creation — 279
Speculations about the Supramental Descent — 280

Section Two
The Supramental Descent and Transformation

The Descent of the Supermind
Inevitability of the Descent — 287
A Beginning, Not a Completion — 288
Clarifications about the Supramental Descent — 292

Descent and Transformation
A World-Changing Yoga — 294
The Vital World and the Supramental Descent — 297
The Nature and Scope of the Transformation — 297
The Earth, the Earth Consciousness and
 the Supramental Creation — 298
The Supramental Change and the Ananda Plane — 299

The Supramental Transformation
Preparatory Steps towards the Supramental Change — 301
The Supramental Influence and Supramentalisation — 301
Premature Claims of Possession of the Supermind — 303

Transformation and the Body
The Transformation of the Body — 305
The Transformation of the Body in Other Traditions — 306
Transforming the Body Consciousness — 309
Death and the Supramental Transformation — 310
The Conquest of Death — 312
The Reproductive Method of the Supramental — 315

CONTENTS

PART FOUR
PROBLEMS OF PHILOSOPHY, SCIENCE, RELIGION AND SOCIETY

Section One
Thought, Philosophy, Science and Yoga

The Intellect and Yoga
Intellectual Truth and Spiritual Experience	321
Intellectual Arguments against Spirituality	324
The Valley of the False Glimmer	330

Doubt and Faith
Doubt and Yoga	337
Faith in Spiritual Things	348

Philosophical Thought and Yoga
Metaphysical Thinkers, East and West	351
World-Circumstances and the Divine	355
Intellectual Expression of Spiritual Experience	357
Comments on Thoughts of J. M. E. McTaggart	368
Comments on Terms Used by Henri Bergson	374
Metaphysics, Science and Spiritual Experience	375

Science and Yoga
Science, Yoga and the Agnostic	380
Science and Spirituality	381
Science and the Supernormal	385
Science and Superstition	388
The Limitations of Science	391
Physics and Metaphysics	395
Space and Time	401
Matter	404
Animals	406
Plants	407
Life on Other Planets	408

CONTENTS

Section Two
Religion, Idealism, Morality and Yoga

Religion and Yoga
Religion and the Truth — 411
Religion in India — 412
Religious Ceremonies — 413
Religious Fanaticism — 415

Idealism and Spirituality
Human Perfection and Spirituality — 416
The Collapse of Twentieth-Century Idealism — 417

Morality and Yoga
The Spiritual Life and the Ordinary Life — 419
Morality — 422
Vice and Virtue — 423
The Sattwic Man and the Spiritual Man — 424
Selfishness and Unselfishness — 428
Humility — 429
Sacrifice — 432
Ahimsa, Destruction and Violence — 434
War and Conquest — 436
Poverty — 437
Natural Calamities — 437

Social Duties and the Divine
Family, Society, Country and the Divine — 438
Philanthropy — 441
Humanitarianism — 441
Social and Political Activism — 444

CONTENTS

PART FIVE
QUESTIONS OF SPIRITUAL AND OCCULT KNOWLEDGE

Section One
The Divine and the Hostile Powers

Terminology
- The Dynamic Divine, the Gods, the Asuras — 449
- The Soul, the Divine, the Gods, the Asuras — 449
- Terms in *The Mother* — 450

The Gods
- The Gods or Divine Powers — 456
- The Gods and the Overmind — 457
- Vedic Gods of the Indian Tradition — 458
- Post-Vedic Gods of the Indian Tradition — 459

The Hostile Forces and Hostile Beings
- The Existence of the Hostile Forces — 461
- The Nature of the Hostile Forces — 463
- The Conquest of the Hostile Forces — 464
- Asuras, Rakshasas and Other Vital Beings — 465

Section Two
The Avatar and the Vibhuti

The Meaning and Purpose of Avatarhood
- The Avatar or Incarnation — 471
- The Divine and Human Sides of the Avatar — 472
- Human Judgments of the Divine — 474
- The Work of the Avatar — 476
- The Avatar: Historicity and Symbols — 478
- The Avatar and the Vibhuti — 485

Specific Avatars and Vibhutis
- The Ten Avatars as a Parable of Evolution — 487
- Rama as an Avatar — 489
- Krishna as an Avatar — 499
- Buddha as an Avatar — 500

CONTENTS

Mahomed and Christ — 501
Ramakrishna — 501
Augustus Caesar and Leonardo da Vinci — 502
Napoleon — 502

Human Greatness
Greatness — 504
Greatness and Vices — 505

Section Three
Destiny, Karma, Death and Rebirth

Fate, Free Will and Prediction
Destiny — 509
Free Will and Determinism — 510
Predictions and Prophecy — 515
Astrology and Yoga — 519

Karma and Heredity
Karma — 520
Karma and Heredity — 521
Evolution, Karma and Ethics — 522

Death
Death and Karma — 526
Death and Grieving — 528
The After-Death Sojourn — 529

Rebirth
The Psychic's Choice at the Time of Death — 532
Assimilation in the Psychic World — 533
The Psychic Being and the Progression from Life to Life — 536
The New Birth — 541
Reincarnation and Soul Evolution — 542
What Survives and What Does Not — 544
Lines of Force and Consciousness — 546
Beings of the Higher Planes — 547
Fragments of a Dead Person that Reincarnate — 547

CONTENTS

Connections from Life to Life   548
Lines of Sex in Rebirth   548
Asuric Births   549
Animals and the Process of Rebirth   550
Remembering Past Lives   551
Unimportance of Past-Life Experience in Yoga   552
Speculating about Past Lives   553
Traditional Indian Ideas about Rebirth and
    Other Worlds   554
European Resistance to the Idea of Reincarnation   554

Section Four
Occult Knowledge and Powers

Occult Knowledge
Occultism and the Supraphysical   559
Occult Forces   559
The Play of Forces   560
The Place of Occult Knowledge in Yoga   565
Spiritism   567
Séances   568
Ghosts   569

Occult Powers or Siddhis
General Remarks   571
Occult Powers Not the Object of Our Yoga   573
Ethical Rules for the Use of Occult Powers   577
Thought Reception and Thought Reading   577
Occult Powers and Health   578
The Power of Healing   579
Miracles   580
Magic   580

NOTE ON THE TEXTS   581

Part One

The Divine, the Cosmos and the Individual

Section One

The Divine, Sachchidananda, Brahman and Atman

Chapter One

The Divine and Its Aspects

The Divine

The Divine is the Supreme Truth because it is the Supreme Being from whom all have come and in whom all are.

*

The Divine is that from which all comes, in which all lives, and to return to the truth of the Divine now clouded over by Ignorance is the soul's aim in life. In its supreme Truth, the Divine is absolute and infinite peace, consciousness, existence, power and Ananda.

*

The Divine is everywhere on all the planes of consciousness seen by us in different ways and aspects of his being. But there is a Supreme which is above all these planes and ways and aspects and from which they come.

*

The Divine is neither personal nor impersonal, formless nor formed. He is the Divine. You talk of these distinctions as if they separated the Divine into so many separate Divines which have nothing to do with each other.

The Divine Consciousness

By the Divine Consciousness we mean the spiritual consciousness to which the Divine alone exists, because all is the Divine and by which one passes beyond the Ignorance and the lower nature into unity with the Divine and the Divine Nature.
    Here in the Ignorance we are not aware of the Divine and we obey the lower nature.

*

All that is true Truth is the direct expression in one way or another of the Divine Consciousness. Life is the dynamic expression of Consciousness-Force when thrown outward to realise itself in concrete harmonies of formation; Love is an intense self-expression of the soul of Ananda, and Light is what always accompanies the Supramental Consciousness and its most essential power.

The Divine: One in All

The Divine is everywhere and in all — but this is a world of Ignorance in which each one is separated from the Divine within him by his ego and he acts according to the ego and not according to the Divine. When he sees the Divine in all, then he begins to have the right consciousness and be free.

*

All things are the Divine because the Divine is there, but hidden not manifest; when the mind goes out to things, it is not with the sense of the Divine in them, but for the appearances only which conceal the Divine. It is necessary therefore for you as a sadhak to turn entirely to the Mother in whom the Divine is manifest and not run after the appearances, the desire of which or the interest in which prevents you from meeting the Divine. Once the being is consecrated, then it can see the Divine everywhere — and then it can include all things in the one consciousness without a separate interest or desire.

*

Wherever the Divine is, everything is — it is only concealed, not non-existent. The Divine is there below in the inconscience itself — mind and life are concealed in Matter, so is Supermind and Sachchidananda. The below is not something outside the Divine Existence. But as mind manifested in Matter only after the descent of Mind opened it into creation, so it is with Supermind.

Aspects of the Divine

The Divine is infinite and a single experience or poise of experience cannot exhaust all the truth of the Divine. The seers have experienced each some aspect or aspects of the Divine Reality. Their mental differences have been illustrated in the apologue of the blind men who all felt the elephant and described it in different figures according to the part they felt. One must go beyond mind altogether, even beyond the spiritualised mind, to have the real complete experience. "Rare", says Sri Krishna, "are the few among the seekers who know me in my totality in all the truth of my being." In fact, it is only in the supramental light that all opposition disappears and the aspects are indivisibly united in the Whole. One must go on enlarging knowledge, adding experience to experience till all the limitation disappears.

The Transcendent, Cosmic and Individual Divine

The Divine has three aspects for us:

1. It is the Cosmic Self and Spirit that is in and behind all things and beings, from which and in which all is manifested in the universe — although it is now a manifestation in the Ignorance.

2. It is the Spirit and Master of our own being within us whom we have to serve and learn to express his will in all our movements so that we may grow out of the Ignorance into the Light.

3. The Divine is transcendent Being and Spirit, all bliss and light and divine knowledge and power, and towards that highest divine existence and its Light we have to rise and bring down the reality of it more and more into our consciousness and life.

In the ordinary nature we live in the Ignorance and do not know the Divine. The forces of the ordinary nature are undivine forces because they weave a veil of ego and desire and unconsciousness which conceals the Divine from us. To get into the higher and deeper consciousness which knows and lives consciously in the Divine, we have to get rid of the forces of the lower nature and open to the action of the Divine Shakti which will transform our consciousness into that of the Divine Nature.

This is the conception of the Divine from which we have to start — the realisation of its truth can only come with the opening of the consciousness and its change.

*

The distinction between the Transcendental, the Cosmic, the Individual Divine is not my invention, nor is it native to India or to Asia — it is on the contrary a recognised European teaching current in the esoteric tradition of the Catholic Church where it is the authorised explanation of the Trinity, — Father, Son and Holy Ghost, — and it is very well-known to European mystic experience. In essence it exists in all spiritual disciplines that recognise the omnipresence of the Divine — in Indian Vedantic experience and in Mahomedan Yoga (not only the Sufi, but other schools also) — the Mahomedans even speak of not two or three but many levels of the Divine until one reaches the Supreme. As for the idea in itself, surely there is a difference between the individual, the cosmos in space and time, and something that exceeds this cosmic formula or any cosmic formula. There is a cosmic consciousness experienced by many which is quite different in its scope and action from the individual consciousness, and if there is a consciousness beyond the cosmic, infinite and essentially eternal, not merely extended in Time, that also must be different from these two. And if the Divine is or manifests Himself in these three, is it not conceivable that in aspect, in His working, He may differentiate Himself so much that we are driven, if we are not to confound all truth of experience, if we are not to limit ourselves to a mere static experience of something indefinable, to speak of a triple aspect of the Divine?

In the practice of Yoga there is a great dynamic difference in one's way of dealing with these three possible realisations. If I realise only the Divine as that, not my personal self, which yet moves secretly all my personal being and which I can bring forward out of the veil, or if I build up the image of that Godhead in my members, it is a realisation but a limited one. If it is the

Cosmic Godhead that I realise, losing in it all personal self, that is a very wide realisation, but I become a mere channel of the universal Power and there is no personal or divinely individual consummation for me. If I shoot up to the transcendental realisation only, I lose both myself and the world in the transcendental Absolute. If on the other hand my aim is none of these things by itself, but to realise and also to manifest the Divine in the world, bringing down for the purpose a yet unmanifested Power, — such as the Supermind, — a harmonisation of all three becomes imperative. I have to bring it down, and from where shall I bring it down — since it is not yet manifested in the cosmic formula — if not from the unmanifest Transcendence, which I must reach and realise? I have to bring it into the cosmic formula and, if so, I must realise the cosmic Divine and become conscious of the cosmic self and the cosmic forces. But I have to embody it here, — otherwise it is left as an influence only and not a thing fixed in the physical world — and it is through the Divine in the individual alone that this can be done.

These are elements in the dynamics of spiritual experience and I am obliged to admit them if a divine work has to be done.

*

The European type of monism is usually pantheistic and weaves the universe and the Divine so intimately together that they can hardly be separated. But what explanation of the evil and misery can there be there? The Indian view is that the Divine is the inmost substance of the Universe, but he is also outside it, transcendent; good and evil, happiness and misery are only phenomena of cosmic experience due to a division and diminution of consciousness in the manifestation, but are not part of the essence or of the undivided whole-consciousness either of the Divine or of our own spiritual being.

*

I know what is your difficulty about the Cosmic Divine. It was not present to my mind because I look at these things from the point of view of facts as they are both to our spiritual and our outward experience — whereas the point of view on which you lay stress is that they are not what they ought to be or what the mind, ethical feeling and the vital in man feel that they ought to be. That this world is full of queer, ugly and inharmonious things is the very plain and self-evident fact with which we have to start, — wherever we may want or hope to arrive. But the whole question is there, whether there is something behind, something that warrants this hope to arrive at something better. For the spiritual experience there is — and this something behind is to it as undeniable a fact as the very apparent character of this world in its surface aspect as a world of Ignorance, tribulation, suffering, disharmony, disorder, obscure Inconscience. To spiritual experience it is not a speculation but a fact that there is a Godhead immanent within behind this flawed and imperfect human nature into some likeness to which this nature can try to grow; there is something behind the cosmic movement with all its disorder which is of the nature of abiding peace, calm, strength, joy and all-embracing universality and to enter into it and abide in it is possible for our consciousness also. It is also a part of spiritual experience that there is something Beyond in which this Divinity — or whatever other name you may give to it — is above the contradiction offered to it by this world of disorder and ignorance; that is the meaning of the Transcendence. Whatever wide differences there may be between different ways of spiritual experience or whatever names may be put on these things, so much is fairly universal. If there were not these certitudes, there could be no assured spiritual life or endeavour.

*

The transcendent [*is the state beyond the universal forces*] — which for the purposes of our universe would mean the Sachchidananda planes and the supramental as a link with the present manifestation.

Of course the absolutely transcendent would be beyond all planes altogether.

Personal and Impersonal Sides of the Divine

There is always the personal and the impersonal side of the Divine and the Truth and it is a mistake to think the impersonal alone true or important — for that leads to a void incompleteness in part of the being while only one side is given satisfaction. Impersonality belongs to the intellectual mind and the static self, personality to the soul and heart and dynamic being. Those who disregard the personal Divine ignore something which is profound and essential.

In X's case there exists a conflict between his ideas of the Truth and his heart. But in following the heart in its purer impulses one follows something that is at least as precious as the mind's loyalty to its own conceptions of what the Truth may be.

*

Many have had communion with the Personal Divine, through the mind and the heart — but that is not the complete or supreme realisation.

*

The usual experience of the Impersonal is that It is everywhere, without form or limitation in any place or time.

*

The impersonal Divine has no abode and cannot have; it is all-pervading. If anybody says the impersonal Divine has its abode in the heart he can be asked what he means by the impersonal Divine.

*

Whatever impersonal Truth or Light there is, you have to find it, use it, do what you can with it. It does not trouble itself to hunt after you. It is the Buddhist idea that you must do everything for yourself, that is the only way.

*

When one follows after the impersonal Self, one is moving

between two opposite principles — the silence and purity of the impersonal inactive Atman and the activity of the ignorant Prakriti. One can pass into the Self, leaving the ignorant Nature or reducing it to silence. Or else, one can live in the peace and freedom of the Self and watch the action of Nature as a witness. Even one may put some sattwic control, by tapasya, over the action of the Prakriti; but the impersonal Self has no power to change or divinise the Nature. For that one has to go beyond the impersonal Self and seek after the Divine who is both personal and impersonal and beyond these two aspects. If, however, you practise living in the impersonal Self and can achieve a certain spiritual impersonality, then you grow in equality, purity, peace, detachment, you get the power of living in an inner freedom not touched by the surface movement or struggle of the mental, vital and physical nature, and this becomes a great help when you have to go beyond the impersonal and to change the troubled nature also into something divine.

The Divine and the Atman

The Divine is more than the Atman. It is Nature also, it contains everything in Itself.

*

It is the individual being that is a portion of the Divine. The universal self or Atman which is the same in all, is not a portion but an aspect of the Divine.

The Divine and the Supermind

One can become one with the Divine on the mental plane. The Supermind is necessary for manifesting the Divine on earth.

*

The Divine can be and is everywhere, masked or half-manifest or beginning to be manifest, in all the planes of consciousness; in the Supramental it begins to be manifest without disguise or veil in its own *svarūpa*.

Chapter Two

Sachchidananda: Existence, Consciousness-Force and Bliss

Sachchidananda

Sachchidananda is the One with a triple aspect. In the Supreme the three are not three but one — existence is consciousness, consciousness is bliss, and they are thus inseparable, not only inseparable but so much each other that they are not distinct at all. In the superior planes of manifestation they become triune — although inseparable, one can be made more prominent and base or lead the others. In the lower planes below they become separable in appearance, though not in their secret reality, and one can exist phenomenally without the others so that we become aware of what seems to us an inconscient or a painful existence or a consciousness without Ananda. Indeed without this separation of them in experience pain and ignorance and falsehood and death and what we call inconscience could not have manifested themselves — there could not have been this evolution of a limited and suffering consciousness out of the universal nescience of Matter.

*

The Sachchidananda is not in itself an active consciousness, it is simply pure existence, consciousness and bliss. By a Truth Consciousness is meant a knowledge consciousness which is immediately, inherently and directly aware of Truth in manifestation and has not to seek for it like Mind. Sachchidananda is everywhere behind the manifestation and supporting it as well as above it and can be experienced below the supermind — even in mind and vital it can be experienced.

*

The original substance of the spirit is pure existence carrying in it pure self-existent consciousness (or consciousness-force) and pure self-existent Ananda.

*

There is no plane beyond Sachchidananda.

*

People say like that [*the Transcendent is something beyond Sachchidananda*] because the transcendent Absolute is not only what to us is existence but also what to us is non-existence. But there is really no such thing as non-existence. So the Transcendent can be conceived as transcendent Sat, transcendent Chit, transcendent Ananda.

Sat or Pure Existence

You must remember that there are reflections of the higher worlds in the lower planes which can easily be experienced as supreme for that stage of the evolution. But the supreme Sachchidananda is not a world, it is supracosmic. The Sat (Satyaloka) world is the highest of the scale connected with this universe.

*

Substance and being are the same thing. In the creation they can be looked at as two aspects of the Spirit.

*

The Pure Existence is not something abstract, but substantial and concrete. Moreover it is descending into the body, so it is quite natural to feel it materially.

Chit or Consciousness

You seem to want to reduce everything to a catalogue and a scientific analysis. Nobody has ever been able to do that with the working of the consciousness. The elements of a condition of consciousness cannot be classified like the "elements" of Matter.

*

I had intended to give only a concise answer to your question about consciousness but it began to develop itself at great length and I could not as yet finish it. I send you for the moment a more summary reply.[1]

Consciousness is not, to my experience, a phenomenon dependent on the reactions of personality to the forces of Nature and amounting to no more than a seeing or interpretation of these reactions. If that were so, then when the personality becomes silent and immobile and gives no reactions, as there would be no seeing or interpretative action, there would therefore be no consciousness. That contradicts some of the fundamental experiences of Yoga, e.g., a silent and immobile consciousness infinitely spread out, not dependent on the personality but impersonal and universal, not seeing and interpreting contacts but motionlessly self-aware, not dependent on the reactions, but persistent in itself even when no reactions take place. The subjective personality itself is only a formation of consciousness which is a power inherent, not in the activity of the temporary manifested personality, but in the being, the Self or Purusha.

Consciousness is a reality inherent in existence. It is there even when it is not active on the surface, but silent and immobile; it is there even when it is invisible on the surface, not reacting on outward things or sensible to them, but withdrawn and either active or inactive within; it is there even when it seems to us to be quite absent and the being to our view unconscious and inanimate.

Consciousness is not only power of awareness of self and things, it is or has also a dynamic and creative energy. It can determine its own reactions or abstain from reactions; it can not only answer to forces, but create or put out from itself forces. Consciousness is Chit but also Chit Shakti.

---

[1] *Sri Aurobindo's incomplete draft reply, which "began to develop itself at great length", is reproduced immediately after the present letter.* — Ed.

Consciousness is usually identified with mind, but mental consciousness is only the human range which no more exhausts all the possible ranges of consciousness than human sight exhausts all the gradations of colour or human hearing all the gradations of sound — for there is much above or below that is to man invisible and inaudible. So there are ranges of consciousness above and below the human range, with which the normal human has no contact and they seem to it unconscious, — supramental or overmental and submental ranges.

When Yajnavalkya says there is no consciousness in the Brahman state, he is speaking of consciousness as the human being knows it. The Brahman state is that of a supreme existence supremely aware of itself, *svayamprakāśa*, — it is Sachchidananda, Existence-Consciousness-Bliss. Even if it be spoken of as beyond that, *parātparam*, it does not mean that it is a state of Non-existence or Non-consciousness, but beyond even the highest spiritual substratum (the "foundation above" in the luminous paradox of the Rig Veda) of cosmic existence and consciousness. As it is evident from the description of Chinese Tao and the Buddhist Shunya that that is a Nothingness in which all is, so with the negation of consciousness here. Superconscient and subconscient are only relative terms; as we rise into the superconscient we see that it is a consciousness greater than the highest we yet have and therefore in our normal state inaccessible to us and, if we can go down into the subconscient, we find there a consciousness other than our own at its lowest mental limit and therefore ordinarily inaccessible to us. The Inconscient itself is only an involved state of consciousness which like the Tao or Shunya, though in a different way, contains all things suppressed within it so that under a pressure from above or within all can evolve out of it — "an inert Soul with a somnambulist Force".

The gradations of consciousness are universal states not dependent on the outlook of the subjective personality; rather the outlook of the subjective personality is determined by the grade of consciousness in which it is organised according to its typal nature or its evolutionary stage.

It will be evident that by consciousness is meant something which is essentially the same throughout but variable in status, condition and operation, in which in some grades or conditions the activities we call consciousness can exist either in a suppressed or an unorganised or a differently organised state; while in other states some other activities may manifest which in us are suppressed, unorganised or latent or else are less perfectly manifested, less intensive, extended and powerful than in those higher grades above our highest mental limit.

*

If your definition is correct, consciousness cannot be a self-existent reality; it is a result, a phenomenon dependent on the reactions of something — you say a personality, but what is a personality apart from consciousness? — to the universal forces of Nature. We can take a purely external view and say that consciousness is the result of a mass of reactions to the impact of outward physical things on the brain and nerves of a physical being. In this case consciousness is a sort of effective hallucination — there is no real and permanent consciousness but only a subjective impression created by a constant activity of reactions. As a number of dancing fires may create a glow in the sky, so consciousness is created by these reactions and is suspended or disappears when they halt or cease. In your definition you add a real (?) subjective personality and supplement the reactions of physical outward things by reactions of inner things or things from above or below. But still the consciousness is only a seeing or interpretation of reactions, — it is a result of them, a phenomenon. If there are no more reactions, consciousness ceases to exist — for what other basis has it or standing place than the impermanent reaction to forces? Unless it is something intrinsic and inherent in the "subjective personality"; but then it is not a result of the reactions or a seeing and interpretation of them, but rather the reactions are the result of a pre-existent consciousness and the seeing or interpretation is merely an activity, perhaps only a very partial and surface activity, of the consciousness already and always inherent in the "personality". Even if there were no impact of forces and no reactions, the consciousness would still be there, but static and inactive. But again this activity of consciousness might not be limited to an interpretation or a passive reaction to forces; it might also, if it chose, be the creator or determinant of its reactions — as for instance to a blow on the body or the vital it might refuse the natural reactions of pain or anger and remain still and immobile or it might return an unusual reaction of love or pleasure. Also this consciousness might not be only a recipient and seer of forces, but a creator or putter out of forces — it might be not only a knower, but an energy, a dynamis. In this view, your definition becomes totally inadequate. Farther, the word personality is misleading; for what we usually know as personality is itself only a formation of consciousness. Behind it we are aware of a Person or Purusha who puts forward the mutable surface formation we call personality and who may even have many personalities at a time or different personalities at different times. This Purusha would be then a being and consciousness, would be not a result or an activity, but a constant reality, an intrinsic power of awareness and action inherent in the being, — as the being is self-existent, so the consciousness self-existent in the being, the Purusha. This is the realisation we have of it in Yogic experience, eternal reality of consciousness inherent in the eternal reality of existence, as in the concept and experience of Sachchidananda.

This is the crucial point in the question, what is consciousness, whether it is a temporary phenomenon of Nature or a reality in itself fundamental to existence. The first is the conclusion that is drawn, and must be drawn, from normal experience on the surface. The other is at best a metaphysical speculation or an instinctive feeling in humanity unless we go beyond the normal experience, deepen and widen the range of our present consciousness and test its inner depths and inferior abysses and supernormal heights, until we can touch its fundamental or its ultimate or its total reality as is done in Yoga. To judge from only normal and superficial experience as the ordinary mind does with phenomena is to miss the truth of things — we have to go behind the surface phenomenon to find the reality of what a thing is. There are no gradations of consciousness if the ordinary phenomenon of consciousness is taken, unless perhaps we distinguish two gradations, the animal and the human; the differences created by the variations of subjective personality amount only to degrees of power of the same human-animal consciousness, a better or worse, cruder or more complex organisation of the instruments by which it receives or reacts to the contacts of Nature. If, on the contrary, consciousness is an inherent power of existence present even when it is not apparent to us or active on the surface, then we can conceive of it arranging its own manifestation in gradations which rise or fall between what seem to us now the subconscient depths and superconscient summits of existence.

The ordinary view of consciousness is based on normal superficial experience plus science. For physical science consciousness is a temporary phenomenon in an unconscious world, something evolved in an animate organisation that somehow develops in an originally inanimate and unconscious Matter. It is not inherent in life, for the plant has it not, it is rather a growing flicker that, once established, lasts intermittently through sleep and waking while life lasts and disappears with the dissolution of life. The ordinary mind identifies consciousness with human waking consciousness possibly shared by the animal — though that is not certain, for many refuse consciousness to the animal. A man is conscious while he lives, when he is dead consciousness disappears, when he is asleep, stunned, drugged, anaesthetised, in trance, then his consciousness is suspended; he is temporarily unconscious. How far is this scientific-superficial view correct or maintainable? For it raises two fundamental questions — is the waking surface consciousness the only form of consciousness possible? and again, is the consciousness synonymous with mind, is all consciousness mental or are other forms of it, supramental or submental, possible?

Outer Consciousness and Inner Consciousness

Consciousness is inherent in Being, though it is here involved and concealed in things so that it has to emerge out of an apparent unconsciousness and organise itself in individual life. But this is only on the surface which is all of which we are aware because we live on the surface of ourselves. This surface (the ordinary waking mind of man) is what we think to be ourselves, the whole of us, because living awake on the surface we are conscious of that only. But within, with a sort of wall of obscurity or oblivion between it and the outer being, there is an inner being, an inner mind, vital, physical and an inmost or psychic being of which we are not aware. We are only aware of what comes up from there to the surface and do not know its source or how it comes. By Yoga the wall is slowly broken down and we become aware of this inner and inmost being — by doing so we build up a new, a Yogic, consciousness which is able to communicate direct with the universal consciousness around and the higher spiritual above.

As the individual has a consciousness of his own, so too there is a universal consciousness, a cosmic Being, a universal Mind, a universal Life, a universal physical conscious Nature. We are unaware of it because we are shut up in our outer physical selves. By the inner awakening and the opening above we become aware of this cosmic consciousness, cosmic Nature and cosmic Self and its movements; our consciousness can widen and become one with it. The forces of universal Nature are always working on us without our knowing how they act or being able to get any general control over their action on us. By becoming conscious of the universal we are able to detect this working and control it.

*

It all depends upon where the consciousness places itself and centralises itself. If the consciousness places or associates itself within the ego, you are identified with the ego — if in the mind, it is identified with the mind and its activities and so on. If the consciousness puts its stress outside, it is said to live in the external being and becomes oblivious of its inner mind and vital and inmost psychic; if it goes inside, puts its centralising stress there, then it knows itself as the inner being or, still deeper, as the psychic being; if it ascends out of the body to the planes where self is naturally conscious of its wideness and freedom, it knows itself as the self and not the mind, life or body. It is this stress of consciousness that makes all the difference. That is why one has to concentrate the consciousness in heart or mind in order to go within or go above. It is the disposition of the consciousness that determines everything, makes one predominantly mental, vital, physical or psychic, bound or free, separate in the Purusha or involved in the Prakriti.

*

Good heavens! what a magnificent muddle [*in the correspondent's response to the preceding letter*]! The Jivatman is on the supramental plane and the Jiva is the psychic? It is the consciousness with a clear individual "I" that disposes variously the centralising stress on one part or another of the being and yet the quality of this "I" is determined by the part with which it identifies itself — therefore it must be a pure conscious I? All that has no basis whatever and does not hang together. I never said that the Jivatman belongs to the supramental plane or is situated there. The word Jiva in its ordinary sense is the living creature, but in its philosophic sense it is often used as a short way of speaking of the Jivatman, the individual being. Neither can it be said that the psychic being is the Jiva. Nor is it the fact that it is the consciousness with a clear individual "I" that disposes variously the centralising stress on one part or another of the being. Consciousness has no need of a clear individual "I" to dispose the stress, — it can do that of itself; wherever the stress is put the "I" attaches itself to that, so that one thinks of oneself as a mental being or physical being or whatever it may be. The consciousness in me can be utterly free of any sense of an individual "I" and yet dispose its stress in this way or the other way — it may go down into the physical and work there in the physical nature keeping all the rest behind or above for the time or it may go up into the overhead level and stand above mind, life and body seeing them as instrumental lower forms of itself; or it may not see them at all but rather immerge in the free undifferentiated Self; or it may throw itself into an active dynamic cosmic consciousness and identify with that or do any number of other things without resorting to the help of this much overrated and meddlesome fly on the wheel which you call the clear individual "I". The real "I" — if you want to use that word — is not a "clear individual", that is, a clear-cut limited separative ego, — it is as wide as the universe and wider, and can contain the universe in itself; it is not the *ahaṅkāra*, it is the Atman.

Consciousness is a fundamental thing, it is the fundamental thing in existence — it is the energy, the action, the movement of consciousness that creates the universe and all that is in it — not only the macrocosm, but the microcosm is nothing but consciousness arranging itself. For instance when consciousness in its movement, or rather a certain stress of movement, forgets itself in the action it becomes an apparently "unconscious" energy; when it forgets itself in the form it becomes the electron, the atom, the material object. In reality it is still consciousness that works in the energy and determines the form and the evolution of form. When it wants to liberate itself, slowly, evolutionarily, out of matter, but still in the form, it emerges as life, as the animal, as man and it can go on evolving itself still farther out of its involution and become something more than mere man. If you can grasp that, then it ought not to be difficult to see farther that it can subjectively formulate itself as a physical, a vital, a mental, a psychic consciousness — all these are present in man, but as they are all mixed up together in our external being and their real status is hidden behind in our inner secret nature one can only become fully aware of them by releasing the original limiting stress of the consciousness which makes us live in our external selves and becoming awake and centred within in the inner being. As the consciousness in us, by its external concentration or stress, has put all these things behind — behind a wall or veil — it has to break down the wall or veil and get back in its stress into these inner parts of existence — that is what we call living within; then our external being seems to us something small and superficial, we are or can become aware of the large and rich and inexhaustible kingdoms within. So also consciousness in us has drawn a lid or covering or whatever one likes to call it between the lower planes of mind, life, body supported by the psychic and the higher planes which contain the spiritual kingdoms where the self is always free and limitless, — and it can break or open the lid or covering and ascend there and become the Self free and wide and luminous or else bring down the influence, reflection, finally even the presence and power of the higher consciousness into the lower nature.

Now that is what consciousness is — it is not composed of parts, it is fundamental to being and itself formulates any parts it chooses to manifest — developing them from above downward by a progressive coming down from spiritual levels towards the evolution in matter or formulating them in an upward working in the front by this process that we call evolution. If it chooses to work in you through the sense of ego, you think that it is the clear-cut individual I that does everything; if it begins to release itself from that limited working, then you too either begin to expand your sense of I till it bursts into infinity and no longer exists or to shed it and flower into spiritual wideness. Of course this is not what is spoken of in modern materialistic thought as consciousness, because that thought is governed by science. Science sees consciousness only as a phenomenon which emerges out of inconscient Matter and consists of certain reactions of the system to outward things. But that is phenomenon of consciousness, it is not consciousness itself, it is even only a very small part of the possible phenomena of consciousness and can give no clue to the true nature of Consciousness, the spiritual Reality which is of the very essence of existence.

That is all at present. You will have to fix yourself in that — for it is fundamental — before it can be useful to go any farther.

*

Certainly, the mind and the inner being are consciousness. For human beings who have not got deeper into themselves mind and consciousness are synonymous. Only when one becomes more aware of oneself by a growing consciousness, then one can see different degrees, kinds, powers of consciousness, mental, vital, physical, psychic, spiritual. The Divine has been described as Being-Consciousness-Ananda, even as a Consciousness (Chaitanya), as putting out a force or energy, Shakti, that creates worlds. The mind is a modified consciousness that puts forth a mental energy. But the Divine can stand back from his energy and observe it at its work, it can be the Witness Purusha watching the works of Prakriti. Even the mind can do that — a man can stand back in his mind-consciousness and watch the mental energy doing things, thinking, planning, etc.; all introspection is based upon that fact that one can so divide oneself into a consciousness that observes and an energy that acts. These are quite elementary things supposed to be known to everybody. Anybody can do that merely by a little practice; anybody who observes his own thoughts, feelings, actions has begun doing it already. In Yoga we make the division complete, that is all.

Consciousness and Force or Energy

Consciousness is made up of two elements, awareness of self and things and forces and conscious power. Awareness is the first thing necessary, you have to be aware of things in the right consciousness, in the right way, seeing them in their truth; but awareness by itself is not enough. There must be a Will and a Force that make the consciousness effective. Somebody may have the full consciousness of what has to be changed, what has to go and what has to come in its place, but may be helpless to make the change. Another may have the will-force, but for want of a right awareness may be unable to apply it in the right way at the right place. The advantage of being in the psychic consciousness is that you have the right awareness and its will being in harmony with the Mother's will, you can call in the Mother's Force to make the change. Those who live in the mind and the vital are not so well able to do this; they are obliged to use mostly their personal effort and as the awareness and will and force of the mind and vital are divided and imperfect, the work done is imperfect and not definitive. It is only in the supermind that Awareness, Will, Force are always one movement and automatically effective.

*

If consciousness and energy are the same thing, there would be no use in having two different words for them. In that case instead of saying, "I am conscious of my defects", one can say, "I am energetic of my defects." If a man is running fast, you can say of him, "He is running with great energy." Do you think it would mean the same if you said, "He is running with great consciousness"? Consciousness is that which is aware of things — energy is a force put in action which does things. Consciousness may have energy and keep it in or put it out, but that does not mean that it is only another word for energy and that it has to go out when the energy goes out and that it cannot stand back and observe the energy in action. You have plenty of inertia in you but that does not mean that you and inertia are the same and when inertia rises and swamps you it is you who rise and swamp yourself.

Force, Energy, Power, Shakti

There is a force behind each action acting in a manner appropriate to that action. It takes all these many forms for the necessity of the working, but it is one Force.

*

I have never classified the different forms [of *Force*] — they can be hundreds or thousands in number. Force varies its form according to the work it has to do.

*

A passive Force has no meaning — Force is always dynamic. Only a Force can act on a basis of calm passivity just as in the material world the Force acts on the basis of inertia.

*

Static and dynamic in reality always go together — it is in appearance that anything seems only dynamic or only static.

*

In each atom of the being there is an Energy, a Shakti — just as there is in every material atom a great material energy. When you see like that, you become aware of these energies. They are neither good nor bad — it depends on how they are used or how they act.

*

Power means strength and force, Shakti, which enables one to face all that can happen and to stand and overcome, also to carry out what the Divine Will proposes. It can include many things, power over men, events, circumstances, means etc. But all this not of the mental or vital kind, but by an action through unity of consciousness with the Divine and with all things and beings. It is not an individual strength depending on certain personal capacities, but the Divine Power using the individual as an instrument. It has no special relation to occult siddhis.

*

Force is the essential Shakti; Energy is the working drive of the Force, its active dynamism; Power is the capacity born of the Force; Strength is energy consolidated and stored in the Adhar.

*

The Divine Force can act on any plane — it is not limited to the Supramental Force. The Supramental is only one aspect of the power of the Divine.

*

The Supreme cannot create through the Transcendent because the Transcendent is the Supreme. It is through the Cosmic Shakti that the Divine creates.

Ananda

Ananda is a thing to be felt — it cannot be defined except negatively that it is not mere joy, but something much more deep and essential.

*

It is the statement of the Upanishad that there is an ether of Ananda in which all breathe and live; if it were not there, none could breathe or live.

*

It is fundamentally true for most people that the pleasure of life, of existence in itself, predominates over the troubles of life; otherwise most people would want to die whereas the fact is that everybody wants to live — and if you proposed to them an easy means of eternal extinction they would decline without thanks. That is what X is saying and it is undeniable. It is also true that this comes from the Ananda of existence which is behind everything and is reflected in the instinctive pleasure of existence. Naturally, this instinctive essential pleasure is not the Ananda, — it is only a pale and dim reflection of it in an inferior life-consciousness — but it is enough for its purpose. I have said that myself somewhere and I do not see anything absurd or excessive in the statement.

*

Why should the joy of creation be unyogic? Every creator feels the joy of creation — including the Divine Creator.

Chapter Three

Brahman

The Impersonal Brahman

You speak of the Impersonal as if it were a Person. The Impersonal is not He, it is It. How can an It guide or help? The Impersonal Brahman is inactive, aloof, indifferent, not concerned with what happens in the universe. Buddha's Permanent is the same.

*

There is no thought in the pure Impersonal, it is silent — but it is true that divine Truth can manifest in the background of the silence. This is of course the truth of things up to the Overmind.

The Inactive Brahman and the Active Brahman

The inactive Brahman and the active personal Brahman are two aspects of the Divine. In the Supreme these are fused into each other, not separate.

*

There are two aspects of the Divine — the static Peace and the dynamic Force. In the end they unite.

*

It is in the inactive Brahman that one merges if one seeks laya or Moksha. One can dwell in the Personal Divine but does not merge in Him. As for the Supreme, He holds in Himself the world-existence and it is in His Consciousness that it moves; so by entering into the Supreme one rises above subjection to Nature, but one does not disappear from all consciousness of world-existence.

*

The immutable Brahman is only a base for the transcendent action which comes down into its peace and silence and fills it with power also and Ananda and the light of knowledge.

Spirit and Life

In the sphere of the Spirit are only the eternal truths — all is eternally itself there, there is no development, nothing unrealised or striving to be fulfilled. There are no such things as possibilities therefore.

In life on the other hand all is a play of possibilities — nothing is realised, all is seeking to be realised — or if not yet seeking, then waiting behind the veil for that. Nothing is realised in its highest form, in its truth or completeness, but all is possible. All these possibilities are derived from the truths above — e.g., the possibility of knowledge, the possibility of love, the possibility of joy etc.

Intellect, will etc. are intermediaries which try to catch something of the hidden higher truths and bring them into life or else raise life to them — so that the possibilities of life here may become the complete realities that are already there above.

Chapter Four
The Self or Atman

The Self

It [*the self*] is being, not a being. By self is meant the conscious essential existence, one in all.

*

The self is the Divine itself in an essential aspect; it is not a portion. There is no meaning in the phrase "not even a portion" or "only an aspect". An aspect is not something inferior to a portion.

*

Do you not know what "essential" means? There is a difference between the essence of a thing which is always the same and its formations and developments which vary. There is, for instance, the essence of gold and there are the many forms which gold can take.

*

Essence can never be defined — it simply is.

*

Everything acts in the self. The whole play of Nature takes place in the self, in the Divine. The self contains the universe.

The Cosmic Spirit or Self

The Cosmic Spirit or Self contains everything in the cosmos — it upholds cosmic Mind, universal Life, universal Matter as well as the Overmind. The Self is more than all these things which are its formulations in Nature.

*

It [*the Cosmic Spirit*] uses Truth and Falsehood, Knowledge and Ignorance and all the other dualities as elements in the manifestation and works out what has to be worked out till all is ready for a higher working.

*

The Cosmic Spirit contains the Supermind, but it keeps it above and works for the present between the Overmind and the physical. It is only when the Ignorance is removed that the Supramental becomes directly a dynamic part of the workings of cosmic Nature here. Till then there are only reflections of it.

*

The Self is essentially universal; the individualised self is only the universal experienced from an individual centre. If what you have realised is not felt to be one in all, then it is not the "Atman"; possibly it is the central being not yet revealing its universal aspect as Atman.

*

The Self is felt as either universal, one in all, or a universalised individual the same in essence as others, extended everywhere from each being but centred here. Of course centre is a way of speaking, because no physical centre is usually felt — only all the action takes place around the individual.

*

All is in the self; when identified with the universal self, all is in you.
 Also, the microcosm reproduces the macrocosm — so all is present in each, though all is not expressed (and cannot be) in the surface consciousness.

The Atman, the Soul and the Psychic Being

The Atman is one in all, is not born, does not evolve or change.
 The soul is something that comes from the Divine into the evolution and as the psychic being it evolves and assumes

different personalities from life to life.

*

To live in the consciousness of the Atman is to live in the calm, unity and peace that is above things and separate from the world even when pervading it. But for the psychic consciousness there are two things, the world and itself acting in the world. The Jivatman has not come down into the world, it stands above, always the same — supporting the different beings, mental etc. which act here. The psychic is what has come down here — its function is to offer all things to the Divine for transformation.

The Self and Nature or Prakriti

The Self or Atman is inactive, Nature (Prakriti) or Shakti acts. When the Self is realised it is first an infinite existence, wideness, silence, freedom, peace that is felt — that is called Atman or Self. When action takes place, it is according to the realisation either felt as forces of Nature working in that wideness, as the Divine Shakti working or as the cosmic Divine or various powers of him working. It is not felt that the Self is acting.

*

One may be aware of the silent static self without relation to the play of the cosmos. Again, one may be aware of the universal static self omnipresent in everything without being supra-sensuously awake to the movement of the dynamic *viśva-prakṛti*. The first realisation of the Self or Brahman is often a realisation of something that separates itself from all form, name, action, movement, exists in itself only, regarding the cosmos as only a mass of cinematographic shapes unsubstantial and empty of reality. That was my own first complete realisation of the Nirvana in the Self. That does not mean a wall between Self and Brahman, but a scission between the essential self-existence and the manifested world.

*

The Self or Atman

In the experience of Yoga the self or being is in essence one with the Divine or at the least it is a portion of the Divine and has all the divine potentialities. But in manifestation it takes two aspects, the Purusha and Prakriti, conscious being and Nature. In Nature here the Divine is veiled, and the individual being is subjected to Nature which acts here as the lower Prakriti, a force of Ignorance, Avidya. The Purusha in itself is divine, but exteriorised in the ignorance of Nature it is as the individual apparent being imperfect with her imperfection. Thus the soul or psychic essence, which is the Purusha entering into the evolution and supporting it, carries in itself all the divine potentialities, but the individual psychic being which it puts forth as its representative assumes the imperfection of Nature and evolves in it till it has recovered its full psychic essence and united itself with the Self above of which the soul is the individual projection in the evolution. This duality in the being on all its planes, for it is true in different ways not only of the Self and the psychic but of the mental, vital and physical Purushas, has to be grasped and accepted before the experiences of the Yoga can be fully understood.

The Being is one throughout, but on each plane of Nature, it is represented by a form of itself which is proper to that plane, the mental Purusha in the mental plane, the vital Purusha in the vital, the physical Purusha in the physical. The Taittiriya Upanishad speaks of two other planes of the being, the Knowledge or Truth plane and the Ananda plane, each with its Purusha, but although influences may come down from them these are superconscient to the human mind and their nature is not yet organised here.

Section Two

The Cosmos: Terms from Indian Systems

Chapter One
The Upanishadic and Puranic Systems

Virat

Virat is the outer manifestation and if we take all that as Brahman without knowing what is behind the manifestation we shall fall into the intellectual error of Pantheism, not realising that the Divine is more than this outer manifestation and cannot be known by it alone. In the vital we may fall into the error of accepting what is dark and imperfect on the same terms as that which makes for the light and divine perfection. There may be many other consequent errors also.

Visva or Virat, Hiranyagarbha or Taijasa, Prajna or Ishwara

These two sets of three names each mean the same things. Visva or Virat = the Spirit of the external universe, Hiranyagarbha or Taijasa (the Luminous) = the Spirit in the inner planes, Prajna or Ishwara = the Superconscient Spirit, Master of all things and the highest Self on which all depends. The Mental cannot be Ishwara.

*

It is the external consciousness, the inner consciousness, the superconscient that are meant [*by* vaiśvānara, taijasa *and* prājña *in the Mandukya Upanishad*]. The terms waking, dream, sleep are applied because in the ordinary consciousness of man the external only is awake, the inner being is mostly subliminal and acts directly only in a state of sleep when its movements are felt like things of dream and vision; while the superconscient (supermind, overmind, etc.) is beyond even that range and is to the mind like a deep sleep.

Vaisvanara, Taijasa, Prajna, Kutastha

But why do you want to connect these things with the soul? These four names [*vaiśvānara, taijasa, prājña, kūṭastha*] are given to four conditions of transcendent and universal Brahman or Self, — they are merely conditions of Being and Consciousness — the Self that supports the Waking State or *sthūla* consciousness, the Self that supports the Dream State or subtle consciousness, the Self that supports the Deep Sleep State or Causal consciousness, *kāraṇa*, and the Self in the supracosmic consciousness. The individual of course participates, but these are conditions of the Self, not the Self and soul. The meaning of these expressions is fixed in the Mandukya Upanishad.

Karana, Hiranyagarbha, Virat

Three planes —
(1) Karana (2) Hiranyagarbha (3) Virat
The parallel between Vijnana or Karana Jagat of the Upanishad presided over by Prajna and equated with Sushupti, as the Hiranyagarbha world with Swapna and things subtle, does not altogether equate with my account of the Supermind. But it might be said that to the normal mind approaching or entering the Supramental plane it becomes a state of Sushupti. If the writer had put the superconscient sleep of Supermind — for so the supramental state appears to the untransformed mind when it touches or apprehends it, for it falls inevitably into such a superconscious sleep — then the difference would be cured.

The Seven Worlds

1. Bhu — Physical[1]
2. Bhuvah — Vital
3. Swar — Mental

---

[1] *The correspondent asked for the terms in Sri Aurobindo's yoga system corresponding to the planes mentioned in the ancient yoga systems of India. — Ed.*

4. Mahat — Vijnana (supramental)
5. Jana — Ananda world
6. Tapah — World of Chit-tapas } Sachchidananda worlds
7. Satya — World of Sat

The Worlds of the Lower Hemisphere

The *bhuvarloka* is not part of the material universe — it is the vital world that goes by that name. *Dyuloka* = mind world, *bhuvarloka* = vital world, *bhūrloka* = material world. *Svarloka* is the highest region of the *dyuloka*, but it came to be regarded as identical with it.

Tapoloka and the Worlds of Tapas

That is the original Tapoloka in which the principle is Chit and its power of Tapas, but there are other worlds of Tapas on the other planes below. There is one in the mental, another in the vital range. It is one of these Tapas worlds from which the being you saw must have come.

Chapter Two
The Sankhya-Yoga System

Purusha

Purusha is the conscious Being who supports all the action of Nature. There is no fixed place, but as the central being he usually stands above the adhar — he becomes also the mental, vital, physical, psychic being.

*

The word being is used with all kinds of significances — it is a very imprecise word and can embrace everything. Purusha has a precise significance. It is the Soul or Spirit side of the being as opposed to the Nature side.

*

There is one Purusha — its action is according to the position and need of the consciousness at the time.
    It is the nature of the action above the ordinary mind or in the cosmic consciousness which is many-sided.

*

The Purusha is one thing and the ordinary mental will and force are another. The latter may be unsuccessful in their action. When you are in the Purusha consciousness, that of itself implies a state of concentration and receptivity.

*

By development of the inner will it [*the Purusha*] can become active.

*

The Purusha in men is normally passive not active. It is the Prakriti that is active.

Purusha and Prakriti

There is a Purusha or essential being for each plane of the consciousness — just as each has its prakriti (nature, especial force of action and movement), so each has its Purusha, a part of the being which supports and observes and experiences and can also control the movements of Prakriti.

*

It is Prakriti (Nature) that sends these impulses [to *act*] — Nature sends all kinds of forces and experiences to each. It is for you as a conscious being (Purusha) to choose whether you shall do or not do — you should reject what you see to be wrong, accept only what is true and right. In Nature there is the higher and the lower, the true and the false. What the Divine wants of you is that you should grow in the Truth and the higher Nature, reject the false and the lower Nature.

*

As you have indulged the Prakriti for the last ten thousand lives or so, it has been accustomed to impose its own way on the Purusha. To be separate is only the first step. Also I fancy the Purusha in you is still very mental in its will.

*

In order to get the dynamic realisation it is not enough to rescue the Purusha from subjection to Prakriti; we must transfer the allegiance of the Purusha from the lower Prakriti with its play of ignorant Forces to the Supreme Divine Shakti, the Mother.
   It is a mistake to identify the Mother with the lower Prakriti and its mechanism of forces. Prakriti here is a mechanism only which has been put forth for the working of the evolutionary Ignorance. As the ignorant mental, vital or physical being is not itself the Divine, although it comes from the Divine — so the mechanism of Prakriti is not the Divine Mother. No doubt something of her is there in and behind this mechanism maintaining it for its evolutionary purpose — but what she is in herself is not

a Shakti of Avidya, but the Divine Consciousness, Power, Light, Para Prakriti to whom we turn for the release and the divine fulfilment.

The realisation of the Purusha Consciousness calm, free, observing the play of forces but not attached or involved in them is a means of liberation. The calm, the detachment, a peaceful strength and joy (*ātmarati*) must be brought down into the vital and physical as well as into the mind. If this is established, one is no longer a prey to the turmoil of the vital forces. But this calm, peace, silent strength and joy is only the first descent of the Power of the Mother into the Adhar. Beyond that is a Knowledge, an executive Power, a dynamic Ananda which is not that of the ordinary Prakriti even at its best and most sattwic, but divine in its nature.

First, however, the calm, the peace, the liberation is needed. To try to bring down the dynamic side too soon is not advisable — for then it would be a descent into a troubled and impure nature unable to assimilate it and serious perturbations might be the consequence.

*

There is a constant movement (Prakriti) and a constant silence (Purusha).

*

It is the Purusha and Prakriti sides of the nature — one leading to pure conscious existence, static, the other to pure conscious force, dynamic. The past darkness they have come out of is that of ignorance, the future darkness that is felt above is superconscience. But of course the superconscience is really luminous — only its light is not seen. The three forms of consciousness are the three sides of Nature represented by the three gunas — force of subconscious tamas, Inertia, which is the law of Matter, force of half-conscious desire, Kinesis, which is rajas, which is the law of Life, force of sattwic Prakasha, which is the law of Intelligence.

Prakriti

Prakriti is a name given to the Force that works out everything in the person and in the world; it takes the form of mental, vital, psychic, physical and other forces, of all sorts of powers and qualities, movements, forms, thoughts, sensations, feelings, actions — all that is the result of Prakriti. It is as when a machine is moved by forces of electricity or steam or gas — so the world may be regarded as a huge and complicated machine worked by the forces of Prakriti. It is what is called in English "Nature", and they say everything in the world is the work of Nature.

*

It is Prakriti or Nature that acts; the Divine does not compel people to do anything. Nothing can happen without the presence and support of the Divine, for Nature or Prakriti is the Divine Force and it is this that works out things, but it works them out according to the nature and through or with the will of each man which is full of ignorance — that goes on until men turn to the Divine and become conscious of Him and united with Him. Then only can it be said that all begins to be done in them by the direct Will of the Divine.

*

The lower Prakriti is the ordinary consciousness of man with its ignorance, desires and bondage. I suppose you know that one has to transcend this ordinary consciousness of the lower Nature and arrive at a higher divine consciousness, if one wants to be free?

*

By Prakriti [*in a passage in* Bases of Yoga] is meant universal Prakriti. Universal Prakriti entering into the vital being creates desires which appear by its habitual response as an individual nature; but if the habitual desires she throws in are rejected and exiled, the being remains but the old individual prakriti of vital desire is no longer there, — a new nature is formed responding to the Truth above and not to the lower Nature.

*

Universal Prakriti determined it [*the habit of response to vital movements*] and the soul or Purusha accepted it. In the acceptance lies the responsibility. The Purusha is that which sanctions or refuses. The vital being responds to the ordinary life waves in the animal; man responds to them but has the power of mental control. He has also as the mental Purusha is awake in him the power to choose whether he shall have desire or train his being to surmount it. Finally, there is the possibility of bringing down a higher nature which will not be subject to desire but act on another vital principle.

Prakriti and Shakti or Chit-Shakti

What is meant by Prakriti or Nature is the outer or executive side of the Shakti or Conscious Force which forms and moves the worlds. This outer side appears here to be mechanical, a play of the forces, gunas etc. Behind it is the living Consciousness and Force of the Divine, the divine Shakti. The Prakriti itself is divided into the lower and higher, — the lower is the Prakriti of the Ignorance, the Prakriti of mind, life and matter separated in consciousness from the Divine; the higher is the Divine Prakriti of Sachchidananda with its manifesting power of Supermind, always aware of the Divine and free from Ignorance and its consequences. Man so long as he is in the ignorance is subject to the lower Prakriti, but by spiritual evolution he becomes aware of the higher Nature and seeks to come into contact with it. He can ascend into it and it can descend into him — such an ascent and descent can transform the lower nature of mind, life and matter.

*

Prakriti is only the executive or working force — the Power behind Prakriti is Shakti. It is the Chit-Shakti in manifestation: that is the spiritual consciousness.

*

All energies derive from the Chit-Shakti; but they differentiate from it as they descend.

This much is true that Life is characteristically Force — the Physical is characteristically substance; but the dynamism of both derives from Chit — mind dynamism also, all dynamism.

Purusha, Prakriti and Action

It is more difficult for the Prakriti [*to separate itself from outer action than for the Purusha*] as its ordinary play is that of the surface being. It has to divide itself into two to separate from that. The Purusha on the contrary is in its nature silent and separate — so it has only to go back to its original nature.

*

It [*Prakriti*] divides itself into an inner Force that is free from its action (free from rajas, tamas etc.) and the outer Prakriti which it is using and changing.

*

If ego and desire are different things from the gunas, then there can be an action of the gunas without ego and desire and therefore without attachment. That is the nature of the action of the gunas in the unattached liberated Yogi. If it were not possible, then it would be nonsense to talk of the Yogis being unattached, for there would remain still attachment in part of their being. To say that they are unattached in the Purusha, but attached in the Prakriti, therefore they are unattached, is to talk nonsense. Attachment is attachment in whatever part of the being it may be. In order to be unattached one must be unattached everywhere, in the mental, vital, physical action and not only in the silent soul somewhere inside.

*

You seem to think that action and Prakriti are the same thing and where there is no action there can be no Prakriti! Purusha and Prakriti are separate powers of the being. It is not that Purusha

= quiescence and Prakriti = action, so that when all is quiescent, there is no Prakriti and when all is active there is no Purusha. When all is active, there is still the Purusha behind the active Nature and when all is quiescent there is still the Prakriti, but the Prakriti at rest.

*

The outer being is also detached [*when a Yogi engages in detached action*] — the whole being is without desire or attachment and still action is possible. Action without desire is possible, action without attachment is possible, action without ego is possible.

It is not the inner Purusha only that remains detached then — the inner Purusha is always detached, only one is not conscious of it in the ordinary state. It is the Prakriti also that is not disturbed by the action of the gunas or attached to it — the mind, the vital, the physical (which are Prakriti) begin to get the same quietude, unperturbed peace and detachment as the Purusha, but it is a quietude, not a cessation of all action, it is quietude in action itself. If it were not so, my statement in the *Arya* that there can be a desireless or liberated action on which I found the possibility of a free (*mukta*) action would be false. The whole being, Purusha-Prakriti, becomes detached (having no desire or attachment) even in the action of the gunas.

*

Prakriti is the Force that acts. A Force may be in action or in quiescence, but when it rests, it is as much a Force as when it acts. The gunas are an action of the Force, they are in the Force itself. The sea is there and the waves are there, but the waves are not the sea and when there are no waves and the sea is still, it does not stop being the sea.

The Gunas or Qualities of Nature

Prakriti and Nature are the same thing — the gunas are modes or processes of Nature (Prakriti).

*

If the gunas are quiescent, then Prakriti ceases to act — unless the gunas are transformed into their divine equivalents, — then Prakriti becomes the higher or divine Nature.

*

I don't think it[1] is correct myself. It is supposed that when the three qualities are not in an equalised condition, when there is a diversity and movement of variation, then creation is active — otherwise all becomes quiescent original Prakriti. It is doubtful if it is actually so.

*

Transcendence of the three gunas is a state of liberation in which one is not affected by the action of the gunas; but even before that is attained there can be a complete and living faith in the Divine.

Transformation of the Gunas

The three gunas become purified and refined and changed into their divine equivalents: sattwa becomes *jyotiḥ*, the authentic spiritual light; rajas becomes *tapas*, the tranquilly intense divine force; tamas becomes *śama*, the divine quiet, rest, peace.

*

You cannot drive out rajas and tamas, you can only convert them and give the predominance to sattwa. Tamas and rajas disappear only when the higher consciousness not only comes down but controls everything down to the cells of the body. They then change into the divine rest and peace and the divine energy or Tapas; finally sattwa also changes into the divine Light. As for remaining quiet when tamas is there, there can also be a tamasic quiet.

*

---

[1] *The correspondent asked for an explanation of an aphorism in the Sankhya Sutra (1.61):* sattvarajastamasāṁ sāmyāvasthā prakṛtiḥ. *— Ed.*

The Prakriti can be psychicised and spiritualised and the gunas yet remain, but with the sattwa dominant and the rajas and tamas enlightened by the sattwa. As the transformation increases, the gunas change more and more towards their divine equivalents, but it is only when the supramental comes that there is the full change.

*

The transformation of the gunas is necessary for the *perfection* of the nature, not for liberation. Liberation comes by loss of ego and desire.

Sattwa and Liberation

When the consciousness as well as the action is free from ego and desire, there is always a fundamental calm. This calm remains whether sattwa predominates or not. Sattwa need not always predominate, because to become sattwic is not the object of sadhana. To need to be always sattwic would be a limitation. Whatever guna predominates in the action, to be free, desireless, calm behind all actions, is the condition of the liberated man.

*

The sattwa predominates [*when action is done without desire and ego*], the rajas acts as a kinetic movement under the control of sattwa until the tamas imposes the need of rest. That is the usual thing. But even if the tamas predominates and the action is weak or the rajas predominates and the action is excessive, neither the Purusha nor the Prakriti get disturbed, there is a fundamental calm in the whole being and the action is no more than a ripple or an eddy on the surface.

Transformation of Rajas and Tamas

It is possible that the fatigue or lethargy comes as the wrong condition which has to be replaced by the peace. As rajas, kinetic passion, has to be replaced by *tapas*, the spiritual force, so tamas, the obscure inertia, has to be replaced by *śama*, the luminous quietude and peace.

*

The peace (*śama*) is the pure form, tamas is its degraded or perverted form — just as rajas is the degraded or perverse form of Tapas. When there is the transformation, tamas can be got rid of — but till then there is always a possibility of its mixing with the peace or stillness so long as that is not perfect and all-pervading.

*

A dynamic descent brings *tapas* not *śama*. It is a greater and greater descent of peace that brings *śama* — the dynamic descent helps it by dispersing the element of rajasic disturbance and changing rajas into *tapas*.

Transformation of Tamas into *Śama*

The tamas is part of the general physical Nature and so long as that is not fully changed and illumined, something of it remains; but one has only to go on opening oneself to the Mother's consciousness and in time the tamas too will change into the inner divine rest and peace.

*

All undesirable things are a mistranslation in the Ignorance of something that on a higher plane is or might be desirable. Inertia, tamas, is the mistranslation of the divine *śama*, rest, quietude, peace; pain is a mistranslation of Ananda, lust of love etc. It is only when the lower perversions are got rid of that the higher things in their truth can reign.

*

It is the tendency of the physical to substitute its own inertia for the emptiness. The true emptiness is the beginning of what I call in the *Arya śama* — the rest, calm, peace of the eternal Self —

which has finally to replace tamas, the physical inertia. Tamas is the degradation of *śama*, as rajas is the degradation of Tapas, the Divine Force. The physical consciousness is always trying to substitute its own inertia for the calm, peace or rest of the true consciousness, just as the vital is always trying to substitute its rajas for the true action of the Force.

*

It [*sleepiness*] is the physical tamas trying to push itself into the place of the calm. Part of the transformation consists in replacing the element of tamas in the nature by the *śama* or true calm, peace, rest, of which tamas or inertia is the degradation or perversion in the lower nature (for each of the three gunas has its divine counterpart in the higher nature). But tamas being the settled habit of the inferior nature tries to persist and keep or get back its place. That is the reason why this kind of alternation takes place between the two.

*

Inert *śama* is *śama* still mixed with tamas — a quietude that has no force of action (*tapas*) in it, no positive principle of happy ease, no positive light of knowledge — but is still calm, repose, release from all disturbance.

*

It [*tamas*] has to be transformed into *śama*, the peace and rest of the higher Prakriti, and then filled with *tapas* and *jyotiḥ*. But this can only be done completely in the physical when the physical is finally transformed by the supramental Power.

Mahat

Mahat is, I suppose, the essential and original matrix of consciousness (involved, not evolved) in Prakriti out of which individuality and formation come.

Tanmatra

Tanmatra is only the basis of matter. In the Sankhya the basis is Pradhana (of Prakriti) out of which come Buddhi and everything else. In the Vedanta it is spiritual substance out of which all comes.

Section Three

The Jivatman and the Psychic Being

Chapter One

The Jivatman in the Integral Yoga

The Jivatman or Individual Self

By Jivatma we mean the individual self. Essentially it is one self with all others, but in the multiplicity of the Divine it is the individual self, an individual centre of the universe — and it sees everything in itself or itself in everything or both together according to its state of consciousness and point of view.

*

The self, Atman, is in its nature either transcendent or universal (Paramatma, Atma); when it individualises and becomes a central being, it is then the Jivatman. The Jivatman feels his oneness with the universal but at the same time his central separateness as a portion of the Divine.

*

The individual Self is usually described as a portion of the Transcendent and cosmic Self — in the higher and subtler ranges of the consciousness it knows itself as that, but in the lower where the consciousness is more and more clouded it identifies itself with surface forms of personality, creations of Prakriti, and becomes unaware of its divine origin. Self, when one becomes aware of it, is felt as something self-existent and eternal which is not identified with forms of mental, vital and physical personality, — these are only small expressions of its potentialities in Nature. What people call themselves now is only the ego or the mind or the life-force or the body, but that is because they think in the terms of the formations of Prakriti and do not see behind them.

*

For the most part the Supreme acts through the Jiva and its

nature and the Jiva and the nature act through the ego and the ego acts through the outer instruments — that is the play of the Ignorance.

*

Essentially one Jiva has the same nature as all — but in manifestation each puts forth its own line of Swabhava.

*

The Jivatma is above all planes. It has no fixed form or colour, though it may represent itself in a form.

*

The Jivatma has always calm and peace — it is the nature (prakriti) that is not quiet.

The Jivatman, the Psychic Being and Prakriti

The Spirit is the Atman, Brahman, Essential Divine.

When the one Divine manifests its ever inherent multiplicity, this essential Self or Atman becomes for that manifestation the Jivatman, the central being who presides from above over the evolution of its personalities and terrestrial lives here, but is itself an eternal portion of the Divine and prior to the terrestrial manifestation — *parā prakṛtir jīvabhūtā*.

In this lower manifestation, *aparā prakṛti*, this eternal portion of the Divine appears as the soul, a spark of the Divine Fire, supporting the individual evolution, supporting the mental, vital and physical being. The psychic being is the spark growing into a Fire, evolving with the growth of the consciousness. The psychic being is therefore evolutionary, not like the Jivatman, prior to the evolution.

But man is not aware of the self or Jivatman, he is aware only of his ego, or he is aware of the mental being which controls the life and the body. But more deeply he becomes aware of his soul or psychic being as his true centre, the Purusha in the heart; the psychic is the central being in the evolution, it proceeds from and represents the Jivatman, the eternal portion of the

Divine. When there is the full consciousness, the Jivatman and the psychic being join together.

The ego is a formation of Nature; but it is not a formation of physical nature alone, therefore it does not cease with the body. There is a mental and vital ego also.

The base of the material consciousness here is not only the Ignorance, but the Inconscience — that is, the consciousness is involved in form of matter and energy of matter. It is not only the material consciousness but the vital and the mental too that are separated from the Truth by the Ignorance.

*

The body is not the individual Self — it is the basis of the external personality or of the physical self, if you like so to express it; but that is not the individual Self. The individual Self is the central being (Jivatma) manifesting in the lower nature as the psychic being — it is directly a portion of the Divine.

*

The soul, representative of the central being, is a spark of the Divine supporting all individual existence in Nature; the psychic being is a conscious form of that soul growing in the evolution — in the persistent process that develops first life in matter, mind in life, until finally mind can develop into overmind and overmind into the supramental Truth. The soul supports the nature in its evolution through these grades, but is itself not any of these things.

The lower Nature, Apara Prakriti, is this external objective and superficial subjective apparent Nature which manifests all these minds, lives and bodies. The supreme Nature, Para Prakriti, concealed behind it is the very nature of the Divine — a supreme Consciousness-Force which manifests the multiple Divine as the Many. These Many are in themselves eternal selves of the Supreme in his supreme Nature, Para Prakriti. Here in relation to this world they appear as the Jivatmas supporting the evolution of the natural existences, *sarvabhūtāni*, in the mutable Becoming which is the life of the Kshara (mobile or mutable)

Purusha. The Jiva (= Jivatma) and the creatures, *sarvabhūtāni*, are not the same thing. The Jivatmas really stand above the creation even though in it, the natural existences, *sarvabhūtāni*, are the creatures of Nature. Man, bird, beast, reptile are natural existences, but the individual self in them is not even for a moment characteristically man, bird, beast or reptile; in its evolution it is the same through all these changes, a spiritual being that consents to the play of Nature.

What is original and eternal for ever in the Divine is the Being, what is developed in consciousness, conditions, forces, forms, etc., by the Divine Power is the Becoming. The eternal Divine is the Being, the universe in Time and all that is apparent in it is a Becoming. The eternal Being in its superior nature, Para Prakriti, is at once One and Many; but the eternal Multiplicity of the Divine when it stands behind the created existences, *sarvabhūtāni*, appears as (or as we say, becomes) the Jiva. That is the meaning of the *parā prakṛtir jīvabhūtā*. In the psychic on the other hand there are two aspects, the psychic existence or soul behind and in front the form of individuality it takes in its evolution in Nature.

The soul or psychic is immutable only in the sense that it contains all the possibility of the Divine within it, but this it has to evolve and in its evolution it assumes the form of a developing psychic individual evolving in the manifestation the individual Prakriti and taking part in the evolution. It is the spark of the Divine Fire that grows behind the mind, vital and physical by means of the psychic being until it is able to transform the Prakriti of Ignorance into a Prakriti of Knowledge. This evolving psychic being is not therefore at any time all that the soul or essential psychic existence bears within it; it temporalises and individualises what is eternal in potentiality, transcendent in essence in this projection of the spirit.

The central being is the being which presides over the different births one after the other but is itself unborn, for it does not descend into the being but is above it — it holds together the mental, vital and physical being and all the various parts of the personality and it controls the life either through the mental being and the mental thought and will or through the psychic, whichever may happen to be most in front or most powerful in action. If it does not exercise its control, then the consciousness is in great disorder and every part of the personality acts for itself so that there is no coherence in the thought, feelings or action.

The psychic is not above, but behind — its seat is behind the heart; its power is not knowledge but an essential or spiritual feeling — it has the clearest sense of the truth and a sort of inherent perception of it which is of the nature of soul-feeling. It is our inmost being and supports all the others, mental, vital, physical, but it is also much veiled by them and has to act upon them as an influence rather than by its sovereign right of direct action; its direct action becomes normal and preponderant only at a high stage of development or by Yoga. It is not the psychic being which, you feel, gives you the intuitions of things to be or warns you against the results of certain actions; that is some part of the inner being, sometimes the inner mental, sometimes the inner vital, sometimes, it may be, the inner or subtle physical Purusha. The inner being — inner mind, inner vital, inner or subtle physical — knows much that is unknown to the outer mind, the outer vital, the outer physical, for it is in a more direct contact with the secret forces of Nature. The psychic is the inmost being of all; a perception of truth which is inherent in the deepest substance of the consciousness, a sense of the good, true, beautiful, the Divine, is its privilege.

The central being — the Jivatman which is not born nor evolves, but presides over the individual birth and evolution — puts forward a representative of himself on each plane of the consciousness. On the mental plane it is the true mental being, *manomaya puruṣa*, on the vital plane the true vital being, *prāṇamaya puruṣa*, on the physical plane the true physical being, *annamaya puruṣa*. Each being therefore is, so long as the Ignorance lasts, centred round his mental, vital or physical Purusha, according to the plane on which he predominantly lives, and that is to him his central being. But the true representative all the time is concealed behind the mind, vital and physical — it is the psychic, our inmost being.

When the inmost knowledge begins to come, we become aware of the psychic being within us and it comes forward and leads the sadhana. We become aware also of the Jivatman, the individual Self or Spirit above the manifestation of which the psychic is the representative here.

The Central Being and the Psychic Being

The central being is above the Adhara — most people are not aware of their central being (Jivatma) — they are aware only of the ego.

The psychic is the soul — it is a portion of the Divine that supports the mind, life and body in the evolution. The psychic gets the Divine's help directly from the Divine.

*

The central being is that which is not born, does not evolve, but presides over all the individual manifestation. The psychic is its projection here — for the psychic being is in the evolution and from within supports our whole evolution; it receives the essence of all experience and by that develops the personality Godward.

The Self is at once one in all and many — one in its essence, it manifests also as the individual self which may be described as in Nature an eternal portion of the Divine; in spirit a centre of the manifestation, individual but extending into universality and rising into transcendence.

*

It is the central being above the evolution (always the same) that we call the Jivatma — the psychic being is the same in the evolution, it is the spark of the Divine there growing into its full divinity as a portion of the Divine.

*

The central being and the soul are both in different ways portions of the Divine. They are in fact two aspects of the same entity, but one is unevolving above Nature, the other evolves a psychic being in Nature.

*

The phrase "central being" in our Yoga is usually applied to the portion of the Divine in us which supports all the rest and survives through death and birth. This central being has two forms — above, it is the Jivatman, our true being, of which we become aware when the higher self-knowledge comes, — below, it is the psychic being which stands behind mind, body and life. The Jivatman is above the manifestation in life and presides over it; the psychic being stands behind the manifestation in life and supports it.

The natural attitude of the psychic being is to feel itself as the child, the son of God, the Bhakta; it is a portion of the Divine, one in essence, but in the dynamics of the manifestation there is always even in identity a difference. The Jivatman, on the contrary, lives in the essence and can merge itself in identity with the Divine; but it too, the moment it presides over the dynamics of the manifestation, knows itself as one centre of the multiple Divine, not as the Parameshwara. It is important to remember this distinction; for, otherwise, if there is the least vital egoism, one may begin to think of oneself as an Avatara or lose balance like Hriday with Ramakrishna.

The Surrender of the Central Being

The central being is that on which all the others depend. If it makes its surrender, that is, renounces its separate fulfilment in order to be an instrument of the Divine, then it is easier for the mental, vital and physical to surrender.

*

It [*the central being's surrender to the Divine*] has nothing to do with suitable circumstances. If the will of the central being turns towards union with the Divine, then it renounces its separate fulfilment.

The Central Being after Liberation

What will remain [*after liberation*] is the central being — not the ego. The central being will live in the consciousness of the Divine everywhere and in all other beings also; so it will not have the consciousness of a separate ego but of one centre among many of the Divine Multiplicity.

*

On the higher spiritual planes there is no ego, because the oneness of the Divine is felt, but there may be the sense of one's true person or individual being — not ego, but a portion of the Divine.

The Karana Purusha

The Karana Purusha is what is called the central being by us, the Jiva. It stands above the play, supporting it always.

The Jivatman and the *Caitya Puruṣa*

Jivatma is not psychic being — we have fixed on *caitya puruṣa* as the equivalent in Sanskrit of the psychic being. Jivatma is the individual Self — the central being.

*

Caitya puruṣa means rather the Purusha in the *cit*, the fundamental (inner) consciousness.

Jiva is the fundamental, or as we call it, the central being. But the fundamental being is not *combined* of the mental, vital, psychic etc., these are only expressions of the Jivatman; the Jivatman itself is self-existent in the Divine; *essential* in its being, it cannot be regarded as a combination of things.

The Jivatman and the Mental Purusha

When the Atman is individualised — i.e. supporting from above the play of individual being, it is called the Purusha or sometimes the Jivatman. It is the central being. Usually however it is the mental Purusha one first becomes aware of and through that the nature is led. To become aware of the psychic being or the central Purusha is more difficult.

*

The mental being within watches, observes and passes judgment on all that happens in you. The psychic does not watch and observe in this way like a witness, but it feels and knows spontaneously in a much more direct and luminous way by the very purity of its own nature and the divine instinct within it, and so, whenever it comes to the front it reveals at once what are the right and what the wrong movements in your nature.

The being of man is composed of these elements — the psychic behind supporting all, the inner mental, vital and physical, and the outer, quite external nature of mind, life and body which is their instrument of expression. But above all is the central being (Jivatman) which uses them all for its manifestation; it is a portion of the Divine Self, but this reality of himself is hidden from the external man who replaces this inmost self and soul of him by the mental and vital ego. It is only those who have begun to know themselves that become aware of their true central being; but still it is always there standing behind the action of mind, life and body and is most directly represented by the psychic which is itself a spark of the Divine. It is by the growth of the psychic element in one's own nature that one begins to come into conscious touch with one's central being above. When that happens and the central being uses a conscious will to control and organise the movements of the nature, it is then that one has a real, a spiritual as opposed to a partial and merely mental or moral self-mastery.

*

I don't think the Jivatma is concentrated anywhere, — except in this sense that in the waking state it is the mental Purusha that leads and the seat of the mental Purusha is in the head, behind the centre between the eyebrows. In the dream state what remains active in the body is the externalising consciousness (or something of it) and the centre of that is in the neck (throat). In the *suṣupti*, if it is real *suṣupti*, not merely unconscious of dreams, but absence of dreams, the consciousness is deep within in the heart centre or behind it — for that is the veiled centre of the innermost being.

The Jivatman, Spark-Soul and Psychic Being

The Jivatman, spark-soul and psychic being are three different forms of the same reality and they must not be mixed up together, as that confuses the clearness of the inner experience.

The Jivatman or spirit is self-existent above the manifested or instrumental being — it is superior to birth and death, always the same; it is the individual self or Atman, the eternal true being of the individual.

The soul is a spark of the Divine in the heart of the living creatures of Nature. It is not seated above the manifested being; it enters into the manifestation of the self, consents to be a part of its natural phenomenal becoming, supports its evolution in the world of material Nature. It carries with it at first an undifferentiated power of the divine consciousness, containing all possibilities, but at first unevolved possibilities, which have not yet taken form but to which it is the function of evolution to give form. This spark of Divinity is there in all terrestrial living beings from the earth's highest to its lowest creatures.

The psychic being is a spiritual personality put forward by the soul in its evolution; its growth marks the stage which the spiritual evolution of the individual has reached and its immediate possibilities for the future. It stands behind the mental, the vital, the physical nature, grows by their experiences, carries the consciousness from life to life. It is the psychic Person, *caitya puruṣa*. At first it is veiled by the mental, vital and physical parts, limited by them in its self-expression by their limitations, bound to the reactions of Nature, but, as it grows, it becomes capable of coming forward and dominating the mind, life and body. In the ordinary man it still depends on them for expression and is not able to take them up and freely use them. The life of the being is animal and human, not divine. When the psychic being can by sadhana become dominant and freely use its instruments, then the impulse towards the Divine becomes complete and the transformation of mind, vital and body, not merely their liberation, becomes possible.

As the Self or Atman is free and superior to birth and death, the experience of the Jivatman and its unity with the supreme or universal Self is sufficient to bring the sense of liberation; but for the transformation of the life and nature the full awareness and awakening of our psychic being also is indispensable.

The psychic being realises at this stage its oneness with the true being, the Self, but it does not disappear or change into it; it remains as its instrument for psychic and spiritual self-expression, a divine manifestation in Nature.

The *bindu* seen by you above may be a symbolic way of seeing the Jivatman, the individual self as a drop of the Sea, an individual portion of the universal Divine; the aspiration on that level would naturally be for the opening of the higher consciousness so that the being may dwell there and not in the ignorance. The Jivatman is already one with the Divine in reality, but its spiritual demand may be for the rest of the consciousness also to realise it.

The aspiration of the psychic being would then translate this demand entirely for the opening of the whole lower nature, mind, vital, body to the Divine, for the love and union with the Divine, for its presence and power within the heart, for the transformation of the mind, life and body by the descent of the higher consciousness into this instrumental being and nature.

Both aspirations are necessary for the fullness of this Yoga, the demand of the self on the nature from above, the psychic aspiration of the nature from below. When the psychic imposes its aspiration on the mind, vital and body, then they too aspire and this is what was felt by you as the aspiration from the level of the lower being. The aspiration felt above is that of the Jivatman for the higher consciousness with its realisation of the One to manifest in all the being. Both aspirations help and are necessary to each other. But the seeking of the lower being is at first intermittent and oppressed by the obscurity and limitations of the ordinary consciousness. It has by sadhana to become clear, constant, strong and enduring; it then compels realisation, makes it inevitable.

The sense of peace, purity and calm felt by you is brought about by a union or strong contact of the lower with the higher consciousness; it cannot be permanent at first, but it can become so by an increased frequency and durability of the calm and peace and finally by the full descent of the eternal peace and calm and silence of the higher consciousness into the lower nature.

The Jivatman in a Supramental Creation

I have used the words Jiva and Jivatman in these and all the passages[1] in exactly the same sense — it never occurred to me that there could be a difference. If I had so intended it, I would have drawn the distinction — the two words being similar — very clearly and not left it to be gathered by inference.

In the passage from the chapter [*in* The Life Divine] on the triple status of the Supermind I was describing how the Supermind working as a force of the highest self-determination of the Divine manifested it in three poises and what was the consciousness of the Jivatman in a supramental creation. There is no statement that the place of the Jivatman is in the supramental plane alone — if that were so, man could have no knowledge of his individual Self or Spirit before he rose to the supramental plane; he could not have any experience of the Self, though he may have the sense of the dissolution of his ego in something Universal. But he can become aware of his unborn non-evolving Self, a centre of the Divine Consciousness, long before that; the Self cosmic or individual is experienced long before rising to Supermind. If it were not so, spiritual experience of that high

---

[1] *The correspondent cited passages from two of Sri Aurobindo's works:* The Life Divine, *volume 21 of* THE COMPLETE WORKS OF SRI AUROBINDO, *p. 157, and* Essays on the Gita, *volume 19, p. 445 and p. 542.*

kind would be impossible to mental man, liberation would be impossible; he would first have to become a supramental being. As for the Purusha it is there on all planes; there is a mental Purusha, *manomaya*, leader of the life and body, as the Upanishad puts it, a vital, a physical Purusha; there is the psychic being or Chaitya Purusha which supports and carries all these as it were. One may say that these are projections of the Jivatman put there to uphold Prakriti on the various levels of the being. The Upanishad speaks also of a supramental and a Bliss Purusha, and if the supramental and the Bliss Nature were organised in the evolution on earth we could become aware of them upholding the movements here.

As for the psychic being it enters into the evolution, enters into the body at birth and goes out of it at death; but the Jivatman, as I know it, is unborn and eternal although upholding the manifested personality from above. The psychic being can be described as the Jivatman entering into birth, if you like, but if the distinction is not made, then the nature of the Atman is blurred and a confusion arises. This is a necessary distinction for metaphysical knowledge and for something that is very important in spiritual experience. The word "Atman" like "spirit" in English is popularly used in all kinds of senses, but both for spiritual and philosophical knowledge it is necessary to be clear and precise in one's use of terms so as to avoid confusion of thought and vision by confusion in the words we use to express them.

If I had meant that it is an individual consciousness that determines all this working, as you tell me, then I should be in contradiction with my own teaching of the Divine as the Master of all and the need of surrender — for an individual who can do everything himself, can carry out his own salvation — he has no need of surrender.

Chapter Two

The Jivatman in Other Indian Systems

The Jivatman in Other Schools

The word Jiva has two meanings in the Sanskritic tongues — "living creature"[1] and the spirit individualised and upholding the living being in its evolution from birth to birth. In the latter sense the full term is Jivatma — the Atman, spirit or eternal self of the living being. It is spoken of figuratively by the Gita as "an eternal portion of the Divine" — but the word fragmentation (used by you) is too strong, it could be applicable to the forms, but not to the spirit in them. Moreover the multiple Divine is an eternal reality antecedent to the creation here. An elaborate description of the Jivatma would be: "the multiple Divine manifested here as the individualised self or spirit of the created being". The Jivatma in its essence does not change or evolve, its essence stands above the personal evolution; within the evolution itself it is represented by the evolving psychic being which supports all the rest of the nature.

The Adwaita Vedanta (Monism) declares that the Jiva has no real existence, as the Divine is indivisible. Another school attributes a real but not an independent existence to the Jiva — it is, they say, one in essence, different in manifestation, and as the manifestation is real, eternal and not an illusion, it cannot be called unreal. The dualistic schools affirm the Jiva as an independent category or stand on the triplicity of God, soul and Nature.

The Jivatman and the Pure "I" of the Adwaita

Well, it is a little difficult to explain. Perhaps the best thing is to

---

[1] In Bengal when one is about to kill a small animal, people often protest saying, "Don't kill — it is Krishna's Jiva (his living creature)."

The Jivatman in Other Indian Systems

break up my answer into a number of separate statements, for the whole thing has got too complicated to do otherwise.

(1) It is impossible to equate my conception or experience of the Jivatman with the pure "I" of the Adwaita, by which you mean, I suppose, something which says, "I am He" and by that perception merges itself into the Brahman. According to the Adwaita of the Mayavadins this Jivatman, like the Ishwara himself, is simply an appearance of the Brahman in illusory Maya. There is no Ishwara, Lord of the world, because there is no world — except in Maya; so too there is no Jivatman, only the Paramatman illusorily perceived as an individual self by the lower (illusory) consciousness in Maya. Those, on the other hand, who wish to unite with the Ishwara, regard or experience the Jiva either as a separate being dependent on the Ishwara or as something one in essence with him, yet different, but this difference like the essential oneness is eternal — and there are also other ideas of the Jivatman and its relation to the Divine or Supreme. So this pure "I", if that is how it is to be described, presents itself differently, in different aspects, one may say, to different people. The Overmind presents the truth of things in all sorts of aspects and mind, even the spiritual mind, fastens on one or the other as the very truth, the one real truth of the matter. It is the mind that makes these differences, but that does not matter, because, through its own way of seeing and experiencing the soul or individualised consciousness or whatever you may like to call it, the mental being goes where it has to go. I hope this much is clear as the first step in the matter.

(2) I do not dispute at all the fact that one can realise the Self, the Brahman or the Ishwara without going into the overhead regions, the dynamic spiritual planes, or stationing oneself permanently above the body as happens in this Yoga. Even if it is done through the Sahasrara, well, the Sahasrara extends to the spiritualised mind and can be felt on the top of the head, so any ascent above is not indispensable. But, apart from that, one can very well, as you say, realise the Atman if one stands back from the mind and heart, detaches oneself from the parts of Prakriti, ceases to identify oneself with mind, life and body, falls

into an inner silence. One need not even explore the kingdoms of the inner mind or inner vital, still less is it compulsory to spread one's wings in ranges above. The Self is everywhere and by entering into full detachment and silence, or even by either detachment or silence, one can get anywhere some glimpse, some reflection, perhaps even a full reflection, or a sense of the Self's presence or of one's own immergence in that which is free, wide, silent, eternal, infinite. Obviously if it is a pure "I", of whatever nature, which gets the experience, it must be looked on by the consciousness that has the realisation as the individual self of the Being, Jivatman.

(3) One can also have the experience of oneself as not the mind but the thinker, not the heart but the self or "I" which supports the feelings, not the life but that which supports life, not the body but that which assumes a body. This self can be obviously dynamic as well as silent; or else you may say that, even though still and immobile, from its silence it originates the dynamism of Nature. One can also feel this to be the Spirit one in all as well as the true "I" in oneself. All depends on the experience. Very usually, it is the experience of the Purusha, often felt first as the Witness silent, upholding all the nature; but the Purusha can also be experienced as the Knower and the Ishwara. Sometimes it is as or through the mental Purusha in one centre or another, sometimes as or through the vital Purusha that one can become aware of one's self or spirit. It is also possible to become aware of the secret psychic being within by itself as the true individual; or one can be aware of the psychic being as the pure "I" with these others standing in mind or vital as representatives in these domains or on these levels. According to one's experience one may speak of any of these as the Jiva or pure "I" (this last is a very dubious phrase) or the true Person or true Individual who knows himself as one with or a portion of or wholly dependent on the universal or transcendent Being and seeks to merge himself in that or ascend to that and be it or live in oneness with it. All these things are quite possible without any need of the overhead experience or of the stable overhead Permanence.

(4) One may ask, first, why not then say that the Jivatman which can be realised in this way is the pure "I" of which the lower self has the experience and through which it gets its salvation; and, secondly, what need is there of going into the overhead planes at all? Well, in the first place, this pure "I" does not seem to be absolutely necessary as an intermediary of the liberation whether into the impersonal Self or Brahman or into whatever is eternal. The Buddhists do not admit any soul or self or any experience of the pure "I"; they proceed by dissolving the consciousness into a bundle of sanskaras, getting rid of the sanskaras and so are liberated into some Permanent which they refuse to describe or some Shunya. So the experience of a pure "I" or Jivatman is not binding on everyone who wants liberation into the Eternal but is content to get it without rising beyond the spiritualised mind into a higher Light above. I myself had my experience of Nirvana and silence in the Brahman, etc. long before there was any knowledge of the overhead spiritual planes; it came first simply by an absolute stillness and blotting out as it were of all mental, emotional and other inner activities — the body continued indeed to see, walk, speak and do its other business but as an empty automatic machine and nothing more. I did not become aware of any pure "I" — nor even of any self, impersonal or other, — there was only an awareness of That as the sole Reality, all else being quite unsubstantial, void, non-real. As to what realised that Reality, it was a nameless consciousness which was not other than That;[2] one could perhaps say this, though hardly even so much as this, since there was no mental concept of it, but no more. Neither was I aware of any lower soul or outer self called by such and such a personal name that was performing this feat of arriving at the consciousness of Nirvana. Well then, what becomes of your pure "I" and lower "I" in all that? Consciousness (not this or that part of consciousness or an "I" of any kind) suddenly emptied itself of all inner contents and remained aware only of unreal surroundings and of Something

---

[2] Mark that I did not think these things, there were no thoughts or concepts nor did they present themselves like that to any Me; it simply just was so or was self-apparently so.

real but ineffable. You may say that there must have been a consciousness aware of some perceiving existence, if not of a pure "I", but, if so, it was something for which these names seem inadequate.

(5) I have said the overhead ascension is not indispensable for the usual spiritual purposes, — but it is indispensable for the purposes of this Yoga. For its aim is to become aware of and liberate and transform and unite all the being in the light of a Truth-consciousness which is above and cannot be reached if there is no entirely inward-going and no transcending and upward-going movement. Hence all the complexity of my psychological statements as a whole, not new in essence — for much of it occurs in the Upanishads and elsewhere, but new in its fullness of collective statement and its developments directed towards an integral Yoga. It is not necessary for anyone to accept it unless he concurs in the aim; for other aims it is unnecessary and may very well be excessive.

(6) But when one *has* made the inner exploration and the ascension, when one's consciousness is located above, one cannot be expected to see things precisely as they are seen from below. The Jivatman is for me the Unborn who presides over the individual being and its developments, associated with it but above it and them and who by the very nature of his existence knows himself as universal and transcendent no less than individual and feels the Divine to be his origin, the truth of his being, the master of his nature, the very stuff of his existence. He is plunged in the Divine and one with the Eternal for ever, aware of his own expression and instrumental dynamism which is the Divine's, dependent in love and delight, with adoration, on That with which yet through that love and delight he is one, capable of relation in oneness, harmonic in this many-sidedness without contradiction, because this is another consciousness and existence than that of the mind, even of the spiritualised mind; it is an intrinsic consciousness of the Infinite, infinite not only in essence but in capacity, which can be to its own self-awareness all things and yet for ever the same and one. This triune realisation, therefore, full of difficulties for the mind, is quite natural, easy,

indisputable to the supramental consciousness or, generally, to the consciousness of the upper hemisphere. It can be seen and felt as knowledge in all the spiritual planes, but the completely indivisible knowledge, the full dynamics of it can only be realised through the supramental consciousness itself on its own plane or by its descent here.

(7) The description of a pure "I" is quite insufficient to describe the realisation of the Jivatman — it is rather describable as the true Person or Divine Individual, though that too is not adequate. The word "I" always comes with an undersuggestion of ego, of separativeness; but there is no separativeness in this self-vision, for the individual here is a spiritual living centre of action for the One and feels no separation from all that is the One.

(8) The Jivatman has its representative power in the individual nature here; this power is the Purusha upholding the Prakriti — centrally in the psychic, more instrumentally in the mind, vital and physical being and nature. It is therefore possible to regard these or any of them as if they were the Jiva here. All the same I am obliged to make a distinction not only for clear thinking but because of the necessity of experience and integral dynamic self-knowledge without which it is difficult to carry through this Yoga. It is not indispensable to formulate mentally to oneself all this, one can have the experience and, if one sees clearly with an inner perception, it is sufficient for progress towards the goal. Nevertheless if the mind is clarified without falling into mental rigidity and error, things are easier for the sadhak of the Yoga. But plasticity must be preserved, for loss of plasticity is the danger of a systematic intellectual formulation; one must look into the thing itself and not get tied up in the idea. Nothing of all this can be really grasped except by the actual spiritual experience.

Part Two

The Parts of the Being and the Planes of Consciousness

Section One

The Organisation of the Being

Chapter One

The Parts of the Being

Men Do Not Know Themselves

Men do not know themselves and have not learned to distinguish the different parts of their being; for these are usually lumped together by them as mind, because it is through a mentalised perception and understanding that they know or feel them; therefore they do not understand their own states and actions, or, if at all, then only on the surface. It is part of the foundation of Yoga to become conscious of the great complexity of our nature, see the different forces that move it and get over it a control of directing knowledge. We are composed of many parts each of which contributes something to the total movement of our consciousness, our thought, will, sensation, feeling, action, but we do not see the origination or the course of these impulsions; we are aware only of their confused pell-mell results on the surface upon which we can at best impose nothing better than a precarious shifting order.

The remedy can only come from the parts of the being that are already turned towards the Light. To call in the light of the Divine Consciousness from above, to bring the psychic being to the front and kindle a flame of aspiration which will awaken spiritually the outer mind and set on fire the vital being, is the way out.

*

What you see and know at present is not the whole of what exists. You do not see your mind and you know only a little part of it — yet your mind exists and is part of your being. There are other parts of your being which you don't know at all — the subconscient for instance. Your sexual impulse or feeling comes out of this subconscient and yet you don't know how or from where it comes in spite of your own will — yet that too is part of your being. But it is possible to know and control. Only a man must give up the pride of his ignorance and have faith in what he does not yet know — then it is possible for him to have the experience.

Many Parts, Many Personalities

The being is made up of many parts. One part may know, the other may not care for the knowledge or act according to it. The whole being has to be made one in the light so that all parts may act harmoniously according to the Truth.

*

The consciousness has in it many parts and many movements and in different conditions and different activities it changes position and arranges its activities in a different way so as to suit what it is doing — but most people are not aware of this because they live only on the surface and do not look into themselves. By sadhana you have become conscious and so you notice these differences.

*

Everybody is an amalgamation not of two but of many personalities. It is a part of the Yogic perfection in this Yoga to accord and transmute them so as to "integrate" the personality.

*

The "tragi-ridiculous" inconsistency you speak of comes from the fact that man is not made up of one piece but of many pieces and each part of him has a personality of its own. That is a thing which people yet have not sufficiently realised — the psychologists have begun to glimpse it, but recognise only when there is a marked case of double or multiple personality. But all men are like that, in reality. The aim should be in Yoga to develop (if one has it not already) a strong central being and harmonise under it all the rest, changing what has to be changed. If this central being is the psychic, there is no great difficulty. If it is the mental being, *manomayaḥ puruṣaḥ prāṇa-śarīra-netā*, then it is more difficult — unless the mental being can learn to be always in contact with and aided by the greater Will and Power of the Divine.

*

Each part of the being has its own nature or even different natures contained in the same part.

*

Each part [*of the being*] has to be kept clear from the other and do its own work and each has to get the truth in it from the psychic or above. The Truth descending from above will more and more harmonise their action, though the perfect harmony can come only when there is the supramental fulfilment.

Chapter Two

Classification of the Parts of the Being

Different Categories in Different Systems

1. The soul and the psychic being are practically the same, except that even in things which have not developed a psychic being, there is still a spark of the Divine which can be called the soul. The psychic being is called in Sanskrit the Purusha in the heart or the Chaitya Purusha. (The psychic being is the soul developing in the evolution.)

2. The distinction between Purusha and Prakriti is according to the Sankhya System — the Purusha is the silent witness consciousness which observes the actions of Prakriti — Prakriti is the force of Nature which one feels as doing all the actions, when one gets rid of the sense of the ego as doer. Then there is the realisation of these two entities. This is quite different from the psychic being. It is felt in the mind, vital, physical — most easily in the mind where the mental being (Purusha) is seated and controls the others (*manomayaḥ puruṣaḥ prāṇa-śarīra-netā*).

3. Prajna, Taijasa etc. are a different classification and have to do, not with the different parts of the being, but with three different states (waking, dream, sleep — gross, subtle, causal).

I think one ought not to try to relate these different things to each other — as that may lead to confusion. They belong to different categories — and to a different order of experiences.

The Concentric and Vertical Systems

I do not think exact correlations can always be traced between one system of spiritual and occult knowledge and another. All deal with the same material, but there are differences of standpoint, differences of view-range, a divergence in the mental idea

Classification of the Parts of the Being 83

of what is seen and experienced, disparate pragmatic purposes and therefore a difference in the paths surveyed, cut out or followed; the systems vary, each constructs its own schema and technique.

In the ancient Indian system there is only one triune supernal, Sachchidananda. Or if you speak of the upper hemisphere as the supernal, there are three, Sat plane, Chit plane and Ananda plane. The Supermind could be added as a fourth, as it draws upon the other three and belongs to the upper hemisphere. The Indian systems did not distinguish between two quite different powers and levels of consciousness, one which we can call Overmind and the other the true Supermind or Divine Gnosis. That is the reason why they got confused about Maya (Overmind-Force or Vidya-Avidya) and took it for the supreme creative power. In so stopping short at what was still a half-light they lost the secret of transformation — even though the Vaishnava and Tantra Yogas groped to find it again and were sometimes on the verge of success. For the rest, this, I think, has been the stumbling-block of all attempts at the discovery of the dynamic divine Truth; I know of none that has not imagined, as soon as it felt the Overmind lustres descending, that this was the true illumination, the gnosis, — with the result that they either stopped short there and could get no farther, or else concluded that this too was only Maya or Lila and that the one thing to do was to get beyond it into some immovable and inactive Silence of the Supreme.

Perhaps, what may be meant by supernals [*in a text submitted by the correspondent*] is rather the three *fundamentals* of the present manifestation. In the Indian system, these are Ishwara, Shakti and Jiva, or else Sachchidananda, Maya and Jiva. But in our system which seeks to go beyond the present manifestation, these could very well be taken for granted and, looked at from the point of view of the planes of consciousness, the three highest — Ananda (with Sat and Chit resting upon it), Supermind and Overmind — might be called the three Supernals. Overmind stands at the top of the lower hemisphere, and you have to pass through and beyond Overmind if you would reach

Supermind, while still above and beyond Supermind are the worlds of Sachchidananda.

You speak of the gulf below the Overmind. But is there a gulf — or any other gulf than human unconsciousness? In all the series of the planes or grades of consciousness there is nowhere any real gulf, always there are connecting gradations and one can ascend from step to step. Between the Overmind and the human mind there are a number of more and more luminous gradations; but, as these are superconscient to human mind (except one or two of the lowest of which it gets some direct touches), it is apt to regard them as a superior Inconscience. So one of the Upanishads speaks of the Ishwara consciousness as *suṣupta*, deep Sleep, because it is only in Samadhi that man usually enters into it, so long as he does not try to turn his waking consciousness into a higher state.

There are in fact two systems simultaneously active in the organisation of the being and its parts; — one is concentric, a series of rings or sheaths with the psychic at the centre; another is vertical, an ascension and descent, like a flight of steps, a series of superimposed planes with the Supermind-Overmind as the crucial nodus of the transition beyond the human into the Divine. For this transition, if it is to be at the same time a transformation, there is only one way, one path. First, there must be a conversion inwards, a going within to find the inmost psychic being and bring it out to the front, disclosing at the same time the inner mind, inner vital, inner physical parts of the nature. Next, there must be an ascension, a series of conversions upwards and a turning down to convert the lower parts. When one has made the inward conversion, one psychicises the whole lower nature so as to make it ready for the divine change. Going upwards, one passes beyond the human mind and at each stage of the ascent there is a conversion into a new consciousness and an infusion of this new consciousness into the whole of the nature. Thus rising beyond intellect through illuminated higher mind to the intuitive consciousness, we begin to look at everything not from the intellect range or through intellect as an instrument, but from a greater intuitive height and through an intuitivised will, feeling, emotion, sensation and physical contact. So, proceeding from intuition to a greater overmind height, there is a new conversion and we look at and experience everything from the overmind consciousness and through a mind, heart, vital and body surcharged with the overmind thought, sight, will, feeling, sensation, play of force and contact. But the last conversion is the supramental, for once there, once the nature is supramentalised, we are beyond the Ignorance and conversion of consciousness is no longer needed, though a farther divine progression, even an infinite development is still possible.

*

The inner consciousness means the inner mind, inner vital, inner physical and behind them the psychic which is their inmost being. But the inner mind is not the higher mind; it is more in touch with the universal forces and more open to the higher consciousness and capable of an immensely deeper and larger range of action than the outer or surface mind — but it is of the same essential nature. The higher consciousness is that above the ordinary mind and different from it in its workings; it ranges from higher mind through illumined mind, intuition and overmind up to the border line of the supramental.

If the psychic were liberated, free to act in its own way, there would not be all this stumbling in the Ignorance. But the psychic is covered up by the ignorant mind, vital and physical and compelled to act through them according to the law of the Ignorance. If it is liberated from this covering, then it can act according to its own nature with a free aspiration, a direct contact with the higher consciousness and a power to change the ignorant nature.

*

Higher Mind is one of the planes of the spiritual mind, the first and lowest of them; it is above the normal mental level. Inner mind is that which lies behind the surface mind (our ordinary mentality) and can only be directly experienced (apart from its vrittis in the surface mind such as philosophy, poetry, idealism etc.) by sadhana, by breaking down the habit of being on the surface and by going deeper within.

Larger mind is a general term to cover the realms of mind which become our field whether by going within or widening into the cosmic consciousness.

The true mental being is not the same as the inner mental — true mental, true vital, true physical being means the Purusha of that level freed from the error and ignorant thought and will of the lower Prakriti and directly open to the knowledge and guidance from above.

Higher vital usually refers to the vital mind and emotive being as opposed to the middle vital which has its seat in the navel and is dynamic, sensational and passionate and the lower which is made up of the smaller movements of human life-desire and life-reactions.

Section Two

The Concentric System: Outer to Inner

Chapter One

The Outer Being and the Inner Being

The Outer and the Inner Being and Consciousness

There are always two different consciousnesses in the human being, one outward in which he ordinarily lives, the other inward and concealed of which he knows nothing. When one does sadhana, the inner consciousness begins to open and one is able to go inside and have all kinds of experiences there. As the sadhana progresses, one begins to live more and more in this inner being and the outer becomes more and more superficial. At first the inner consciousness seems to be the dream and the outer the waking reality. Afterwards the inner consciousness becomes the reality and the outer is felt by many as a dream or delusion, or else as something superficial and external. The inner consciousness begins to be a place of deep peace, light, happiness, love, closeness to the Divine or the presence of the Divine, the Mother. One is then aware of two consciousnesses, this inner one and the outer which has to be changed into its counterpart and instrument — that also must become full of peace, light, union with the Divine. At present you are moving between the two and in this period all the feelings you have are quite natural. You need not be at all anxious about that, but wait for the full development of the inner consciousness in which you will be able to live.

*

There is always a double nature in human beings, the inner (psychic and spiritual) which is in touch with the Divine; the outer, mental, vital and physical, which has been brought up in the Ignorance and is full of defects, imperfections and impurities. It is for this reason that in sadhana things cannot be changed in a moment. The inner experience grows and extends and fills more and more of the nature, but till all is filled, the imperfections remain somewhere.

*

It is a usual experience — to live within in one consciousness while the external being (mind, life, body) goes on of itself under the impulsion of the cosmic Force, doing quietly whatever is necessary to do. This is part of the Yogic consciousness and to have it means a very real and considerable advance on the path of Yoga.

*

You have been accustomed to feel your outer consciousness as if it were yourself and so, when you are in your inner realisation, you feel as if you were not in this old accustomed self. As you grow in the sadhana, you must learn to live in this inner being and to feel the outer as something a little outside and this inner being as your real self.

*

The inner parts in everybody remain vulgar or become high according as they are turned to the outward forces of the Ignorance or towards the higher forces from above and the inner impulsion of the psychic. All forces can play there. It is the outer being that is fixed in a certain character, certain tendencies, certain movements.

*

The outer consciousness is shut up in the body limitation and in the little bit of personal mind and sense dependent on the body — it sees only the outward, sees only things. But the inner consciousness can see behind the thing, it is aware of the play of forces, personal or universal — for it is in conscious touch with the universal action.

*

The Outer and the Inner Being

The outer consciousness is that which usually expresses itself in ordinary life. It is the external mental, vital, physical. It is not connected very much with the inner being except in a few — until one connects them together in the course of the sadhana.

*

The exterior being is the physical which is connected in an ignorant way with the physical universe. It is this physical being which has developed an external mind and vital. The inner mind and vital are on the contrary in direct contact with the universal mental and vital and their forces; the inner subtle physical can also be in direct touch with the cosmic forces of the physical universe. But the exterior being is not in direct touch with the universal or cosmic — only through the outer mind and senses.

*

It is the outer nature that is obscure and when it is at ease, feels no necessity of remembering the Mother — when the difficulty comes, then it feels the necessity and remembers. But the inner being is not like that.

*

The inner being is not usually unquiet but it can be quiet or unquiet like the outer.

The Inner, the Outer and the Process of Yoga

It is only by virtue of the inner consciousness that the outer can awaken to the Divine Influence at all — it receives the inner urge even when it is not aware whence it comes.

*

They [*the inner mind and vital*] exercise an influence and send out their powers or suggestions which the outer sometimes carries out as best it can, sometimes does not follow. How much they work on the outer depends on how far the individual has an inner life. E.g. the poet, musician, artist, thinker, live much from within — men of genius and those who try to live according to an ideal also. But there are plenty of people who have very little inner life and are governed entirely by the forces of Nature.

*

As one gathers experience from life to life, mental or vital, the inner mind and vital also develop according to the use made of our experiences and the extent to which they are utilised for the growth of the being.

*

You are mistaken in thinking that your external being alone is like that. Hardly anybody has the external being of a Yogi — it is the inner being that has the Yogic turn — the external has to be converted and transformed.

*

If the inner being does not manifest or act, the outer being will never get transformed.

*

If the inner being is safe, then there is no longer any struggle or overpowering [*of the outer being*] by inertia or depression or other fundamental difficulties. The rest can be done progressively and quietly, including the coming down of the Force. The outer being becomes merely a machinery or an instrumentation to be set right. It is not so easy to be entirely *mukta* in the inner being.

*

When the inner being once thoroughly establishes its separateness, even oceans of inertia cannot prevent it from keeping it. It is the first thing to be done in order to have a secure basis in the Yoga, to establish thoroughly this separateness. It comes most usually when the peace is thoroughly fixed in all inner parts, that the separateness also becomes fixed and permanent.

The Inner Being

The inner being is the inner mind, inner vital, inner physical with the psychic behind them. The [term] higher being is used to denote the conscious self on planes higher than the ordinary human consciousness.

*

Do you not know that the inner being means the inner mind, inner vital, inner physical with the psychic behind as the inmost? How can there be one centre for all that?

*

The inner being cannot be "located" above, it can only join with the above, penetrate it and be penetrated by it. If it were located above, then there would be no inner being.

*

The inner being has its own time which is sometimes slower, sometimes faster than the physical.

The Inner Being, the Antaratma and the Atman

The word Antaratma is very vaguely used like the word soul in English — so used, it covers all the inner being, inner mind, inner vital, inner physical even, as well as the inmost being, the psychic.

*

Our inner being is in touch with the universal mind, life, matter, a part of all that, but by that very fact it cannot be in possession of liberation and peace. You are thinking probably of the Atman and confusing it with the inner being.

The Inner Being and the Psychic Being

I did not mean by the inner being the psychic or inmost being. It is the psychic being that feels love, bhakti and union with the

Mother. I was speaking of the inner mental, inner vital, inner physical; in order to reach the hidden seat of the psychic one has first to pass through these things. When one leaves the outer consciousness and goes inside, it is here that one enters — some or most entering into the inner vital first, others into the inner mental or inner physical; the emotional vital is the most direct road, for the seat of the psychic is just behind the emotional in the heart centre. It is absolutely necessary for our purpose that one should become conscious in these inner regions, for if they are not awake, then the psychic being has no proper and sufficient instrumentation for its activities; it has then only the outer mind, outer vital and body for its means and these are too small and narrow and obscure. You as yet have been able only to enter the outskirts of the inner vital and are still insufficiently conscious there. By becoming more conscious there and going deeper one can reach the psychic — the safe refuge, *nirāpad sthāna*, of which you speak, and you will not be disturbed by the confused visions and experiences of the inner vital outskirts.

*

The psychic stands behind the inner mind, inner vital and inner physical and supports them all — they are the inner, this the inmost being.

*

I do not know what you mean by its [*the inner being's*] being "around" the psychic. It is obviously nearer to the psychic than the outer mind, vital or physical, but that does not ensure its being open to the psychic only and not to other universal forces.

*

The psychic can have peace behind it — but the inner mind, vital and physical are not necessarily silent — they are full of movements. It is the higher consciousness that has a basis of peace.

*

The Outer and the Inner Being

The psychic being is described in the Upanishads as no bigger than the size of one's thumb! That of course is a symbolic image. For usually when one sees anybody's psychic being in a form, it is bigger than that. As for the inner being, one feels it big because the true mental or the true vital or even the true physical being is much wider in consciousness than the external consciousness which is limited by the body. If the external parts seem to occupy the whole consciousness, it is when one comes down into the physical and feels all the activities of Nature playing in it — even the mental and vital movements are then felt through the physical and not as things of a separate plane. But when one lives in the inner being then one is aware of a consciousness which begins to spread into the universal and the external is only a surface movement thrown up by the universal forces.

The Outer Being and Consciousness

The outer being is a means of expression only, not one's self. One must not identify with it, for what it expresses is a personality formed by the old ignorant Nature. If not identified, one can change it so as to express the true inner personality of the Light.

*

They [*the outer mind, vital and body*] are small, but not unimportant in spite of their apparent insignificance — because they are a necessary passage of transmission between the soul and the outer world.

*

You take the outer waking consciousness as if it were the real person or being and conclude that if it is not this but something else that has the realisation or abides in the realisation, then no one has it — for there is no one here except this waking consciousness. That is the very error by which the ignorance lasts and cannot be got rid of. The very first step in getting out of the ignorance is to accept the fact that this outer consciousness is not one's soul, not oneself, not the real person, but only a temporary formation on the surface for the purposes of the surface play. The soul, the person is within, not on the surface — the outer personality is the person only in the first sense of the Latin word *persona* which meant originally a mask.

Chapter Two

The True Being and the True Consciousness

The True Being

The true being may be realised in one or both of two aspects — the Self or Atman and the soul or *antarātman*, psychic being or *caitya puruṣa*. The difference is that one is felt as universal, the other as individual supporting the mind, life and body. When one first realises the Atman one feels it separate from all things, existing in itself and detached, and it is to this realisation that the image of the dry coconut fruit may apply. When one realises the psychic being, it is not like that; for this brings the sense of union with the Divine and dependence upon it and sole consecration to the Divine alone and the power to change the nature and discover the true mental, the true vital, the true physical being in oneself. Both realisations are necessary for this Yoga.

The "I" or the little ego is constituted by Nature and is at once a mental, vital and physical formation meant to aid in centralising and individualising the outer consciousness and action. When the true being is discovered, the utility of the ego is over and this formation has to disappear — the true being is felt in its place.

*

The psychic is the true being here — the ego is simply a mental, vital, physical formation of the mobile consciousness in Nature which is wrongly taken for our true being so long as the psychic is veiled and the consciousness is in the Ignorance.

*

As to the change of nature, the first step is to become conscious and separate from the old surface nature. For this rajasic vital nature is a surface creation of Prakriti, it is not the true being; however persistent it seems, it is only a temporary combination of vital movements. Behind is the true mental and vital being supported by the psychic — this true being is calm, wide, peaceful. By drawing back and becoming separate one creates the possibility of living in the peace of this inner Purusha no longer identified with the surface Prakriti. Afterwards it will be much easier to change, by the force of the psychic perception and the Peace and Power and Light from above, the surface being.

*

The outward disturbances cannot touch the true being. If one is in the true being, they are not felt as belonging to oneself, but as outside or surface movements which leave one unmoved and unidentified with them.

*

The true inner being — the true mental, the true vital, the true physical represent each on its plane and answer to the central being, but the whole of the nature and especially the outer nature does not nor the ordinary mental, vital or physical personality. The psychic being is the central being for the purposes of the evolution — it grows and develops; but there is a central being above of which the mind is not aware which presides unseen over the existence and of which the psychic being is the representative in the manifested nature. It is what is called the Jivatman.

*

The true being mental, vital or subtle physical has always the greater qualities of its plane — it is the Purusha and like the psychic, though in another way, the projection of the Divine, therefore in connection with the Higher Consciousness and reflects something of it, though it is not altogether that — it is also in tune with the cosmic Truth.

The True Consciousness

The condition you describe[1] is the true consciousness, psychic and spiritual, which will become the base of the sadhana. If it is only for a brief time that it comes, it is always so at the beginning of its coming, but afterwards it fixes and becomes a pervading basis. It is a sign of the psychic opening and when the psychic fully opens and inspires the mind and heart, the love you wish to have will undoubtedly be there. Aspire and persevere and all will come with the growing consciousness.

*

The consciousness that is aware of the Divine and the Truth and does not look at things from the ego [*is the true consciousness*] — it is wide and calm and strong and aspires to union and surrender — it is many things besides, but this is the essential.

*

It [*an experience reported by the correspondent*] is the true Yogic consciousness in which one feels the oneness and lives in it, not touched by the outer being and its inferior movements, but looking on them with a smile at their ignorance and smallness. It will become much more possible to deal with these outer things if that separateness is maintained always.

*

Living in the true consciousness is living in a consciousness in which one is spiritually in union with the Divine in one way or another. But it does not follow that by so living one will have the complete, exact and infallible truth about all ideas, all things and all persons.

*

It is the true consciousness growing within that gives the power [*to be free from the vital forces*]. As it grows, these vital forces

---

[1] *The correspondent's letter is not available.* — Ed.

get more and more externalised and foreign to the nature. It is only by the power of past habit that they rise.

*

This [*vast consciousness above the head*] was the true consciousness that must establish itself, but before it can establish itself it must come down below the head and take full possession of the navel and two lower centres and pervade the body down to the feet and even below. Once established, it holds the ego-forces outside or, even if they come, whether in rajasic or tamasic obstructive form, keeps the inner being totally detached and unmoved all the time by their environmental presence.

*

The consciousness of the mind, life, body in each person is ordinarily shut up in itself; it is narrow, not wide, sees itself as the centre of everything, judges all things according to its own impressions — it does not know anything as it really is. But when by Yoga one begins to open to the true consciousness, then this barrier begins to break down. One feels the mind grow wider, even in the end the physical consciousness grows wider and wider, until you feel all things in yourself, yourself one with all things. You then become one with the Mother's universal Consciousness. That is why you feel the mind becoming wide. But also there is much above the human mind and it is this which you feel like a world above your head. All these are the ordinary experiences of our Yoga. It is only a beginning. But in order that it may go on developing, you must become more and more quiet, more and more able to hold whatever comes without getting too eager and excited. Peace and calmness are the first thing, and with it wideness — in the peace you can bear whatever love or Ananda comes, whatever strength comes or whatever knowledge.

*

To feel quietude, peace, the force working *is* to be conscious; the unconscious condition comes only by confusion and admitting wrong suggestions and restlessness; if you reject these things, the true consciousness will grow in you. Naturally, the consciousness you have now is nothing to what you will have hereafter when it has grown; but it has to begin in this way and increase by quietude. You cannot have the full complete consciousness now and it is no use repining and doubting because it is not complete or fully established as yet; that fretting only delays and hinders. Open yourself; remain quiet; let it grow.

*

There is no insincerity in asking me again and again for the right condition — the feeling of connection and the true consciousness and the psychic state. It is most important that you should have them and become able to keep them. It is indeed the one thing needful for you.

Chapter Three
The Psychic Being

The Psychic and the Divine

They [*the psychic being and the Divine Presence in the heart*] are quite different things. The psychic being is one's own individual soul-being. It is not the Divine, though it has come from the Divine and develops towards the Divine.

*

It [*the psychic*] is constantly in contact with the immanent Divine — the Divine secret in the individual.

*

It is the psychic that is in direct relation with the transcendent Divine and leads the nature upwards towards the Supreme.

*

The Divine is always in the inner heart and does not leave it.

*

The psychic is not, by definition,[1] that part [*of the being*] which is in direct touch with the supramental plane, — although, once

---

[1] Someone had asked what the psychic being was, whether it could be defined as that part of the being which is always in direct touch with the supramental. I replied that it could not be so defined. For the psychic being in animals or in most human beings is not in direct touch with the supramental — therefore it cannot be so described, *by definition*.

But once the connection between the supramental and the human consciousness is made, it is the psychic being that gives *the readiest response* — more ready than the mind, the vital or the physical. It may be added that it is also a purer response; the mind, vital and physical can allow other things to mix with their reception of the supramental influence and spoil its truth. The psychic is pure in its response and allows no such mixture.

The supramental change can take place only if the psychic is awake and is made the chief support of the descending supramental power.

the connection with the supramental is made, it gives to it the readiest response. The psychic part of us is something that comes direct from the Divine and is in touch with the Divine. In its origin it is the nucleus pregnant with divine possibilities that supports this lower triple manifestation of mind, life and body. There is this divine element in all living beings, but it stands hidden behind the ordinary consciousness, is not at first developed and, even when developed, is not always or often in the front; it expresses itself, so far as the imperfection of the instruments allows, by their means and under their limitations. It grows in the consciousness by Godward experience, gaining strength every time there is a higher movement in us, and, finally, by the accumulation of these deeper and higher movements there is developed a psychic individuality, — that which we call usually the psychic being. It is always this psychic being that is the real, though often the secret cause of man's turning to the spiritual life and his greatest help in it. It is therefore that which we have to bring from behind to the front in the Yoga.

The word "soul", as also the word "psychic", is used very vaguely and in many different senses in the English language. More often than not in ordinary parlance no clear distinction is made between mind and soul and often there is an even more serious confusion, for the vital being of desire — the false soul or desire-soul — is intended by the words "soul" and "psychic" and not the true soul, the psychic being. The psychic being is quite different from the mind or vital; it stands behind them where they meet in the heart. Its central place is there, but behind the heart rather than in the heart; for what men call usually the heart is the seat of emotion, and human emotions are mental-vital impulses, not ordinarily psychic in their nature. This mostly secret power behind, other than the mind and the life-force, is the true soul, the psychic being in us. The power of the psychic, however, can act upon the mind and vital and body, purifying thought and perception and emotion (which then becomes psychic feeling) and sensation and action and everything else in us and preparing them to be divine movements.

The psychic being may be described in Indian language as the Purusha in the heart or the *caitya puruṣa*;[2] but the inner or secret heart must be understood, *hṛdaye guhāyām*, not the outer vital-emotional centre. It is the true psychic entity (distinguished from the vital desire-mind) — the psyche — spoken of on the page of the *Arya* to which you make reference.

*

The psychic is the soul, the divine spark animating matter and life and mind and as it grows it takes form and expresses itself through these three touching them to beauty and fineness — it works even before humanity in the lower creation leading it up towards the human, in humanity it works more freely though still under a mass of ignorance and weakness and coarseness and hardness leading it up towards the Divine. In Yoga it becomes conscious of its aim and turns inward to the Divine. It sees behind and above it — that is the difference.

*

The psychic is the spark of the Divine involved here in the individual existence. It grows and evolves in the form of the psychic being — so obviously it cannot have already the powers of the Divine. Only its presence makes it possible for the individual to open to the Divine and grow towards the Divine Consciousness and when it acts it is always in the sense of the Light and the Truth and with the push towards the Divine.

---

[2] The chitta and the psychic part are not in the least the same. Chitta is a term in a quite different category, something from which are thrown up to be combined and set in action the main movements of our external consciousness, and to know it we need not go deep behind our surface or external nature. Category means here another class of psychological factors, *tattva-vibhāga*. The psychic belongs to one class or category — supermind, mind, life, psychic, physical — which covers both the inner and the outer nature. Chitta belongs to quite another class or category — buddhi, manas, chitta, prana etc. — which is the classification made by ordinary Indian psychology; it covers only the psychology of the external being. In this category it is the main functions of our external consciousness only that are coordinated and put in their place by the Indian thinkers; chitta is one of these main functions of the external consciousness and, therefore, to know it we need not go behind the external nature.

The Self or Spirit and the Psychic or Soul

The Spirit is the consciousness above mind, the Atman or self, which is always in oneness with the Divine — a spiritual consciousness is one which is always in unity or at least in contact with the Divine.

The psychic is a spark come from the Divine which is there in all things and as the individual evolves it grows in him and manifests as the psychic being, the soul seeking always for the Divine and the Truth and answering to the Divine and the Truth whenever and wherever it meets it.

*

All contact with the Divine through the essential substance of the consciousness is spiritual and it is that consciousness in the essential substance — what is called self — that is the spiritual consciousness. The soul or psychic being is a spark of the Divine that grows and evolves through successive lives and leads the rest towards the Divine. The spirit or self is the same always.

*

The self feels always its unity with the Divine and is always the same. The soul is a portion of the Divine that comes down into the evolution and evolves a psychic being more and more developed through experiences of successive lives until it is ready for the divine realisation here.

*

There is no distinction between the Self and the spirit. The psychic is the soul that develops in the evolution — the spirit is the Self that is not affected by the evolution, it is above it — only it is covered or concealed by the activity of mind, vital and body. The removal of this covering is the release of the spirit — and it is removed when there is a full and wide spiritual silence.

*

The soul in evolution is only a power for the evolution, it

contains everything in potentiality; but that can only be worked out by the psychic being. It is quite different from the condition of the self.

*

There is a difference between the psychic and the self. The self is the Atman above which is one in all, remains always wide, free, pure, untouched by the action of life in its ignorance. Its nature is peace, freedom, light, wideness, Ananda. The psychic (*antarātmā*) is the individual being which comes down into life and travels from birth to birth and feels the experiences and grows by them till it is able to join itself with the free Atman above.

*

The psychic being is concealed in the depths behind the heart-centre.
    The Self has no separate place — it is everywhere. Your self and the self of all beings is the same.

*

Love, joy and happiness come from the psychic. The Self gives peace or a universal Ananda.

The Atman, the Jivatman and the Psychic

The Jiva is realised as the individual Self, Atman, the central being above the Nature, calm, untouched by the movements of Nature but supporting their evolution though not involved in it. Through this realisation silence, freedom, wideness, mastery, purity, a sense of universality in the individual as one centre of this divine universality become the normal experience. The psychic is realised as the Purusha behind the heart. It is not universalised like the Jivatman, but is the individual soul supporting from its place behind the heart-centre the mental, vital, physical, psychic evolution of the being in Nature. Its realisation brings Bhakti, self-giving, surrender, turning of all the movements Godward, discrimination and choice of all that belongs to the Divine Truth, Good, Beauty, rejection of all that is false, evil, ugly, discordant, union through love and sympathy with all existence, openness to the Truth of the Self and the Divine.

*

The psychic is a spark of the Divine — but I do not know that it can be called a portion of the Jivatma — it is the same put forward in a different way.

*

The *bindu* of which you speak is not the psychic being, but the soul or spark of the Divine which supports each existence; the psychic being is usually seen in form as a Purusha. The psychic being is the soul or spark of the Divine developing a form of itself in the evolution which travels from life to life. The Jivatma and the soul are the same, but in two different statuses. The Jivatma is the Ansha of the Divine standing above the consciousness as the individual self and unchanged by the evolution — the soul is the same descended into the evolution and developing its consciousness from life to life until in the opening of knowledge the psychic being realises its oneness with the self above.

The ego is quite different — it is a creation of Prakriti and part of Prakriti, which centralises the thoughts, desires, passions etc. of the nature and is involved in them entirely. The ego is not a real and eternal existence, but only a formation of Nature. It has to disappear by the coming of knowledge and be replaced by the true psychic and spiritual self.

*

The psychic is the soul in evolution; the Atman is the self above the evolution.

*

There is always a part of the mind, of the vital, of the body which is or can be influenced by the psychic; they can be called the psychic-mental, the psychic-vital, the psychic-physical. According to the personality or the degree of evolution of each person, this part can be small or large, weak or strong, covered up and inactive or prominent and in action. When it acts the movements of the mind, vital or physical accept the psychic motives or aims, partake of the nature of the psychic or follow its aims but with a modification in the manner which belongs to the mind, vital or physical. The psychic-vital seeks after the Divine, but it has a demand in its self-giving, desire, vital eagerness the psychic has not, for the psychic has instead pure self-giving, aspiration, intensity of psychic fire. The psychic-vital is subject to pain and suffering, which there is not in the psychic.

Atma is not the same as psychic — Atma is the self which is one in all, calm, wide, ever at peace, always free. The psychic being is the soul within that experiences life and develops with evolving mind and life and body. The psychic does not suffer like the vital or body, it has not pain or anguish or despair; but it has a psychic sorrow which is different from these things. It has a kind of quiet sweet sadness of yearning which it feels when things go against the Divine, when the obscurity and obstacles are too heavy, when the mind, vital and physical follow after other things, when evil and falsehood and darkness seem to be too strong for the Light. It does not despair, but feels that these things ought not to be and the psychic yearning for it to be otherwise becomes so intense that it is felt as if something akin to sadness.

As for the psychic not being in front, that cannot be brought about all at once; the other parts of the being must be prepared for the change and the veil between must become thinner and thinner. It is for that experiences come and there is the working on the inner mind and vital and physical as well as on the outer nature.

*

What do you mean by a personal vital? What people call personality is a formation. There is no unchangeable vital personality. There is a Presence called the Purusha, something projected by the Self or Atman, which supports on each plane the formation of the personalities on that plane, but the Purusha is not a personality and it has no name or form. But it is best for you not to speculate too much about these subtle things at present; you have not sufficient experience to grasp correctly the complexity of the truth. The one thing you are concerned with is that you have a soul, a psychic being, which stands for your centre of existence, a part of the Divine. Become aware of that and put all your mental, vital and physical nature in relation to it, in order that they may become purified, harmonised, divinised, and the supramental being and nature may descend and be manifested in you — for until this is done, this conscious linking and relation with the psychic centre, there can be no supramental descent.

The Words "Soul" and "Psychic"

The European mind, for the most part, has never been able to go beyond the formula of soul + body — usually including mind in soul and everything except body in mind. Some occultists make a distinction between spirit, soul and body. At the same time there must be some vague feeling that soul and mind are not quite the same thing, for there is the phrase "This man has no soul", or "he is a soul" meaning he has something in him beyond a mere mind and body. But all that is very vague. There is no clear distinction between mind and soul and none between mind and vital and often the vital is taken for the soul.

*

Psychic is ordinarily used in the sense of anything relating to the inner movements of the consciousness or anything phenomenal in the psychology; in this case I have made a special use of it, relating it to the Greek word psyche meaning soul; but ordinarily people make no distinction between the soul and the mental-vital consciousness; for them it is all the same.

*

"Psychic" in the sense in which it is used commonly by people has no definite meaning — it is applied to anything non-physical or supraphysical. In the language of our Yoga it refers always to the inner soul. Therefore the use of the words "psychic significance" is incorrect here. One can say "occult significance" or "symbolic significance" or "inner significance". "Psychic significance" we can say only of experiences belonging to the psychic as opposed to the mental, vital and physical planes.

The Psychic or Soul and Traditional Indian Systems

It appears the Maharshi at the time supposed that by the psychic being I meant the enlightened ego! But people do not understand what I mean by the psychic being, because the word psychic has been used in English to mean anything of the inner mental, inner vital or inner physical or anything abnormal or occult or even the more subtle movements of the outer being, all in a jumble — also occult phenomena are often called psychic. The distinction between these different parts of the being is unknown. Even in India the old knowledge of the Upanishads in which they are distinguished has been lost. The Jivatman, psychic being (*puruṣo antarātmā*), the *manomaya puruṣa*, the *prāṇamaya puruṣa* are all confused together.

*

The *antarātman* is the soul, the portion of the Divine that is at the inmost basis of the evolving individual and supports the mind and life and body which are the instrumental parts of nature through which it tries to grow from the material Inconscience towards the divine Light and Immortality which are its proper being. The limitations of its instruments impose upon it an acceptance of the lower movements and a compromise between soul and nature which retard this movement even while it gets its means of advance from that interchange. The psychic being is the soul-form or soul-personality developing through this evolution and passing from life to life till all is ready for the higher evolution beyond the Ignorance.

*

The psychic being is the Soul, the Purusha in the secret heart supporting by its presence the action of the mind, life and body. The vital is the Pranamaya Purusha spoken of in the Taittiriya Upanishad — the being behind the Force of Life; in its outer form in the Ignorance it generates the desire soul which governs most men and which they mistake often for the real soul.

The Atma is the Self or Spirit that remains above, pure and stainless, unaffected by the stains of life, by desire and ego and ignorance. It is realised as the true being of the individual, but also more widely as the *same being* in all and as the Self of the cosmos; it has also a self-existence above the individual and cosmos and it is then called the Paramatma, the supreme Divine Being. This distinction has nothing to do with the distinction between the psychic and the vital; the vital being is not what is known as the Atma.

The vital as the desire-soul and desire-nature controls the consciousness to a large extent in most men because men are governed by desire. But even in the surface human nature the proper ruler of the consciousness is the mental being, the *manomayaḥ puruṣaḥ prāṇa-śarīra-netā* of the Upanishad. The psychic influences the consciousness from behind, but one has to go out of the ordinary consciousness into the inmost being to find it and make it the ruler of the consciousness as it should be. To do that is one of the principal aims of the Yoga. The vital should be an instrument of the consciousness, not its ruler.

The vital being is not the I — the ego is mental, vital, physical. Ego implies the identification of our existence with outer self, the ignorance of our true self above and our psychic being within us.

In a certain sense the various Purushas or beings in us, psychic, mental, vital, physical, are projections of the Atma, but that gets its full truth only when we get into our inner being and know the inner truth of ourselves. On the surface in the Ignorance, it is the mental, vital, physical Prakriti that acts and the Purusha is disfigured, as it were, in the action of Prakriti. It is not our true mental being, our true vital being, our true physical being even that we are aware of; these remain behind, veiled and silent. It is the mental, vital, physical ego that we take for our being until we get knowledge.

*

The psychic being in the old systems was spoken of as the Purusha in the heart (the secret heart — *hṛdaye guhāyām*) which corresponds very well to what we define as the psychic being behind the heart centre. It was also this that went out from the body at death and persisted — which again corresponds to our teaching that it is this which goes out and returns, linking new life to former life. Also we say that the psychic is the divine portion within us — so too the Purusha in the heart is described as Ishwara of the individual nature in some places.

The word soul is very vaguely used in English — as it often refers to the whole non-physical consciousness including even the vital with all its desires and passions. That is why the word psychic being has to be used so as to distinguish this divine portion from the instrumental parts of the nature.

*

I do not know what is exactly meant by this phrase.[3] It is too vague and limited for a description of the psychic. Antahkarana usually means the mind and vital as opposed to the body — the body being the outer instrument and *manaḥ-prāṇa* the inner instrument of the soul. By psychic I mean something different from a purified mind and vital. A purified mind and vital are the result of the action of the awakened and liberated psychic being but it is not itself the psychic.

Again it depends on what is meant by Ahambhava. But the psychic is not a "bhava"; it is a being, a Purusha. Ahambhava is a formation of Prakriti, it is not a being or a Purusha. Ahambhava can disappear and yet the Purusha will be there.

By liberated psychic being, I mean that it is no longer obliged to express itself under the conditions of the obscure and ignorant instruments, from behind a veil, but is able to come forward,

---

[3] *The correspondent's letter is not available to identify the phrase. — Ed.*

control and change the action of mind and vital and body. Purified and perfected are not epithets that can properly be applied to the psychic — the psychic is always pure and has no positive imperfection. The thing that has to be perfected is its control over the instruments. If it is perhaps sometimes spoken of as purified or perfected, what must be meant is the psychic action in the mind, vital and physical instruments. A purified inner being does not mean a purified psychic, but a purified inner mental, vital and physical. The epithets I used for the psychic were "awakened and liberated".

Spiritual individuality is rather a vague term and might be variously interpreted. I have written about the psychic being that the psychic is the soul or spark of the Divine Fire supporting the individual evolution on the earth and the psychic being is the soul-consciousness developing itself or rather its manifestation from life to life with the mind, vital and body as its instruments until all is ready for the union with the Divine. I don't know that I can add anything to that.

*

The mental being spoken of by the Upanishad is not part of the mental nervous physical composite — it is the *manomayaḥ puruṣaḥ prāṇa-śarīra-netā*, the mental being leader of the life and body. It could not be so described if it were part of the composite. Nor can the composite or part of it be the Purusha, — for the composite is composed of Prakriti. It is described as *manomaya* by the Upanishad because the psychic being is behind the veil and man being the mental being in the life and body lives in his mind and not in his psychic, so to him the *manomaya puruṣa* is the leader of the life and body, — of the psychic behind supporting the whole he is not aware or dimly aware in his best moments. The psychic is represented in man by the Prime Minister, the *manomaya*, itself being a mild constitutional king; it is the *manomaya* to whom Prakriti refers for assent to her actions. But still the statement of the Upanishad gives only the apparent truth of the matter, valid for man and the human stage only — for in the animal it would be rather the *prāṇamaya puruṣa* that is the *netā*, leader of mind and body.

*

Purusha Prakriti is the Kshara Purusha — standing back from it is the Akshara Purusha.

Ego-sense and Purusha are two quite different things — ego-sense is a mechanism of Prakriti, Purusha is the conscious being.

The psychic being evolves, so it is not the immutable.

The psychic being is especially the soul of the individual evolving in the manifestation the individual Prakriti and taking part in the evolution. It is that spark of the Divine Fire that grows behind the mind, vital and physical as the psychic being until it is able to transform the Prakriti of Ignorance into a Prakriti of Knowledge. These things are not in the Gita, but we cannot limit our knowledge by the points in the Gita.

The Soul and the Psychic Being

A distinction[4] has to be made between the soul in its essence and the psychic being. Behind each and all there is the soul which is the spark of the Divine — none could exist without that. But it is quite possible to have a vital and physical being supported by such a soul essence but without a clearly evolved psychic being behind it.

There is indeed an inner being composed of the inner mental, inner vital, inner physical, — but that is not the psychic being. The psychic is the inmost being of all and quite distinct from these. The word psychic is indeed used in English to indicate anything that is other or deeper than the external mind, life and body or it indicates sometimes anything occult or supraphysical; but that is a use which brings confusion and error and we have almost entirely to discard it.

---

[4] *The original text of this letter was revised by Sri Aurobindo on two different occasions. As the two revised versions differ considerably at places, both of them are published here, one after the other. — Ed.*

The Psychic Being

The psychic being is veiled by the surface movements and expresses itself as best it can through the three outer instruments which are more governed by the outer forces than by the inner being or the psychic entity. But that does not mean that they are entirely isolated from the soul. The soul is in the body in the same way as the mind or vital — but the body is not this gross physical body only, but the subtle body also. When the gross body falls away, the vital and mental sheaths of the body still remain as the soul's vehicle till these too dissolve.

The soul of a plant or an animal is not dormant — only its means of expression are less developed than those of a human being. There is much that is psychic in the plant, much that is psychic in the animal. The plant has only the vital-physical elements evolved in its form; the consciousness behind the form of the plant has no developed or organised mentality capable of expressing itself, — the animal takes a step farther; it has a vital mind and some extent of self-expression, but its consciousness is limited, its mentality limited, its experiences are limited; the psychic essence too puts forward to represent it a less developed consciousness and experience than is possible in man. All the same, animals have a soul and can respond very readily to the psychic in man.

The "ghost" of a man is of course not his soul. It is either the man appearing in his vital body or it is a fragment of his vital structure that is seized on by some force or being of the vital world for its own purpose. For normally the vital being with its personality exists after the dissolution of the physical body for some time only; afterwards it passes away into the vital plane where it remains till the vital sheath dissolves. Next one passes in the mental sheath, to some mental world; but finally the soul leaves its mental sheath also and goes to its place of rest. If the mental is strongly developed, then the mental being can remain and so also can the strongly developed vital, provided they are organised by and centred around the true psychic being — they then share the immortality of the psychic. But ordinarily this does not happen; there is a dissolution of the mental and vital as well as the physical parts and the soul in rebirth assumes a new mind, life and body and not, as is often supposed, a replica of its old nature-self. Such a repetition would be meaningless and useless and would defeat the purpose of rebirth which is a progression of the nature by experience, an evolutionary growth of the soul in nature towards its self-finding. At the same time the soul preserves the impression of what was essential in its past lives and personalities and the new birth and personality are a balance between this past and the soul's need for its future.[5]

*

A distinction has to be made between the soul in its essence and the psychic being. Behind each and all there is the soul which is the spark of the Divine — none could exist without that. But it is quite possible to have a vital and physical being without a clearly evolved psychic being behind it. Still, one cannot make general statements that no aboriginal has a soul or there is no display of soul anywhere.

The inner being is composed of the inner mental, inner vital, inner physical, — but that is not the psychic being. The psychic is the inmost being and quite distinct from these. The word psychic is indeed used in English to indicate anything that is other or deeper than the external mind, life and body, anything occult or supraphysical, but that is a use which brings confusion and error and we entirely discard it when we speak or write about Yoga. In ordinary parlance we may sometimes use the word psychic in the looser popular sense or in poetry, which is not bound to intellectual accuracy, we may speak of the soul sometimes in the ordinary and more external sense or in the sense of the true psyche.

The psychic being is veiled by the surface movements and expresses itself as best it can through these outer instruments which are more governed by the outer forces than by the inner influences of the psychic. But that does not mean that they are

---

[5] There are cases in which there is a rapid rebirth of the exterior being with a continuation of the old personality and even the memory of its past life, but this is exceptional and happens usually when there is a frustration by premature death and a strong will in the vital to continue its unfinished experience.

entirely isolated from the soul. The soul is in the body in the same way as the mind or vital — but the body it occupies is not this gross physical frame only, but the subtle body also. When the gross sheath falls away, the vital and mental sheaths of the body still remain as the soul's vehicle till these too dissolve.

The soul of a plant or an animal is not altogether dormant — only its means of expression are less developed than those of a human being. There is much that is psychic in the plant, much that is psychic in the animal. The plant has only the vital-physical evolved in its form, so it cannot express itself; the animal has a vital mind and can, but its consciousness is limited and its experiences are limited, so the psychic essence has a less developed consciousness and experience than is present or at least possible in man. All the same, animals have a soul and can respond very readily to the psychic in man.

The ghost is of course not the soul. It is either the man appearing in his vital body or it is a fragment of his vital that is seized on by some vital force or being. The vital part of us normally exists after the dissolution of the body for some time and passes away into the vital plane where it remains till the vital sheath dissolves. Afterwards it passes, if it is mentally evolved, in the mental sheath to some mental world and finally the psychic leaves its mental sheath also and goes to its place of rest. If the mental is strongly developed, then the mental part of us can remain; so also can the vital, provided they are organised by and centred around the true psychic being — for they then share the immortality of the psychic. Otherwise the psychic draws mind and life into itself and enters into an internatal quiescence.

*

There is the divine spark from the beginning, the soul, in all things, but it takes a long time and a long evolution for it to arrive at a conscious expression and form of manifested being — what we call the psychic being.

*

The soul is described as a spark of the Divine Fire in life and matter, that is an image. It has not been described as a spark of consciousness.

There is mental, vital, physical consciousness — different from the psychic. The psychic being and consciousness are not identical.

When the soul or "spark of the Divine Fire" begins to develop a psychic individuality, that psychic individuality is called the psychic being.

The soul or spark is there before the development of an organised vital and mind. The soul is something of the Divine that descends into the evolution as a divine Principle within it to support the evolution of the individual out of the Ignorance into the Light. It develops in the course of the evolution a psychic individual or soul individuality which grows from life to life, using the evolving mind, vital and body as its instruments. It is the soul that is immortal while the rest disintegrates; it passes from life to life carrying its experience in essence and the continuity of the evolution of the individual.

It is the whole consciousness, mental, vital, physical also, that has to rise and join the higher consciousness and, once the joining is made, the higher has to descend into them. The psychic is behind all that and supports it.

*

The soul is always pure, but the knowledge and force in it are involved and come out only as the psychic being evolves and grows stronger.

*

The psychic being is the soul evolving in the course of birth and rebirth and the soul is a portion of the Divine — but with the soul there is always the veiled Divine.

*

The psychic being is the developing soul consciousness manifested for the created being as it evolves. At first, the soul is something essential behind the veil, not developed in front. In front there is only the body, life, mind. In the evolution the soul consciousness develops more and more in the created being until it is so developed that it can come entirely in front and govern mind, life and body.

*

The difference [*between one psychic being and another*] is one of evolution. The psychic being is more developed in some, but the soul-principle is the same in all.

*

The soul and the psychic are the same — only as there is a vital being supported by the vital and expressing itself through it, so there is a growing psychic being supported on the psychic and expressing itself through the soul-nature.

*

But, hang it all, the psychic is part of the human nature or of ordinary nature, — it has been there even before the human began.

The Form of the Psychic Being

Formed souls enter only into formed organisms — in the protoplasm etc. it is only the spark of the Divine that is there, not the formed soul.

*

As there is in us a mind which one does not see in form but is aware of and as there is at the same time a mental being which one can see in form, so there is a soul and a psychic being. The soul is the same always, the psychic being is what it develops in the evolution.

*

The soul is not limited by any form, but the psychic being puts out a form for its expression, just as the mental, vital and subtle physical Purushas do — that is to say, one can see or another person can see one's psychic being in such and such a form. But this seeing is of two kinds — there is the standing characteristic form taken by this being in this life and there are symbolic forms, such as when one sees the psychic as a newborn child in the lap of the Mother. If the sadhak in question really saw his psychic in the form of a woman it can only have been a constructed appearance expressing some quality or attitude of the psychic.

*

Yes, the psychic being has a form. But that does not appear from the photo [*of a person*]; for the psychic has not always or usually a form closely resembling that of the physical body, it is sometimes even quite different. When looking at the photo [*with Yogic vision*] what is seen is not a form, but something of the consciousness that either is expressed in the body or comes through somehow; one perceives or feels it there through the photo.

The Psychic Being and the Intuitive Consciousness

No, the intuitive self is quite different [*from the psychic*], or rather the intuitive consciousness — that is somewhere above the mind. The psychic stands behind the being — a simple and sincere devotion to the Divine, single-hearted, an immediate sense of what is right and helps towards the Truth and the Divine, an instinctive withdrawal from all that is the opposite are its most visible characteristics.

The Psychic Being and the External Being

What you experience is the first condition of the Yogic consciousness and self-knowledge. The ordinary mind knows itself only as an ego with all the movements of the nature in a jumble and, identifying itself with these movements, thinks "I am doing this, feeling that, thinking, in joy or in sorrow etc." The first beginning of real self-knowledge is when you feel yourself separate from the nature in you and its movements and then you see that there are many parts of your being, many personalities each acting on its own behalf and in its own way. The two different beings you feel are — one, the psychic being which draws you towards the Mother, the other the external being mostly vital which draws you outward and downwards towards the play of the lower nature. There is also in you behind the mind the being who observes, the witness Purusha, who can stand detached from the play of the nature, observing it and able to choose. It has to put itself always on the side of the psychic being and assent to and support its movements and to reject the downward and outward movement of the lower nature, which has to be subjected to the psychic and changed by its influence.

The Psychic or Soul and the Lower Nature

All belongs to Nature — the soul itself acts under the conditions and by the agency of Nature.

*

The moral of the condition you describe is not that Yoga should not be done but that you have to go on steadily healing the rift between the two parts of the being. The division is very usual, almost universal in human nature, and the following of the lower impulse in spite of the contrary will in the higher parts happens to almost everybody. It is the phenomenon noted by Arjuna in his question to Krishna, "Why does one do evil, even though one wishes not to do it, as if compelled to it by force?", and expressed sententiously by Ovid, "*video meliora proboque, Deteriora sequor*".[6] By constant effort and aspiration one can arrive at a turning point when the psychic asserts itself and what seems a very slight psychological change or reversal alters the whole balance of the nature.

*

Every soul is not awake and active; nor is every soul turned directly to the Divine before practising Yoga. For a long time

---

[6] "I see the better and approve of it, I follow the worse." Metamorphoses 7.20 — Ed.

it seeks the Divine through men and things much more than directly.

*

In the ordinary consciousness in which the mind etc. are *not* awakened, the psychic acts as well as it can through them, but according to the laws of the Ignorance.

*

These things, love, compassion, kindness, bhakti, Ananda are the nature of the psychic being, because the psychic being is formed from the Divine Consciousness, it is the divine part within you. But the lower parts are not yet accustomed to obey or value the influence and control of the psychic for in men the vital and physical are accustomed to act for themselves and do not care for what the soul wants. When they do care and obey the psychic, that is their conversion — they begin to put on themselves the psychic or divine nature.

*

The psychic is the support of the individual evolution; it is connected with the universal both by direct contact and through the mind, vital and body.

*

It may be said of the psychic that it is that [*the luminous part of our being*], because the psychic is in touch with the Divine and a projection of the Divine into the lower nature. But the inner mind, vital and physical are a part of the universal and open to the dualities — only they are wider than the external mind, life and body and can receive more largely and easily the divine influence.

*

The psychic is deep within in the inner heart-centre behind the emotional being. From there it stretches upward to form the psychic mind and below to form the psychic vital and psychic physical, but usually one is aware of these only after the mind, vital and physical are subjected and put under the psychic influence.

The Psychic Being or Soul and the Vital or Life

The soul and the life are two quite different powers. The soul is a spark of the Divine Spirit which supports the individual nature; mind, life, body are the instruments for the manifestation of the nature. In most men the soul is hidden and covered over by the action of the external nature; they mistake the vital being for the soul, because it is the vital which animates and moves the body. But this vital being is a thing made up of desires and executive forces good and bad; it is the desire-soul, not the true thing. It is when the true soul (psyche) comes forward and begins first to influence and then govern the actions of the instrumental nature that man begins to overcome vital desire and grow towards a greater divine nature.

*

We are concerned with the growth of the soul out of the Ignorance, not its plunge into it. The lower nature is the nature of the Ignorance, what we seek is to grow into the nature of the Truth. How do you make out that when the soul has looked towards the Truth and is moving towards it, a pull-back by the vital and the ego towards the Ignorance is a glorious action of the soul and not a revolt of the lower nature? I suppose you are floundering about in the confusion of the idea that the "desire-soul" in the vital is the true psyche of man. If you like — but that is no part of my explanation of things; I make a clear distinction between the two, so I refuse to sanctify the revolt of the lower nature by calling it the sanction of the soul. If it is the soul that wants to fail, why is there any struggle or sorrow over the business? It would be a perfectly smooth affair.

*

The psychic being is not the fulfiller of desires — it is the spark of the Divine in all things manifested here that grows into the psychic being and supports the evolution. It is that which survives the dissolution of the vital and physical sheaths and returns to birth again.

*

The two feelings you have are that of two different personalities or parts in the being, one which has the feeling of service is in the vital, the other which has the feeling of the child and of the self-giving is psychic. In the progress of the sadhana these different parts or personalities get developed or transformed and harmonised with each other — all becoming parts of the ultimate perfection of the being in the Mother's consciousness.

The Psychic Being and the Ego

There is individuality in the psychic being but not egoism. Egoism goes when the individual unites himself with the Divine or is entirely surrendered to the Divine.

*

It is the psychic inmost being that replaces the ego. It is through love and surrender to the Divine that the psychic being becomes strong and manifest, so that it can replace the ego.

The Psychic World or Plane

There is a psychic world — a sort of Heaven of peace and beauty and harmony. It is also a place of rest for the soul between two incarnations in which it absorbs its past experiences and becomes ready for another birth.

*

What you describe [*lying calmly in a realm of peace, joy and oneness*] is what we mean by the psychic being in its own plane of existence, for the psychic plane is like that. The psychic stands behind the rest of the being supporting it with its own purity, truth and joy.

Section Three

The Vertical System:
Supermind to Subconscient

Chapter One

The Planes or Worlds of Consciousness

The System of Planes or Worlds

What we speak of are planes of consciousness — the physical is the lowest, above it the ordinary vital, above it the emotional (heart), above it the mental, above the mental are other planes. There is a psychic plane behind the emotional which influences all the others.

*

The physical is not the only world; there are others that we become aware of through dream records, through the subtle senses, through influences and contacts, through imagination, intuition and vision. There are worlds of a larger subtler life than ours, vital worlds; worlds in which Mind builds its own forms and figures, mental worlds; psychic worlds which are the soul's home; others above with which we have little contact. In each of us there is a mental plane of consciousness, a psychic, a vital, a subtle physical as well as the gross physical and material plane. The same planes are situated in the consciousness of general Nature. It is when we enter or contact these other planes that we come into connection with the worlds above the physical. In sleep we leave the physical body, only a subconscient residue remaining, and enter all planes and all sorts of worlds. In each we see scenes, meet beings, share in happenings, come across formations, influences, suggestions which belong to these planes. Even when we are awake, part of us moves in these planes, but their activity goes on behind the veil; our waking minds are not aware of it. Dreams are often only incoherent constructions of our subconscient, but others are records (often much mixed and distorted) or transcripts of experiences in these supraphysical planes. When we do sadhana, this kind of dream becomes very common; then subconscious dreams cease to predominate.

The forces and beings of the vital world have a great influence on human beings. The vital world is on one side a world of beauty, — the poet, artist, musician are in close contact with it; it is also a world of powers and passions, lusts and desires, — our own lusts and desires, and passions and ambitions can put us into connection with the vital worlds and their forces and beings. It is again a world of things dark, dangerous and horrible. Nightmares like X's are contacts with this side of the vital plane. Its influences are also the source of much in men that is demoniac, dirty, cruel and base.

*

It is good that you were able to overcome the difficulty and have a good meditation. Your observation that the difficulty is only in the head and throat and mainly in the latter is very significant. These are the mental centres and it is evident therefore that the difficulty comes from the physical mind. The higher part of the mind belongs to the thinking mind proper, the buddhi, that which understands and observes and guides; the throat is the centre of the externalising mind, that which deals with outer and physical things and responds to them. Its activity is always one of the chief difficulties of the sadhana. If it is quiet it is easier, as you have seen, for the whole being to be quiet.

The last of the four experiences, that of the being within arranged in layers one under the other like the steps of a ladder, is also very significant and very true. It is so that inner consciousness is arranged. There are five main divisions of this ladder. At the top above the head are layers (or as we call them planes) of which we are not conscious and which become conscious to us only by sadhana — those above the human mind — that is the higher consciousness. Below from the crown of the head to the throat are the layers (there are many of them) of the mind, the three principal being one at the top of the head communicating with the higher consciousness, another between the eyebrows where is the thought, sight and will, a third in the throat which is the externalising mind. A second division is from the shoulders to the navel, these are the layers of the higher vital presided over by the heart centre where is the emotional being with the psychic hidden behind it. From the navel downwards is the rest of the vital being containing several layers. From the bottom of the spine downward are the layers of the physical consciousness proper, the material, and below the feet is the subconscient which has also many levels.

The experience of the splitting of the forehead from the middle and the pouring out of light signified the opening of the centre of thought, will and vision there. When this opens, there is the opening of the inner mind consciousness through which the light of the higher can pour out — here it is the Mother's white light that was pouring out through the opening.

The lights you saw were the many lights (powers, forces full of light) of the higher consciousness, the Truth consciousness or divine consciousness. Their pouring down was preceded and made possible by the appearance of the moon, the spiritual light. It is when the spiritual light is there that the presence of the Mother is revealed and her action brings down the powers of the Truth, the Divine and she gives them to the sadhak.

*

If we regard the gradation of worlds or planes as a whole, we see them as a great connected complex movement; the higher precipitate their influences on the lower, the lower react to the higher and develop or manifest in themselves within their own formula something that corresponds to the superior power and its action. The material world has evolved life in obedience to a pressure from the vital plane, mind in obedience to a pressure from the mental plane. It is now trying to evolve supermind in obedience to a pressure from the supramental plane. In more detail, particular forces, movements, powers, beings of a higher world can throw themselves on the lower to establish appropriate and corresponding forms which will connect them with the material domain and, as it were, reproduce or project their action here. And each thing created here has, supporting it, subtler envelopes or forms of itself which make it subsist and connect it with forces acting from above. Man, for instance, has, besides his gross physical body, subtler sheaths or bodies by which he lives behind the veil in direct connection with supraphysical planes of consciousness and can be influenced by their powers, movements and beings. What takes place in life has always behind it preexistent movements and forms in the occult vital planes; what takes place in mind presupposes preexistent movements and forms in the occult mental planes. That is an aspect of things which becomes more and more evident, insistent and important, the more we progress in a dynamic Yoga.

But all this must not be taken in too rigid and mechanical a sense. It is an immense plastic movement full of the play of possibilities and must be seized by a flexible and subtle tact or sense in the seeing consciousness. It cannot be reduced to a too rigorous logical or mathematical formula. Two or three points must be pressed in order that this plasticity may not be lost to our view.

First, each plane, in spite of its connection with others above and below it, is yet a world in itself, with its own movements, forces, beings, types, forms existing as if for its and their own sake, under its own laws, for its own manifestation without apparent regard for other members of the great series. Thus, if we regard the vital or the subtle physical plane, we see great ranges of it (most of it) existing in themselves, without any relation with the material world and with no movement to affect or influence it, still less to precipitate a corresponding manifestation in the physical formula. At most we can say that the existence of anything in the vital, subtle physical or any other plane creates a possibility for a corresponding movement of manifestation in the physical world. But something more is needed to turn that static or latent possibility into a dynamic potentiality or an actual urge towards a material creation. That something may be a call from the material plane, e.g. some force or someone in the physical existence entering into touch with a supraphysical power or world or part of it and moved to bring it down into the earth life. Or it may be an impulse in the vital or other plane itself, e.g. a vital being moved to extend his action towards the earth and establish there a kingdom for himself or the play of the forces for which he stands in his own domain. Or it may be a pressure from above, let us say some supramental or mental power precipitating its formation from above and developing forms and movements on the vital level as a means of transit to its self-creation in the material world. Or it may be all these things acting together, in which case there is the greatest possibility of an effective creation.

Next, as a consequence, it follows that only a limited part of the action of the vital or other higher planes is concerned with the earth-existence. But even this creates a mass of possibilities which is far greater than the earth can at one time manifest or contain in its own less plastic formulas. All these possibilities do not realise themselves; some fail altogether and leave at the most an idea that comes to nothing; some try seriously and are repelled and defeated and, even if in action for a time, come to nothing. Others effectuate a half manifestation, and this is the most usual result, the more so as these vital or other supraphysical forces come into conflict and have not only to overcome the resistance of the physical consciousness and of matter, but their own internecine resistance to each other. A certain number succeed in precipitating their results in a more complete and successful creation, so that if you compare that creation with its original in the higher plane, there is something like a close resemblance or even an apparently exact reproduction or translation from the supraphysical to the physical formula. And yet even there the exactness is only apparent; the very fact of translation into another substance and another rhythm of manifestation makes a difference. It is something new that has manifested and it is that that makes the creation worth while. What for instance would be the utility of a supramental creation on earth if it were just the same thing as a supramental creation on the supramental plane? It is that, in principle, but yet something else, a triumphant new self-discovery of the Divine in conditions that are not elsewhere.

No doubt, the subtle physical is closest to the physical, and most like it. But yet the conditions are different and the thing too different. For instance, the subtle physical has a freedom, plasticity, intensity, power, colour, wide and manifold play (there are thousands of things there that are not here) of which as yet we have no possibility on earth. And yet there is something here, a potentiality of the Divine which the other in spite of its greater liberties has not, something which makes creation more difficult, but in the last result justifies the labour.

*

Each plane of consciousness contains the others in itself in principle. In the physical consciousness there is a physical mind, a vital force and action which we call the vital physical, and the physical proper or material.

*

Mind has its own realms and life has its own realms just as matter has. In the mental realms life and substance are entirely subordinated to Mind and obey its dictates. Here on earth there is the evolution with matter as the starting point, life as the medium, mind emerging from it. There are many grades, realms, combinations in the cosmos — there are even many universes. Ours is only one of many.

The Planes and the Body

The heavenly worlds are above the body. What the parts of the body correspond to are planes — subtle physical, higher, middle and lower vital, mental. Each plane is in communication with various worlds that belong to it.

*

The appearance of the being in other planes is not the same necessarily as that of the physical body. Very often the form taken by the vital or psychic or mental being is very different from the physical form. Even when they resemble on the whole, there is always some difference.

Chapter Two

The Supermind or Supramental

Supermind and the Purushottama

Purushottama of the Gita is the supreme being; the supermind is a power of the Supreme — or proceeding from him, if you like.

*

Supermind is not *the* Purushottama consciousness, it is *a* Purushottama consciousness, a certain level and power of being which he can share with his "eternal portions", aṁśāḥ sanātanāḥ, provided they can climb out of the Ignorance. As for embodying it, it is certainly difficult but not impossible.

Supermind and Sachchidananda

Supermind is between the Sachchidananda planes and the lower creation. It contains the self-determining Truth of the Divine Consciousness and is necessary for a Truth creation.
    One can of course realise Sachchidananda in relation to the mind, life, body also — but then it is something stable, supporting by its presence the lower Prakriti, but not transforming it. The supermind alone can transform the lower nature.

*

In the supramental consciousness, there are no problems — the problem is created by the division set up by the Mind. The Supramental sees the Truth as a single whole and everything falls into its place in that whole. The Supramental is also spiritual, but the old Yogas reach Sachchidananda through the spiritualised mind and depart into the eternally static oneness of Sachchidananda or rather pure Sat (Existence) absolute and eternal or else a pure Non-existence absolute and eternal. Ours having realised Sachchidananda in the spiritualised mind plane proceeds to realise it in the supramental plane.

The supreme supra-cosmic Sachchidananda is above all. Supermind may be described as its power of self-awareness and world-awareness, the world being known as within itself and not outside. So to live consciously in the supreme Sachchidananda one must pass through the Supermind. If one is in the supra-cosmic apart from the manifestation, there is no place for problems or solutions. If one lives in the transcendence and the cosmic view at the same time, that can only be by the supramental consciousness in the supreme Sachchidananda consciousness — so why should the question arise? Why should there be a difference between the supreme Sachchidananda version of the cosmos and the Supermind's version of it? Your difficulty probably comes from thinking of both in terms of the mind.

The Supermind is an entirely different consciousness not only from the spiritualised Mind, but from the planes above spiritualised Mind which intervene between it and the supramental plane. Once one passes beyond Overmind to Supermind, one enters into a consciousness to which the norms of the other planes do not at all apply and in which the same Truth, e.g. Sachchidananda and truth of this universe, is seen in quite a different way and has a different dynamic consequence. This necessarily results from the fact that Supermind has an indivisible knowledge, while Overmind proceeds by union in division and Mind by division taking division as the first fact, for that is the natural process of its knowledge.

In all planes the essential experience of Sachchidananda, pure Existence, Consciousness, Bliss is the same and Mind is often contented with it as the sole Truth and dismisses all else as part of the grand Illusion, but there is also a dynamic experience of the Divine or of Existence (e.g. as One and Many, Personal and Impersonal, the Infinite and Finite etc.) which is essential for the integral knowledge. The dynamic experience is not the same in the lower planes as in the higher, in the intermediate spiritual planes and in the Supramental. In these the oppositions can only be put together and harmonised, in the Supermind they fuse together and are inseparably one; that makes an enormous difference.

The universe is dynamism, movement — the essential experience of Sachchidananda apart from the dynamism and movement is static. The full dynamic truth of Sachchidananda and the universe and its consequence cannot be grasped by any other consciousness than the Supermind, because the instrumentation in all other (lower) planes is inferior and there is therefore a disparity between the fullness of the static experience and the incompleteness of the dynamic power, knowledge, result of the inferior light and power of other planes. This is the reason why the consciousness of the other spiritual planes even if it descends can make no radical change in the earth-consciousness, it can only modify or enrich it. The radical transformation needs the descent of a supramental power and nature.

One cannot speak of two classes of Sachchidananda, for Sachchidananda is the same always — but the knowledge of Sachchidananda and the universe differs according to the degree of the consciousness which has the experience.

The personal realisation of the Divine may be sometimes with Form, sometimes without Form. Without Form, it is the Presence of the living Divine Person, felt in everything. With Form, it comes with the image of the One to whom worship is offered. The Divine can always manifest himself in a form to the bhakta or seeker. One sees him in the form in which one worships or seeks him or in a form suitable to the Divine Personality who is the object of the adoration. How it manifests depends on many things and it is too various to be reduced to a single rule. Sometimes it is in the heart that the Presence with the form is seen, sometimes in any of the other centres, sometimes above and guiding from there; sometimes it is seen outside and in front as if an embodied Person. Its advantages are an intimate relation and constant guidance or if felt or seen within, a very strong and concrete realisation of the constant Presence. But one must be very sure of the purity of one's adoration and seeking — for the disadvantage of this kind of embodied relation is that other Forces can imitate the Form or counterfeit the voice and the guidance and this gets more force if it is associated with a constructed image which is not the true thing. Several have been misled in this way because pride, vanity or desire was strong in them and robbed them of the finer psychic perception that is not mental and can at once turn the Mother's light on such misleadings or errors.

*

It is the supramental Power that transforms mind, life and body — not the Sachchidananda consciousness which supports impartially everything. But it is by having experience of the Sachchidananda, pure existence-consciousness-bliss, that the ascent to the supramental and the descent of the supramental become (at a much later stage) possible. For first one must get free from the ordinary limitation by the mental, vital and physical formations, and the experience of the Sachchidananda peace, calm, purity and wideness gives this liberation.

The supermind has nothing to do with passing into a blank. It is the Mind overpassing its own limits and following a negative and quietistic way to do it that reaches the big blank. The Mind, being the Ignorance, has to annul itself in order to enter into the supreme Truth — or, at least, so it thinks. But the supermind being the Truth-Consciousness and the Divine Knowledge has no need to annul itself for the purpose.

*

The Will of Sachchidananda can act under different conditions in the Knowledge or the Ignorance. The Supermind is the Truth Consciousness, the Knowledge, and the will there works out spontaneously the unmixed Knowledge — whereas below the Supermind it allows the forces to play in quite another way and supports them or intervenes according to the need of the play in the Ignorance.

*

In the supermind, consciousness is existence eternally aware both *that it is* and of what it is and also of what it intends to do with itself and become for its own Ananda. Consciousness and knowledge there are one.

The Supracosmic, the Supramental, the Overmind and Nirvana

(1) I mean by the supracosmic Reality the supreme Sachchidananda who is above this and all manifestations, not bound by any, yet from whom all manifestation proceeds and all universe.

(2) The supramental and the supracosmic are not the same. If it were so there could be no supramental world and no descent of the supramental principle into the material world — we would be brought back to the idea that the divine Truth and Reality can only exist beyond and the universe, any universe can only be a half-truth or an illusion of ignorance.

(3) I mean by the supramental the Truth-Consciousness whether above or in the universe by which the Divine knows not only his own essence and being but his manifestation also. Its fundamental character is knowledge by identity, by that the Self is known, the Divine Sachchidananda is known, but also the truth of the manifestation is known, because this too is That — *sarvaṁ khalvidaṁ brahma, Vāsudevaḥ sarvam* etc. Mind is an instrument of the Ignorance trying to know — Supermind is the Knower possessing knowledge because one with it and the known, therefore seeing all things in the Light of His own Truth, the light of their true Self which is He. It is a dynamic and not only a static Power, not only a Knowledge, but a Will according to Knowledge — there is a supramental Power or Shakti which can manifest directly its world of Light and Truth in which all is luminously based on the harmony and unity of the One, not disturbed by a veil of Ignorance or any disguise. The Supermind therefore does not transcend all manifestation, but it is above the triplicity of mind, life and matter which is our present experience of this manifestation.

(4) The Overmind is a sort of delegation from the Supermind (this is a metaphor only) which supports the present evolutionary universe in which we live here in Matter. If Supermind were

to start here from the beginning as the direct creative Power, a world of the kind we see now would be impossible; it would have been full of the divine Light from the beginning, there would be no involution in the inconscience of Matter, consequently no gradual striving evolution of consciousness in Matter. A line is therefore drawn between the higher half of the universe of consciousness, *parārdha*, and the lower half, *aparārdha*. The higher half is constituted of Sat, Chit, Ananda, Mahas (the supramental) — the lower half of mind, life, Matter. This line is the intermediary Overmind which, though luminous itself, keeps from us the full indivisible supramental Light, depends on it indeed, but in receiving it, divides, distributes, breaks it up into separated aspects, powers, multiplicities of all kinds, each of which it is possible by a further diminution of consciousness such as we reach in Mind to regard as the sole or the chief Truth and all the rest as subordinate or contradictory to it. To this action of the Overmind may be applied the words of the Upanishad, "The face of the Truth is covered by a golden Lid", or those of the Vedic *ṛtena ṛtam apihitam*. Here there is the working of a sort of *vidyā-avidyāmayī māyā* which makes possible the predominance of *avidyā*. It is by this primitive divisional principle that the Mind is enabled to regard for example the Impersonal as the Truth and the Personal as only a mask or the personal Divine as the greatest Truth and impersonality as only an aspect; it is so too that all the conflicting philosophies and religions arise, each exalting one aspect or potentiality of Truth presented to Mind as the whole sufficient explanation of things or exalting one of the Divine's Godheads above all others as the true God than whom there can be no other or none so high or higher. This divisionary principle pursues man's mental knowledge everywhere and even when he thinks he has arrived at the final unity and harmony, it is only a constructed unity based on an Aspect. It is so that the scientist seeks to found the unity of knowledge on some original physical aspect of things, Energy or Matter, Electricity or Ether, or the Mayavadin thinks he has arrived at absolute Adwaita by cutting existence into two and calling the upper side Brahman and the lower side Maya. It is the reason why mental knowledge can never arrive at a final solution of anything, for the aspects of Existence as distributed by Overmind are numberless and one can go on multiplying philosophies and religions for ever.

In the Overmind itself there is not this confusion, for the Overmind knows the One as the support, essence, fundamental power of all things, but in the dynamic play proper to it it lays emphasis on its divisional power of multiplicity and seeks to give each Power or Aspect its full chance to manifest, relying on the underlying Oneness to prevent disharmony or conflict. Each Godhead, as it were, creates his own world, but without conflict with others; each Aspect, each Idea, each Force of things can be felt in its full separate energy or splendour and work out its values, but this does not create a disharmony because the Overmind has the sense of the Infinite and in the true (not spatial) Infinite many concording infinities are possible. This peculiar security of Overmind is however not transferable to the lower planes of consciousness which it supports and governs, because as one descends in the scale the stress on division and multiplicity increases and in the Mind the underlying oneness becomes vague, abstract, indeterminate and indeterminable and the only apparent concreteness is that of the phenomenal which is by its nature a form and representation — the self-view of the One has already begun to disappear. Mind acts by representations and constructions, by the separation and weaving together of its constructed data; it can make a synthetic construction and see it as the whole, but when it looks for the reality of things, it takes refuge in abstractions — it has not the concrete vision, experience, contact sought by the mystic and the spiritual seeker. To know Self and Reality directly or truly, it has to be silent and reflect some light of these things or undergo self-exceeding and transformation, and this is only possible either by a higher Light descending into it or by its ascent, the taking up or immergence of it into a higher Light of existence. In Matter, descending below Mind, we arrive at the acme of the principle of fragmentation and division; the One, though secretly there, is lost to knowledge and we get the fullness of the Ignorance, even a fundamental Inconscience out of which the universe has to evolve consciousness and knowledge.

(5) If we regard Vaikuntha or Goloka each as the world of a Divinity, Vishnu or Krishna, we would be naturally led to seek its place or its origin in the Overmind plane. The Overmind is the plane of the highest worlds of the Gods. But Vaikuntha and Goloka are human conceptions of states of being that are beyond humanity. Goloka is evidently a world of Love, Beauty and Ananda full of spiritual radiances (the cow is the symbol of spiritual light) of which the souls there are the keepers or possessors, Gopas and Gopis. It is not necessary to assign any single plane to this manifestation — in fact there can be a reflection or possession of it or of its conditions on any plane of consciousness — the mental, vital or even the subtle physical plane. The explanation of it which you mention is not therefore excluded, it is quite feasible.

(6) It is not possible to situate Nirvana as a world or plane, for the Nirvana push is to a withdrawal from world and world-values; it is therefore a state of consciousness or rather of superconsciousness without habitation or level. There is more than one kind of Nirvana (extinction or dissolution) possible. Man being a mental being in a body, *manomaya puruṣa*, makes this attempt at retreat from the cosmos through the spiritualised mind, he cannot do otherwise and it is this that gives it the appearance of an extinction or dissolution, *laya*, *nirvāṇa*; for extinction of the mind and all that depends on it including the separative ego in something Beyond is the natural way, almost the indispensable way for such a withdrawal. In a more affirmative Yoga seeking transcendence but not withdrawal there would not be this indispensability, for there would be the way already alluded to of self-exceeding or transformation of the mental being. But it is possible also to pass to that through a certain experience of Nirvana, an absolute silence of mind and cessation of its activities, constructions, representations which can be so complete that not only to the silent mind but also to the passive senses the whole world is emptied of its solidity and reality and things appear only as unsubstantial forms without

any real habitations or else floating in something that is a nameless Infinite: this Infinite or else something still beyond is That which alone is real; an absolute calm, peace, liberation would be the resulting state. Action would continue, but no initiation or participation in it by the silent liberated consciousness; a nameless Power would do all until there began the descent from above which would transform the consciousness, making its silence and freedom a basis for a luminous knowledge, action, Ananda. But such a passage would be rare; ordinarily a silence of the mind, a liberation of the consciousness, a renunciation of its belief in the final value or truth of the mind's imperfect representations or constructions would be enough for the higher working to be possible.

(7) Now about the cosmic consciousness and Nirvana. Cosmic consciousness is a complex matter. To begin with, there are two sides to it, the experience of the Self free, infinite, silent, inactive, one in all and beyond all and the direct experience of the cosmic Energy and its forces, workings and formations, this latter experience not being complete till one has the sense of being commensurate with the universe or pervading, exceeding and containing it. Till then there may be direct contacts, communications, interchanges with cosmic forces, beings, movements, but not the full unity of mind with the cosmic Mind, of life with the cosmic Life, of body and physical consciousness with the cosmic material Energy and its substance. Again there may be a realisation of the Cosmic Self which is not followed by the realisation of the dynamic universal oneness. Or on the contrary there may be some dynamic universalising of consciousness without the experience of the free static Self omnipresent everywhere, — the preoccupation with and pleasure of the greater energies that one would thus experience would stop the way to that liberation. Also the identification or universalisation may be more on one plane or level of consciousness than on another, predominantly mental or predominantly emotional (through universal sympathy or love) or vital of another kind (experience of the universal life forces) or physical. But in any case, even with the full realisation and experience it should be evident that this

cosmic play would be something that one would finally feel as limited, ignorant, imperfect from its very nature. The free soul might regard it untouched and unmoved by its imperfections and vicissitudes, do some appointed work, try to help all or be an instrument of the Divine, but neither the work nor the instrumentation would have anything like the perfection or even the full light, power, bliss of the Divine. This could only be gained by an ascension into higher planes of cosmic existence or their descent into one's consciousness — and, if this were not envisaged or accepted, the push to Nirvana would still remain as a way of escape. The other way would be the ascent after death into these higher planes, — the heavens of the religions signify after all nothing but such an urge to a greater, luminous, beatific Divine Existence.

But, one might ask, if the higher planes or if the Overmind itself were to manifest their consciousness with all that power, light, freedom and vastness and these things were to descend into an individual consciousness here, would not that make unnecessary both the cosmic negation or the Nirvanic push and the urge towards some Divine Transcendence? But in the result, though one might live in a union with the Divine in a luminous wide free consciousness embracing the universe in itself and be a channel of great energies or creations, spiritual or external, yet this world here would remain fundamentally the same — there would be a gulf of difference between the Spirit within and its medium and stuff on which it acted, between the inner consciousness and the world in which it was working. The achievement inner, subjective, individual might be perfect, but the dynamic outcome insufficient, disparate, a mixture, not a perfect harmony of the inner and the outer, a new integral rhythm of existence here that could be called truly divine. Only a consciousness like the supramental, unconditioned and in perfect unity with its source, a Truth-Consciousness empowered to create its own free determinations would be able to establish some perfect harmony and rhythm of the higher hemisphere in this lowest rung of the lower hemisphere. Whether it is to do so or not depends on the significance of the evolutionary existence; it depends on whether that existence is something imperfect in its very nature and doomed to frustration — in which case either a negative way of transcendence by some kind of Nirvana or a positive way of transcendence, perhaps by breaking the shining lid of Overmind, *hiraṇmaya pātra*, into what is above it, would be the final end of the soul escaping from this meaningless universe; unless indeed like the Amitabha Buddha one were held by compassion or else the Divine Will within to continue helping and sharing the upward struggle towards the Light of those here still in the darkness of the Ignorance. If on the contrary this world is a Lila of spiritual involution and evolution in which one power after another up to the highest is to appear as Matter, Life and Mind have already appeared out of an apparent indeterminate Inconscience, then another culmination is possible.

The push to Nirvana has two motive forces behind it. One is the sense of the imperfection, sorrow, death, suffering of this world — the original motive force of the Buddha. But for escape from these afflictions Nirvana might not be necessary, if there are higher worlds into which one can ascend where there is no such imperfection, sorrow, death or suffering. But this other possibility of escape is met by the idea that these higher worlds too are transient and part of the Ignorance, that one has to return here always till one overcomes the Ignorance, that the Reality and the cosmic existence are as Truth and Falsehood, opposite, incompatible. This brings in the second motive force, that of the call to Transcendence. If the Transcendent is not only supracosmic but an aloof Incommunicable, *avyavahāryam*, which one cannot reach except by a negation of all that is here, then some kind of Nirvana, an absolute Nirvana even is inevitable. If on the other hand the Divine is transcendent but not incommunicable, the call will still be there and the soul will leave the chequered cosmic play for the beatitude of the transcendent existence, but an absolute Nirvana would not be indispensable; a beatific union with the Divine offers itself as the way before the seeker. This is the reason why the Cosmic Consciousness is not sufficient and the push away from it is so strong, — it is only if the golden lid of the Overmind is overpassed and opened and the dynamic contact with the Supermind and a descent of its Light and Power here is intended that it can be otherwise.

Supermind and Other Planes

The words supermind and supramental were first used by me, but since then people have taken up and are using the word supramental for anything above the mind.

*

The highest or true Vijnana is the supramental plane — the plane of the Divine Knowledge — it is only at the end of the sadhana, when there is the full siddhi that one can have free connection with that plane.

*

The Supramental is a higher level of consciousness than the mind in which one gets the direct truth of the Supreme and the whole truth. One can meet the One in the mind, but it is an imperfect knowledge and experience.

*

It is only the supramental that is all Knowledge. All below that from Overmind to Matter is Ignorance — an Ignorance growing at each level nearer to the full Knowledge. Below Supermind there may be Knowledge but it is not all Knowledge.

*

I have not said that everything is falsehood except the supramental Truth. I said that there was no complete Truth below the supramental. In the Overmind the Truth of supermind which is whole and harmonious enters into a separation into parts, many Truths fronting each other and moved each to fulfil itself, to make a world of its own or else to prevail or take its share in worlds made of a combination of various separated Truths and Truth-forces. Lower down in the scale, the fragmentation becomes more and more pronounced, so as to admit of positive error, falsehood, ignorance, finally, inconscience like that of Matter. This world here has come out of the Inconscience and developed the Mind which is an instrument of Ignorance trying to reach out to the Truth through much limitation, conflict, confusion and error. To get back to Overmind, if one can do it completely, which is not easy for physical beings, is to stand on the borders of the supramental Truth with the hope of entry there.

*

If the supermind were not to give us a greater and completer truth than any of the lower planes, it would not be worth while trying to reach it. Each plane has its own truths. Some of them are no longer true on a higher plane; e.g. desire and ego are truths of the mental, vital and physical Ignorance — a man there without ego or desire would be a tamasic automaton. As we rise higher, ego and desire appear no longer as truths, they are falsehoods disfiguring the true person and the true will. The struggle between the Powers of Light and the Powers of Darkness is a truth here — as we ascend above, it becomes less and less of a truth and in the supermind it has no truth at all. Other truths remain but change their character, importance, place in the whole. The difference or contrast between the Personal and Impersonal is a truth of the Overmind — there is no separate truth of them in the supermind, they are inseparably one. But one who has not mastered and lived the truths of Overmind cannot reach the supramental Truth. The incompetent pride of man's mind makes a sharp distinction and wants to call all else untruth and leap at once to the highest truth whatever it may be — but that is an ambitious and arrogant error. One has to climb the stairs and rest one's feet firmly on each step in order to reach the summit.

*

Each plane is true in itself but only in partial truth to the Supermind. When these higher truths come into the physical they try to realise themselves there but can do so only in part and under the conditions of the material plane. It is only the Supermind that can overcome this difficulty.

*

Supermind is not organised in the lower planes as the others are. It is only a veiled influence. Otherwise the supramental realisation would be easy.

Supermind and Overmind

Supermind is not merely a step higher than Overmind — it is beyond the line, that is, a different consciousness and power beyond the mental limit.

*

It is hardly possible to say what the Supermind is in the language of Mind, even spiritualised Mind, for it is a different consciousness altogether and acts in a different way. Whatever may be said of it is likely to be not understood or misunderstood. It is only by growing into it that one can know what it is and this also cannot be done until after a long process by which mind heightening and illuminating becomes pure Intuition (not the mixed thing that ordinarily goes by that name) and Intuition widens and masses itself into Overmind; after that Overmind can be lifted into and suffused with Supermind till it undergoes a transformation.

In the Supermind all is self-known self-luminously, there are no divisions, oppositions or separated aspects as in Mind whose principle is division of Knowledge into parts and setting each part against another. Overmind approaches this at its top and is often mistaken for Supermind, but it cannot reach it — except by uplifting and transformation.

*

By the Supermind is meant the full Truth-consciousness of the Divine Nature in which there can be no place for the principle of division and ignorance; it is always a full light and knowledge superior to all mental substance or mental movement. Between the

The Supermind or Supramental

Supermind and the human mind are a number of ranges, planes or layers of consciousness — one can regard it in various ways — in which the element or substance of mind and consequently its movements also become more and more illumined and powerful and wide. The Overmind is the highest of these ranges; it is full of lights and powers; but from the point of view of what is above it, it is the line of the soul's turning away from the complete and indivisible knowledge and its descent towards the Ignorance. For although it draws from the Truth, it is here that begins the separation of aspects of the Truth, the forces and their working out as if they were independent truths and this is a process that ends, as one descends to ordinary Mind, Life and Matter, in a complete division, fragmentation, separation from the indivisible Truth above. There is no longer the essential, total, perfectly harmonising and unifying knowledge, or rather knowledge for ever harmonious because for ever one, which is the character of Supermind. In the Supermind mental divisions and oppositions cease, the problems created by our dividing and fragmenting mind disappear and Truth is seen as a luminous whole. In the Overmind there is not yet the actual fall into Ignorance, but the first step is taken which will make the fall inevitable.

*

The Supermind is the One Truth deploying and determining the manifestation of its Powers — all these Powers working as a multiple Oneness, in harmony, without opposition or collision, according to the One Will inherent in all. The Overmind takes these Truths and Powers and sets each working as a force in itself with its necessary consequences — there can be harmony in their action, but the Overmind's harmonies are synthetic and partial rather than inherent, total and inevitable and, as one descends from the highest Overmind, separation, collision and conflict of forces increase, separability dominates, ignorance grows, existence becomes a clash of possibilities, a mixture of conflicting half-truths, an unsolved and apparently unsolvable riddle and puzzle.

*

The Supermind is the Truth-Consciousness; below it there intervenes the Overmind of which the principle is to receive the powers of the Divine and try to work them out separately, each acting in its own right and working to realise a world of its own or, if it has to act with others, enforcing its own principle as much as possible. Souls descending into the Overmind act in the same way. The principle of separated Individuality is from here. At first still aware of its divine origin, it becomes as it descends still more and more separated and oblivious of it, governed by the principle of division and ego. For Mind is farther removed from the Truth than Overmind, Vital Nature is engrossed in the realisation of ignorant forces, while in Matter the whole passes into what seems an original Inconscience. It is the Overmind Maya that governs this world, but in Matter it has deepened into Inconscience out of which consciousness reemerges and climbs again bringing down into Matter life and mind, and opening in mind to the higher reaches — which are still in some direct connection with the Truth (Intuition, Overmind, Supermind).

*

At the time when these chapters [*the last chapters of* The Synthesis of Yoga] were written, the name "overmind" had not been found, so there is no mention of it. What is described in these chapters is the action of the supermind when it descends into the overmind plane and takes up the overmind workings and transforms them.[1] It was intended in later chapters to show how difficult even this was and how many levels there were between human mind and supermind and how even supermind, descending, could get mixed with the lower action and turned into something that was less than the true Truth. But these later chapters were not written.

*

The distinction [*between the Supermind and the Overmind*] has

---

[1] The highest Supermind or Divine Gnosis existent in itself is something that lies beyond still and quite above.

not been made in the *Arya* because at that time what I now call the Overmind was supposed to be an inferior plane of the Supermind. But that was because I was seeing them from the Mind. The true defect of Overmind, the limitation in it which gave rise to a world of Ignorance, is seen fully only when one looks at it from the physical consciousness, from the result (Ignorance in Matter) to the cause (Overmind division of the Truth). In its own plane Overmind seems to be only a divided, many-sided play of the Truth, so can easily be taken by the Mind as a supramental province. Mind also when flooded by the Overmind lights feels itself living in a surprising revelation of divine Truth. The difficulty comes when we deal with the vital and still more with the physical. Then it becomes imperative to face the difficulty and to make a sharp distinction between Overmind and Supermind — for it then becomes evident that the Overmind Power (in spite of its lights and splendours) is not sufficient to overcome the Ignorance because it is itself under the law of Division out of which came the Ignorance. One has to pass beyond and supramentalise Overmind so that mind and all the rest may undergo the final change.

*

The Supermind is the total Truth Consciousness; the Overmind draws down the truths separately and gives them a separate activity — e.g. in the Supermind the Divine Peace and Power, Knowledge and Will are one. In the Overmind each of these becomes a separate aspect which can exist or act on its own lines apart from the others. When it comes down to Mind, this turns into an ignorance and incapacity — because Knowledge can come without a Will to support it or Peace can be disturbed by the action of Power etc.

*

Supermind by the way is synthetic only in the lowest spaces of itself where it has to prepare the principles of Overmind — synthesis is necessary only where analysis has taken place; one has dissected everything, put in pieces (analysis) so one has to piece together. But Supermind is unitarian, has never divided up, so it does not need to add and piece together the parts and fragments. It has always held the conscious Many together as the conscious One.

*

To return to the supramental — the supramental is simply the direct self-existent Truth Consciousness and the direct self-effective Truth Power. There can therefore be no question of jugglery about it. What is not true is not supramental. As for calm and silence, there is no need of the supramental to get that. One can get it even on the level of Higher Mind which is the next above the human intelligence. I got these things in 1908, twenty-seven years ago and I can assure you they were solid enough and marvellous enough without any need of supramentality to make it more so! Again, a calm that "seems like motion" is a phenomenon of which I know nothing. A calm or silence which can support or produce action — that I know and that is what I have had — the proof is that out of an absolute silence of the mind I edited the *Bande Mataram* for four months and wrote $6\frac{1}{2}$ volumes of the *Arya*, not to speak of all the letters and messages etc. etc. I have written since. If you say that writing is not an action or motion but only something that seems like it, a jugglery of the consciousness, — well, still out of that calm and silence I conducted a pretty strenuous political activity and have also taken my share in keeping up an Asram which has at least an appearance to the physical senses of being solid and material! If you deny that these things are material or solid (which of course metaphysically you can), then you land yourself plump into Shankara's illusionism, and there I will leave you.

You will say however that it is not the Supramental but at most the Overmind that helped me to these non-nebulous motions. But the Supermind is by definition a greater dynamic activity than mind or Overmind. I have said that what is not true is not supramental; I will add that what is ineffective is not supramental. And finally I will conclude by saying that I have not told X that I have taken possession of the supramental — I only admit to be very near to it, or at least to its tail. But "very near" is — well, after all a relative phrase like all human phrases.

*

One must have already become intuitively conscious to know about the overmind and the supermind. To give "signs" is useless, for the mind would only make mistakes in trying to judge by the "signs" — one has to become conscious within and know directly.

Knowledge and Will in the Supermind

That [*the division between knowledge and will*] is true of mental knowledge and will, but not of the higher knowledge-will. In the Supermind knowledge and will are one.

*

Knowledge and will have naturally to be one before either can act perfectly.

*

Force and Knowledge are two different things and in the consciousness below supermind may go together or may not.

Chapter Three

The Overmind

Overmind and the Cosmic Consciousness

Overmind is the highest source of the cosmic consciousness available to the embodied being in the Ignorance. It is part of the cosmic consciousness — but the human individual when he opens into the cosmic usually remains in the cosmic Mind-Life-Matter receiving only inspirations and influences from the higher planes of Intuition and Overmind. He receives through the spiritualised higher and illumined mind the fundamental experiences on which spiritual knowledge is based; he can become even full of intuitive mind movements, illuminations, various kinds of powers and illumined light, liberation, Ananda. But to rise fully into the Intuition is rare, to reach the Overmind still rarer — although influences and experiences can come down from there.

*

It is (sometimes directly, sometimes indirectly) by the power of the Overmind releasing the mind from its close partitions that the cosmic consciousness opens in the seeker and he becomes aware of the cosmic spirit and the play of the cosmic forces.

It is from or at least through the overmind plane that the original prearrangement of things in this world is effected; for from it the determining vibrations originally come. But there are corresponding movements on all the planes, the mind, the vital, the physical even, and it is possible in a very clear or illumined condition of the lower consciousness to become aware of these movements and understand the plan of things and be a conscious instrument or even, to a limited extent, a determinant Will or Force. But the stuff of the lower planes always mixes with the overmind forces and diminishes or even falsifies and perverts their truth and power.

It is even possible for the Overmind to transmit to the lower planes of consciousness something of the supramental Light; but, so long as the Supermind does not directly manifest, its Light is modified in Overmind itself and still further modified in the application by the needs, the demands, the circumscribing possibilities of the individual nature. The success of this diminished and modified Light, e.g. in purifying the physical, cannot be immediate and absolute as the full and direct supramental action would be; it is still relative, conditioned by the individual nature and the balance of the universal forces, resisted by adverse powers, baulked of its perfect result by the unwillingness of the lower workings to cease, limited either in its scope or in its efficacy by the want of a complete consent in the physical nature.

*

Probably what X calls overmind is the first "above-mind" layers of consciousness. Or it may be experiences from the larger Mind or Vital ranges. To the human mind all these are so big that it is easy to take them for overmind or even supermind. One can get indirect overmind touches if one opens into the cosmic consciousness, still more if one enters freely into that consciousness. Direct overmind experience cannot come unless part of the being at least is seated in the wideness and peace.

*

You cannot do it [*recognise the different planes of the Overmind*] at present. Only those who have got fully into the cosmic consciousness can do it and even they cannot do it at first. One must first go fully through the experience of higher mind and illumined mind and intuition before it can be done.

Planes of the Overmind

There are different planes of the Overmind. One is mental, directly creative of all the formations that manifest below in the mental world — that is the mental Overmind. Above is the overmind Intuition. Still above are the planes of overmind that are more and more connected with the supermind and have a partly supramental character. Highest in the overmind ranges is the supramental Overmind or Overmind gnosis. But these are things you cannot understand until you get a higher experience.

*

It [*the overmind*] can for convenience be divided into four planes — mental overmind and the three you have written [*intuitive overmind, true overmind and supramental overmind*] — but there are many layers in each and each of these can be regarded as a plane in itself.

*

There are many stages in the transition from mental overmind to supramentalised overmind and then from that to supramental overmind and from that to supermind. Do not be in a hurry to say, "This is the last highest overmind."

*

What you call supramental overmind[1] is still overmind — not a part of the true Supermind. One cannot get into the true Supermind (except in some kind of trance or Samadhi) unless one has first objectivised the overmind Truth in life, speech, action, external knowledge and not only experienced it in meditation and inner experience.

The Overmind, the Intuition and Below

The Overmind receives the Divine Truth and disperses it in various formations and diverse play of forces, building thus different worlds out of this dispersion.

In the Intuition the nature of Knowledge is Truth not global or whole, but coming out in so many points, edges, flashes of a Truth that is behind it and supplies it with its direct perceptions.

*

---

[1] This expression is a misnomer since overmind cannot be supramental: it can at most receive some light and truth from the higher source.

It is from the Overmind that all these different arrangements of the creative Truth of things originate. Out of the Overmind they come down to the Intuition and are transmitted from it to the Illumined and higher Mind to be arranged there for our intelligence. But they lose more and more of their power and certitude in the transmission as they come down to the lower levels. What energy of directly perceived Truth they have is lost in the human mind; for to the human intellect they present themselves only as speculative ideas, not as realised Truth, not as direct sight, a dynamic vision coupled with a concrete undeniable experience.

The Overmind and the Supermind Descent

The Overmind has to be reached and brought down before the Supermind descent is at all possible — for the Overmind is the passage through which one passes from mind to Supermind.

The Overmind and the *Kāraṇa Deha*

The *kāraṇa deha* may be simply a form answering to the higher consciousness (overmental, intuitive etc.) and I suppose a being could be there working in that consciousness and body. It is not likely to be the supramental being and supramental body — for in that case the whole consciousness, thought, action subjective and objective would begin to be faultlessly true and irresistibly effective. Nobody has reached that stage yet, even the overmind is, for all but the Mother and myself, either unrealised or only an influence mostly subjective.

The Dividing Aspect of the Overmind

There are no Overmind dangers — it is only the lower consciousness misusing overmind or higher consciousness intimations that can make a danger. There are also no Overmind Falsehoods. The Overmind is part of the Ignorance in this sense that it is the highest knowledge to which the Ignorance can attain, but the knowledge is still divided and so can be a knowledge of parts and aspects of the Truth, not the integral knowledge. As such it can be misused and turned into falsehood by the Mind.

*

What I said was that the scission between the two aspects of the Divine [*Personal and Impersonal*] is a creation of the Overmind which takes various aspects of the Divine and separates them into separate entities. Thus it divides Sat, Chit and Ananda, so that they become three separate aspects different from each other. In fact in the Reality there is no separateness, the three aspects are so fused into each other, so inseparably one that they are a single undivided reality. It is the same with the Personal and Impersonal, the Saguna and Nirguna, the Silent and the Active Brahman. In the Reality they are not contrasted and incompatible aspects; what we call Personality and what we call Impersonality are inseparably fused together in a single Truth. In fact "fused together" even is a wrong phrase, because there they were never separated so that they have to be fused. All the quarrels about either the Impersonal being the only true truth or the Personal being the only highest truth are mind-created quarrels derivative from this dividing aspect of the Overmind. The Overmind does not deny any of the aspects as the Mind does, it admits them all as aspects of the One Truth, but by separating them it originates the quarrel in the more ignorant and more limited and divided Mind, because the Mind cannot see how two opposite things can exist together in one Truth, how the Divine can be *nirguṇo guṇī*; — having no experience of what is behind the two words it takes each in an absolute sense. The Impersonal is Existence, Consciousness, Bliss, not a Person, but a state. The Person is the Existent, the Conscious, the Blissful; consciousness, existence, bliss taken as separate things are only states of his being. But in fact the two (personal being and eternal state) are inseparable and are one reality.

The Overmind and the World

[*How the world appears to one living at the overmind level*:] As a manifestation of the One Divine with a thousand aspects, a development of all the potentialities in the one existence, a play of Forces and Ideas which you can look at from many centres and points of view, each having its own truth in the whole. In the highest overmind all these prepare to meet and reunite themselves in one central Truth which is the Supramental.

Chapter Four

The Higher Planes of Mind

The Higher Planes and Higher Consciousness

The higher planes are the higher mind, illumined, intuitive, overmind, supermind. The psychic, mind, vital, physical belong to the ordinary manifestation.

*

The planes and the body are not the same. Above the head are seen all the planes from the overmind down to the higher mind, but this is only a correlation in the consciousness — not an actual location in space.

*

The spiritual mind is a mind which, in its fullness, is aware of the Self, reflecting the Divine, seeing and understanding the nature of the Self and its relations with the manifestation, living in that or in contact with it, calm, wide and awake to higher knowledge, not perturbed by the play of the Forces. When it gets its full liberated movement, its central station is very usually felt above the head, though its influence can extend downward through all the being and outward through space.

*

It [*higher consciousness*] means the larger spiritual consciousness which contains all these things [*cosmic consciousness, intuitive consciousness, other planes of consciousness between Intuition and mind*] in possibility and once it is there can develop them in their due place or order.

*

The planes below [*the Supermind, from the Overmind to the Higher Mind*] are of the spiritual consciousness but when there is a dynamic action from them, it is always a mixed action, not an action of pure knowledge but of knowledge subduing itself to the rule of the Ignorance, the cosmic necessity in a world of Ignorance. If their action was that of the full Knowledge, there would be no need of any supramental descent.

*

The higher consciousness is a concentrated consciousness, concentrated in the Divine Unity and in the working out of the Divine Will, not dispersed and rushing about after this or that mental idea or vital desire or physical need as is the ordinary human consciousness — also not invaded by a hundred haphazard thoughts, feelings and impulses, but master of itself, centred and harmonious.

The Plane of Intuition

Intuition sees the truth of things by a direct inner contact, not like the ordinary mental intelligence by seeking and reaching out for indirect contacts through the senses etc. But the limitation of the Intuition as compared with the Supermind is that it sees things by flashes, point by point, not as a whole. Also in coming into the mind it gets mixed with the mental movement and forms a kind of intuitive-mind activity which is not the pure truth, but something in between the higher Truth and the mental seeking. It can lead the consciousness through a sort of transitional stage and that is practically its function.

*

Intuition is in direct contact with the higher Truth but not in an integral contact. It gets the Truth in flashes and turns these flashes of Truth-perception into intuitions — intuitive ideas. The ideas of the true Intuition are always correct so far as they go — but when intuition is diluted in the ordinary mind stuff, its truth gets mixed with error.

*

Intuitivising [*of the being*] is not sufficient to prevent a drop [*in consciousness*]; if it is complete (and it is not complete until not only the mind, but the vital and physical are intuitivised) it can make you understand and be conscious of all the processes in you and around but it does not necessarily make you entire master of the reactions. For that Knowledge is not enough — a certain Knowledge-Will (knowledge and will fused together) or Consciousness-Power is needed.

*

One can get intuitions — communications from there [*the intuitive plane*] even while the ego exists — but to live in the wideness of the Intuition is not possible with the limitation of the ego.

*

The Intuition is the first plane on which there is a real opening to the full possibility of realisation — it is through it that one goes farther — first to Overmind and then to Supermind.

*

It [*the individual Self*] is not specially related [*to intuition*] — intuition is the highest power the embodied individual can reach without universalising itself; when it universalises itself it is then possible for it to come in contact with overmind. If by the individual Self is meant the Jivatman, it can be on any plane of consciousness.

*

By the intuitive self I meant the intuitive being, that part which belongs to the intuitive plane or is in connection with it. The intuition is one of the higher planes of consciousness between the human thinking mind and the supramental plane.

*

The difference between intuition and thought is very much like that between seeing a thing and badgering one's brains to find out what the thing can possibly be like. Intuition is truth-sight.

The thing seen may not be the truth? Well, in that case it will at least be one of its hundred tails or at least a hair from one of the tails. The very first step in the supramental change is to transform all operations of consciousness from the ordinary mental to the intuitive, only then is there any hope of proceeding farther, — not to, but towards the supramental.

The Plane of Intuition and the Intuitive Mind

Intuition proper is true in itself (when not interpreted or altered by mind), although fragmentary — intuitive mind is mixed with mind and therefore not infallible because the truth intuition gives may be mixed or imperfectly put by mind.

*

There is the Intuition and below it there is the intuitive mind which may have several degrees or layers. Also there is a partial power of intuition in ordinary mind itself, in the vital, in the physical consciousness, in the material itself.

*

To live in the Intuitive it is necessary first to have the opening into the cosmic consciousness and to live first in the higher and the illumined Mind, seeing everything from there. To receive constantly the intuition from above, that is not necessary — it is sufficient to have the sense of the One everywhere and to get into contact with things and people through the inner mind and senses more than with the outer mind and senses — for the latter meet only the surface of things and are not intuitive.

*

The intuitive "mind" does not get the touch *direct* from the supramental. Above it is the Overmind — in which there is a higher and greater intuition and above that are the supermind ranges.

*

The intuitive mind is a level of consciousness which is touched by the light of higher truths and receives them vividly and conveys them to the consciousness below.

*

I do not think it can be said that there are separate strata in the intuitive for purity, strength and beauty. These are separate powers of the Divine, not separate strata. But of course they can be arranged by the Mind in that way for some organised purpose.

Yogic Intuition and Ordinary Intuitions

Some people have a faculty of receiving impressions about others which is not by any means infallible, but often turns out to be right. That is one thing and the Yogic intuition by which one directly knows or feels what is in a man, his capacities, character, temperament, is another. The first may be a help for developing the other, but it is not the same thing. The Yogic faculty has to be and it can be complete only with a great development of the inner consciousness.

*

To have the true intuition one must get rid of the mind's self-will and the vital's also, their preferences, fancies, fantasies, strong insistences, and eliminate the mental and vital ego's pressure which sets the consciousness to work in the service of its own claims and desires. Otherwise these things will come in with force and claim to be intuitions, inspirations and the rest of it. Or if any intuitions come, they can be twisted and spoiled by the mixture of these forces of the Ignorance.

*

It [*intuition*] is the power of knowing any truth or fact directly without reasoning or sense-proof, by a spontaneous right perception.

*

As for intuition — well! One has to make a distinction — if one can — between a pure intuition and a mixed one. A pure intuition carries in it a truth, even if it is only a fragment or point of truth, and can be trusted. A mixed one carries in it some suggestion of truth which gets coated with mental matter — here one has to use discrimination and separate the true suggestion from the less reliable mental matter. Intuition and discrimination must always go together so long as one mixes in the mental plane — and for some time after.

*

Mental intuitive knowledge catches directly some aspect of a truth but without any completeness or certitude and the intuition is easily mixed with ordinary mental stuff that may be erroneous; in application it may easily be a half truth or be so misinterpreted and misapplied as to become an error. Also, the mind easily imitates the intuition in such a way that it is difficult to distinguish between a true or a false intuition. That is the reason why men of intellect distrust the mental intuition and say that it cannot be accepted or followed unless it is tested and confirmed by the intellect. What comes from the overmind intuition has a light, a certitude, an effective force of Truth in it that the mental intuition at its best even has not.

*

Yes,[1] but it does not *necessarily* come from the original source — the plane of Intuition. There are mental, vital, subtle physical intuitions as well as intuitions from the higher and the illumined Mind.

Powers of the Intuitive Consciousness

Revelation is a part of the intuitive consciousness.

*

---

[1] *The correspondent asked: "Is the knowledge got by the Samyama of Rajayoga of the same kind as one would get by Intuition? Is the source of the knowledge not the same?"* — Ed.

There is a discrimination [*in the intuitive consciousness*] that is not intellectual — a direct perception.

*

No, the world of Knowledge is composed of several planes. It is from one of them that inspiration comes.

The Illumined Mind

Intuition is above illumined Mind — which is simply higher Mind raised to a great luminosity and more open to modified forms of intuition and inspiration.

*

The substance of knowledge is the same [*in the higher mind and the illumined mind*], but the higher mind gives only the substance and form of knowledge in thought and word — in the illumined mind there begins to be a peculiar light and energy and ananda of knowledge which grows as one rises higher in the scale or else as the knowledge comes from a higher and higher source. This light etc. are still rather diluted and diffused in the illumined mind; it becomes more and more intense, clearly defined, dynamic and effective on the higher planes, so much so as to change always the character and power of the knowledge.

The Higher Mind

The higher mind is a thing in itself above the intellect. It is only when something of its power comes down and is modified in the lower mind substance that it acts as part of the intellect.

*

It depends on what is meant by the higher buddhi — whether you use the word to mean the higher part of the intellect or the higher Mind. The higher Mind in itself on its own level knows, but when it is involved in the ordinary human intelligence and works under limitations, it often does not know — or it has the idea merely that it must be so but has not the consciousness of its separate existence. The intellect can rise above its ordinary movements and feel itself as a separate power no longer working under the limitations of the vital and physical mind and the senses. It then begins to reflect something of the action of the higher mind but without the full freedom and greater light and truth of the higher mind.

Chapter Five

The Lower Nature or Lower Hemisphere

The Higher Nature and the Lower Nature

The lower nature is called lower because it is unenlightened — it can't be enlightened and changed by ignoring it, the higher has to be brought there. So one must speak of both, not of the higher alone.

*

But why do you suppose that you alone are made of the lower nature? Every earthly being is so made. The higher nature is there but behind and above. It has to be brought forward from the inner being or brought down from above constantly and persistently till the lower is changed.

The Three Planes of the Lower Hemisphere and Their Energies

There is a vital plane (self-existent) above the material universe which we see; there is a mental plane (self-existent) above the vital and material. These three together, — mental, vital, physical, — are called the triple universe of the lower hemisphere. They have been established in the earth-consciousness by evolution — but they exist in themselves before the evolution, above the earth-consciousness and the material plane to which the earth belongs.

*

Forces, movements are not really planes but lines of consciousness or force which you may feel in that way one over the other. The planes are planes of consciousness and its powers — in the mind there is a mind of Knowledge (higher mind), a mind of will (dynamic mind) and a mind of thought (intellect) which are one above the other and it is these you probably mean. They easily get covered when their forces come down into the ordinary mind — covered by the lower consciousness.

*

It is not possible to give a name to all the energies that act in the being. They are put into several classes. First are the mental thought energies (intelligence, dynamic mind, physical perceptive mind); the vital — 1st emotional vital with all the emotional movements in it; 2nd the central vital (the larger desires, passions, ambitions, forces of work, possession, conquest); 3rd the lower vital (all the small egoistic movements of desire, enjoyment, lust, greed, jealousy, envy, vanity etc. etc.); 4th the physical energies concerned with the material life and its functioning, needs, outer action, instrumental fulfilment of the other powers.

*

It cannot be explained accurately in a few words; but roughly thoughts are of the mind, emotions are of the heart, desires are of the vital. On the surface they are all mixed together, but behind they come from separate parts of the being.

The Adhara

The Adhara is that in which the consciousness is now contained — mind-life-body.

*

The Adhar means the mind, life and body as instruments of the expression of the being — the being is the conscious Existence within which uses mind, life and body as its instruments of thought, feeling and action. But sometimes the word being is used to signify the whole — soul and nature together.

Chapter Six
The Mind

Mind in the Integral Yoga and in Other Indian Systems

The "Mind" in the ordinary use of the word covers indiscriminately the whole consciousness, for man is a mental being and mentalises everything; but in the language of this Yoga, the words mind and mental are used to connote specially the part of the nature which has to do with cognition and intelligence, with ideas, with mental or thought perceptions, the reactions of thought to things, with the truly mental movements and formations, mental vision and will etc. that are part of his intelligence. The vital has to be carefully distinguished from mind, even though it has a mind element transfused into it; the vital is the Life nature made up of desires, sensations, feelings, passions, energies of action, will of desire, reactions of the desire soul in man and of all that play of possessive and other related instincts, anger, fear, greed, lust etc. that belong to this field of the nature. Mind and vital are mixed up on the surface of the consciousness, but they are quite separate forces in themselves and as soon as one gets behind the ordinary surface consciousness one sees them as separate, discovers their distinct action and can with the aid of this knowledge analyse their surface mixtures. It is quite possible and even usual during a time shorter or longer, sometimes very long, for the mind to accept the Divine or the Yogic ideal while the vital is unconvinced and unsurrendered and goes obstinately on its way of desire, passion and attraction to the ordinary life. Their division or their conflict is the cause of most of the more acute difficulties of the sadhana.

*

I don't use these terms [*Manas, Buddhi etc.*] myself as a rule — they are the psychological phraseology of the old Yoga.

*

The terms Manas etc. belong to the ordinary psychology applied to the surface consciousness. In our Yoga we adopt a different classification based on the Yoga experience. What answers to this movement of the Manas there would be two separate things — a part of the physical mind communicating with the physical vital. It receives from the physical senses and transmits to the Buddhi — i.e. to some part or other of the Thought-Mind; it receives back from the Buddhi and transmits idea and will to the organs of sensation and action. All that is indispensable in the ordinary action of the consciousness. But in the ordinary consciousness everything gets mixed up together and there is no clear order or rule. In the Yoga one becomes aware of the different parts and their proper action, and puts each in its place and to its proper action under the control of the higher consciousness or else under the control of the Divine Power. Afterwards all gets surcharged with the spiritual consciousness and there is an automatic right perception and right action of the different parts because they are controlled entirely from above and do not falsify or resist or confuse its dictates.

Manas and Buddhi

Manas is the sense mind, that which perceives physical objects and happenings through the senses and forms mental percepts about them and mental reactions to them; it also observes the reactions of the Chitta, feelings, emotions, sensations etc. (which belong to what in the system of this Yoga is called the vital). Buddhi is the thinking mind which stands above and behind all these things, reflects, judges, decides what is to be thought or done or not done, what is right or wrong, true or false etc. At least that is what it should do in all independence, but usually it is obscured by the vital movements, desires etc. and its ideas and judgments are not pure.

*

In physical mind there can be an action of intelligent reasoning and coordination which is a delegation from the Buddhi and would perhaps not be attributed to the Manas by the old psychology. Still the larger part of the action of physical mind corresponds to that of Manas, but it comprises also much of what we would attribute to vital mind and to the nervous being. It is a little difficult to equate this old nomenclature with that of this Yoga, for the former takes the mixed action of the surface and tries to analyse it — while in this Yoga what is mixed together on the surface gets separated and seen in the light of the deeper working behind which is hidden from the surface awareness. So we have to adopt a different classification.

The physical mind has first to open to the higher consciousness — its limitations are then removed and it admits what is supraphysical and begins to see things in harmony with the higher knowledge. It becomes an instrument for externalising that knowledge in the pragmatic perceptions and actions of the physical life. It sees things as they are and deals with them according to the larger Truth with an automatic rightness of perception and will and reaction to impacts.

*

To sense things and react mentally to objects and convey impressions to the Buddhi etc. [*is the function of Manas*].

*

The right activity of the buddhi is always to observe, discern, discriminate, understand rightly and give the right direction to the vital and the body. But it does it imperfectly so long as it is in the Ignorance; by opening to the Mother it begins to get the true light and direction. Afterwards it is transformed into intuition and from intuition to the instrumental action of the overmind or the supermind Consciousness.

Chitta

The Chitta is the general stuff of mental consciousness which supports Manas and everything else — it is an indeterminate consciousness which gets determined into thoughts and memories and desires and sensations and perceptions and impulses and feelings (*cittavṛtti*).

*

There is no special plane of chitta. Chitta in the language of the old Yogas meant the stuff of consciousness out of which thought, will, memory, emotion, desire, sensation all arise — all these are called chittavritti, movements of the chitta. It was distinguished from Chit, the higher or divine consciousness.

*

Usually the word [*Chitta*] is employed for the general surface consciousness in which thoughts, feelings, desires, emotions, sensations (these being called chittavritti) arise. There is therefore no special location. Its function is to receive the impacts of the world and give back reactions which take the form of thoughts, feelings etc.

*

The Chitta is not near the heart — if you mean the substance of the lower consciousness, it has no particular place. All things of this life are there in this stuff of consciousness, but the memory of past lives is wrapped up and involved elsewhere. The heart is the main centre of this consciousness for most men, so of course you may feel its activities centred on that level.

*

Chitta really means the ordinary consciousness including the mind, vital and physical — but practically it can be taken to mean something central in the consciousness. If that is centred in the Divine, the rest follows more or less quietly as a natural result.

*

The Chitta receives these things [*thoughts, desires, etc.*], gives them for formation to the vital and mind and all is transmitted to the Buddhi, but also it receives thoughts from the Buddhi and turns these into desires and sensations and impulses.

*

Yes, certainly [*the Chitta must stop catching influences from outside at random*] — but as its whole business is to receive from above or below or around, it cannot stop doing it, it cannot of itself determine what it shall or shall not receive. It has to be assisted by the Buddhi, vital will or some higher power. Afterwards when the higher consciousness descends it begins to be transformed and capable of an automatic rejection of what is not true or right or divine or helpful to the growth of the divine in the being.

*

The Chitta does not receive desires and sensations from the Buddhi. It takes thoughts from the Buddhi and turns them into desires.

*

There is always or generally at least a modifying reaction [*to thoughts, desires etc. from outside*] in the chitta — except when it simply receives and stores without passing them on to the instruments.

*

If the word *vāsanā* is used in the original [*the Yogavasishtha*], it does not mean "desire". It means usually the idea or mental feeling rising from the chitta, imaginations, impressions, memories etc., impressions of liking and disliking, of pain and pleasure. What Vasishtha wants to say is that while the ideas, impressions, impulsions that lead to action in an ordinary man rise from the chitta, those that rise in the Jivanmukta come straight from the *sattva* — from the essential consciousness of the being — in other words they are not mental but spiritual formations. As one might say, instead of *cittavṛtti* they are *sattvapreraṇā*, direct indications from the inner being of what is to be thought, felt or done. When the chitta is no longer active and the mind silent — which happens when the *mukti* comes and no one can be Jivanmukta without that — then what remains and perceives and does things is felt as an essential consciousness, the consciousness of the true self or true being.

*

There is a subconscient action of the chitta which keeps the past impression of things and sends up forms of them to the consciousness in dream or else keeps the habit of old movements and sends up these whenever it finds an opportunity.

*

The chitta is the consciousness out of which all is formed, but the formation is made by the mind or vital or other force — which are, as it were, the instruments of the chitta for self-expression.

Western Ideas of Mind and Spirit

St. Augustine was a man of God and a great saint, but great saints are not always — or often — great psychologists or great thinkers. The psychology here[1] is that of the most superficial schools, if not that of the man in the street; there are as many errors in it as there are psychological statements — and more, for several are not expressed but involved in what he writes. I am aware that these errors are practically universal, for psychological enquiry in Europe (and without enquiry there can be no sound knowledge) is only beginning and has not gone very far, and what has reigned in men's minds up to now is a superficial statement of the superficial appearances of our consciousness as they look to us at first view and nothing more. But knowledge only begins when we get away from the surface phenomena and look behind them for their true operations and causes. To the superficial view of the outer mind and senses the sun is a little fiery ball circling in mid air round the earth and the stars twinkling little things stuck in the sky for our benefit at night.

[1] *In St. Augustine's* Confessions *8.9.21.* — Ed.

Scientific enquiry comes and knocks this infantile first view to pieces. The sun is a huge affair (millions of miles away from our air) around which the small earth circles and the stars are huge members of huge systems indescribably distant which have nothing apparently to do with the tiny earth and her creatures. All science is like that, a contradiction of the sense view or superficial appearances of things and an assertion of truths which are unguessed by the common sense and the uninstructed reason. The same process has to be followed in psychology if we are really to know what our consciousness is, how it is built and made and what is the secret of its functionings or the way out of its disorders.

There are several capital and common errors here —

(1) That mind and spirit are the same thing.

(2) That all consciousness can be spoken of as "mind".

(3) That all consciousness therefore is of a spiritual substance.

(4) That the body is merely matter, not conscious, therefore something quite different from the spiritual part of the nature.

First, the spirit and the mind are two different things and should not be confused together. The mind is an instrumental entity or instrumental consciousness whose function is to think and perceive — the spirit is an essential entity or consciousness which does not need to think or perceive either in the mental or the sensory way, because whatever knowledge it has is direct or essential knowledge, *svayaṁprakāśa*.

Next, it follows that all consciousness is not necessarily of a spiritual make and it need not be true and is not true that the thing commanding and the thing commanded are the same, are not at all different, are of the same substance and therefore are bound or at least ought to agree together.

Third, it is not even true that it is the mind which is commanding the mind and finds itself disobeyed by itself. First there are many parts of the mind, each a force in itself with its formations, functionings, interests, and they may not agree. One part of the mind may be spiritually influenced and like to think of the Divine and obey the spiritual impulse, another part may be rational or scientific or literary and prefer to follow the formations, beliefs or doubts, mental preferences and interests which are in conformity with its education and its nature. But quite apart from that, what was commanding in St. Augustine may very well have been the thinking mind or reason while what was commanded was the vital, and mind and vital, whatever anybody may say, are not the same. The thinking mind or buddhi lives, however imperfectly in man, by intelligence and reason, and tries to act or makes the rest act under that law as far as and in the way that it has conceived the law of intelligence and reason. The vital on the other hand is a thing of desires, impulses, force-pushes, emotions, sensations, seekings after life fulfilment, possession and enjoyment; these are its function and its nature; — it is that part of us which seeks after life and its movements for their own sake and it does not want to leave hold of them even if they bring it suffering as well as or more than pleasure; it is even capable of luxuriating in tears and suffering as part of the drama of life. What then is there in common between the thinking intelligence and the vital and why should the latter obey the mind and not follow its own nature? The disobedience is perfectly normal instead of being, as Augustine suggests, unintelligible. Of course man can establish a mental control over his vital and in so far as he does it he is a man, — because the thinking mind is a nobler and more enlightened entity and consciousness than the vital and ought therefore to rule and, if the mental will is strong, can rule. But this rule is precarious, incomplete and established and held only by much self-discipline. For if the mind is more enlightened, the vital is nearer to earth, more intense, vehement, more directly able to touch the body. There is too a vital mind which lives by imagination, thoughts of desire, will to act and enjoy from its own impulse and this is able to seize on the reason itself and make it its auxiliary and its justifying counsel and supplier of pleas and excuses. There is also the sheer force of Desire in man which is the vital's principal support and strong enough to sweep off the reason as the Gita says, "like a boat in stormy waters", *nāvam ivāmbhasi*.

Finally, the body obeys the mind automatically in those

things in which it is formed or trained to obey it, but the relation of the body to the mind is not in all things that of an automatic perfect instrument. The body also has a consciousness of its own and, though it is a submental instrument or servant consciousness, it can disobey or fail to obey as well. In many things, in matters of health and illness for instance, in all automatic functionings, the body acts on its own and is not a servant of the mind. If it is fatigued, it can offer a passive resistance to the mind's will. It can cloud the mind with tamas, inertia, dullness, fumes of the subconscient so that the mind cannot act. The arm lifts itself no doubt when it gets the suggestion, but at first the legs do not obey when they are asked to walk; they have to learn how to leave the crawling attitude and movement and take up the erect and ambulatory habit. When you first ask the hand to draw a straight line or to play music, it can't do it and won't do it. It has to be schooled, trained, taught, and afterwards it does automatically what is required of it. All this proves that there is a body consciousness different from the mind consciousness which can do things at the mind's order but has to be awakened, trained, made a good and conscious instrument. It can even be so trained that a mental will or suggestion can cure the illnesses of the body. But all these things, these relations of mind and body, stand on the same footing in essence as the relation of mind to vital and it is not so easy or primary a matter as Augustine would have it.

This puts the problem on another footing with the causes more clear and, if we are prepared to go far enough, it suggests the way out, the way of Yoga.

P. S. All this is quite apart from the contributing and very important factor of plural personality of which psychological enquiry is just beginning rather obscurely to take account. That is a more complex affair.

*

The non-materialistic European idea [*of the true soul or person*] makes a distinction between soul and body — the body is perishable, the mental-vital consciousness is the immortal soul and remains always the same (horrible idea!) in heaven as on earth or if there is rebirth it is also the same damned personality that comes back and makes a similar fool of itself.

The Psychic Mind

When the mind is turned towards the Divine and the Truth and feels and responds to that only or mainly, it can be called a psychic mind — it is something formed by the influence of the psychic being on the mental plane.

*

Psychic mind and mental psychic are the same thing practically. When there is a movement of the mind in which the psychic influence predominates, it is called the psychic in the mind or the psychic mind.

The Mind Proper

Above the physical mind and the vital mind is the mental intelligence, the mind proper. Beyond the ordinary thinking mind or intellect is the higher mind; beyond the higher mind is the illumined mind and beyond that is the intuitive mind. Above the intuitive mind are the Intuition and the Overmind.

*

The Mind proper is divided into three parts — thinking Mind, dynamic Mind, externalising Mind — the former concerned with ideas and knowledge in their own right, the second with the putting out of mental forces for realisation of the idea, the third with the expression of them in life (not only by speech, but by any form it can give). The word "physical mind" is rather ambiguous, because it can mean this externalising mind and the mental in the physical taken together.

Vital mind proper is a sort of mediator between vital emotion, desire, impulsion etc. and the mental proper. It expresses the desires, feelings, emotions, passions, ambitions, possessive and active tendencies of the vital and throws them into mental forms (the pure imaginations or dreams of greatness, happiness etc. in which men indulge are one peculiar form of the vital mind activity). There is a still lower stage of the mental in the vital which merely expresses the vital stuff without subjecting it to any play of intelligence. It is through this mental vital that the vital passions, impulses, desires rise up and get into the Buddhi and either cloud or distort it.

As the vital Mind is limited by the vital view and feeling of things (while the dynamic Intelligence is not, for it acts by the idea and reason), so the mind in the physical or mental physical is limited by the physical view and experience of things, it mentalises the experience brought by the contacts of outward life and things and does not go beyond that (though it can do that much very cleverly), unlike the externalising mind which deals with them more from the reason and its higher intelligence. But in practice these two usually get mixed together. The mechanical mind is a much lower action of the mental physical which, left to itself, would only repeat customary ideas and record the natural reflexes of the physical consciousness to the contacts of outward life and things.

The lower vital as distinguished from the higher is concerned only with the small greeds, small desires, small passions etc. which make up the daily stuff of life for the ordinary sensational man — while the vital physical proper is the nervous being giving vital reflexes to contacts of things with the physical consciousness.

*

It is quite usual for the dynamic and formative part of the mind to be more quick to action than the reflective and discriminative part to control it. It is a question of getting a kind of balance and harmony between them.

The Thinking Mind and the Vital Mind

The thinking mind does not lead men, does not influence them the most — it is the vital propensities and the vital mind that predominate. The thinking mind with most men is, in matters of life, only an instrument of the vital.

*

Vital thought expresses vital movements, the play of vital forces. It does not think freely and independently of them as the thinking mind can do. The true thinking mind can stand above the vital movements, watch and observe and judge them freely as it would observe and judge outside things. In most men however the thinking mind (reason) is invaded by the vital mind and not free.

The Thinking Mind and the Physical Mind

The true thinking mind does not belong to the physical, it is a separate power. The physical mind is that part of the mind which is concerned with the physical things only — it depends on the sense mind, sees only objects, external actions, draws its ideas from the data given by external things, infers from them only and knows no other Truth — until it is enlightened from above.

*

The physical mind can deal only with outward things. One has to think and decide in other things with the mind itself (buddhi), not with the physical part of it.

The Vital Mind

There is a part of the nature which I have called the vital mind; the function of this mind is not to think and reason, to perceive, consider and find out or value things, for that is the function of the thinking mind proper, *buddhi*, — but to plan or dream or imagine what can be done. It makes formations for the future which the will can try to carry out if opportunity and circumstances become favourable or even it can work to make them favourable. In men of action this faculty is prominent and a leader of their nature; great men of action always have it in a very high measure. But even if one is not a man of action or practical realisation or if circumstances are not favourable or one can do only small and ordinary things, this vital mind is there. It acts in them on a small scale, or if it needs some sense of largeness, what it does very often is to plan in the void knowing that it cannot realise its plans or else to imagine big things, stories, adventures, great doings in which oneself is the hero or the creator. What you describe as happening in you is the rush of this vital mind or imagination making its formations; its action is not peculiar to you but works pretty much in the same way in most people — but in each according to his turn of fancy, interest, favourite ideas or desires. You have to become master of its action and not to allow it to seize your mind and carry it away when and where it wants. In sadhana when the experiences begin to come, it is exceedingly important not to allow this power to do what it likes with you; for it then creates false experiences according to its nature and persuades the sadhak that these experiences are true or it builds unreal formations and persuades him that this is what he has to do. Some have been taken away by this misleading force used by powers of Falsehood who persuaded them through it that they had a great spiritual, political or social work to do in the world and led them away to disappointment and failure. It is rising in you in order that you may understand what it is and reject it. For there are several things you had to get out of the vital plane before the deeper or greater spiritual experiences could safely begin or safely continue.

The descent of the peace is often one of the first major positive experiences of the sadhana. In this state of peace the normal thought-mind (*buddhi*) is apt to fall silent or abate most of its activity and, when it does, very often either this vital mind can rush in, if one is not on one's guard, or else a kind of mechanical physical or random subconscient mind can begin to come up and act; these are the chief disturbers of the silence. Or else the lower vital mind can try to disturb; that brings up the ego and passions and their play. All these are signs of elements that have to be got rid of, because if they remain and other of the higher powers begin to descend, Power and Force, Knowledge, Love or

Ananda, those lower things may come across with the result that either the higher consciousness retires or its descent is covered up and the stimulation it gives is misused for the purposes of the lower nature. This is the reason why many sadhaks after having big experiences fall into the clutch of a magnified ego, upheavals, ambition, exaggerated sex or other vital passions or distortions. It is always well therefore if a complete purification of the vital can either precede or keep pace with the positive experience — at least in natures in which the vital is strongly active.[2]

The Physical Mind

It [*the true physical mind*] is the instrument of understanding and ordered action on physical things. Only instead of being obscure and ignorant and fumbling as now or else guided only by an external knowledge it has to become conscious of the Divine and to act in accordance with an inner light, will and knowledge putting itself into contact and an understanding unity with the physical world.

*

It [*the true physical mind*] can press upon it [*the physical vital*] the true attitude and feeling, make the incoming of the wrong suggestions and impulsions more difficult and give full force to the true movements. This action of the physical mind is indispensable for the change of the whole physical consciousness even to the most material, though for that the enlightening of the subconscient is indispensable.

*

It is the function of the outward physical mind to deal with external things — that is why it wants always to be busy with them. What it has to learn is to be quiet and to act only when the Will wants to use it, when it is really needed — and also to act only

---

[2] Other letters on the vital mind have been placed under the heading "The Mental Vital or Vital Mind" on pages 189–92. — Ed.

on what the Will wants to deal with, not run about in a random manner. When it becomes quiet, it can then go inside and come into contact and unity with the inner physical consciousness. The wideness and peace as it grows can do much to quiet the physical mind and give it an inward source of deeper action.

*

In the human physical mind there is always a tendency not to understand or to misunderstand and to interpret according to its own notions. That can only be removed by the Light in the mind and the power everywhere which refuses to accept suggestions of disturbance.

*

It is the physical mind that finds it difficult to believe in the reality of supraphysical things — that is due to its ignorance and its belief that only physical things are real.

*

Yes, it [*the physical mind*] reasons, but on the basis of external data mostly — on things as they appear to the outer mind and senses or the habitual ideas to which it is accustomed or to a purely external knowledge.

*

That part of the being [*the physical mind*] has no reason except its whims, its habits or an inclination to be tamasic.

*

The physical mind is in the habit of observing things with or without use.

The Physical Mental or Physical Mind and the Mental Physical or Mechanical Mind

The physical mental or externalising mind is part of the mental consciousness, not part of the physical consciousness. But it is closely connected with the mental physical — so that the two usually act together.

*

The automatic or mechanical mind is called by us the mental physical — and distinguished from the physical mind which is that which deals intelligently with physical things. The other simply stores, associates, repeats, gives reflexes and reactions etc.

*

Repetition is the habit of the mental physical — it is not the true thinking mind that behaves like this, it is the mental physical or else the lowest part of the physical mind.

*

But the main error here is in your description of the physical part of the mind — what you have described there is the mechanical mental physical or body-mind which when left to itself simply goes on repeating the past customary thoughts and movements or at the most adds to them such further mechanical reactions to things and reflexes as are in the round of life. The true physical mind is the receiving and externalising intelligence which has two functions — first, to work upon external things and give them a mental order with a way of practically dealing with them and, secondly, to be the channel of materialising and putting into effect whatever the thinking and dynamic mind sends down to it for the purpose.

*

The vital mind is usually energetic and creative even in its more mechanical rounds, so it must be the physical that is turning. It is that and the mechanical that last longest, but these too fall silent when the peace and silence become massive and complete. Afterwards knowledge begins to come from the higher planes — the Higher Mind to begin with, and this creates a new action of thought and perception which replaces the ordinary mental.

It does that first in the thinking mind, but afterwards also in the vital mind and physical mind, so that all these begin to go through a transformation. This kind of thought is not random and restless, but precise and purposeful — it comes only when needed or called for and does not disturb the silence. Moreover the element of what we call thought there is secondary and what might be called a seeing perception (intuition) takes its place. But so long as the mind does not become capable of a complete silence, this higher knowledge, thought, perception either does not come down or, if partially it does, it is liable to get mixed up with or imitated by the lower, and that is a bother and a hindrance. So the silence is necessary.

*

The automatic mind is a part of the lower action, it can only stop by the acquirement of mental silence or the descent of a higher consciousness.

The Mental World of the Individual

As he [*the human being*] lives in a separative consciousness, he makes a mental world of his own out of his experience of the common world in which all here live. It is built in the same way as that of others and he receives into it the thoughts, feelings of others, without knowing it most often, and uses that too as material for his separate world.

Chapter Seven

The Vital Being and Vital Consciousness

The Vital

Mind and vital are two different processes of one consciousness.

*

It [*vital*] means *prāṇa* — it is the life-force and desire-force in a man and the part of the being that responds to desire and is the instrument of the life-forces.

The True Vital Being and Consciousness

There is behind all the vital nature in man his true vital being concealed and immobile which is quite different from the surface vital nature. The surface vital is narrow, ignorant, limited, full of obscure desires, passions, cravings, revolts, pleasures and pains, transient joys and griefs, exultations and depressions. The true vital being on the contrary is wide, vast, calm, strong, without limitations, firm and immovable, capable of all power, all knowledge, all Ananda. It is moreover without ego, for it knows itself to be a projection and instrument of the Divine; it is the divine Warrior, pure and perfect; in it is an instrumental Force for all divine realisations. It is the true vital being that has become awake and come in front within you. In the same way there is too a true mental being, a true physical being. When these are manifest, then you are aware of a double existence in you; that behind is always calm and strong, that on the surface alone is troubled and obscure. But if the true being behind remains stable and you live in it, then the trouble and obscurity remain only on the surface; in this condition the exterior parts can be dealt with more potently and they also made free and perfect.

*

The true vital is in the inner consciousness, the external is that which is instrumental for the present play of Prakriti in the surface personality. When the change comes, the true vital rejects what is out of tune with its own truth from the external and makes it a true instrument for its expression, a means of expression of its inner will, not a thing of responses to the suggestions of the lower Nature. The strong distinction between the two practically disappears.

*

The higher and lower [*vital*] are divisions of the ordinary vital and equally ignorant. It is the true vital that is in contact with the Divine.

*

The true vital consciousness is one in which the vital makes full surrender, converts itself into an instrument of the Divine, making no demand, insisting on no desire, answering to the Mother's force and to no other, calm, unegoistic, giving an absolute loyalty and obedience, with no personal vanity or ambition, only willing to be a pure and perfect instrument, desiring nothing for itself but that the Truth may prevail within itself and everywhere and the Divine Victory take place and the Divine Work be done.

*

It [*the true vital*] is capable of receiving the movements of the higher consciousness, and afterwards it can be capable of receiving the still greater supramental power and Ananda. If it is not, then the descent of the higher consciousness would be impossible and supramentalisation would be impossible. It is not meant that it possesses these things itself in its own right and that as soon as one is aware of the true vital, one gets all these things as inherent in the true vital.

*

The Vital Being and Vital Consciousness

It is as I told you — only by losing ego and having the sense of the Infinite can one experience the true vital. So you got the experience of the loss of ego and the sense of a true vital existence. But there are all those parts of the human vital nature that are not the true vital and these are full of impurities which have to be thrown in the fire of aspiration burning in the true vital being.

*

It [*the illumined vital*] is in contact with the Divine Power or the higher Truth and seeks to transform itself and become a true instrument — it rejects the ordinary vital movements.

Parts of the Vital Being

There are four parts of the vital being — first, the mental vital which gives a mental expression by thought, speech or otherwise to the emotions, desires, passions, sensations and other movements of the vital being; the emotional vital which is the seat of various feelings such as love, joy, sorrow, hatred, and the rest; the central vital which is the seat of the stronger vital longings and reactions, e.g. ambition, pride, fear, love of fame, attractions and repulsions, desires and passions of various kinds and the field of many vital energies; last, the lower vital which is occupied with small desires and feelings, such as make the greater part of daily life, e.g. food desire, sexual desire, small likings, dislikings, vanity, quarrels, love of praise, anger at blame, little wishes of all kinds — and a numberless host of other things. Their respective seats are (1) the region from the throat to the heart, (2) the heart (it is a double centre, belonging in front to the emotional and vital and behind to the psychic), (3) from the heart to the navel, (4) below the navel.

*

The point about the emotional and the higher vital is a rather difficult one. In one classification in which mind is taken as something more than the thinking, perceiving and willing intelligence, the emotional can be reckoned as part of the mind, the vital in the mental. In another classification it is rather the most mentalised part of the vital nature. In the first case, the term higher vital is confined to that larger movement of the conscious life-force which is concerned with creation, with power and force and conquest, with giving and self-giving and gathering from the world for farther action and expenditure of power, throwing itself out in the wider movements of life, responsive to the greater objects of Nature. In the second arrangement, the emotional being stands at the top of the vital nature and the two together make the higher vital. As against them stands the lower vital which is concerned with the pettier movements of action and desire and stretches down into the vital physical where it supports the life of the more external activities and all physical sensations, hungers, cravings, satisfactions. The term lower must not be considered in a pejorative sense; it refers only to the position in the hierarchy of the planes. For although this part of the nature in earthly beings tends to be very obscure and is full of perversions, — lust, greed of all kinds, vanity, small ambitions, petty anger, envy, jealousy are its ordinary guests, — still there is another side to it which makes it an indispensable mediator between the inner being and the outer life.

It is not a fact that every psychic experience embodies itself in a purified and rightly directed vital current; it does that when it has to externalise itself in action. Psychic experience is in itself a quite independent thing and has its own characteristic forms. The psychic being stands behind all the others; its force is the true soul-power. But if it comes to the front, it can suffuse all the rest; mind, vital, the physical consciousness can take its stamp and be transformed by its influence. When the nature is properly developed, there is a psychic in the mental, a psychic in the vital, a psychic in the physical. It is when that is there and strong, that we can say of someone that he evidently has a soul. But there are some in whom this element is so lacking that we have to use faith in order to believe that they have a soul at all. The centre of the psychic being is behind the centre of the emotional being; it is the emotional that is nearest dynamically to the psychic and in most men it is through the emotional centre that the psychic can be most easily reached and through the psychicised emotion that it can be most easily expressed. Many therefore mistake the one for the other; but there is a world of difference between the two. The emotions normally are vital in their character and not part of the psychic nature.

It must be remembered that while this classification is indispensable for psychological self-knowledge and discipline and practice, it can be used best when it is not made too rigid and cutting a formula. For things run very much into each other and a synthetical sense of these powers is as necessary as the analysis. Mind for instance is everywhere. The physical mind is technically placed below the vital and yet it is a prolongation of the mind proper and can act in its own sphere by direct touch with the higher mental intelligence. And there is too an obscure mind of the body, of the very cells, molecules, corpuscles. Haeckel, the German materialist, spoke somewhere of the will in the atom, and recent Science, dealing with the incalculable individual variation in the activity of the electrons, comes near to perceiving that this is not a figure but the shadow thrown by a secret reality. This body-mind is a very tangible truth; owing to its obscurity and mechanical clinging to past movements and facile oblivion and rejection of the new, we find in it one of the chief obstacles to permeation by the supermind force and the transformation of the functioning of the body. On the other hand, once effectively converted, it will be one of the most precious instruments for the stabilisation of the supramental light and force in material Nature.

The Mental Vital or Vital Mind

It is the mental part of the vital that is there between the throat and the heart. The place of the mind is from the crown of the head to the throat (where is the physical mind); from below the throat to the heart is the emotional heart or the [*higher*] vital (mental emotional, emotional feelings); the navel and abdomen [*are the seats of*] the middle and lower vital.

*

It is not possible to say with any precision what the resistance in the higher vital parts will be, what form it takes, because it may take different forms with different natures. It is quite normal that there should be some resistance almost at every point to the descent of the higher consciousness; for the different parts of the present nature are each more or less attached to their own established way of seeing, acting, feeling, reacting to things and to the habitual movements and formations of their own domain which each individual has made for himself in the past or in his present life. What is needed is a general plasticity of the mind, the vital, the physical consciousness, a readiness to give up all attachment to these things, to accept whatever the higher consciousness brings down with it however contrary to one's own received ideas, feelings, habits of nature. The greater the plasticity in any part of the nature, the less the resistance there.

By the higher vital parts of the nature I mean the vital mind, the emotional nature, the life-force dynamis in the being. The vital mind is that part of the vital being which builds, plans, imagines, arranges things and thoughts according to the life-pushes, desires, will to power or possession, will to action, emotions, vital ego reactions of the nature. It must be distinguished from the reasoning will which plans and arranges things according to the dictates of the thinking mind proper, the discriminating reason or according to the mental intuition or a direct insight and judgment. The vital mind uses thought for the service not of reason but of life-push and life-power and when it calls in reasoning it uses that for justifying the dictates of these powers, imposes their dictates on the reason instead of governing by a discriminating will the action of the life-forces. This higher vital with all its parts is situated in the chest and has the cardiac centre as its main stronghold governing all this part down to the navel. I need not say anything about the emotional nature, for its character and movements are known to all. From the navel downwards is the reign of the vital passions and sensations and all the small life-impulses that constitute the bulk of the ordinary human life and character. This is what we call the lower vital nature. The Muladhara is the main support of the physical consciousness and the material parts of the nature.

*

It [*the vital mind*] is a mind of dynamic (not rationalising) will, action, desire — occupied with force and achievement and satisfaction and possession, enjoyment and suffering, giving and taking, growth, expansion, success and failure, good fortune and ill fortune etc. etc.

*

That [*repetitive imaginative thinking*] is the ordinary activity of the vital mind which is always imagining and thinking and planning what to do about this and how to arrange about that. It has obviously its utility in human nature and human action, but acts in a random and excessive way without discipline, economy of its powers or concentration on the things that have really to be done.

*

The things which come to you in this way in sleep or waking are of the nature of vital mind imaginations and activities about things and work and whatever presents itself to the mind. On all things that present themselves to the mind, the vital imagination in man is able to work, imagining, speculating, building ideas or plans for the future etc. etc. It has its utility for the consciousness in ordinary life, but must quiet down and be replaced by a higher action in Yoga. In sleep it is also the vital plane into which you enter. If properly seen and coordinated, what is experienced in the vital plane has its value and gives knowledge which is useful and control over the vital self and vital plane. But all that is coming to you through the subconscient in an incoherent way — this is the cause of the trouble. The whole thing has to be quieted down and we shall try to get that done. When I spoke of your opening yourself, I meant simply that you should fix it in your mind that the help is coming and have the will to receive it — not necessarily that you should open yourself by an effort.

*

The source from which these imaginations[1] come has nothing to do with the reason and does not care for any rational objections. They come either from the vital mind, the same source from which come all the fine imaginations and long stories which men tell themselves in which they are the heroes and do great things or they come from little entities attached to the physical mind which pick up any random suggestion anywhere and present it to the mind just to see whether it will be accepted. If one watches oneself closely one can find the most queer and extraordinary or nonsensical things crossing the mind or peeping in on it in this way. Usually one laughs or hardly notices and the thing falls back to the world of incoherent thought from which it came.

*

It is again the vital mind. It has no sense of proportion or measure and is eager to be or achieve something big at once.

*

All that [*pleasurable imaginations*] is the vital mind — it has in everybody the habit of such imaginations. It is not very important, but of course it has to be got rid of, as the basis is ego.

*

The vital mind in the ordinary nature cannot get on without these imaginations — so the habit remains for a long time. To be detached and indifferent is the best, then after a time it may get disgusted and drop the habit.

*

That kind of talking [*in one's mind to another person*] is very common with the vital mind. It is a way it has of acting on the subtle plane on things in which it is interested, especially if the physical action is stopped or restricted.

---

[1] *The disciple had imagined that he was the Buddha.* — Ed.

The Emotional Being or Heart

The emotional being is itself a part of the vital.

*

The heart is the centre of the emotional being and the emotions are vital movements. When the heart is purified, the vital emotions change into psychic feelings or else psychicised vital movements.

*

The heart is part of the vital — it has to be controlled in the same way as the rest, by rejection of the wrong movements, by acceptance of the true psychic surrender which prevents all demand and clamour, by calling in the higher light and knowledge. It is not usually however the heart that bothers about mental questions and the answer to them.

*

Pure and true thoughts and emotions and impulsions can rise from the human mind, heart and vital, because all is not evil there. The heart may be unpurified, but that does not mean that everything in it is impure.

*

I make the distinction [*between emotions and lower vital movements*] by noting where these things rise from. Anger, fear, jealousy touch the heart no doubt just as they touch the mind but they rise from the navel region and entrails (i.e. the lower or at highest the middle vital). Stevenson has a striking passage in *Kidnapped* where the hero notes that his fear is felt primarily not in the heart but the stomach. Love, hope have their primary seat in the heart, so with pity etc.

The Central Vital or Vital Proper

Above the heart is the vital mind — sense and the rising of

sensation is lower than the emotion, not higher.
Sensation is much nearer the physical than emotion.
The place of desire is below the heart in the central vital (navel) and in the lower vital, but it invades the emotion and the vital mind.

*

A mistake [*to think that all men seek after happiness*]; many men are not after happiness and do not believe it is the true aim of life. It is the physical vital that seeks after happiness, the bigger vital is ready to sacrifice it in order to satisfy its passions, search for power, ambition, fame or any other motive. If you say it is because of the happiness power, fame etc. gives, that again is not universally true. Power can give anything else, but not happiness; it is something in its very nature arduous and full of difficulty to get, to keep or to use — I speak of course of power in the ordinary sense. A man may know he can never have fame in this life but yet work in the hope of posthumous fame or in the chance of it. He may know that the satisfaction of his passion will bring him everything rather than happiness — suffering, torture, destruction — yet he will follow his impulse. So also the mind as well as the larger vital is not bound by the pursuit of happiness. It can seek Truth rather or the victory of a cause. To reduce all to a single hedonistic strain seems to me very poor psychology. Neither Nature nor the vast Spirit in things are so limited and one-tracked as that.

*

The nervous part of the being is a portion of the vital — it is the vital physical, the life-force closely enmeshed in the reactions, desires, needs, sensations of the body. The vital proper is the life-force acting in its own nature, impulses, emotions, feelings, desires, ambitions etc. having as their highest centre what we may call the outer heart of emotion, while there is an inner heart where are the higher or psychic feelings and sensibilities, the emotions and intuitive yearnings and impulses of the soul. The vital part of us is, of course, necessary to our completeness, but it is a true instrument only when its feelings and tendencies have been purified by the psychic touch and taken up and governed by the spiritual light and power.

The Lower Vital, the Physical Vital and the Material Vital

Below the navel is the lower vital plane, which is ignorant and obscure, the seat of small desires, greeds, passions and enjoyments.

*

As there is a physical mind, so there is a physical vital — a vital turned entirely upon physical things, full of desires and greeds and seekings for pleasure on the physical plane.

*

That [*seeking enjoyment*] is the attitude not of the whole vital but of the physical vital, the animal part of the human being. Of course it cannot be convinced by mental reasoning of any kind. In most men it is the natural and accepted attitude towards life varnished over with some conventional moralism and idealism as a concession to the mind and higher vital. In a few this part of the being is gripped and subordinated to the mental or the higher vital aim, forced to take a subordinate place so that the mind may absorb itself persistently in mental pursuits or idealisms or great political or personal ambitions (Lenin, Hitler, Stalin, Mussolini). The ascetic and the Puritan try to suppress it mostly or altogether. In our Yoga the principle is that all must become an instrument of the Spirit and the parts of enjoyment taste the Ananda in things, not the animal enjoyment of the surface. But the Ananda will not come or will not stay so long as this part is not converted and insists on its own way of satisfaction.

*

Yes — they [*the lower vital, the physical vital and the material vital*] become very clear to the increasing consciousness. And the distinctions are necessary — otherwise one may influence or control the lower vital or a part of the physical vital and then be astonished to find that something intangible but apparently invincible still resists — it is the material vital with so much of the rest as it can influence by its resistance.

*

I don't know about subtle vital. One says subtle physical to distinguish from gross material physical — because to our normal experience all physical is gross, *sthūla*. But the vital is in its nature non-material, so the adjective is superfluous. By material vital, we mean the vital so involved in matter as to be bound by its movements and gross physical character. The action is to support and energise the body and keep in it the capacity of life, growth, movement etc., also of sensitiveness to outer impacts.

A Strong Vital

A strong vital is one that is full of life-force, has ambition, courage, great energy, a force for action or for creation, a large expansive movement whether for generosity in giving or for possession and lead and domination, a power to fulfil and materialise — many other forms of vital strength there are also. It is often difficult for such a vital to surrender itself because of this sense of its own powers — but if it can do so, it becomes an admirable instrument for the Divine Work.

*

No, a weak vital has not the strength to turn spiritually — and being weak more easily falls under a wrong influence and even when it wants, finds it difficult to accept anything beyond its own habitual nature. The strong vital when the will is there can do it much more easily — its one central difficulty is the pride of its ego and the attraction of its powers.

The chest has more connection with the psychic than the vital. A strong vital may have a good physique, but as often it has not — it draws too much on the physical, eats it up as it were.

*

In a mere vampire there is no psychic, for the vampire is a vital being — but in all humans (even if dominated by a vital being or vampire force), there is a psychic veiled behind it all.

The Vital Body

The physical life cannot last without the body nor can the body live without the life force, but the life in itself has a separate existence and a separate body of its own, the vital body, just as the mind has a separate existence and can exist on its own plane. All the organisation is held together by the psychic which is the support of all.

The Vital Nature

It was not your own vital that you saw, but the general vital Nature in the Ignorance that took form and spoke. The battle you saw was the struggle between the Powers of the Light and the Powers of the Darkness for possession of the vital Nature on earth.

Your vital cannot be destroyed, because it is needed as an instrument for the manifestation of the Divine element in you. There can be no life and no manifestation here on earth without the vital. It has not to be destroyed, but purified and changed into the true Vital.

The Vital Plane and the Physical Plane

Things do happen on the vital plane — but they are not *more* important than what happens here because it is here we have to realise and what happens in the vital is only a help.

*

Most things happen in the vital before they happen in the physical, but all that happens in the vital does not realise itself in the physical or not in the same way. There is always or at least usually a change in the form, time, circumstances due to the different conditions of the physical plane.

The Life Heavens

Where do you find in "The Life Heavens"[2] that I say or anybody says the conditions on the earth are glorious and suited to the Divine Life? There is not a word to that effect there! The Life Heavens are the heavens of the vital gods and there is there a perfect harmony but a harmony of the sublimated satisfied senses and vital desires only. If there is to be a Harmony, it must be of all the powers raised to their highest and harmonised together. All the non-evolutionary worlds are worlds of a type limited to its own harmony like the Life Heavens. The Earth on the other hand is an evolutionary world, not at all glorious or harmonious even as a material world (except in certain appearances), but rather most sorrowful, disharmonious, imperfect. Yet in that imperfection is the urge towards a higher and more many-sided perfection. It contains the last finite which yet yearns to the supreme infinite (it is not to be satisfied by sense-joys precisely because in the conditions of earth it is able to see their limitations). God is pent in the mire (mire is not glorious, so there is no claim to glory or beauty here) but that very fact imposes a necessity to break through that prison to a consciousness which is ever rising towards the heights. And so on. That *is* "a deeper power", not a greater actual glory or perfection. All that may be true or not to the mind, but it is the traditional attitude of Indian spiritual experience. Ask any Yogin, he will tell you that the Life Heavens are childish things; even the gods, says the Purana, must come down to earth and be embodied there if they want *mukti*, giving up the pride of their limited perfection — they must enter into the last finite if they want to reach the last infinite. A poem is not a philosophical treatise or a profession of religious faith — it is the expression of a vision or an experience of some kind,

---

[2] A poem by Sri Aurobindo. See Collected Poems, *volume 2 of* THE COMPLETE WORKS OF SRI AUROBINDO, *p. 549. — Ed.*

mundane or spiritual. Here it is the vision of the Life Heavens, its perfection, its limitations and the counterclaim of the Earth or rather the Spirit or Power behind the earth consciousness. It has to be taken at that, as an expression of a certain aspect of things, an expression of a certain kind of experience, not of a mental dogma. There is a deep truth behind it, though it may not be the whole truth of the matter. In the poem, also, there is no question of a Divine Life here, though that is hinted at as the unexpressed possible result of the ascent — because the Earth is not put aside ("Earth's heart was felt beating below me still"); nevertheless the poem expresses only the ascent towards the Highest, far beyond the Life Heavens, and the Earth-Spirit claims that power and does not speak of any descent of a Divine Life. I say so much in order to get rid of that misconception so as not to have to go back to it when dealing with Earth's disharmonies.

*

They wouldn't be heavens if they were not immune [*from attacks by hostile powers*] — a heaven with fear in it would be no heaven. The Life Heavens have an influence on earth and so have the Life Hells, but it does not follow that they influence each other in their own domain. Overmind can influence earth, so can the hostile Powers, but it does not follow that hostile Powers can penetrate the Overmind — they can't: they can only spoil what it sends to the earth. Each power of the Divine (life like mind and matter are powers of the Divine) has its own harmony inherent in the purity of its own principle — it is only if it is disturbed or perverted that it produces disorder. That is another reason why the evolution could have been a progressing harmony, not a series of discords through which harmony of a precarious and wounded kind has to be struggled for at each step: for the Divine Principle is there within. Each plane therefore has its heavens; there are the subtle physical heavens, the vital heavens, the mental heavens. If Powers of disharmony got in, they would cease to be heavens.

Chapter Eight
The Physical Consciousness

The Physical Consciousness and Its Parts

The physical consciousness is that part which directly responds to physical things and physical Nature, sees the outer only as real, is occupied with it — not like the thinking mind with thought and knowledge, or like the vital with emotion, passion, subtler satisfaction of desire. If this part is obscure, then it is difficult to bring into it the consciousness of deeper or spiritual things, feelings etc. even when the mind or the vital are after these deeper things.

*

You ask whether the mind and vital do not come in the way as well as the physical. Yes, but when I speak of the physical consciousness, I mean the physical mind and the physical vital as well as the body consciousness proper. This physical mind and physical vital are concerned with the small ordinary movements of life and are governed by a very external view of things and by habitual small reactions and do not respond at once to the inner consciousness not because they are in active opposition to it, as the vital mind and vital proper can be, but because they find it difficult to change their habitual movements. It is this now that you feel and that makes you think you have a poor responsiveness to the inner experience. But that is not a fact; in your mind and in a great part of your vital there is a considerable capacity of response. As for the physical its difficulty is universal in everybody and not peculiar to you. It has come up because it always comes up in the sadhana when the physical consciousness has to be worked upon for the necessary change. As soon as that is done, the difficulty you feel will first diminish and then go.

It is this work that is going on and when you felt the white light in meditation and the result which lasted even after opening the eyes, the head and eyes cool and all vast and wide, it was this working taking place in your physical mind to change it. The rest of the physical consciousness was still undergoing another kind of working and so felt heat and not this release and wideness. But afterwards the working can go down first to the heart and then still lower and to all the body and the same release and wideness come there. Naturally, at present these results are not permanent but only for a time, they come as experiences, not lasting realisations. But it cannot be otherwise at the present stage. These experiences, however passing, are meant to prepare and do prepare the different parts of the nature.

*

They [*the physical mind and vital physical*] are very near to it [*the Inconscient*] — except that part of the physical mind which is trained to deal with physical objects and affairs. But that is agile and active and competent only in its own limits. When it has to deal with supraphysical things it becomes incompetent, often imbecile and yet positive and arrogant and dogmatic in its ignorance. The rest of the physical consciousness is near to the inconscient. Here again in its own field it can have accurate perceptions and instincts if it is able to act spontaneously; but usually in the human being it is not allowed to do so, for the mind and vital intervene. The vital physical is entirely irrational in its action — even when it is right, it cannot explain why; for it is made more of automatic or habitual instincts, impulses, sensations and feelings than anything else. It is the mind that gives reasons and justifications to its movements and if the mind stands back and judges and questions, the vital physical can only answer "I want", "I like", "I dislike", "I feel like that".

*

Each plane of our being — mental, vital, physical — has its own consciousness, separate though interconnected and interacting; but to our outer mind and sense, in our waking experience, they are all confused together. The body, for instance, has its own consciousness and acts from it, even without any conscious mental will of our own or even against that will, and our surface mind knows very little about this body consciousness, feels it only in an imperfect way, sees only its results and has the greatest difficulty in finding out their causes. It is part of the Yoga to become aware of this separate consciousness of the body, to see and feel its movements and the forces that act upon it from inside or outside and to learn how to control and direct it even in its most hidden and (to us) subconscient processes. But the body consciousness itself is only part of the individualised physical consciousness in us which we gather and build out of the secretly conscious forces of universal physical Nature.

There is the universal physical consciousness of Nature and there is our own which is a part of it, moved by it, and used by the central being for the support of its expression in the physical world and for a direct dealing with all these external objects and movements and forces. This physical consciousness-plane receives from the other planes their powers and influences and makes formations of them in its own province. Therefore we have a physical mind as well as a vital mind and the mind proper; we have a vital physical part in us — the nervous being — as well as the vital proper; and both are largely conditioned by the gross material bodily part which is almost entirely subconscient to our experience.

The physical mind is that which is fixed on physical objects and happenings, sees and understands these only, and deals with them according to their own nature, but can with difficulty respond to the higher forces. Left to itself, it is sceptical of the existence of supraphysical things, of which it has no direct experience and to which it can find no clue; even when it has spiritual experiences, it forgets them easily, loses the impression and result and finds it difficult to believe. To enlighten the physical mind by the consciousness of the higher spiritual and supramental planes is one object of this Yoga, just as to enlighten it by the power of the higher vital and higher mental elements of the being is the greatest part of human self-development, civilisation and culture.

The vital physical on the other hand is the vehicle of the

nervous responses of our physical nature; it is the field and instrument of the smaller sensations, desires, reactions of all kinds to the impacts of the outer physical and gross material life. This vital physical part (supported by the lowest part of the vital proper) is therefore the agent of most of the lesser movements of our external life; its habitual reactions and obstinate pettinesses are the chief stumbling-block in the way of the transformation of the outer consciousness by the Yoga. It is also largely responsible for most of the suffering and disease of mind or body to which the physical being is subject in Nature.

As to the gross material part it is not necessary to specify its place, for that is obvious, but it must be remembered that this too has a consciousness of its own, the obscure consciousness proper to the limbs, cells, tissues, glands, organs. To make this obscurity luminous and directly instrumental to the higher planes and to the divine movement is what we mean in our Yoga by making the body conscious, — that is to say, full of a true, awake and responsive awareness instead of its own obscure, limited half-subconscience.

There is an inner as well as an outer consciousness all through our being, upon all its levels. The ordinary man is aware only of his surface self and quite unaware of all that is concealed by the surface. And yet what is on the surface, what we know or think we know of ourselves and even believe that that is all we are, is only a small part of our being and far the larger part of us is below the surface, the frontal consciousness. Or, more accurately, it is behind the frontal consciousness, behind the veil, occult and known only by an occult knowledge. Modern psychology and psychic science have begun to perceive this truth just a little. Materialistic psychology calls this hidden part the Inconscient, although practically admitting that it is far greater, more powerful and profound than the surface conscious self, — very much as the Upanishads called the superconscient in us the Sleep self, although this Sleep self is said to be an infinitely greater Intelligence, omniscient, omnipotent, Prajna, the Ishwara. Psychic science calls this hidden consciousness the subliminal self, and, here too, it is seen that this subliminal self has more powers, more knowledge, a freer field of movement than the smaller self that is on the surface. But the truth is that all this that is behind, this sea of which our waking consciousness is only a wave or series of waves, cannot be described by any one term, for it is very complex. Part of it is subconscient, lower than our waking consciousness; part of it is on a level with it but behind and much larger than it; part is above and superconscient to us. What we call our mind is only an outer mind, a surface mental action, instrumental for the partial expression of a larger mind behind of which we are not ordinarily aware and can only know by going inside ourselves. So too what we know of the vital in us is only the outer vital, a surface activity partially expressing a larger secret vital which we can only know by going within. Equally, what we call our physical being is only a visible projection of a greater and subtler invisible physical consciousness which is much more complex, much more aware, much wider in its receptiveness, much more open and plastic and free.

If you understand and experience this truth, then only you will be able to realise what is meant by the inner mental, the inner vital, the inner physical consciousness. But it must be noted that this term "inner" is used in two different senses. Sometimes it denotes the consciousness behind the veil of the outer being, the mental or vital or physical within, which is in direct touch with the universal mind, the universal life forces, the universal physical forces. Sometimes, on the other hand, we mean an inmost mental, vital, physical, more specifically called the true mind, the true vital, the true physical consciousness which is nearest to the soul and can most easily and directly respond to the Divine Light and Power. There is no real Yoga possible, still less any integral Yoga, if we do not go back from the outer self and become aware of all this inner being and inner nature. For then alone can we break the limitations of the ignorant external self which receives consciously only the outer touches and knows things indirectly through the outer mind and senses, and become directly aware of the universal consciousness and the universal forces that play through us and around us. And then only too can we hope to be directly aware of the Divine in us and directly in touch with the Divine Light and the Divine Force. Otherwise we can feel the Divine only through external signs and external results and that is a difficult and uncertain way and very occasional and inconstant, and it leads only to belief and not to knowledge, not to the direct consciousness and awareness of the constant presence.

As for instances of the difference, I may give you two from the opposite poles of experience, one from the most external phenomena showing how the inward opens to the awareness of universal forces, one of spiritual experience indicating how the inward opens to the Divine. Take illness. If we live only in the outward physical consciousness, we do not usually know that we are going to be ill until the symptoms of the malady declare themselves in the body. But if we develop the inward physical consciousness, we become aware of a subtle environmental physical atmosphere and can feel the forces of illness coming towards us through it, feel them even at a distance and, if we have learned how to do it, we can stop them by the will or otherwise. We sense too around us a vital physical or nervous envelope which radiates from the body and protects it, and we can feel the adverse forces trying to break through it and can interfere, stop them or reinforce the nervous envelope. Or we can feel the symptoms of illness, fever or cold for instance, in the subtle physical sheath before they are manifest in the gross body and destroy them there, preventing them from manifesting in the body. Take now the call for the Divine Power, Light, Ananda. If we live only in the outward physical consciousness, it may descend and work behind the veil but we shall feel nothing and only see certain results after a long time. Or at most we feel a certain clarity and peace in the mind, a joy in the vital, a happy state in the physical and infer the touch of the Divine. But if we are awake in the inward physical, we shall feel the light, power or Ananda flowing through the body, the limbs, nerves, blood, breath and, through the subtle body, affecting the most material cells and making them conscious and blissful and we shall sense directly the Divine Power and Presence. These are only two instances out of a thousand that are possible and can be constantly experienced by the sadhaka.

Living in the Physical Consciousness

So far as it [*living in the physical consciousness*] can be said to be distinguishable by outward signs, it is a state of fundamental passivity in which one is and does what the forces of the physical plane make one be and do. When one lives in the mind, there is an active mental intelligence and mental will that tries to control and shape action and experience and life and everything else. When one is in the vital one is full of energy and enthusiasm and passion and force which may be right or wrong, but is very much alive. These things in the physical inertia either disappear or become weak or are forces that act upon the system occasionally but are not possessed by it. This condition may not be absolute, for one has a mind and a vital, but it is what predominates. There are two ways of getting out of this — one is to rise above in the self and see the physical from there as an instrument, not oneself, the other is to bring down the divine Force from above and make the physical the instrument of that Force.

*

The forces of the physical mind, vital physical, material consciousness [*are the forces of the physical plane*]. Of course, as I said, the statement must be taken with a qualification, for the true mind and vital are also there, but in this condition [*of passivity and inertia*] it is the forces of the physical consciousness that predominate and determine the general condition which is a proneness to *aprakāśa* and sometimes *apravṛtti*.

The Opening of the Physical Consciousness

The physical consciousness? It opens just like the rest, receives a new consciousness, obeys the Force, feels a change even in the cells, aspires to and seeks self-giving and union with the Divine.

The True Activity of the Senses

It [*the true activity of the senses*] is to record the divine or true appearance of things and return to them the reaction of an equal Ananda without dislike or desire.

The Physical Parts of the Mind and Emotional Being

Everything has a physical part — even the mind has a physical part; there is a mental physical, a mind of the body and the material. So the emotional being has a physical part. It has no location separate from the rest of the emotional. One can only distinguish it when the consciousness becomes sufficiently subtle to do so.

The Mental Physical or Mechanical Mind

That is the nature of the mental physical to go on repeating without use the movement that has happened. It is what we call the mechanical mind — it is strong in childhood because the thinking mind is not developed and has besides a narrow range of interests. Afterwards it becomes an undercurrent in the mental activities. It must now have risen up with the other characteristics of the mental physical because it is in the physical that the action has come down. Sometimes also when there is silence of the mind, these things come up till they also are quieted down.

*

The mechanical mind is a sort of engine — whatever comes to it it puts into the machine and goes on turning it round and round — no matter what it is.

*

From what you describe it seems that you have got into contact with the mechanical mind whose nature is to go on turning round in a circle on the thoughts that come into it. This sometimes happens when the thinking mind is quiet. This is part of the physical mind and you should not be disturbed or alarmed by its rising up, but see what it is and quiet it down or get control of its movements.

*

What is called the mechanical mind is necessary for the maintenance (in the physical) of things gained — it is by conservation and repetition that Nature does that. The subconscient is the basis of conservation and the mechanical mind is the means of repetition. Only they have to be enlightened and change and conserve and repeat the new divine things and not the old undivine ones.

*

If there is a strong activity of the higher parts of the consciousness, the possibility of the mechanical mind working is very much diminished. It may come up in moments of relaxation or fatigue but usually it is active only in a subordinate way that does not attract notice.

*

When the higher consciousness takes hold of the mechanical mind, it ceases to be mechanical.

The Vital Physical

The physical vital is the being of small desires and greeds etc. — the vital physical is the nervous being; they are closely connected together.

*

The vital physical governs all the small daily reactions to outward things — reactions of the nerves and the body consciousness and the reflex reactions and sensations; it motives much of the ordinary actions of man and joins with the lower parts of the vital proper in producing lust, jealousy, anger, violence etc. In its lowest parts (vital-material) it is the agent of pain, physical illness etc.

*

The vital physical forces can be received from anywhere by the body, from around, below or above. The order of the planes is in reference to each other, not in reference to the body. In reference to each other, the vital physical is below the physical mind, but above the material: but at the same time these powers interpenetrate each other.

*

The body energy is a manifestation of material forces supported by a vital-physical energy which is the vital energy precipitated into matter and conditioned by it.

The Material Consciousness or Body Consciousness

By material is meant the body consciousness, the consciousness of Matter etc. Physical is a wider term. There is for instance a physical mind (which cannot be called material) dealing with outside earthly things.

*

A great part of the body consciousness is subconscient and the body consciousness and the subconscient are closely bound together. The body and the physical do not coincide — the body consciousness is only part of the whole physical consciousness.

*

What you describe is the material consciousness; it is mostly subconscient, but the part of it that is conscious, is mechanical, inertly moved by habits or by the forces of the lower nature. Always repeating the same unintelligent and unenlightened movements, it is attached to the routine and established rule of what already exists, unwilling to change, unwilling to receive the Light or obey the higher Force. Or, if it is willing, then it is unable. Or if it is able, then it turns the action given to it by the Light or the Force into a new mechanical routine and so takes out of it all soul or life. It is obscure, stupid, indolent, full of ignorance and inertia, darkness and slowness of tamas.

It is this material consciousness into which we are seeking to bring first the higher (divine or spiritual) Light and Power and Ananda, and then the supramental Truth which is the object of our Yoga. But there is an obstinate dark and inert resistance both from material Nature and from the physical consciousness of the sadhaks — of which the lower vital and the material consciousness, both of them still unregenerated, are the cause.

*

It [*the material*] is the most physical grade of the physical — there is the mental physical, the vital physical, the material physical.

*

Yes — or at least it [*the material consciousness*] is a separate part of the physical consciousness. Physical mind for instance is narrow and limited and often stupid, but not inert. Matter consciousness is on the contrary inert as well as largely subconscious — active only when driven by an energy, otherwise inactive and immobile. When one first falls into direct contact with this level, the feeling in the body is that of inertia and immobility, in the vital physical exhaustion or lassitude, in the physical mind absence of *prakāśa* and *pravṛtti* or only the most ordinary thoughts and impulses. It took me a long time to get down any kind of light or power into this level. But when once it is illumined, the advantage is that the subconscient becomes conscient and this removes a very fundamental obstacle from the sadhana.

The Gross Physical and the Subtle Physical

By the gross physical is meant the earthly and bodily physical

— as experienced by the outward sense mind and senses. But that is not the whole of Matter. There is a subtle physical also with a subtler consciousness in it which can (for instance) go to a distance from the body and yet feel and be aware of things in a not merely mental or vital way. As for mind and vital they are everywhere — there is an obscure mind and life even in the cells of the body, the stones or in molecules and atoms.

*

It [*the subtle physical*] is difficult to realise without definite experience, e.g. as when light or ananda or force come into the body and one feels it working as if in the cells, yet with a little attention it becomes clear that it is not the material cells, but something more subtle that feels it.

*

There is what is called the nervous envelope surrounding the body — you are probably seeing the *sūkṣma* and the nervous envelope in one view. The *sūkṣma deha* contains the *sthūla deha*. Only it is not bound to itself and can contract or expand unlike the material body.

The Physical Nerves and the Subtle Nerves

The physical nerves are part of the material body, but they are extended into subtle nerves in the subtle body and there is a connection between the two.

*

Yes, there are nerves in the subtle body.

*

The physical nerves have many centres or plexuses. The nervous being proper is part of the physical — and it starts from the physical centre, the Muladhara.

*

The nerves are distributed all over the body — but the vital-physical action is concentrated in its origin between the Muladhara and the centre just above it.

The Sheaths of the Indian Tradition

Yes [*the inner being is made up of sheaths*]. Sheaths is simply a term for bodies, because each is superimposed on the other and acts as a covering and can be cast off. Thus the physical body itself is called the food sheath and its throwing off is what is called death.

*

You can only distinguish [*the different sheaths*] either by intuition or by experience and then you have established direct knowledge of the different sheaths.

Chapter Nine

The Environmental Consciousness

The Environmental Consciousness around the Individual

Everyone carries around him an environmental consciousness or atmosphere through which he is in relation with others or with the universal forces. It is through this that these forces or the thoughts or feelings of others enter.

*

The environmental is not a world — it is an individual thing.

*

The individual is not limited to the physical body — it is only the external consciousness which feels like that. As soon as one gets over this feeling of limitation, one can feel first the inner consciousness which is connected with the body but does not belong to it, afterwards the planes of consciousness above the body — also a consciousness surrounding the body, but part of oneself, part of the individual being, through which one is in contact with the cosmic forces and with other beings. This last is what I have called the environmental consciousness.

*

Each man has his own personal consciousness entrenched in his body and gets into touch with his surroundings only through his body and senses and the mind using the senses.

Yet all the time the universal forces are pouring into him without his knowing it. He is aware only of thoughts, feelings etc. that rise to the surface and these he takes for his own. Really they come from outside in mind waves, vital waves, waves of feeling and sensation etc. which take particular forms in him and rise to the surface after they have got inside.

But they do not get into his body at once. He carries

about with him an environmental consciousness (called by the Theosophists the aura) into which they first enter. If you can become conscious of this environmental self of yours, then you can catch the thought, passion, suggestion or force of illness, or whatever it may be, before it enters and prevent it from entering into you. If things in you are thrown out, they often do not go altogether but take refuge in this environmental atmosphere and from there try to get in again or they go to a distance outside but linger on the outskirts or even perhaps far off, waiting till they get an opportunity to attempt entrance.

*

It [*the environmental consciousness*] can become silent when there is the wideness. One can become conscious of it and deal with what passes through it. A man without it would be without contact with the rest of the world.

The Environmental Consciousness and the Movements of the Lower Nature

These things [*self-esteem, depression, etc.*] usually hide in recesses of the vital or the physical in which there is not yet the full force of the Peace and Light. When they are quite driven out from there, they may lodge in the subconscient and send up suggestions from there. Thrown out altogether they remain in the environmental consciousness and try to act from there, but then they are no longer part of one's own consciousness and are not felt as such but as something trying to come in from outside.

*

One can be free [*from lower vital movements*], but one cannot say that the freedom has been made absolutely complete or secure until the complete transformation takes place. For these things always remain in the environmental consciousness or even at a distance in the universal itself and take any opportunity to come in from there.

*

These [*forces of depression, dullness of mind, etc.*] are things that wander about in the atmosphere and jump upon one without notice. It is often difficult to see where precisely they come from and often there is no reason at all or any inviting cause in oneself. They have simply to be thrown off as when something falls on the body.

*

There is no mystery [*about the power of lower forces to attack*]. These things were violent and obstinate in you for a long time and you were indulging them — hence they acquired a great force to return even after you began rejecting them, first because of habit, secondly because of their belief that they have acquired a right over you, thirdly because of the habit of assent and passive response to them or endurance of them that has been stamped on the physical consciousness. This physical consciousness is not as yet liberated, it has not begun to be as responsive to the higher force as the vital, so it cannot resist their invasion. So these forces when thrown out retreat into the environmental consciousness and remain there concealed and at any opportunity make an attack on the centres accustomed to receive them (external mind and the external emotional) and get in. This happens with most sadhaks. Two things are necessary — (1) to open fully the physical to the higher forces, (2) to reach the stage when even if the forces attack, they cannot come fully in, the inner being remaining calm and free. Then even if there is still a surface difficulty, there will not be these overpowerings.

The Environmental Consciousness and the Subconscient

They [*the environmental consciousness and the subconscient*] are two quite different things. What is stored in the subconscient — impressions, memories, rise up from there into the conscious parts. In the environmental things are not stored up and fixed, although they move about there. It is full of mobility, a field of vibration or passage of forces.

Chapter Ten

The Subconscient and the Inconscient

The Subconscient in the Integral Yoga

In our Yoga we mean by the subconscient that quite submerged part of our being in which there is no wakingly conscious and coherent thought, will or feeling or organised reaction, but which yet receives obscurely the impressions of all things and stores them up in itself and from it too all sorts of stimuli, of persistent habitual movements, crudely repeated or disguised in strange forms can surge up into dream or into the waking nature. For if these impressions rise up most in dream in an incoherent and disorganised manner, they can also and do rise up into our waking consciousness as a mechanical repetition of old thoughts, old mental, vital and physical habits or an obscure stimulus to sensations, actions, emotions which do not originate in or from our conscious thought or will and are even often opposed to its perceptions, choice or dictates. In the subconscient there is an obscure mind full of obstinate sanskaras, impressions, associations, fixed notions, habitual reactions formed by our past, an obscure vital full of the seeds of habitual desires, sensations and nervous reactions, a most obscure material which governs much that has to do with the condition of the body. It is largely responsible for our illnesses; chronic or repeated illnesses are indeed mainly due to the subconscient and its obstinate memory and habit of repetition of whatever has impressed itself upon the body consciousness. But this subconscient must be clearly distinguished from the subliminal parts of our being such as the inner or subtle physical consciousness, the inner vital or inner mental; for these are not at all obscure or incoherent or ill-organised, but only veiled from our surface consciousness. Our surface constantly receives something, inner touches, communications or influences, from these sources but does not know for the most part whence they come.

*

The subconscient is below the waking physical consciousness — it is an automatic, obscure, incoherent, half-unconscious realm into which light and awareness can with difficulty come. The inner vital and physical are quite different — they have a larger, plastic, subtler, freer and richer consciousness than the surface vital and physical, much more open to the Truth and in direct touch with the universal.

*

The subconscient is not the whole foundation of our nature; it is only the lower basis of the Ignorance and governs mostly the lower vital and physical exterior consciousness and these again affect the higher parts of the nature. While it is necessary to see what it is and how it acts, one must not be too preoccupied with this dark side or this apparent aspect of the instrumental being. One should rather regard it as something not oneself, a mask of false nature imposed on the true being by the Ignorance. The true being is the inner with all its vast possibilities of reaching and expressing the Divine and especially the inmost, the soul, the psychic Purusha which is always in its essence pure, divine, turned to all that is good and true and beautiful. The exterior being has to be taken hold of by the inner being and turned into an instrument no longer of the upsurgings of the ignorant subconscient Nature, but of the Divine. It is by remembering always that and opening the nature upwards that the Divine Consciousness can be reached and descend from above into the whole inner and outer existence, mental, vital, physical, the subconscient, the subliminal, all that we overtly or secretly are. This should be the main preoccupation. To dwell solely on the subconscient and the aspect of imperfection creates depression and should be avoided. One has to keep a right balance and stress on the positive side most, recognising the other but only to reject and change it. This and a constant faith and reliance on the Mother are what is needed for the transformation to come.

*

The Subconscient is the basis of much of the lower activities — that is now generally admitted.

*

The subconscious is the evolutionary basis in us, it is not the whole of our hidden nature, nor is it the whole origin of what we are. But things can rise from the subconscient and take shape in the conscious part and much of our smaller vital and physical instincts, movements, habits, character-forms has this source.

There are three occult sources of our action — the superconscient, the subliminal, the subconscient, but of none of them are we in control or even aware. What we are aware of is the surface being which is only an instrumental arrangement. The source of all is the general Nature, — universal Nature individualising itself in each person; for this general Nature deposits certain habits of movement, personality, character, faculties, dispositions, tendencies in us, and that, whether formed now or before our birth, is what we usually call ourselves. A good deal of this is in habitual movement and use in our known conscious part on the surface, a great deal more is concealed in the other unknown three which are below or behind the surface.

But what we are on the surface is being constantly set in motion, changed, developed or repeated by the waves of the general Nature coming in on us either directly or else indirectly through others, through circumstances, through various agencies or channels. Some of this flows straight into the conscious part and acts there, but our mind ignores its source, appropriates it and regards all that as its own; a part comes secretly into the subconscient or sinks into it and waits for an opportunity of rising up into the conscious surface; a good deal goes into the subliminal and may at any time come out — or may not, may rather rest there as unused matter. Part passes through and is rejected, thrown back or thrown out or spilt into the universal sea. Our nature is a constant activity of forces supplied to us out of which (or rather out of a small amount of it) we make what we will or can. What we make seems fixed and formed for good, but in reality it is all a play of forces, a flux, nothing fixed or stable; the appearance of stability is given by constant repetition and recurrence of the same vibrations and formations. That is why our nature can be changed in spite of Vivekananda's saying and Horace's adage and in spite of the conservative resistance of the subconscient, but it is a difficult job because the master mode of Nature is this obstinate repetition and recurrence.

As for the things in our nature that are thrown away from us by rejection but come back, it depends on where you throw them. Very often there is a sort of procedure about it. The mind rejects its mentalities, the vital its vitalities, the physical its physicalities — these usually go back into the corresponding domain of general Nature. It all stays at first, when that happens, in the environmental consciousness which we carry about with us, by which we communicate with the outside Nature, and often it persistently rushes back from there — until it is so absolutely rejected, or thrown far away as it were, that it cannot return upon us any more. But when what the thinking and willing mind rejects is strongly supported by the vital, it leaves the mind indeed but sinks down into the vital, rages there and tries to rush up again and reoccupy the mind and compel or capture our mental acceptance. When the higher vital too — the heart or the larger vital dynamis rejects it, it sinks from there and takes refuge in the lower vital with its mass of small current movements that make up our daily littleness. When the lower vital too rejects it, it sinks into the physical consciousness and tries to stick by inertia or mechanical repetition. Rejected even from there it goes into the subconscient and comes up in dreams, in passivity, in extreme tamas. The Inconscient is the last resort of the Ignorance.

As for the waves that recur from the general Nature, it is the natural tendency of the inferior forces there to try and perpetuate their action in the individual, to rebuild what he has unbuilt of their deposits in him, so they return on him, often with an increased force, even with a stupendous violence, when they find their influence rejected. But they cannot last long once the environmental consciousness is cleared — unless the "Hostiles" take a hand. Even then they can indeed attack, but if the sadhak has established his position in the inner self, they can only attack and retire.

It is true that we bring most of ourselves — or rather most of our predispositions, tendencies of reaction to the universal Nature — from past lives. Heredity only affects strongly the external being; besides, all the effects of heredity are not accepted even there, only those that are in consonance with what we are to be or not preventive of it at least.

*

The subconscient is a concealed and unexpressed inarticulate consciousness which works below all our conscious physical activities. Just as what we call the superconscient is really a higher consciousness above from which things descend into the being, so the subconscient is below the body consciousness and things come up into the physical, the vital and the mind-nature from there.

Just as the higher consciousness is superconscient to us and supports all our spiritual possibilities and nature, so the subconscient is the basis of our material being and supports all that comes up in the physical nature.

Men are not ordinarily conscious of either of these planes of their own being, but by sadhana they can become aware.

The subconscient retains the impressions of all our past experiences of life and they can come up from there in dream forms. Most dreams in ordinary sleep are formations made from subconscient impressions.

The habit of strong recurrence of the same things in our physical consciousness, so that it is difficult to get rid of its habits, is largely due to a subconscient support. The subconscient is full of irrational habits.

When things are rejected from all other parts of the nature, they go either into the environmental consciousness around us through which we communicate with others and with universal

Nature and try to return from there or they sink into the subconscient and can come up from there even after lying long quiescent so that we think they are gone.

When the physical consciousness is being changed, the chief resistance comes from the subconscient. It is constantly maintaining or bringing back the inertia, weakness, obscurity, lack of intelligence which afflict the physical mind and vital or the obscure fears, desires, angers, lusts of the physical vital, or the illnesses, dullnesses, pains, incapabilities to which the body-nature is prone.

If light, strength, the Mother's consciousness is brought down into the body it can penetrate the subconscient also and convert its obscurity and resistance.

When something is erased from the subconscient so completely that it leaves no seed and thrown out of the circumconscient so completely that it can return no more, then only can we be sure that we have finished with it for ever.

*

About the subconscient — it is the submaterial base of the being and is made up of impressions, instincts, habitual movements that are stored there. Whatever movement is impressed on it, it keeps. If one impresses the right movement on it, it will keep and send up that. That is why it has to be cleared of old movements before there can be a permanent and total change in the nature. When the higher consciousness is once established in the waking parts, it goes down into the subconscient and changes that also, makes a bedrock of itself there also. Then no farther trouble from the subconscient will be possible. But even before that one can minimise the trouble by putting the right will and the right habit of reaction on the subconscient parts.

*

All that one does and thinks leaves its trace in the subconscient.

*

Yes, the subconscient is a cosmic as well as an individual plane.

The Subconscient in Traditional Indian Terminology

I don't know that there is any [*term corresponding to the subconscient in Patanjali or the Sankhya*] — this plane was spoken of more as inconscient than subconscient — it is practically the indiscriminate or *jaḍa prakṛti*, perhaps — or the seed state. In the Veda it is symbolised by the cave of the Panis. Perhaps by looking through books like the Yogavasishtha one could find something about the subconscient in fact though not in express terms.

*

You had asked the other day about the subconscient, what it was. In the vision you describe you were shown the universal subconscient in the figure of Patala, a place without light of consciousness and, because universal, therefore without bounds or end — the dark unconscious infinite out of which this material universe has arisen — it is walled with darkness on all sides, it seems also to have no bottom. The Light comes from above from the higher consciousness and coming down through the mind and heart and vital and physical has to pour down into this subconscient and make it luminous.

*

"Patala" [*in an experience described by the correspondent*] is a name for the subconscient — the beings there had no heads, that is to say, there is there no mental consciousness; men have all of them such a subconscient plane in their own being and from there rise all sorts of irrational and ignorant (headless) instincts, impulsions, memories etc. which have an effect upon their acts and feelings without their detecting the real source. At night many incoherent dreams come from this world or plane. The world above is the superconscient plane of being — above the human consciousness — there are many worlds of that kind; they are divine worlds.

The Subconscient and the Superconscient

Below the feet is the subconscient, just as above the head is the superconscient.

The Subconscient and the Subliminal

Subliminal is a general term used for all the parts of the being which are not on the waking surface. Subconscient is very often used in the same sense by European psychologists because they do not know the difference. But when I use the word, I mean always what is *below* the ordinary physical consciousness, not what is behind it. The inner mental, vital, physical, the psychic are not subconscious in this sense, but they can be spoken of as subliminal.

*

What he [*a correspondent*] has written about the subconscient and the outer nature is true. But the role of subliminal forces cannot be said to be small, since from there come all the greater aspirations, ideals, strivings towards a better self and better humanity without which man would be only a thinking animal — as also most of the art, poetry, philosophy, thirst for knowledge which relieve if they do not yet dispel the ignorance.

The role of the superconscient has been to evolve slowly the spiritual man out of the mental half-animal. That also cannot be called an insignificant role.

The Subconscient Memory and Conscious Memory

Exact images are retained by the subliminal memory. All that is subliminal is described by ordinary psychology as subconscient; but in our psychology that cannot be done, for the consciousness that holds them is as precise and far wider and fuller than our waking or surface consciousness, so how can it be called subconscient? Conscious memory is that which can bring up at any moment we like the memory of a thing, it is under our control. Subliminal memory can hold all things, even those which the mind cannot understand, e.g. if you hear somebody talking Hebrew, the subliminal memory can hold that and bring it up accurately in some abnormal state, e.g. the hypnotic. Subconscient memory is a memory of impressions; when they come up as in dream, either the result is something incoherent or fancifully rearranged or it is only the essence of the thing, its psychological deposit that comes up, e.g. sex, fear, some particular libido as the psychoanalysts call it, but the expression given to the latter need not be the same as memory would give; it may repeat the same forms if it gets hold of the mechanical mind in the physical to help its expression, but also it may be quite different from anything in real life.

*

The clear memory of words, images and thoughts is an action of the conscious mind, not the unconscious. Of course the memory goes behind, so to speak, in the back part of the mind, but it can be brought out. Also the memory can be lost or defaced, so that one remembers wrongly or forgets altogether, but that is still an imperfect action of the conscious mind, not an action of the subconscious. What the subconscious keeps is a mass of impressions, not of clear or exact images and these can come up as in dreams in an incoherent jumble distorted altogether or else in the waking state as a mechanical recurrence or repetition of the same suggestions, impulses (subconscient vital) or sensations. There is a recognisable difference between the two functionings.

*

It [*the memory of things*] is not in the mind alone; it is stored in the subconscient (mind, vital and physical) as impressions — also in the inner being all is present but held back as a store of past experience.

*

All that our consciousness meets in day-to-day experience is registered in subconscient memory and from there can be brought up to the mind or come of itself. But what we call memory is when the thing registered is kept in the conscious mind at its back and brought forward at will — that is conscious memory.

*

No — that [*the record of Chitragupta*] is quite different [*from the cosmic subconscient*], since it belongs to something where the records are precise and accurate. The subconscient is a suppressed and obscure seed state where things are emerging out of the indeterminate inconscience of original Nature but are yet fluent and imprecise, having all the potentiality of determination in them, but not yet determinate. The past things fall back into it not as memories, but as impressions which is a quite different thing. When they come up from there it is in all sorts of queer forms with variations and mixtures.

*

There is very often a complaint of this kind [*weakening of memory*] made during the course of the sadhana. I suppose that the usual action of memory is for a time suspended by the mental silence or else by the physical tamas.

*

By the change of consciousness there can be a more conscious and perfect functioning of the memory replacing the old mechanism.

The Subconscient and the Inconscient

The subconscient is universal as well as individual like all the other main parts of the nature. But there are different parts or planes of the subconscient. All upon earth is based on the Inconscient as it is called, though it is not really inconscient at all, but rather a complete "sub"-conscience, a suppressed or involved consciousness, in which there is everything but nothing is formulated or expressed. The subconscient lies in between this Inconscient and the conscious mind, life and body. It contains the potentiality of all the primitive reactions to life which struggle out to the surface from the dull and inert obscurity of Matter and form by a constant development a slowly evolving and self-formulating consciousness; it contains them not as ideas or perceptions or conscious reactions but as the fluid substance of these things. But also all that is consciously experienced sinks down into the subconscient, not as precise though submerged memories but as obscure yet obstinate impressions of experience, and these can come up at any time as dreams, as mechanical repetitions of past thought, feelings, action etc., as "complexes" exploding into action and event etc. etc. The subconscient is the main cause why all things repeat themselves and nothing ever gets changed except in appearances. It is the cause why people say character cannot be changed, the cause also of the constant return of things one hoped to have got rid of for ever. All seeds are there and all the sanskaras of the mind and vital and body, — it is the main support of death and disease and the last fortress (seemingly impregnable) of the Ignorance. All too that is suppressed without being wholly got rid of sinks down there and remains in seed ready to surge up or sprout up at any moment.

Section Four

The Chakras
or Centres of Consciousness

Chapter One

The System of the Chakras

The Functions of the Chakras or Centres

The centres or Chakras are seven in number —
    (1) The thousand-petalled lotus on the top of the head.
    (2) In the middle of the forehead — the Ajna Chakra — (will, vision, dynamic thought).
    (3) Throat centre — externalising mind.
    (4) Heart-lotus — emotional centre. The psychic is behind it.
    (5) Navel — higher vital (proper).
    (6) Below navel — lower vital.
    (7) Muladhara — physical.

All these centres are in the middle of the body; they are supposed to be attached to the spinal cord; but in fact all these things are in the subtle body, *sūkṣma deha*, though one has the feeling of their activities as if in the physical body when the consciousness is awake.

*

Chakras

The thousand-petalled (head) lotus	Chakra or centre of the higher will and knowledge
The lotus in the forehead	Will, vision, mental dynamism
The lotus in the throat	Expression — external mind
The lotus of the heart	Emotion, dynamic vital feeling (behind the heart is the seat of the psychic being)
The lotus of the navel	Higher vital
The lotus of the abdomen	Lower vital
The lotus at the end of the spine (Muladhara)	Physical consciousness

*

In the process of our Yoga the centres have each a fixed psychological use and general function which base all their special powers and functionings. The *mūlādhāra* governs the physical down to the subconscious; the abdominal centre — *svādhiṣṭhāna* — governs the lower vital; the navel centre — *nābhipadma* or *maṇipūra* — governs the larger vital; the heart centre — *hṛtpadma* or *anāhata* — governs the emotional being; the throat centre — *viśuddha* — governs the expressive and externalising mind; the centre between the eyebrows — *ājñācakra* — governs the dynamic mind, will, vision, mental formation; the thousand-petalled lotus — *sahasradala* — above commands the higher thinking mind, houses the still higher illumined mind and at its highest opens to the intuition through which or else by an overflooding directness the overmind can have with the rest communication or an immediate contact.[1]

*

I never heard of two lotuses in the heart centre; but it is the seat of two powers, in front the higher vital or emotional being, behind and concealed the soul or psychic being.

The colours of the lotuses and the numbers of petals are respectively, from bottom to top: — (1) the Muladhara or physical consciousness centre, four petals, red; (2) the abdominal centre, six petals, deeper purple red; (3) the navel centre, ten petals, violet; (4) the heart centre, twelve petals, golden pink; (5) the throat centre, sixteen petals, grey; (6) the forehead centre between the eyebrows, two petals, white; (7) the thousand-petalled lotus above the head, blue with gold light around. The functions are, according to our Yoga, — (1) commanding the physical consciousness and the subconscient; (2) commanding the small vital movements, the little greeds, lusts, desires, the small sense-movements; (3) commanding the larger life-forces and the passions and larger desire-movements; (4) commanding

---

[1] *In a draft of this letter Sri Aurobindo wrote in the opening paragraph: "I have often written of the centres — but without using the Sanskrit names which are intelligible only to Hindus. They are the same but our interpretation and application is not quite identical. We relate them to the psychological levels or planes." — Ed.*

the higher emotional being with the psychic deep behind it; (5) commanding expression and all externalisation of the mind-movements and mental forces; (6) commanding thought, will, vision; (7) commanding the higher thinking mind and the illumined mind and opening upwards to the intuition and overmind. The seventh is sometimes confused with the brain, but that is an error — the brain is only a channel of communication situated between the thousand-petalled and the forehead centre. The former is sometimes called the void centre, *śūnya*, either because it is not in the body, but in the apparent void above or because rising above the head one enters first into the silence of the self or spiritual being.

*

There is one centre below the navel (lower vital), another at the navel (central vital), another in the chest (emotional vital, heart centre), another in the throat (physical mind), another above the head (higher consciousness); besides these there is the centre in the forehead (mind, will, vision) and one at the bottom of the spine (muladhara, physical centre). The working in each will be according to the nature of the centre.

The Chakras in Reference to Yoga

One can speak of the chakras only in reference to Yoga. In ordinary people the chakras are not open, it is only when they do sadhana that they open. For the chakras are the centres of the inner consciousness and belong organically to the subtle body. So much as is active in ordinary people is very little — for in them it is the outer consciousness that is active.

*

The centres of consciousness [*are meant by the term "centres"*], the chakras. It is by their opening that the Yogic or inner consciousness develops — otherwise you are bound to the ordinary outer consciousness.

*

One does not pass through the psychic centre or any centre [*during the sadhana*]. The centres open under the pressure of the sadhana. You can say that the Force descends or ascends into a centre.

*

The spine is the support of the centres and it is through the spine that in the Tantric sadhana the Kundalini rises.

*

Allow me to state my difficulty [*with the idea that the "spirit entity" is lodged in the pineal gland*]. How the devil can a spirit entity be enclosed in a material gland? So far as I know the self or spirit is not enclosed in the body, rather the body is in the Self. When we have the full experience of the Self, we feel it as a wide consciousness in which the body is a very small thing, an adjunct, or a thing contained, not a container. What then is this spirit entity? There can be a small formation which stands for the Self or Spirit, like the Upanishad's Purusha no bigger than a man's thumb. Is this the spirit entity? But even then in which sense, in what relativity of space can it be said to be *in* the very material pineal gland? A spirit confined in a gland and dislodged from it by a pistol shot is a kind of language which I buck at. A spirit touching grey brain matter and so entering into contact with universal mind and touching white matter and so entering into contact with loftier spiritual realities is also too weird a conception for my intelligence. What happens to it when it has no matter to touch? Dissolution? laya?

When we speak of the Purusha in the head, heart etc., we are using a figure. The Muladhara from which the Kundalini rises is not in the physical body, but in the subtle body (the subtle body is that in which the being goes out in deep trance or more radically, at the time of death); so also are all the centres. But as the subtle body penetrates and is interfused with the gross body, there is a certain correspondence between these chakras and certain centres in the physical proper. So figuratively we speak of the Purusha in this or that centre of the body. Owing to this correspondence, again, when the Ananda or anything else comes down into the being, it is the subtle body that it pervades, but it communicates itself through it to the gross body and its consciousness, so that it is felt as if pervading the body. But all that is very different from saying that the spirit is lodged in a gland. The gross body is an engine, a means of communication and action of the spirit upon the world and it is only a small part of the instrumentation. It is absurd to make so much of it as all that. It is a sort of false materialism intended to placate minds that have a scanty knowledge of science. But what is the use of that? Everybody now knows that science is not a statement of the truth of things, but only a language expressing a certain experience of objects, their structure, their mathematics, a coordinated and utilisable impression of their processes — it is nothing more. Matter itself is something (a formation of energy perhaps?) of which we know superficially the structure as it appears to our mind and senses and to certain examining instruments (about which it is now suspected that they largely determine their own results, Nature adapting its replies to the instrument used), but more than that no scientist knows or can know. If the Radhasoami affirmations [*mentioned by the correspondent*] are meant to be another kind of language expressing certain psycho-physical experiences, I have no objection. But why all this pineal glandism and talk about entities and bullets?

N.B. If I say the Purusha is in the heart, do I mean it is there in the physical heart, tumbling about in the flow of the blood or stuck in the valves or muscular portions and when a bullet is lodged in the heart it jumps with an Ooah! and tumbles down dead or goes off skating and swimming into some grey or white matter worlds beyond? Certainly not. I am using a significant language which expresses certain relations between the psychic consciousness and the physical of which we become aware by Yoga.

The Centres and the Planes

Each centre of the system (*cakra, padma*) represents or centralises a plane of experience and each is supported on the spine which is the support of the nervous energies. When the serpent Energy from above and below have free passage through the centres (which is represented by the spine appearing like a serpent) then they open and there is the free wideness of the universal or infinite consciousness on all these planes.

*

All the centres above the Muladhara are connected with the higher worlds above the physical, with the vital, mental, psychic and still higher worlds — the Muladhara and below with the physical and subconscient worlds (subconscient physical and sub-physical). The whole physical body of course belongs to the earth-world, but it is connected through these centres with the other worlds.

*

According to our system the three lower centres are the vital, the lower vital and the physical — but the planes are quite different. The three lower planes are mind, life and matter and it is true that the human mind confines itself to these three activities. But it is not true that its activities are confined to the vital and physical things.

*

What is the fourth centre? In our system the fourth centre is the heart and the Divine is there in the psychic, behind the heart. But the fourth of our seven planes is the supramental which is far above the head, but can be communicated with through the seventh centre, the Sahasradala padma.

The Mind Centres

This must be the psychicised higher mental being — the position above the head points to that. In other words, you have become aware of your higher mental being which is in contact at once with the Divine above and with the psychic behind the heart and is aware of the Truth and has the psychic and spiritual insight and view into things.

Above the head extends the higher consciousness centre, sahasradala padma. But usually there is partial working of the forehead centre also when the sahasradala opens.

The ordinary mind is at the highest the free intelligence, receiving perhaps intuitions and intimations from above which it intellectualises. It is on the surface and sees things from outside except in so far as it is helped by intuition and other powers to see a little deeper. When this ordinary mind opens within to inner mind and psychic and above to higher mind and higher consciousness generally, then it begins to be spiritualised and its highest ranges merge into the spiritual mind-consciousness of which this higher mind can be a beginning. This merging is part of the spiritual transformation.

For the mind there are many centres: (1) the sahasradala which centralises spiritual mind, higher mind, intuitive mind and acts as a receiving station for the intuition proper and overmind, (2) the centre in the forehead for inner thought, will and vision, (3) the throat centre for the externalising or physical mind.

The Sahasradala or Sahasrara or Crown Centre

The thousand-petalled lotus is above the head. It is the seventh and highest centre.

Usually those who take the centres in the body only, count six centres, the Sahasrara being excluded.

*

It is evidently the sahasradala padma through which the higher intuition, illumined mind and overmind all pass their rays.

*

The sahasradala commands all between the ordinary mind and the supermind — therefore its opening necessarily takes long. But opening by itself only creates a connection or communication — to dwell in that centre, one needs to have overpassed the mind and be able to live mainly in the spiritual self.

*

The Supramental is not organised in the body so there is no separate centre for it; but all that comes from above the Mind uses the Sahasrara for its transit and so opens something there.

*

The centre at the crown must be part of the *sahasradala*, the centre of communication direct between the individual being and the Infinite Consciousness above. There is not supposed to be any other main centre of dynamism between that and the Ajna Chakra. But there can be many nerve-centres in various parts of the body, apart from the six or rather seven main centres.

*

The crown centre open removes the difficulty of the lid between the ordinary mind and the higher consciousness above. If the ajnachakra also is open, then it is possible to have a clear communication between the higher consciousness and the inner mind and the outer mind (throat centre) also. That is the condition for the realisation of knowledge and the mental illumination and transformation. The heart centre commands the psychic and vital — that opening enables the psychic influence to work in the vital and ends in the coming forward of the psychic being.

*

It [*the opening at the top of the head*] is the Brahmarandhra through which there is the communication between the higher consciousness and the lower in the body. It is a passage, not a centre. The centre is the thousand-petalled lotus just above the head, at that part.

*

The crown is the place of passage between the body consciousness with all it contains of mind and life and the higher being above the body. It is there that the two consciousnesses begin to meet.

*

The brain is only a centre of the physical consciousness. One feels stationed there so long as one dwells in the physical mind or is identified with the body consciousness, then one receives through the sahasradala into the brain. When one ceases to be stationed in the body, then the brain is not a station but only a passive and silent transmitting channel.

The Ajnachakra or Forehead Centre

There are different centres in the body which are represented in vision by these lotuses — one is between the eyebrows in the forehead, a centre of inner consciousness, will and visions — that is opening in you.

*

If the forehead centre opens, it is fairly certain that the crown centre must have opened sufficiently at least to allow the passage of the higher force which is above it. The psychic is a different matter — it stands behind the centres and the time of its opening varies with different people — in fact it is not so much the opening of a centre as the coming forward of the psychic being.

The usual rule in this Yoga is from above downwards. There may be variations in the preparatory stage. There may for instance be a partial opening first of the heart centre. The higher vital centre may become active first also, but that means much struggle and difficulty.

*

The psychic being is behind the heart-centre — the centre between the eyes is that of inner (occult) thought, will and vision. This inner or occult vision is called by ordinary people psychic vision.

*

It [*the centre between the eyebrows*] is the centre of the inner mind — therefore also of the inner mental will and inner mental vision.

*

The centre of vision is between the eyebrows in the centre of the forehead. When it opens one gets the inner vision, sees the inner forms and images of things and people and begins to understand things and people from within and not only from outside, develops a power of will which also acts in the inner (Yogic) way on things and people etc. Its opening is often the beginning of the Yogic as opposed to the ordinary mental consciousness.

*

In the forehead between the eyes but a little above is the Ajnachakra, the centre of the inner will, also of the inner vision, the dynamic mind etc. (This is not the ordinary outer mental will and sight, but something more powerful, belonging to the inner being.) When this centre opens and the Force there is active, then there is the opening of a greater will, power of decision, formation, effectiveness beyond what the ordinary mind can achieve.

*

The centre Ajnachakra is in the place I indicated [*in the previous letter*], but the pressure can be felt in all the forehead and the eyebrows also or anywhere there. It radiates from the centre.

*

The forehead centre is that of inner mind and vision. It is really through that inner vision that one sees the lights — the open eyes are only a channel for seeing them outside as well as within.

*

The pressure from within upon the forehead centre begins very often after the pressure from above on the forehead — something of the Force has come in sufficiently to exercise this second pressure. That on the back must be a direct pressure on the psychic region (if it is in or near the middle of the back) mainly to prepare the action in the heart. When the centres begin to open, inner experiences such as the seeing of light or images through the subtle vision in the forehead centre or psychic experiences and perceptions in the heart, become frequent — gradually one becomes aware of one's inner being as separate from the outer and what can be called a Yogic consciousness with all its deeper movements develops in the place of the ordinary superficial mental and vital movements.

*

A third eye does open there [*in the centre of the forehead*] — it represents the occult vision and the occult power which goes with that vision — it is connected with the Ajnachakra.

The Throat Centre

The throat centre is the centre of the physical mind, the external will and the expression.

*

Yes [*the throat centre is the physical mind centre*]. It is the centre of externalisation, — speech, expression, the power to deal mentally with physical things etc. Its opening brings the power to open the physical mind to the light of the divine consciousness instead of remaining in the ordinary outward-going mentality.

*

Yes, it is so — it is the physical mind that acts like that [*rising up from the throat centre to cover the mind*]. The centre of the physical mind or externalising mind is in the subtle body in the throat and connected strongly with the speech — but it acts by connection with the brain. All forces that want to cover the consciousness rise up to do it, covering and acting on the mind centres if they can — because otherwise the covering is not complete.

*

Speech comes from the throat centre, but it is associated with whatever is the governing centre or level of the consciousness — wherever one thinks from. If one rises above the head, then thought takes place above the head and one can speak from there, that is to say, the direction of the speech is from there.

The Throat Centre and the Lower Centres

The throat centre is the externalising (physical) mind, the heart is the emotional mind and beginning of the higher vital. If the heart centre is dominated by the physical mind to any extent, it will necessarily be open to the outer attacks that affect the physical and nervous consciousness. The heart has to be in connection with the psychic and the higher consciousness.

*

The centre in the throat is that of the physical mind and all between it and the centre in the heart is the joining place of the mind and the vital-emotional being. If the pain is of the nerves, then there must be some resistance and difficulty there which should go with the full opening.

*

The heart is the centre of the emotional being, the highest part of the vital. The navel is the centre of the dynamic and sensational vital (this is the source of pride, sense of possession, ambition, anger and other passions — but it expresses them often through the heart centre). The centre between the navel and the Muladhara commands the lower vital (physical desires, small greeds, passions etc.). The throat centre is not the vital — it is the physical mind, the expressive externalising consciousness. What you feel may be the vital taking hold of the physical mind and using it for expression.

*

The physical mind centre is in the throat and mouth — the vital physical is between the two lowest centres — the material consciousness is in the *mūlādhāra*.

The Heart Centre

The heart is the centre of the being and commands the rest, as the psychic being or chaitya purusha is there. It is only in that sense that all flows from it, for it is the psychic being who each time creates a new mind, vital and body for himself.

*

There is one centre for the heart, although it is a double centre, in front the emotional, behind the psychic.

*

The apex of the psychic and emotional centre (like the apex of all centres) is in the backbone, the base in front in the middle of the sternum.

*

The physical heart is in the left side, but the heart centre of Yoga is in the middle of the chest — the cardiac centre.

*

I do not quite understand what you mean by soul. The psychic being (which is the soul) does not make centres for itself in the Adhar — the centres are there. The psychic being can take control of the centres that are already there — the heart and the navel centre and the two below the navel. Also the mind and vital are not abolished — they are brought under the psychic influence and psychicised, or they are occupied by the higher consciousness from above and transformed into its instruments.

*

The heart-centre is the emotional centre. The navel is the main vital centre. In the abdomen is the lower vital centre. It is in these two that there is the origination of desire — but desire rises and becomes emotional in the heart and mental in the higher centres above.

The Navel and Abdominal Centres

The navel is the chief vital centre below the emotional — there is another centre of small vital movements below it, between the navel and Muladhara.

*

The navel is the vital centre in the physical body but the natural seat of the vital is in the vital sheath of the subtle body, which sheath it pervades; but for action through the gross body it is centred at the navel and below it.

*

A centre may be opened and still there may be resistances in that part of the nature. If the vital were clear of all difficulties one would be on the point of Yogic perfection. Below the navel is the physical vital.

*

The navel is the seat of the central vital, below it is the lower vital. It must have been the resistance of the lower vital to the fire that you felt.

*

The feeling you have of coming down to the navel corresponds to the actual fact of a change of the centre of consciousness, which one speaks of as a lowering of the consciousness. In this stage of sadhana one must keep always above until one is seated for good in the above-head position and the higher consciousness has pervaded the lower centres and fields down to the Muladhara and the whole body.

The Muladhara

The Muladhara is the centre of the physical consciousness proper, and all below in the body is the sheer physical, which as it goes downward becomes increasingly subconscient, but the real seat of the subconscient is below the body as the real seat of the higher consciousness (superconscient) is above the body. At the same time, the subconscient can be felt anywhere, felt as something below the movement of the consciousness and, in a way, supporting it from beneath or else drawing the consciousness down towards itself. The subconscient is the main support of all habitual movements, especially the physical and lower vital movements. When something is thrown out of the vital or physical, it very usually goes down into the subconscient and remains there as if in seed and comes up again when it can. That is the reason why it is so difficult to get rid of habitual vital movements or to change the character; for, supported or refreshed from this source, preserved in this matrix your vital movements, even when suppressed or repressed, surge up again and recur. The action of the subconscient is irrational, mechanical, repetitive. It does not listen to reason or the mental will. It is only by bringing the higher light and force into it that it can change.

*

The Muladhara is the centre of the physical consciousness, but the legs below represent the special field governed by it — as distinct from the mental and vital parts in the body. So when there is working there, it means a working in the physical proper itself. Of course the physical is half-subconscient, but the field of the subconscient proper is below the feet, just as the field of the superconscient is above the head.

*

The lowest centre at the bottom of the spine [*is the sex centre*]. It contains many other things, but also it is in its front the support of the sexual movements.

*

It [*the end of the spine*] is the place of the physical centre which is also the sex-centre. The apex of it is at the end of the spine and it projects forward from there — commanding the organ and its action.

*

The sex centre is the physical centre — it [*the physical centre*] happens to be the centre for sex and physical propagation also, but it is not separately and solely the centre of sex. If that were so, there would be no centre governing the physical consciousness, but only a centre governing the sex organ.

No Subconscient Centre

There is no subconscient centre. Its plane is below the feet as that of the superconscient is above the head.

*

No, the subconscient is too vague to have a centre. It has a level — below the feet as the superconscient is above, but from there it can surge up anywhere.

Chapter Two

The Parts of the Body and the Centres

The Parts of the Body in Yoga

Different parts of the body indicate for this purpose different parts of the nature. The head is the seat of the mind (buddhi) and the lower part of the mouth, chin, neck are the seat of the external or physical mind. It indicates that the force is working there to change and prepare this part of the mind and get rid of resistance and wrong mental habits.

The Cerebellum

Yes, it [*the cerebellum*] has some connection with the subconscient.

The Ear, Nose, Face and Throat

It cannot be anything physical but only a subtle physical sensation. The ear is the passage of communion between the inner mind centre and the thought-forces or thought-waves of the universal Nature. It sounds like a sensation of opening and enlarging of this passage.

*

The nose is connected with the vital dynamic part of the mental — a man with a strong nose is supposed to have a strong will or a strong mental personality, — though I don't know whether it is invariably true. But the vital physical? Of course the nose is the passage of the Prana and the Prana is the support of the vital physical.

*

The working on the lower part of the face always indicates an action on the externalising mind (physical mental) whose centre is in the throat.

*

The neck and throat and the lower part of the face belong to the externalising mind, the physical mental. The forehead to the inner Mind. Above the head are the higher planes of Mind.

*

The organ of speech is an instrument of the physical mental or expressive externalising mind.

The Chest, Stomach and Abdomen

It is because the centre of your difficulties has been there [*in the chest and stomach*]. The chest = the emotional nature exposed to wrong feelings; the stomach = the dynamic vital centre, exposed to wrong desires, ambitions, sense of possession and vital ego etc. But all that will progressively become things of the past, when the Peace, the Presence, the inner happiness increase and take possession of the external nature.

*

Yogically, psycho-physically etc. etc. stomach, heart and intestine lodge the vital movements, *not* the physical consciousness — it is there that anger, fear, love, hate and all the other psychological privileges of the animal tumble about and upset the physical and moral digestion. The Muladhara is the seat of the physical consciousness proper.

*

As for the lower part of the body, it is the physical and external vital that it represents at present and that has still to be penetrated and held by the Force. But the conditions under which it can be done are growing more complete. The physical opening needs a great quietude which replaces the tamasic inertia of body nature by a true peace. Then all else can be done.

The Legs and Feet

It is the material consciousness that is indicated by the legs and feet. Below the feet is the subconscient. There is no big centre below the Muladhara in the body, but there are minor centres everywhere.

*

The leg indicates the physical (material) consciousness. All below the Muladhara is the range of the physical consciousness proper including the mental physical, vital physical, material physical. This [*aspiration rising from the legs*] would indicate therefore an aspiration from Matter (bodily Matter).

The Sides of the Body

The two sides of the body are supposed to represent two different sides of the being, the side of consciousness and knowledge and the side of force and action. The feeling you had at meditation may have been the sense of the removal of some veil of obscurity covering the mind — the head from the crown to the throat being the seat of the thinking mind.

*

It is usually supposed that the left is the side of power, the right of knowledge.

The ascent from below [*the left foot*] means of course the material and subconscient calling down the higher power — and it is true that there is a correspondence between the depth from which the ascension goes and the height from which the power from above comes.

Part Three

The Evolutionary Process and the Supermind

ial Evolution
Section One

The Supramental Evolution

Chapter One

The Problem of Suffering and Evil

The Riddle of This World

It is not to be denied, no spiritual experience will deny that this is an unideal and unsatisfactory world, strongly marked with the stamp of inadequacy, suffering, evil. Indeed this perception is in a way almost the starting-point of the spiritual urge — except for the few to whom the greater experience comes spontaneously without being forced to seek it by the strong or overwhelming, the afflicting and detaching sense of the Shadow overhanging the whole range of this manifested existence. But still the question remains whether this is indeed, as is contended, the essential character of all manifestation or so long at least as there is a physical world it must be of this nature, so that the desire of birth, the will to manifest or create has to be regarded as the original sin and withdrawal from birth or manifestation as the sole possible way of salvation. For those who perceive it so or with some kindred look — and these have been the majority — there are well-known ways of issue, a straight-cut to spiritual deliverance. But equally it may not be so but only seem so to our ignorance or to a partial knowledge — the imperfection, the evil, the suffering may be a besetting circumstance or a dolorous passage, but not the very condition of manifestation, not the very essence of birth in Nature. And if so, the highest wisdom will lie not in escape, but in the urge towards a victory here, in a consenting association with the Will behind the world, in a discovery of the spiritual gate to perfection which will be at the same time an opening for the entire descent of the Divine Light, Knowledge, Power, Beatitude.

All spiritual experience affirms that there is a Permanent above the transience of this manifested world we live in and this limited consciousness in whose narrow borders we grope and struggle, and that its characters are infinity, self-existence, freedom, absolute Light, absolute Beatitude. Is there then an unbridgeable gulf between that which is beyond and that which is here or are they two perpetual opposites and only by leaving this adventure in Time behind, by overleaping the gulf can men reach the Eternal? That is what seems to be at the end of one line of experience which has been followed to its rigorous conclusion by Buddhism and a little less rigorously by a certain type of Monistic spirituality which admits some connection of the world with the Divine, but still opposes them in the last resort to each other as truth and illusion. But there is also this other and indubitable experience that the Divine is here in everything as well as above and behind everything, that all is in That and is That when we go back from its appearance to its Reality. It is a significant and illumining fact that the knower of Brahman even moving and acting in this world, even bearing all its shocks, can live in some absolute peace, light and beatitude of the Divine. There is then something here other than that mere trenchant opposition, — there is a mystery, a problem which one would think must admit of some less desperate solution. This spiritual possibility points beyond itself and brings a ray of hope into the darkness of our fallen existence.

And at once a first question arises — is this world an unchanging succession of the same phenomena always or is there in it an evolutionary urge, an evolutionary fact, a ladder of ascension somewhere from an original apparent Inconscience to a more and more developed consciousness, from each development still ascending, emerging on highest heights not yet within our normal reach? If so, what is the sense, the fundamental principle, the logical issue of that progression? Everything seems to point to such a progression as a fact — to a spiritual and not merely a physical evolution. Here too there is a justifying line of spiritual experience in which we discover that the Inconscience from which all starts is apparent only, for in it there is an involved Consciousness with endless possibilities, a consciousness not limited but cosmic and infinite, a concealed and self-imprisoned Divine, imprisoned in Matter but with every potentiality held in its secret depths. Out of this apparent Inconscience each potentiality is revealed in its turn, first organised Matter concealing the indwelling Spirit, then Life emerging in the plant and associated in the animal with a growing Mind, then Mind itself evolved and organised in Man. This evolution, this spiritual progression — does it stop short here in the imperfect mental being called Man? Or is the secret of it simply a succession of rebirths whose only purpose or issue is to labour towards the point at which it can learn its own futility, renounce itself and take its leap into some original unborn Existence or Non-Existence? There is at least the possibility, there comes at a certain point the certitude that there is a far greater consciousness than what we call Mind, and that by ascending the ladder still farther we can find a point at which the hold of the material Inconscience, the vital and mental Ignorance ceases; a principle of consciousness becomes capable of manifestation which liberates not partially, not imperfectly, but radically and wholly this imprisoned Divine. In this vision each stage of evolution appears as due to the descent of a higher and higher Power of consciousness, raising the terrestrial level, creating a new stratum, but the highest yet remain to descend and it is by their descent that the riddle of terrestrial existence will receive its solution and not only the soul but Nature herself find her deliverance. This is the Truth which has been seen in flashes, in more and more entirety of its terms by the line of seers whom the Tantra would call the hero-seekers and the divine seekers and which may now be nearing the point of readiness for its full revelation and experience. Then whatever be the heavy weight of strife and suffering and darkness in the world, yet if there is this as its high result awaiting us, all that has gone before may not be counted too great a price by the strong and adventurous for the glory that is to come. At any rate the shadow lifts; there is a Divine Light that leans over the world and is not only a far-off incommunicable Lustre.

It is true that the problem still remains why all this that yet is should have been necessary — those crude beginnings, this long, dark and stormy passage — why should the heavy and tedious price be demanded, why should evil and suffering ever have been there? For to the how of the fall into the Ignorance as opposed to the why, as to the effective cause, there is a substantial agreement in all spiritual experience. It is the division, the separation, the principle of isolation from the Permanent and One that brought it about; it is because the ego set up for itself in the world affirming its own desire and self-affirmation in preference to its unity with the Divine and its oneness with all; it is because instead of the one supreme Force, Wisdom, Light determining the harmony of all forces each Idea, Force, Form of things was allowed to work itself out as far as it could in the mass of infinite possibilities by its separate will and inevitably in the end by conflict with others. Division, ego, the imperfect consciousness and groping and struggle of a separate self-affirmation are the effective cause of the suffering and ignorance of this world. Once consciousnesses separated from the One Consciousness, they fell inevitably into ignorance and the last result of ignorance was Inconscience; from a dark immense Inconscient this material world arises and out of it a soul that by evolution is struggling into consciousness, attracted towards the hidden Light, ascending but still blindly towards the lost Divinity from which it came.

But why should this have happened at all? One common way of putting the question and answering it ought to be eliminated from the first, — the human way and its ethical revolt and reprobation, its emotional outcry. For it is not, as some religions suppose, a supra-cosmic, arbitrary, personal Deity himself altogether uninvolved in the fall who has imposed evil and suffering on creatures made capriciously by his fiat. The Divine we know is an Infinite Being in whose infinite manifestation these things have come — it is the Divine itself that is here, behind us, pervading the manifestation, supporting the world with its oneness; it is the Divine that is in us upholding itself the burden of the fall and its dark consequence. If above it stands for ever in its perfect Light, Bliss and Peace, it is also here; its Light, Bliss and Peace are secretly here supporting all; in ourselves there is a spirit, a central presence greater than the series of surface personalities which, like the supreme Divine itself, is not overborne by the fate they endure. If we find out this Divine within us, if we know ourselves as this spirit which is of one essence and being with the Divine, that is our gate of deliverance and in it we can remain ourselves even in the midst of this world's disharmonies, luminous, blissful and free. That much is the age-old testimony of spiritual experience.

But still what is the purpose and origin of the disharmony — why came this division and ego, this world of a painful evolution? Why must this evil and sorrow enter into the divine Good, Bliss and Peace? It is hard to answer to the human intelligence on its own level, for the consciousness to which the origin of this phenomenon belongs and to which it stands as it were automatically justified in a supra-intellectual knowledge, is a cosmic and not an individualised human intelligence; it sees in larger spaces, it has another vision and cognition, other terms of consciousness than human reason and feeling. To the human mind one might answer that while in itself the Infinite might be free from those perturbations, yet once manifestation began infinite possibility also began and among the infinite possibilities which it is the function of the universal manifestation to work out, the negation, the apparent effective negation — with all its consequences — of the Power, Light, Peace, Bliss was very evidently one. If it is asked why even if possible it should have been accepted, the answer nearest to the Cosmic Truth which the human intelligence can make is that in the relations or in the transition of the Divine in the Oneness to the Divine in the Many, this ominous possible became at a certain point an inevitable. For once it appears it acquires for the Soul descending into evolutionary manifestation an irresistible attraction which creates the inevitability — an attraction which in human terms on the terrestrial level might be interpreted as the call of the unknown, the joy of danger and difficulty and adventure, the will to attempt the impossible, to work out the incalculable, the will to create the new and uncreated with one's own self and life as the material, the fascination of contradictories and their difficult harmonisation — these things translated into another supraphysical, superhuman consciousness, higher and wider than the mental, were the temptation that led to the fall. For to the original being of light on the verge of the descent the one thing unknown was the depths of the abyss, the possibilities of the Divine in the Ignorance and Inconscience. On the other side from the Divine Oneness a vast acquiescence, compassionate, consenting, helpful, a supreme knowledge that this thing must be, that having appeared it must be worked out, that its appearance is in a certain sense part of an incalculable infinite wisdom, that if the plunge into Night was inevitable the emergence into a new unprecedented Day was also a certitude, and that only so could a certain manifestation of the Supreme Truth be effected — by a working out with its phenomenal opposites as the starting-point of the evolution, as the condition laid down for a transforming emergence. In this acquiescence was embraced too the will of the great Sacrifice, the descent of the Divine itself into the Inconscience to take up the burden of the Ignorance and its consequences, to intervene as the Avatar and the Vibhuti walking between the double sign of the Cross and the victory towards the fulfilment and deliverance. A too imaged rendering of the inexpressible Truth? but without images how to present to the intellect a mystery far beyond it? It is only when one has crossed the barrier of the limited intelligence and shared in the cosmic experience and the knowledge which sees things from identity that the supreme realities which lie behind these images — images corresponding to the terrestrial fact — assume their divine forms and are felt as simple, natural, implied in the essence of things. It is by entering into that greater consciousness alone that one can grasp the inevitability of its self-creation and its purpose.

This is indeed only the Truth of the manifestation as it presents itself to the consciousness when it stands on the border line between Eternity and the descent into Time where the relation between the One and the Many in the evolution is self-determined, a zone where all that is to be is implied but not yet in action. But the liberated consciousness can rise higher where the problem exists no longer and from there see it in the light of a supreme identity where all is predetermined in the automatic self-existent truth of things and self-justified to an absolute

The Problem of Suffering and Evil

consciousness and wisdom and absolute Delight which is behind all creation and non-creation and the affirmation and negation are both seen with the eyes of the ineffable Reality that delivers and reconciles them. But that knowledge is not expressible to the human mind; its language of light is too undecipherable, the light itself too bright for a consciousness accustomed to the stress and obscurity of the cosmic riddle and too entangled in it to follow the clue or to grasp the secret. In any case, it is only when we rise in the spirit beyond the zone of the darkness and the struggle that we enter into the full significance of it and there is a deliverance of the soul from its enigma. To rise to that height of liberation is the true way out and the only means of the indubitable knowledge.

But that liberation and transcendence need not necessarily impose a disappearance, a sheer dissolving cut from the manifestation; it can prepare a liberation into action of the highest Knowledge and an intensity of Power that can transform the world and fulfil the evolutionary urge. It is an ascent from which the return is no longer a fall but a winged or self-sustained descent of light, force and Ananda.

It is what is inherent in force of being that manifests as becoming; but what the manifestation shall be, its terms, its balance of energies, its arrangement of principles depends on the consciousness which acts in the creative force, on the power of consciousness which being delivers from itself for manifestation. It is in the nature of being to be able to grade and vary its powers of consciousness and determine according to the grade and variation its world or its degree and scope of self-revelation. The manifested creation is limited by the power to which it belongs and sees and lives according to it and can only see more, live more powerfully, change its world by opening or rising towards or making descend a greater power of consciousness that was above it. This is what is happening in the evolution of consciousness in our world, a world of inanimate matter producing under the stress of this necessity a power of life, a power of mind which bring into it new forms of creation and still labouring to produce, to make descend into it some supramental power. It is farther an operation of creative force which moves between two poles of consciousness. On one side there is a secret consciousness within and above which contains in it all potentialities — there eternally manifest, here awaiting delivery — of light, peace, power and bliss. On the other side there is another outward on the surface and below that starts from the apparent opposite of unconsciousness, inertia, blind stress, possibility of suffering and grows by receiving into itself higher and higher powers which make it always recreate its manifestation in larger terms, each new-creation of this kind bringing out something of the inner potentiality, making it more and more possible to bring down the Perfection that waits above. At last the line will be crossed that will make possible the entire reversion and the manifestation in the terms of ensouled Matter of That which is above. As long as the outward personality we call ourselves is centred in the lower powers of consciousness, the riddle of its own existence, its purpose, its necessity is to it an insoluble enigma; if something of the truth is at all conveyed to this outward mental man, he but imperfectly grasps it and perhaps misinterprets and misuses and mislives it. His true staff of walking is made more of a fire of faith than any ascertained and indubitable light of knowledge. It is only by rising toward a higher consciousness beyond the line and therefore superconscient now to him that he can emerge from his inability and his ignorance. His full liberation and enlightenment will come when he crosses the line into the light of a new superconscient existence. That is the transcendence which was the object of aspiration of the mystics and the spiritual seekers.

But in itself this would change nothing in the creation here; the evasion of a liberated soul from the world makes to that world no difference. But this crossing of the line if turned not only to an ascending but to a descending purpose would mean the transformation of the line from what it now is, a lid, a barrier, into a passage for the higher powers of consciousness of the Being now above it. It would mean a new creation on earth, a bringing in of the ultimate powers which would reverse the conditions here, in as much as that would produce a creation raised into the full flood of spiritual and supramental light in place of one emerging into a half-light of mind out of a darkness of material inconscience. It is only in such a full flood of the realised spirit that the embodied being could know, in the sense of all that was involved in it, the meaning and temporary necessity of his descent into the darkness and its conditions and at the same time dissolve them by a luminous transmutation into a manifestation here of the revealed and no longer of the veiled and disguised or apparently deformed Divine.

*

I suppose you have not read my "Riddle of This World",[1] but it is a similar solution I put there. X's way of putting it is a trifle too "Vedantic-Theistic" — in my view it is a transaction between the One and the Many. In the beginning it was you (not the human you who is now complaining but the central being) which accepted or even invited the adventure of the Ignorance; sorrow and struggle are a necessary consequence of the plunge into the Inconscience and the evolutionary emergence out of it. The explanation is that it had an object, the eventual play of the Divine Consciousness and Ananda not in its original transcendence but under conditions for which the plunge into the Inconscience was necessary. It is fundamentally a cosmic problem and can be understood only from the cosmic consciousness. If you want a solution which will be agreeable to the human mind and feelings, I am afraid there is none. No doubt if human beings had made the universe, they would have done much better; but they were not there to be consulted when they were made. Only your central being was there and that was much nearer in its temerarious foolhardiness to Vivekananda's or X's than to the repining prudence of your murmuring and trembling human mentality of the present moment — otherwise it would never have come down into the adventure. Or perhaps it did not realise what it was in for? It is the same with the wallowers

---

[1] *The preceding letter was published under the heading* "The Riddle of This World" *in a book of the same name in 1933.* — Ed.

under their cross. Even now they wallow because something in them likes the wallowing and bears the cross because something in them chooses to suffer. So?

The Disharmonies of Earth

That brings me to your second question[2] about the missing Harmony and the actual disharmonies of earth, a dissonance out of which like most people you build a justification for a saving flight towards Nirvana, — although in the true theory of Mayavada harmony and disharmony are of equal value or rather equal non-value: for the glory of Heaven and the joy of the gods are as much an illusion and, if anything, a greater illusion than any ugliness of life or redundancy of human suffering. But I agree with you that disharmony is what is the matter with the world here and it is harmony that is the one thing desirable. Then the whole question is whether harmony is intended to be found or not or whether the very nature and condition and grain of life is a disharmony that, because the very root of life is ego and division, is incurable. The Mayavadin contends that it is; Buddha also decided that the only way out of suffering and disharmony was out of life into the permanence or perhaps the nothingness of Nirvana. But the question is whether what is now is the base of existence or only a temporary phase of existence here. Is life radically just an expression of ego and division? and is there nothing else, is there not behind it the unity of the Divine? and cannot it be brought out, — cannot we get rid in the end of the little things on the surface and express these greater things behind it? If, as spiritual experience shows us, the unity of the Divine is there at the very base and if as both ancient and modern knowledge declare, there has been a spiritual evolution from down upwards, — though the modern speaks only of an evolution of the body with the consciousness

---

[2] The first question of the correspondent concerned "the results of the manifestation of a new supramental principle in the earth-consciousness". See Sri Aurobindo's letters beginning "There is not much profit" and "As I have said" on pages 280–84. — Ed.

The Problem of Suffering and Evil

depending on it and the ancient, as in the Tantras, only of a spiritual evolution of the soul from vegetable life-form to the human mind-life, — then there is no reason why this spiritual evolution should not arrive beyond its present incomplete and therefore still disharmonious consciousness in man to its logical consummation, an expression of the Divine. There is not only no reason why it should not, but such an arrival is inevitably pointed to both by the logic of reason and the gaze of intuition. Not only so, but the first step towards solution has been taken by the Yogin's extension of consciousness beyond ego and division; spiritual experience has shown that the embodied soul can arrive beyond ego and division to consciousness governed by the unity of the one Self or the Divine; and the existence of the Jivanmukta proves that one can thus exceed ego and division and yet live and act, so that life in the Divine is not an imagination or a fable.

The ascension above ego and division is no doubt only a first step achieved in rare individuals, but in evolution it is the first step which counts and makes all the rest possible. Also, no doubt, to stand above an egoistic and divided world and act on it from the egoless heights of the spirit is not enough — a power is needed and a process, — the descent of a power that can bring harmony because in its nature it is at once superior, fundamental and comprehensive and a discovery of the process that fits the power. All achievement in embodied life has been made possible by the discovery of the necessary power and the effective process. It must so also be done in the achievement of harmony in a still discordant earth-nature.

Is there any conclusive reason for declaring such an achievement or spiritual evolution impossible? The only argument you advance amounts to this only that it has not been done yet and that shows that it cannot be done. That reasoning has not much value. It is the usual logic of the physical intellect which is bound by what is and believes that to be definitive. It has been used against all new or yet unaccomplished ideas or achievements and, when they have been accomplished, still urged against their successors. The physical mind always comes in with its fixed line of the present and "No farther" and when the fixed line of the present is unfixed and overpassed, it again erects a new line and cries "No farther". If an "elemental" who had attained to the physical mind had been present at the different stages of the earth-history he would have argued like that. When only matter was there and there was no life, if told that there would soon be life on earth embodied in matter, he would have cried out, "What is that? It is impossible, it cannot be done. Life is possible only in a subtle body. It has never been and never will be embodied in gross matter. What, this mass of electrons, gases, chemical elements, this heap of mud and water and stones and inert metals, how are you going to get life in that? Will the metal walk? can the stone live? will you take mud and water and make out of it a body that can move, feel, act, desire?" But life came in spite of the impossibility and living forms were developed — plant and tree and living bodies were built out of the protoplasm and molecule; some ingenious force or being evolved slowly out of that through millions of years with an amazing patience, using chemical and biological elements alike, gene and gland and heart and brain and nerve and cell and living tissue and the animal walked and bounded and man arose evolving through tens of thousands, perhaps millions of years in the body of an erect two-footed animal. There again the physical-minded elemental would have intervened and cried out, "What is this that is being attempted? No, no, impossible. Such a thing has never been done. Reflexes, memories, associations, instinctive combinations of life and action, these things of course are possible; but reason, intelligent will, conscious planning and creation, art, poetry, philosophy in this savage shambling creature? An animal cannot evolve powers and activities which have never been possessed except by the gods and the Asuras. How can this material animal organism ever be capable of such a [*incomplete*]

Chapter Two

Spiritual Evolution and the Supramental

Human History and Spiritual Evolution

There have been times when the seeking for spiritual attainment was, at least in certain civilisations, more intense and widespread than now or rather than it has been in the world in general during the past few centuries. For now the curve seems to be the beginning of a new turn of seeking which takes its start from what was achieved in the past and projects itself towards a greater future. But always, even in the age of the Vedas or in Egypt, the spiritual achievement or the occult knowledge was confined to a few; it was not spread in the whole mass of humanity. The mass of humanity evolves slowly, containing in itself all stages of the evolution from the material and the vital man to the mental man. A small minority has pushed beyond the barriers, opening the doors to occult and spiritual knowledge and preparing the ascent of the evolution beyond mental man into spiritual and supramental being. Sometimes this minority has exercised an enormous influence as in Vedic India, Egypt or, according to tradition, in Atlantis, and determined the civilisation of the race, giving it a strong stamp of the spiritual or the occult; sometimes they have stood apart in their secret schools or orders, not directly influencing a civilisation which was sunk in material ignorance or in chaos and darkness or in the hard external enlightenment which rejects spiritual knowledge.

The cycles of evolution tend always upward, but they are cycles and do not ascend in a straight line. The process therefore gives the impression of a series of ascents and descents, but what is essential in the gains of the evolution is kept or, even if eclipsed for a time, reemerges in new forms suitable to the new ages.

The Creation has descended all the degrees of being from

the Supermind to Matter and in each degree it has created a world, reign, plane or order proper to that degree. In the creating of the material world there was a plunge of this descending Consciousness into an apparent Inconscience and an emergence of it out of that Inconscience, degree by degree, until it recovers its own highest spiritual and supramental summits and manifests their powers here in Matter. But even in the Inconscience there is a secret Consciousness which works, one may say, by an involved and hidden Intuition proper to itself. In each stage of Matter, in each stage of Life, this Intuition assumes a working proper to that stage and acts from behind the veil, supporting and enforcing the immediate necessities of the creative Force. There is an intuition in Matter which holds the action of the material Energy together and dictates the organisation of the material world from the electron to the sun and planet and their contents. There is an intuition in Life which similarly supports and guides the play and development of life in matter till it is ready for the mental evolution of which man is the vehicle. In man also the creation follows the same upward process, — the intuition within develops according to the stage he has reached in his progress. Even the precise intellect of the scientist, who is inclined to deny the separate existence or the superiority of intuition, yet cannot really move forward unless there is behind him a mental intuition which enables him to take a forward step or to divine what has to be done. Intuition therefore is present at the beginning of things and in their middle as well as at their consummation.

But Intuition takes its proper form only when one goes beyond the mental into the spiritual domain, for there only it comes fully forward from behind the veil and reveals its true and complete nature. Along with the mental evolution of man there has been going forward the early process of another evolution which prepares the spiritual and supramental being. This has had two lines, one the discovery of the occult forces secret in Nature and of the hidden planes and worlds concealed from us by the world of Matter and the other the discovery of man's soul and spiritual self. If the tradition of Atlantis is correct, it is that

Spiritual Evolution and the Supramental   267

of a progress which went to the extreme of occult knowledge but could go no farther. In the India of Vedic times we have the record left of the other line of achievement, that of spiritual self-discovery; occult knowledge was there but kept subordinate. We may say that here in India the reign of Intuition came first, intellectual Mind developing afterwards in the later philosophy and science. But in fact the mass of men at the time, it is quite evident, lived entirely on the material plane, worshipped the Godheads of material nature, sought from them entirely material objects. The effort of the Vedic mystics revealed to them the things behind through a power of inner sight and hearing and experience which was confined to a limited number of seers and sages and kept carefully secret from the mass of humanity — secrecy was always insisted on by the mystics. We may very well attribute this flowering of intuition on the spiritual plane to a rapid reemergence of the essential gains brought down from a previous cycle. If we analyse the spiritual history of India we shall find that after reaching this height there was a descent which attempted to take up each lower degree of the already evolved consciousness and link it to the spiritual at the summit. The Vedic age was followed by a great outburst of intellectual philosophy which yet took spiritual truth as its basis and tried to reach it anew, not through a direct intuitive or occult process as did the Vedic seers, but by the power of the mind's reflective, speculative, logical thought; at the same time processes of Yoga were developed which used the thinking mind as a means of arriving at spiritual realisation, spiritualising this mind itself at the same time. Then followed an era of the development of philosophies and Yoga processes which more and more used the emotional and aesthetic being as the means of spiritual realisation and spiritualised the emotional level in man through the heart and feeling. This was accompanied by Tantric and other processes which took up the mental will, the life-will, the life of sensations and made them at once the instruments and the field of spiritualisation. In Hathayoga and in the various attempts at divinisation of the body there is also a line of endeavour which attempted to arrive at the same achievement with regard to living matter; but this still awaits the discovery of the true characteristic method and power of spirit in the body. We may say therefore that the universal Consciousness after its descent into Matter has conducted the evolution there along two lines, one of ascent to the discovery of the self and spirit, the other of descent through the already evolved levels of mind, life and body so as to bring down the spiritual consciousness into these also and to fulfil thereby some secret intention in the creation of the material universe. Our Yoga is in its principle a taking up and summarising and completing of this process, an endeavour to rise to the highest possible supramental level and bring down its consciousness and powers into mind, life and body.

The condition of present-day civilisation, materialistic with an externalised intellect and life-endeavour, which you find so painful, is an episode, but one which was perhaps inevitable. For if the spiritualisation of mind, life and body is the thing to be achieved, the conscious presence of the Spirit even in the physical consciousness and material body, an age which puts Matter and the physical life in the forefront and devotes itself to the effort of the intellect to discover the truth of material existence, had perhaps to come. On one side, by materialising everything up to intellect itself it has created the extreme difficulty of which you speak for the spiritual seeker; but on the other hand it has given the life in Matter an importance which the spirituality of the past was inclined to deny to it. In a way it has made the spiritualisation of it a necessity for spiritual seeking and so aided the descent movement of the evolving spiritual Consciousness in the earth-nature. More than that we cannot claim for it; its conscious effect has been rather to stifle and almost extinguish the spiritual element in humanity; it is only by the divine use of the pressure of contraries and an intervention from above that there will be the greater spiritual outcome.

*

All the phases of human history may be regarded as a working out of the earth-consciousness in which each phase has its place and significance, so this materialistic-intellectual phase had to come and has had, no doubt, its purpose and significance. One may also hold that one of its uses was as an experiment to see how far and whither the human consciousness would go through an intellectual and external control of Nature with physical and intellectual means only and without the intervention of any higher consciousness and knowledge — or that it may help by resistance to draw the spiritual consciousness that is growing behind all vicissitudes to attempt the control of Matter and turn it towards the Divine, as the Tantriks and Vaishnavas tried to do with the emotional and lower vital nature, not contenting themselves with the Vedantic turning of the mind towards the Supreme. But it is difficult to go farther than that or to hold that this materialism is itself a spiritual thing or that the dark, confused and violent state of contemporary Europe was an indispensable preparation for the descent of the Spirit. This darkness and violence which seems bent on destroying such light of mental idealism and desire of harmony as had succeeded in establishing itself in the mind of humanity, is obviously due to a descent of fierce and dark vital Powers which seek to possess the human world for their own, not for a spiritual purpose. It is true that such a precipitation of Asuric forces from the darker vital worlds has been predicted by some occultists as one first result of the pressure of the Divine Descent on their vital domain, but it was regarded as a circumstance of the battle, not as something helping towards the Divine Victory. The churning of Matter by the attempt of the human intellect to conquer material Nature and use it for its purposes may break something in the passivity and inertia, but it is done for material ends, in a rajasic spirit, with a denial of spirituality as its mental basis. Such an attempt may end, seems to be ending indeed in chaos and a disintegration, while the new attempts at creation and reintegration seem to combine the obscure rigidity of material Nature with a resurgence of the barbaric brutality and violence of a half animal vital Nature. How are the spiritual Forces to deal with all that or make use of such a churning of the energies of the material universe? The way of the Spirit is the way of peace and light and harmony; if it has to battle it is precisely because of the presence of such forces which seek either to extinguish or to pervert the spiritual light. In the spiritual change inertia has to be replaced by the divine peace and calm, the rajasic troubled energy by a tranquil and potent, pure and liberated dynamis, while the mind must be kept plastic for the workings of a higher Light of Knowledge. How will the activity of Materialism lend itself to that change?

Materialism can hardly be spiritual in its basis because its basic method is just the opposite of the spiritual way of doing things. The spiritual works from within outward, the way of materialism is to work from out inwards. It makes the inner a result of the outer, fundamentally a phenomenon of Matter and it works upon that view of things. It seeks to "perfect" humanity by outward means and one of its main efforts is to construct a perfect social machine which will train and oblige men to be what they ought to be. The loss of the ego in the Divine is the spiritual ideal; here it is replaced by the immolation of the individual to the military and industrial State. Where is there any spirituality in all that? Spirituality can only come by opening of the mind, vital and physical to the inmost soul, to the higher Self, to the Divine, and their subordination to the spiritual forces and instrumentation as channels of the inner light, the higher Knowledge and Power. Other things, mental, aesthetic, vital, are often misnamed spirituality, but they lack that essential character without which the word loses its true significance.

*

All that you say only amounts, on the general issue, to the fact that this is a world of slow evolution in which man has emerged out of the beast and is still not out of it, light out of darkness, a higher consciousness out of first a dead and then a struggling and troubled unconsciousness. A spiritual consciousness is emerging and it is through this spiritual consciousness that one can meet the Divine. Religions, full of mental and vital mixed, troubled and ignorant stuff, can only get glimpses of the Divine; positivist reason with its questioning based upon things as they are and refusing to believe in anything that may or will be cannot get

Spiritual Evolution and the Supramental

any vision of it at all. The spiritual is a new consciousness that has to evolve and has been evolving. It is quite natural that at first and for a long time only a few should get the full light, while a greater number but still only a few compared with the mass of humanity, should get it partially. But what has been gained by the few can at a stage of the evolution be completed and more generalised and that is the attempt which we are making. But if this greater consciousness of light, peace and joy is to be gained, it cannot be by questioning and scepticism which can only fall back on what is and say, "It is impossible, impossible — what has not been in the past cannot be in the future; what is so imperfectly realised as yet, cannot be better realised in the future." A faith, a will or at least a persistent demand and aspiration are needed — a feeling that with this and this alone I can be satisfied and a push towards it that will not cease till it is done. That is why a spirit of denial and scepticism stands in the way, because they stand against the creation of the conditions under which spiritual experience can unroll itself. In the absence of faith and firm will to achieve, the Divine has to manifest in conditions which are the most adverse to that manifestation. It can be done, but you cannot expect it to be easily done.

*

I do not know what Mahatma Gandhi means by complete realisation.[1] If he means a realisation with nothing more to realise, no farther development possible, then I agree — I have myself spoken of farther divine progression, an infinite development. But the question is not that; the question is whether the Ignorance can be transcended, whether a complete essential realisation turning the consciousness from darkness to light, from an instrument of the Ignorance seeking for Knowledge into an instrument or rather a manifestation of Knowledge proceeding to greater

---

[1] *These observations were made with regard to a statement by Mahatma Gandhi: "I hold that complete realisation is impossible in this embodied life. Nor is it necessary. A living immovable faith is all that is required for reaching the full spiritual height attainable by human beings." This statement appeared in an article submitted to Sri Aurobindo by the correspondent. — Ed.*

Knowledge, Light enlarging, heightening into greater Light, is or is not possible. My view is that this conversion is not only possible, but inevitable in the spiritual evolution of the being here. The embodiment of life has nothing to do with it. This embodiment is not of life, but of consciousness and its energy, of which life is only one phase or force. As life has developed mind, and the embodiment has modified itself to suit this development (mind is precisely the main instrument of ignorance seeking for knowledge), so mind can develop supermind which is in its nature knowledge not seeking for itself, but manifesting itself by its own automatic power, and the embodiment can again modify itself or be modified from above so as to suit this development. Faith is a necessary means for arriving at realisation because we are ignorant and do not yet know that which we are seeking to realise; faith is indeed knowledge giving the ignorance an intimation of itself previous to its own manifestation, it is the gleam sent before by the yet unrisen Sun. When the Sun shall rise there will be no longer any need of the gleam. The supramental knowledge supports itself, it does not need to be supported by faith; it lives by its own certitude. You may say that farther progression, farther development will need faith. No, for the farther development will proceed on a basis of knowledge, not of Ignorance. We shall walk in the light of knowledge towards its own wider vistas of self-fulfilment.

*

I do not see what answer you can give to your uncle that would satisfy him, as he is evidently living in the mentality of the past and would not readily understand anything about spiritual evolution, the supermind and the Divine Manifestation in life and matter. You can perhaps tell him casually that it is not our hope to transform suddenly the whole human race. Your object is precisely to lead a higher life away from the ordinary world, only it is not solitary; there is a collective side to it and a side, not only of meditation, but of work, action and creation. There is nothing in this that is impossible.

*

It is quite possible that there have been periods of harmony on different levels, not supramental, which were afterwards disturbed — but those could only be a stage or resting place in a world of spiritual evolution out of the Ignorance.

*

This is a world of evolution in Matter. If everything were supramental from the beginning, there would be no place for evolution.

*

The evolution I speak of is not the evolution of the Darwinian theory.

Spiritual and Supramental

Spiritual and supramental are not the same thing. The spiritual planes from higher mind to Overmind are accessible to the old sadhanas so there is no difficulty about that. If they were not accessible there would have been no Yoga at all and no Yogis in the past in India.

*

If spiritual and supramental were the same thing, as you say my readers imagine, then all the sages and devotees and Yogis and sadhaks throughout the ages would have been supramental beings and all I have written about the supermind would be so much superfluous stuff, useless and otiose. Anybody who had spiritual experiences would then be a supramental being; the Asram would be chock-full of supramental beings and every other Asram in India also. Spiritual experiences can fix themselves in the inner consciousness and alter it, transform it, if you like; one can realise the Divine everywhere, the Self in all and all in the Self, the universal Shakti doing all things; one can feel merged in the Cosmic Self or full of ecstatic bhakti or Ananda. But one may and usually does still go on in the outer active parts of Nature thinking with the intellect or at best the intuitive mind, willing with a mental will, feeling joy and sorrow on the vital surface, undergoing physical afflictions and suffering the struggle of life in the body with death and disease. The change then only will be that the inner self will watch all that without getting disturbed or bewildered, with a perfect equality, taking it as an inevitable part of Nature, inevitable at least so long as one does not withdraw to the Self out of Nature. That is not the transformation I envisage. It is quite another power of knowledge, another kind of will, another luminous nature of emotion and aesthesis, another constitution of the physical consciousness that must come in by the supramental change.

*

Spiritual realisation can be had on any plane by contact with the Divine (who is everywhere) or by perception of the Self within, which is pure and untouched by the outer movements. The Supermind is something transcendent — a dynamic Truth consciousness which is not here yet and has to be brought down from above.

The Overmind and the Supramental

There are many aspects of the Divine and of existence manifested as separate by the Overmind. Different minds are drawn by different aspects and each follows its own path to its own goal. Each is free to follow its own path and is not bound by another.

As for the Supramental, it is by definition a consciousness above the Overmind in which all aspects are infused in the integral Divine. But none is bound to seek after the Supramental consciousness if his tendency is elsewhere.

The manifestation is complex and there are beings in it who belong to various levels. If a soul wishes to plunge into the Divine through Nirvana or seeks spiritual fulfilment in a world of the Gods, such as Vaikuntha or Goloka, it has the freedom to do so, to follow its own tendency.

The discovery of the Supramental is especially important for the spiritual evolution on the earth. If the souls here have to reach it eventually, no doubt the Divine will evolve them to seek it. There is nothing compelling all to reach it by a progress towards it in direct line or by the same path and stages. It is possible for them to be satisfied with another path and intermediary partial fulfilment. If it is their destiny, they may return afterwards to pursue the further ascent to the Supramental level.

The Gita accepted the current belief that freedom from birth was the consequence of reaching the highest state. It is a natural deduction from the belief that this is not only a world of Ignorance but cannot be ever anything else.

*

Yes, there has been some progress in that respect [*psychicisation*] and all progress in the psychic or spiritual consciousness of the sadhaks makes the descent more easy. But the main cause [*of the descent of Light and Power*] is that the Overmind principle which is the immediate secret support of the present earth-nature with all its limitations is more and more undergoing the pressure of the Supramental and letting through a greater Light and Power. For so long as the Overmind intervenes (the principle of the Overmind being a play of forces, each trying to realise itself as the Truth) the law of struggle remains and with it the opportunity for the adverse Forces.

*

It is not immortality *of* the body, but the consciousness of immortality *in* the body that can come with the descent of Overmind into Matter or even into the physical mind or with the touch of the modified Supramental Light on the physical mind-consciousness. These are preliminary openings, but they are not the supramental fulfilment in Matter.

Involution and Evolution

The involution is of the Divine in the Inconscience and it is done by the interposition of intermediate planes (Overmind etc., mind, vital) — then the plunge into the Inconscient which is the origin of matter. But all that is not a process answering to the evolution in the inverse sense — for there is no need for that, but a gradation of consciousness which is intended to make the evolution upwards possible.

*

Man has evolved from Matter — or rather Nature has evolved first the plant, then the animal, then Man in a regular succession out of Matter. What is involved is not Man, but mind and life and spirit. "Involved" means that they are there even though there seems to be no mental activity (as in the tree) and no mental or vital activity (as in the stone); as the evolution goes on the involved life appears and begins to organise itself and the plants appear and then the animals; next mind, first in the animal, and then man appears.

*

Everything here that belongs strictly to the earth plane is evolved out of the Inconscient, out of Matter — but the essential mental being exists already, not involved on the mental plane. It is only the personal mental that is evolved here by something rising out of the Inconscient and developing under a pressure from above.

*

What is meant here[2] is the Divine in its essential manifestation which reveals itself to us as Light and Consciousness, Power, Love and Beauty. But in its actual cosmic manifestation the Supreme, being the Infinite and not bound by any limitation, can manifest in itself, in its consciousness of innumerable possibilities, something that seems to be the opposite of itself, something in which there can be Darkness, Inconscience, Inertia, Insensibility, Disharmony and Disintegration. It is this that we see at the basis of the material world and speak of nowadays as the Inconscient — the inconscient Ocean of the Rigveda in which the One was hidden and arose in the form of this Universe, —

---

[2] *The statement is not available. — Ed.*

Spiritual Evolution and the Supramental

or, as it is sometimes called, the non-being, Asat. The Ignorance which is the characteristic of our mind and life is the result of this origin in the Inconscience. Moreover, in the evolution out of inconscient existence there rise up naturally powers and beings which are interested in the maintenance of all negations of the Divine, error and unconsciousness, pain, suffering, obscurity, death, weakness, illness, disharmony, evil. Hence the perversion of the manifestation here, its inability to reveal the true essence of the Divine. Yet in the very base of this evolution all that is divine is there involved and pressing to evolve, Light, Consciousness, Power, Perfection, Beauty, Love. For in the Inconscient itself and behind the perversions of the Ignorance Divine Consciousness lies concealed and works and must more and more appear, throwing off in the end its disguises. That is why it is said that the world is called to express the Divine.

Your statement about the supramental evolution is correct except that it does not follow that humanity as a whole will become supramental. What is more likely to happen is that the supramental principle will be established in the evolution by the descent just as the mental principle was established by the appearance of thinking Mind and Man in earthly life. There will be a race of supramental beings on the earth just as now there is a race of mental beings. Man himself will find a greater possibility of rising to the planes intermediary between his mind and supermind and making their powers effective in his life, which will mean a great change in humanity on earth, but it is not likely that the mental stage will disappear from the ascending ladder and, if so, the continued existence of a mental race will be necessary so as to form a stage between the vital and the supramental in the evolutionary movement of the spirit.

Such a descent of higher beings as you suggest may be envisaged as a part of the process of the change. But the main part of the change will be the appearance of the supramental being and the organisation of a supramental nature here, as a mental being has appeared and a mental nature organised itself during the last stage of the evolution. I prefer nowadays not to speak of the descent of the higher beings because my experience is that it leads in the minds of the sadhaks to a vain and often egoistic romanticism which distracts the attention from the real work, that of the realisation of the Divine and the transformation of the nature.

*

In the descent it [*falsehood*] begins with Mind, in the evolutionary ascent it is difficult to say where it begins — for here the beginning is Inconscience and Ignorance; but I suppose we may say that conscious falsehood begins with the beginnings of mind still involved in Life or appearing out of it.

*

An evolution from the Inconscient need not be a painful one if there is no resistance; it can be a deliberately slow and beautiful efflorescence of the Divine. One ought to be able to see how beautiful outward Nature can be and usually is, although it is itself apparently "inconscient". Why should the growth of consciousness in inward Nature be attended by so much ugliness and evil spoiling the beauty of the outward creation? Because of a *perversity* born from the Ignorance, which came in with Life and increased in Mind — that is the Falsehood, the Evil that was born because of the starkness of the Inconscient's sleep separating its action from the luminosity of the secret Conscient that was all the time within it. But it need not have been so except for the overriding Will of the Supreme which meant that the possibility of Perversion by inconscience and ignorance should be manifested in order to be eliminated through being given their chance, since all possibility has to manifest somewhere: once it is eliminated, the Divine Manifestation in Matter will be greater than it otherwise could be because it will gather all the possibilities involved in this difficult creation and not some of them as in an easier and less strenuous creation might naturally be.

"From beauty to greater beauty, from joy to intenser joy, by an especial adjustment of the senses" — yes, that would be the normal course of a divine manifestation, however gradual, in

Matter. "Discordant sound and offensive odour" are creations of a disharmony between consciousness and Nature and do not exist in themselves; they would not be present to a liberated and harmonised consciousness for they would be foreign to its being, nor would they afflict a rightly developing harmonised soul and Nature. Even the "belching volcano, crashing thunderstorm and whirling typhoon" are in themselves grandiose and beautiful things and only harmful or horrible to a consciousness unable to meet or deal with them or make a pact with the spirits of the Wind and Fire. You are assuming that the manifestation from the Inconscient must be what it is now and here and that no other kind of world of Matter was possible, but the harmony of material Nature in itself shows that it need not necessarily be a discordant, evil, furiously perturbed and painful creation — the psychic being, if allowed to manifest from the first in Life and lead the evolution instead of being relegated behind the veil, would have been the principle of a harmonious outflowering; everyone who has felt the psychic at work within him, freed from the vital intervention, can at once see that this would be its effect because of its unerring perception, true choice, harmonic action. If it has not been so, it is because the dark Powers have made Life a claimant instead of an instrument. The reality of the Hostiles and the nature of their role and trend of their endeavour cannot be doubted by anyone who has had his inner vision unsealed and made their unpleasant acquaintance.

The Supermind and the Lower Creation

It [*the Supermind*] can act directly on everything if it is brought down into the material consciousness — at present in the arrangement of things here it is latent behind and acts through other media.

*

No, one can't say that [*there is a direct supramental action at work in plants*]. It is the vital force that works, but there is a sort of underlying Intuition in this Life-Force which is behind the whole action and that is what one might call a reflection or delegated Power at the back of which is latent Supermind.

*

There is no reason why the vegetable, animal and human life should not evolve in the Truth and not in the Ignorance — if once the Knowledge is there in the earth-plane.

Speculations about the Supramental Descent

It is not perhaps very useful to forecast by the mind what will be the precise results of the descent of a supramental consciousness into a world in which up to now the mental intelligence has been the highest evolutionary product and leading power. For the supermind is a consciousness which will work in a very different way from the mind and the lines laid down for it by the latter are not likely to be respected by the greater energy in its self-organisation and operation here.

*

There is not much profit in mental and intellectual speculations about what precisely the results would be of the introduction of a supramental principle and a supramental organisation and order in the earth-consciousness and the earth-life. In all probability the speculations would be quite beside the mark or, even where they hit on some broad lines, would draw them wrong and all awry and out of proportion; for the intellectual mind is a different and inferior power of consciousness; it is analytical and synthetic, pulling things to pieces and putting them together in order to understand and deal with them, proceeding by representation and abstraction and formulas and schematic figures; it imposes a rigid logic on an illogical world in order to bring about a fixed and mechanical order; it cuts up, divides, compares, contrasts, confronts one element of existence contradictorily with another; classifies according to similarity and difference. In the end it produces a system of things explained and intelligible; but each such system is only a segment of truth dried up into a formula. Life compelled into these systems either escapes and flows through its hard set lines and undermines and slowly or quickly upsets or transmogrifies the system till it is no longer what it pretends to be or else it remains fossilised and cramped within until it dies or until an explosion of its suppressed forces liberates it into a new order. Supermind is a totally different power. It has a whole-vision and an essential vision; it reposes on an all-seeing authority of Truth which spontaneously produces harmony according to the inner truth of the One and the inner truth of the Many in the One. Out of things that to the mind are opposites and incompatible contrasts it takes in each its essence and joins them harmoniously into a single piece. This it does by raising them beyond their separated appearances and putting them in the light of the one Truth where they can find their reality and their reconciling principle. The things that in the mind are in constant conflict or with only a patched-up truce between them, liberty and order, commonalty and individuality and the rest will in supermind find their natural harmony because they are not only indispensable aspects of the essential whole, but themselves one. But for this our existing materials mind, life, body must be supramentalised; otherwise the discordances and oppositions of mind will remain oppositions and discords, the confusions and conflicts of life will remain confused and conflicting, the cramps and limits of form will prevent plastic change, perfection, fulfilment. Mind has failed to liberate and perfect life, because it has imperfectly mentalised life and form, without finding their secret by which they can find themselves and their perfection through a higher light than their own half-conscious self-feeling. Supermind will supramentalise fully mind, life and body and in the very doing of it liberate their own perfection because it is in supermind that the full and perfect secret of mind, life and form are treasured and await their time of descent into terrestrial nature.

*

As I have said [*in the preceding letter*], speculation on the results of the manifestation of a new supramental principle in the earth-consciousness organising itself there as mind, life and matter have already organised themselves — for that is what it comes to — is a little perilous and premature, because we must do it with the mind and the mind has not the capacity to forecast the action of what is above itself — just as a merely animal or vital perception of things could not have forecast what would be the workings of Mind and a mentalised race of beings here. The supermind is a different order of consciousness far removed from the mental — there are in fact several grades of higher consciousness between the human mind and the supramental. If the earth were not evolutionary but a typal world, then indeed one could predict that the descent of a higher type of consciousness would swallow up or abolish the existing type. Ignorance would end and the creation in the ignorance disappear either by transmutation or by annihilation and replacement. The human mental kingdom would be transformed into the supramental; the vital and subhuman, if it existed in the typal world, would also be changed and become supramental. But, earth being an evolutionary world, the supramental descent is not likely to have such a devastating completeness. It would be only the establishment of a new principle of consciousness and a new order of conscious beings and this new principle would evolve its own forms and powers in the terrestrial order. Even the whole human kingdom need not and would not be transformed at once or to the whole supramental extent. But at the same time the beginning of a supramental creation on earth is bound to have a powerful effect on the rest of terrestrial existence. Its first effect on mankind would be to open a way between the order of the Truth-light and the orders of the Ignorance here on earth itself, a sort of realised gradation by which it would be possible for mental man to evolve more easily and surely from the Ignorance towards the Light and, as he went, organise his existence according to these steps. For at present the grades of consciousness between mind and supermind act only as influences (the highest of them very indirect influences) on human mind and consciousness and cannot do more. This would change. An organised higher human consciousness could appear or several degrees of it, with the supermind-organised consciousness as the leader at the top influencing the others and drawing them towards itself. It is likely that as the supramental principle evolved itself the evolution would more and more take on another aspect — the Daivic nature would predominate, the Asuro-Rakshaso-Pishachic prakriti which now holds so large a place would more and more recede and lose its power. A principle of greater unity, harmony and light would emerge everywhere. It is not that the creation in the Ignorance would be altogether abolished, but it would begin to lose much of its elements of pain and falsehood and would be more a progression from lesser to higher Truth, from a lesser to a higher harmony, from a lesser to a higher Light, than the reign of chaos and struggle, of darkness and error that we now perceive. For according to all occult teaching the evolutionary creation could have been such but for the intervention of the Powers of Darkness — all traditions including that of the Veda and Upanishads point under different figures to the same thing. In the Upanishads it is the Daityas that smite with evil all that the gods create, in the Zoroastrian tradition it is Ahriman coming across the work of Ahura Mazda, the Chaldean tradition uses a different figure. But the significance is the same; it is the perception of something that has struck across the harmonious development of creation and brought in the principle of darkness and disorder. The occult tradition also foresees the elimination of this disturbing element by the descent of a divine Principle or Power on earth, but gives to it usually a sudden and dramatic form. I conceive that the supramental descent would effect the same event by a progressive elimination of the darkness and evolution of the Light, but with what rate of rapidity it would be rash to try to forecast or prefigure.

This is a very general statement, but perhaps it is a sufficient answer to your first question. I need only add that there is nothing to prevent the supramental creation, the creation in the higher Truth-Light from being evolutionary, a continuous efflorescence of the Divine Truth and Harmony in a manifold variety, not a final and decisive creation in a single fixed type. What would be decisive would be the crossing of the border between twilight and Light, the transference of the base of development from the consciousness in the Ignorance to the Truth-consciousness. That would be, on this level, final. The transition into a world of spirits would only effectuate itself, first, if the whole earth-consciousness became thoroughly supramentalised, secondly, if after that the turn were to a realisation here of the principle of those worlds of Sachchidananda where determination disappears in the interpenetration of All-in-All. But that would be to look too far into the potentialities of the future. In short, if the supramental principle came down it would not be in order to reproduce Heaven here under celestial conditions but to "create a new Heaven and a new earth" in the earth-consciousness itself, completing and transmuting but not abolishing the earth order.

It is evident that the creative process here could be greatly modified and transmuted by the appearance of the supramental principle. What would be its exact forms is a more difficult question, for the principle of a supramental creation is obvious but the possibilities of its manifestation are many and it is only the dynamic Truth itself that can choose and determine.

Section Two

The Supramental Descent and Transformation

Chapter One

The Descent of the Supermind

Inevitability of the Descent

The descent of the supramental is an inevitable necessity in the logic of things and is therefore sure. It is because people do not understand what the supermind is or realise the significance of the emergence of consciousness in a world of "inconscient" Matter that they are unable to realise this inevitability. I suppose a matter-of-fact observer if there had been one at the time of the unrelieved reign of inanimate Matter in the earth's beginning would have criticised any promise of the emergence of life in a world of dead earth and rock and mineral as an absurdity and a chimaera; so too afterwards he would have repeated his mistake and regarded the emergence of thought and reason in an animal world as an absurdity and a chimaera. It is the same now with the appearance of supermind in the stumbling mentality of this world of human consciousness and its reasoning ignorance.

*

If the supramental descent is decreed, nothing can prevent it; but all things are worked out here through a play of forces, and an unfavourable atmosphere or conditions can delay even when they cannot prevent. Even when the thing is destined, it does not present itself as a certitude in the consciousness here (Overmind-mind-vital-physical) till the play of forces has been worked out up to a certain point at which the descent not only is, but appears as inevitable.

*

The descent of the supermind is a long process or at least a process with a long preparation and one can only say that the work is going on sometimes with a strong pressure for completion, sometimes retarded by the things that rise from below and have to be dealt with before farther progress can be made. The process is a (spiritual) evolutionary process concentrated into a brief period — it could be done otherwise (by what men would regard as a miraculous intervention) only if the human mind were more flexible and less attached to its ignorance than it is. As we envisage it, it must manifest in a few first and then spread, but it is not likely to sweep over the earth in a moment. It is not advisable to discuss too much what it will do and how it will do it, because these are things the Supermind itself will fix, acting out of that Divine Truth in it, and the mind must not try to fix for it grooves in which it will run. Naturally, the release from subconscient ignorance and from disease, duration of life at will, and a change in the functioning of the body must be among the ultimate results of a supramental change; but the details of these things must be left for the supramental Energy to work out according to the truth of its own nature.

A Beginning, Not a Completion

What we are doing, if and when we succeed, will be a beginning, not a completion. It is the foundation of a new consciousness on earth — a consciousness with infinite possibilities of manifestation. The eternal progression is in the manifestation and beyond it there is no progression.

If the redemption of the soul from the physical vesture be the object, then there is no need of supramentalisation. Spiritual Mukti and Nirvana are sufficient. If the object is to rise to supraphysical planes, then also there is no need of supramentalisation. One can enter into some heaven above by devotion to the Lord of that heaven. But that is no progression. The other worlds are typal worlds, each fixed in its own kind and type and law. Evolution takes place on the earth and therefore the earth is the proper field for progression. The beings of the other worlds do not progress from one world to another. They remain fixed to their own type.

The purely monistic Vedantist says, all is Brahman, life is a dream, an unreality, only Brahman exists. One has Nirvana or

Mukti, then one lives only till the body falls — after that there is no such thing as life.

They do not believe in transformation, because mind, life and body are an ignorance, an illusion — the only reality is the featureless, relationless Self or Brahman. Life is a thing of relations; in the pure Self, all life and relations disappear. What would be the use or the possibility of transforming an illusion that can never be anything else (however transformed) than an illusion? There is no such thing for them as a "Nirvanic life".

It is only some Yogas that aim at a transformation of any kind except that of ignorance into knowledge. The idea varies, — sometimes a divine knowledge or power or else a divine purity or an ethical perfection or a divine love.

What has to be overcome is the opposition of the Ignorance that does not want the transformation of the nature. If that can be overcome, then old spiritual ideas will not form an obstacle.

It is not intended to supramentalise humanity at large, but to establish the principle of the supramental consciousness in the earth-evolution. If that is done, all that is needed will be evolved by the supramental Power itself. It is not therefore important that the mission should be widespread. What is important is that the thing should be done at all in however small a number; that is the only difficulty.

If the transformation of the body is complete, that means no subjection to death — it does not mean that one will be bound to keep the same body for all time. One creates a new body for oneself when one wants to change, but how it will be done cannot be said now. The present method is by physical birth — some occultists suppose that a time will come when that is not necessary — but the question must be left for the supramental evolution to decide.

The questions about the supermind cannot be answered profitably now. Supermind cannot be described in terms that the mind will understand, because the terms will be mental and mind will understand them in a mental way and mental sense and miss their true import. It would therefore be a waste of time and energy which should be devoted to the preliminary work

— psychicisation and spiritualisation of the being and nature without which no supramentalisation is possible. Let the whole dynamic nature led by the psychic make itself full of the dynamic spiritual light, peace, purity, knowledge, force; let it afterwards get experience of the intermediate spiritual planes and know, feel and act in their sense; then it will be possible to speak last of the supramental transformation.

*

All that [*ideas such as "everything will soon be spiritualised"*] is absurd. The descent of the supramental means only that the Power will be there in the earth consciousness as a living force just as the thinking mental and the higher mental are already there. But an animal cannot take advantage of the presence of the thinking mental Power or an undeveloped man of the presence of the higher mental Power — so too everybody will not be able to take advantage of the presence of the supramental Power. I have also often enough said that it will be at first for the few, not for the whole earth, — only there will be a growing influence of it on the earth life.

*

It [*the world*] wants and it does not want something that it has not got. All that the supramental could give, the inner mind of the world would like to have, but its outer mind, its vital and physical do not like to pay the price. But after all I am not trying to change the world all at once but only to bring down centrally something into it it has not yet, a new consciousness and power.

*

Not in their entirety [*will cosmic Mind, Life and Matter be transformed*] — for that is not our business. It is ourselves that we have to transform and change the earth consciousness by bringing in the supramental principle into the evolution there. Once there it will necessarily have a powerful influence on the whole earth-life — as mind has had through the evolution of men, but much greater.

*

It is not possible for a force like the Supramental to come down without making a large change in earth conditions. It does not follow that all will become supramentalised and it is not necessary — but mind itself will be influenced as life has been influenced by the development of mind on earth.

*

Nothing permanent can be done without the real Supramental Force. But the result of its descent would be that in human life intuition would become a greater and more developed force than it now is and the other intermediate powers between Mind and Supermind would become also more common and develop an organised action.

*

It is not for considerations of gain or loss that the Divine Consciousness acts — that is a human standpoint necessary for human development. The Divine, as the Gita says, has nothing to gain and nothing that it has not, yet it puts forth its power of action in the manifestation. It is the earth-consciousness, not the supramental world that has to gain by the descent of the supramental principle — that is sufficient reason for it to descend. The supramental worlds remain as they are and are in no way affected by the descent.

*

It [*the descent of the Supermind*] would not necessarily be known by everybody beforehand. Besides even if the descent were here one would have to be ready before one could get the final change.

*

It is the supermind we have to bring down, manifest, realise. Anything higher than that is impossible at this stage of the evolution except as a reflection in the consciousness or a power delegated and modified in its descent.

*

The descent of the Supramental can hasten things, but it is not going to act as a patent universal medicine or change everything in the twinkle of an eye.

Clarifications about the Supramental Descent

But what will happen when the supramental comes down is a matter for the supramental to decide — no use laying down laws for it beforehand with the mind. It is the Truth-consciousness, sir — it will act according to the divine Truth behind things.

*

It is the very principle of this Yoga that only by the supramentalisation of the consciousness which means rising above mind to supermind and the descent of the supermind into the nature can the final transformation be made. So if nobody can rise above mind to supermind or obtain the descent of the supermind, then logically this Yoga becomes impossible. Every being is in essence one with the Divine and in his individual being a portion of the Divine, so there is no insuperable bar to his becoming supramental. It is no doubt impossible for the human nature being mental in its basis to overcome the Ignorance and rise to or obtain the descent of the Supermind by its own unaided effort, but by surrender to the Divine it can be done. One brings it down into the earth Nature through his own consciousness and so opens the way for the others, but the change has to be repeated in each consciousness to become individually effective.

*

There need not be [*catastrophes when the Supramental descends*]. There will necessarily be great changes but they are not bound to be catastrophic. When there is a strong pressure from Overmind forces for change, then there are likely to be catastrophes because of the resistance and clash of forces. The supramental has a greater, in its fullness a complete mastery of things and power of harmonisation which can overcome resistance by other means than dramatic struggle and violence.

*

There are three powers of the cosmos to which all things are subject — creation, preservation and destruction; whatever is created lasts for a time, then begins to crumble down. The taking away of the power of destruction implies a creation that will not be destroyed but last and develop always. In the Ignorance destruction is necessary for progress — in the Knowledge, the Truth-creation, the law is that of a constant unfolding without any Pralaya.

*

It is not by a general descent that people come out of the physical mind. If one chooses to remain in the physical mind, one million descents can come down and make no difference to him.

*

The Supermind coming down on earth will change nothing in a man if he clings to the ego.

Chapter Two
Descent and Transformation

A World-Changing Yoga

What is a perfect technique of Yoga or rather of a world-changing and Nature-changing Yoga? Not one that takes a man by a little bit of him somewhere, attaches a hook and pulls him up by a pulley into Nirvana or Paradise. The technique of a world-changing Yoga has to be as multiform, sinuous, patient, all-including as the world itself. If it does not deal with all the difficulties or possibilities and carefully deal with each necessary element, has it any chance of success? And can a perfect technique which everybody can understand do that? It is not like writing a small poem in a fixed metre with a limited number of modulations. If you take the poem simile, it is the Mahabharata of a Mahabharata that has to be done. And what, compared with the limited Greek perfection, is the technique of the Mahabharata?

Next, what is the use of *vicārabuddhi* in such a case? If one has to get to a new consciousness which surpasses the reasoning intellect, can one do it on lines which are to be judged and understood by the reasoning intellect, controlled at every step by it, told by the intellect what it is to do, what is the measure of its achievements, what its steps must be and what their value? If one does that, will one ever get out of the range of the reasoning intelligence into what is beyond it? And if one does, how shall others judge what one is doing by the intellectual measure? How can one judge what is beyond the ordinary consciousness when one is oneself in the ordinary consciousness? Is it not only by exceeding yourself that you can feel, experience, judge what exceeds you? What is the value of a judgment without the feeling and experience?

What the Supramental will do the mind cannot foresee or lay down. The mind is Ignorance seeking for the Truth, the

Descent and Transformation

Supramental by its very definition is Truth Consciousness, Truth in possession of itself and fulfilling itself by its own power. In a supramental world imperfection and disharmony are bound to disappear. But what we propose just now is not to make the earth a supramental world but to bring down the Supramental as a power and established consciousness in the midst of the rest — to let it work there and fulfil itself as Mind descended into Life and Matter and has worked as a Power there to fulfil itself in the midst of the rest. This will be enough to change the world and to change Nature by breaking down her present limits. But what, how, by what degrees it will do it is a thing that ought not to be said now — when the Light is there, the Light will itself do its work — when the Supramental Will stands on earth, that Will will decide. It will establish a perfection, a harmony, a Truth-creation — for the rest, well, it will be the rest — that is all.

*

I certainly hope to bring down an effective power of the Truth which will replace eventually the Falsehood that has governed the minds and hearts of men for so long. The liberation of a few individuals is a thing that is always possible and has always been done — but, to my seeing, it cannot be the sole aim of existence. Whatever the struggles and sufferings and blunders of humanity, there is still in it an urge towards the Light, an impulse towards a greater Truth not only of the soul but the life. If it has not been done yet, it is surely because those who reached the Light and the greater Truth, rested there and saw in it more a means of escape for the soul than a means of transformation for the life. The liberation of the spirit is necessary, nothing can be done without it — but the transformation is also possible.

*

You have missed altogether the qualifying words which I put with great care and prominent emphasis[1] — if you don't read

---

[1] *In a letter published in* Letters on Himself and the Ashram, *volume 35 of* THE COMPLETE WORKS OF SRI AUROBINDO, *p. 649.* — Ed.

carefully, you will necessarily misunderstand what I write. I said "*This transformation* cannot be done individually *in a solitary way only.*" No individual solitary transformation apart from the work for the earth (which means more than any individual transformation) would be either possible or useful. (Also no individual human being can by his own power alone work out the transformation, nor is it the object of the Yoga to create an individual superman here and there.) The object of the Yoga is to bring down the supramental consciousness on earth, to fix it there, to create a new race with the principle of the supramental consciousness governing the inner and outer individual and collective life. Therefore the existence of the Asram, whatever difficulties it created for ourselves or for the individual, was inevitable. The method was the preparation of the earth consciousness in the human being as represented by the members of the Asram and others (with also a certain working in the general earth consciousness) so as to make the descent of the supramental Force possible. That Force accepted by individual after individual according to their preparation would establish the supramental consciousness in the physical world and so create a nucleus for its own expansion.

*

As far as I can see, once the supramental is established in Matter, the transformation will be possible under much less troublesome conditions than now are there. These bad conditions are due to the fact that the Ignorance is in possession and the hostile Powers an established authority, as it were, who do not care to give up their hold and there is no full force of Light established in the earth consciousness which would not only meet but outweigh their full force of darkness.

*

It is the darkest nights that prepare the greatest dawns — and it is so because it is into the deep inconscience of material life that we have to bring, not an intermediate glimmer, but the full glory of the divine Light.

The Vital World and the Supramental Descent

When there is a pressure on the vital world due to the preparing Descent from above, that world usually precipitates something of itself into the human. The vital world is very large and far exceeds the human in extent. But usually it dominates by influence not by descent. Of course the effort of this part of the vital world is always to maintain humanity under its sway and prevent the higher Light.

*

The vital descent cannot prevent the supramental — still less can the possessed nations do it by their material power, since the supramental descent is primarily a spiritual fact which will bear its necessary outward consequences. What previous vital descents have done is to falsify the Light that came down as in the history of Christianity where it took possession of the teaching and distorted it and deprived it of any widespread fulfilment. But the supermind is by definition a Light that cannot be distorted if it acts in its own right and by its own presence. It is only when it holds itself back and allows inferior Powers of consciousness to use a diminished and already deflected Truth that the knowledge can be seized by the vital Forces and made to serve their own purpose.

The Nature and Scope of the Transformation

When the mind, life and body are entirely divine and supramentalised, that is the perfect transformation and the true transformation is the process that leads towards it.

*

It is not a question of "can" or "cannot" [*the Divine Force transform someone*] — it is a question of what is necessary for the true transformation. Theoretically the Force can transform you in one hundredth of a second from an animal to a god, but that would not be transformation or the working out of a spiritual evolution, it would be mere thaumaturgy, i.e. miracle working without a significance or purpose.

*

The whole of humanity cannot be changed at once. What has to be done is to bring the Higher Consciousness down into the earth-consciousness and establish it there as a constant realised force, just as mind and life have been established and embodied in Matter, so to establish and embody the Supramental Force.

*

It would not be possible to change all that [*ordinary life on earth*] in a moment — we have always said that the whole of humanity will not change the moment there is the Descent. But what can be done is to establish the higher principle in the earth consciousness in such a way that it will remain and go on strengthening and spreading itself in the earth-life. That is how a new principle in the evolution must necessarily work.

*

There is no proposal to transform the whole earth consciousness — it is simply to introduce the supramental principle there which will transform those who can receive and embody it.

The Earth, the Earth Consciousness and the Supramental Creation

The earth is the place of evolution in which all these [*universal*] forces meet and try to manifest and out of their working something has to develop. On the other planes (the mental, vital etc.) there is not the evolution — there each acts separately according to its own law.

*

It [*the earth*] contains all the potentialities which come out in the beings of earth and also much that is unexpressed.

*

It is first through the individual that it [*the supramental activity*] becomes part of the earth consciousness and afterwards it spreads from the first centres and takes up more and more of the global consciousness till it becomes an established force there.

*

The consciousness of this Earth alone [*is the earth consciousness.*]. There is a separate global consciousness of the earth (as of other worlds) which evolves with the evolution of life on the planet.

*

Yes, all that [*humans, animals, vegetables, minerals*] is the earth consciousness — mineral = matter, vegetable = the vital-physical creation, animal = the vital creation, man = the mental creation. Into the earth consciousness so limited to mind, vital, matter has to come the supramental creation. Necessarily *at first* it cannot be in a great number — but even if it is only in a few at first, that does not mean that it will have no effect on the rest or will not change the whole balance of the earth-nature.

The Supramental Change and the Ananda Plane

The supramental change is the ultimate stage of siddhi and it is not likely to come so soon; but there are many levels between the normal mind and the supermind and it is easy to mistake an ascent into one of them or a descent of their consciousness or influence for a supramental change.

It is quite impossible to ascend to the real Ananda *plane* (except in a profound trance), until after the supramental consciousness has been entered, realised and possessed; but it is quite possible and normal to feel some form of Ananda *consciousness* on any level. This consciousness wherever it is felt is a derivation from the Ananda plane, but it is very much diminished in power and modified to suit the lesser power of receptivity of the inferior levels.

*

I presume it is the development of the Truth Power and the Ananda Power in the overmind consciousness that is being pursued. The transcendent Ananda in itself could descend only after the complete Supramentalisation of the being and would mean a stupendous change in the earth consciousness. It is the divine Truth in the overmind and the divine Ananda in the overmind that can now prepare their manifestation and it is that which is being indicated in these experiences.

Chapter Three

The Supramental Transformation

Preparatory Steps towards the Supramental Change

It is not possible to have the direct supramental working now. The Adhar is not yet ready. First one must accept an indirect working which prepares the lower planes for the supramental change.

*

The gate of the supramental cannot be smashed open like that. The Adhar has to be steadily prepared, changed, made fit for the supramental Descent. There are several powers between the ordinary mind and the supramental and these must be opened up and absorbed by the consciousness — only then is the supramental change possible.

*

To speak of "receiving power from the supramental when we are not conscious" is strange. When one is not conscious, one can still receive a *higher* force; the Divine Shakti works often from behind the veil, otherwise in the ignorant and unconscious condition of the human being she would not be able to work at all. But the nature of the force or action is modified to suit the condition of the sadhak. One must develop a very full consciousness before one can receive anything from the direct supramental Power and one must be very advanced in consciousness even to receive something of it modified through the Overmind or other intermediate region.

The Supramental Influence and Supramentalisation

Who told you that it [*the supermind*] was descending on the physical consciousness without touching the mind and vital?

Certainly no part of the Nature has been supramentalised — that is not possible, until the whole being has been put under the supramental influence. The supramental influence must come first, the supramental transformation can only come afterwards.

*

A touch or influence of the supramental is not the same thing as supramentalisation. To suppose that the physical can be supramentalised before the mental and vital is an absolute absurdity. What I said was that the mind and vital could not be supramentalised so long as the physical was left as it was, untouched by the supramental descent.

*

It is quite impossible for the supramental to take up the body before there has been the full supramental change in the mind and the vital. X and others seem always to expect some kind of unintelligible miracle — they do not understand that it is a concentrated evolution, rapid but following the law of creation, that has to take place. A miracle can be only a moment's wonder. A change according to the Divine Law can alone endure.

*

If the supramental can stand in the mind and vital, then it must stand in the physical also. If it does not stand in the physical, it cannot stand in the mind and vital also; it will be something else, not the supramental.

*

It [*the supermind*] cannot be brought down into the mind and vital without being brought down into the physical also. One can feel its influence or get something from it, but bringing down means much more than that.

*

The supermind is a harmonious whole — it is not a mixture of light and ignorance. If the physical mind is not supramentalised, then there will be in mind a mixture of ignorance, but then it will not be supermind there, but something else. So also with the vital. All that can manifest in the mind separately is a partly supramentalised overmind.

*

There can be no conquest of the other planes by the supermind, but only an influence, so long as the physical is not ready.

*

Aspiration is necessary in all spiritual aims from whatever part of the consciousness. The supermind can descend into the physical only if there is brought down into it the power of higher and higher levels till the supramental intensity is possible.

Premature Claims of Possession of the Supermind

It is very unwise for anyone to claim prematurely to have possession of the supermind or even a taste of it. The claim is usually accompanied by an outburst of superegoism, some radical blunder of perception or a gross fall into wrong condition and wrong movement. A certain spiritual humility, a serious un-arrogant look at oneself and quiet perception of the imperfections of one's present nature and, instead of self-esteem and self-assertion, a sense of the necessity of exceeding one's present self, not from egoistic ambition, but from an urge towards the Divine would be, it seems to me, for this frail terrestrial and human composition far better conditions for proceeding towards its supramental change.

*

He is using the word supermind too easily. What he describes as supermind is a higher illumined consciousness; a modified supramental light may touch it, but not the full power of the supermind; and, in any case, it is not the supermind. He speaks of a supramental part which is unreceptive, — that is impossible, the supramental cannot be unreceptive. The supermind is the

Truth-consciousness itself; it already possesses the Truth and does not even need to receive it. The word *vijñāna* is sometimes used for the higher illumined Intelligence in communication with the Truth, and this must be the part in himself which he felt — but this is not the supermind. One can enter into supermind only at the very end of the sadhana, when all difficulties have disappeared and there is no obstacle any longer in the way of the realisation.

*

The question arose and always arises because of an eagerness in the vital to take any stage of strong experience as the final stage, even to take it for the overmind, supermind, full siddhi. The supermind or the overmind either is not so easy to reach as that, even on the side of Knowledge or inner experience only. What you are experiencing belongs to the spiritualised and liberated mind. At this stage there may be intimations from the higher mind levels, but these intimations are merely isolated experiences, not a full change of consciousness. The supermind is not part of mind or a higher level of mind — it is something entirely different. No sadhak can reach the supermind by his own efforts and the effort to do it by personal tapasya has been the source of many mishaps. One has to go quietly stage by stage until the being is ready and even then it is only the Grace that can bring the real supramental change.

*

The action that took place was not supramental; the fact that you were aware of a centre in the brain shows that it was through the mind that it was done. The force that acted was the Divine Power which can work in this way on any plane, supramental, mental, vital or physical or on all the planes together. The supramental action can only be achieved after a long discipline of Yoga directed towards that end; it cannot be an initial experience.

That there was no mental expectation was all to the good; if there had been an expectation, the mind might have been active and interfered and either prevented the experience or else stood in the way of its being pure and complete.

Chapter Four
Transformation and the Body

The Transformation of the Body

It is quite true that the surrender and the consequent transformation of the whole being is the aim of the Yoga — the body is not excluded, but at the same time this part of the endeavour is the most difficult and doubtful — the rest, though not facile, is comparatively less difficult to accomplish. One must start with an inner control of the consciousness over the body, a power to make it obey more and more the will or the force transmitted to it. In the end as a higher and higher Force descends and the plasticity of the body increases, the transformation becomes possible.

*

It is absolutely idle to think of transforming the body when other things that are so much easier to do — though of course none is easy — are not done. The inner must change before the outermost can follow. So what is the use of such a concentration — unless one thinks that everything else is perfect, which would be a rather astonishing claim. What has to be done with the body at first is to make it open to the Force, so as to receive strength against illness and fatigue — when they come, there must be the power to react and throw them off and to keep a constant flow of force into the body. If that is done, the rest of the bodily change can wait for its proper time.

*

The supramental perfection means that the body becomes conscious, is filled with consciousness and that as this is the Truth consciousness all its actions, functionings etc. become by the power of the consciousness within it harmonious, luminous, right and true — without ignorance or disorder.

The Hathayogic method is to bring an immense vital force into the body and by this and by certain processes keep it strong and in good health and a capable instrument.

The Transformation of the Body in Other Traditions

It [*a body of light seen by the correspondent in a vision*] is the luminous body spoken of in the Veda as possessed by the beings of the higher planes. It is supposed by certain schools of Yoga in the East and West that in the final transformation on earth man will develop a body having these qualities. It was called the *corps glorieux*, "body of glory", by the Mother's first spiritual instructor.

*

It has been the idea of many who have speculated on the subject that the body of the future race will be a luminous body (*corps glorieux*) and that might mean radio-active.[1] But also it has to be considered (1) that a supramental body must necessarily be one in which the consciousness determines even the physical action and reaction to the most material and these therefore are not wholly dependent on material conditions or laws as now known, (2) that the subtle process will be more powerful than the gross, so that a subtle action of Agni will be able to do the action which would now need a physical change such as increased temperature.

*

I did not intend to evade anything, except that in so far as I do not yet know what will be the chemical constitution of the changed body, I could not answer anything to that. That was why I said it needed investigation.

I was simply putting my idea on the matter which has always been that it is the supramental which will create its own

---

[1] *The correspondent asked whether the chemicals in a transformed body would become "more Peace-active, Light-active, Force-active (as we say, radio-active)". — Ed.*

physical basis. If you mean that the supramental cannot *fulfil itself* in the present body with its present processes that is true. The processes will obviously have to be altered. How far the constitution of the body will be changed and in what direction is another question. As I said it may become as you suggest radio-active: Théon (Mother's teacher in occultism) spoke of it as luminous, *le corps glorieux*. But all that does not make it impossible for the supramental to act in the present body for change. It is what I am looking forward to at present.

Of course a certain preliminary transformation is necessary, just as the psychic and spiritual transformation precedes the supramental. But this is a change of the physical consciousness down to the submerged consciousness of the cells so that they may respond to higher forces and admit them and to a certain extent a change or at least a greater plasticity in the processes. The rules of food etc. are meant to help that by minimising obstacles. How far this involves a change of the chemical constitution of the body I cannot say. It seems to me still that whatever preparatory changes there may be, it is only the action of the supramental Force that can confirm and complete them.

*

If the consciousness cannot determine the physical action and reaction in the present body, if it needs a different basis, then that means this different basis must be prepared by different means. By what means? Physical? The old Yogis tried to do it by physical tapasya; others by seeking the elixir of life etc. According to this Yoga, the action of the higher Force and consciousness which includes the subtle action of Agni has to open and prepare the body and make it more responsive to Consciousness-Force instead of being rigid in its present habits (called laws). But a different basis can only be created by the supramental action itself. What else but the supermind can determine its own basis?

*

I read the Bible, — very assiduously at one time. When I have looked at it, it has always given me a sense of imprecision in the thought-substance, in spite of the vividness of the expression, and that makes it very difficult to be sure about these things. This passage about the body, for instance—although St. Paul had remarkable mystic experiences and, certainly, much profound spiritual knowledge (profound rather than wide, I think) —I would not swear to it that he is referring to the supramentalised body (*physical body*). Perhaps to the supramental body or to some other luminous body in its own space and substance, which he found sometimes as if enveloping him and abolishing this body of death which he felt the material envelope to be. This verse like many others is capable of several interpretations and might refer to a quite supraphysical experience. The idea of a transformation of the body occurs in different traditions, but I have never been quite sure that it meant the change in this very matter. There was a Yogi some time ago in this region who taught it, but he hoped when the change was complete, to disappear in light. The Vaishnavas speak of a divine body which will replace this one when there is the complete siddhi. But, again, is this a divine physical or supraphysical body? At the same time there is no obstacle in the way of supposing that all these ideas, intuitions, experiences point to, if they do not exactly denote, the physical transformation.

*

The physical Nature does not mean the body alone but the phrase includes the transformation of the whole physical mind, vital, material nature — not by imposing siddhis on them, but by creating a new physical nature which is to be the habitation of the supramental being in a new evolution. I am not aware that this has been done by any Hathayogic or other process. Mental or vital occult power can only bring siddhis of the higher plane into the individual life — like the Sannyasi who could take any poison without harm, but he died of a poison after all when he forgot to observe the conditions of the siddhi. The working of the supramental power envisaged is not an influence on the physical giving it abnormal faculties, but an entrance and permeation changing it wholly into a supramentalised physical. I did not learn the idea from Veda or Upanishad, and I do not know if there is anything of the kind there. What I received about the supermind was a direct, not a derived knowledge given to me; it was only afterwards that I found certain confirmatory revelations in the Upanishad and Veda.

Transforming the Body Consciousness

That [*stopping at each stage of transformation in order to deal with the body*] is hardly possible. The body consciousness is there and cannot be ignored, so that one can neither transform the higher parts completely leaving the body for later dealing nor make each stage complete in all its parts before going to the next. I tried that method but it never worked. A predominant overmentalisation of mind and vital is the first step, for instance, when overmentalising, but the body consciousness retains all the lower movements unovermentalised and until these can be pulled up to the overmental standard, there is no overmental perfection, always the body consciousness brings in flaws and limitations. To perfect the overmind one has to call in the supramental force and it is only when the overmind has been partially supramentalised that the body begins to be more and more overmental. I do not see any way of avoiding this process, though it is what makes the thing so long.

*

The fallacy of the argument [*that after supramentalisation severe attacks on the body will still be possible*] lies in the premiss laid down in the beginning that even after supramentalisation difficulties and attacks will continue. In the supramental consciousness such attacks are not possible — the coexistence of the supramental and the lower darkness in the same being and body is not possible. It is precisely for that reason that the supramentalisation of the body consciousness is laid down as the condition of the successful transformation. If attacks continue and can come in successfully, it means that the body consciousness is not yet supramentalised.

Death and the Supramental Transformation

The change of the consciousness is the necessary thing and without it there can be no physical siddhi. But the fullness of the supramental change is not possible if the body remains as it is, a slave of death, disease, decay, pain, unconsciousness and all the other results of the ignorance. If these are to remain the descent of the supramental is hardly necessary — for a change of consciousness which would bring mental-spiritual union with the Divine, the Overmind is sufficient, even the Higher Mind is sufficient. The supramental descent is necessary for a dynamic action of the Truth in mind, vital and body. This would imply as a final result the disappearance of the unconsciousness of the body; it would no longer be subject to decay and disease. That would mean that it would not be subject to the ordinary processes by which death comes. If a change of body had to be made, it would have to be by the will of the inhabitant. This (not an obligation to live 3000 years, for that too would be a bondage) would be the essence of physical immortality. Still, if one wanted to live 1000 years or more, then supposing one had the complete siddhi, it should not be impossible.

*

Death is necessary in the evolution, because the body can progress no longer — cannot suffice any longer as an instrument for the progress or evolution of the consciousness — it has to change its physical instrument and get a new one. If something can be brought into the body that will make it a plastic instrument for the soul, then only death is no longer necessary. If the supramental transformation is complete that is what should happen.

*

It [*death*] has no separate existence by itself, it is only a result of the principle of decay in the body and that principle is there already — it is part of the physical nature. At the same time it is not inevitable; if one could have the necessary consciousness and force, decay and death is not inevitable. But to bring that consciousness and force into the whole of the material nature is the most difficult thing of all — at any rate in such a way as to annul the decay principle.

*

Immunity from death by anything but one's own will to leave the body, immunity from illness are things that can be achieved only by a complete change of consciousness which each man has to develop in himself, — there can be no automatic immunity without that achievement.

*

That[2] is the argument of the Mayavadin to whom all manifestation is useless and unreal because it is temporary — even the life of the gods is no use because it is in Time, not in the Timeless. But if manifestation is of any use, then it is worthwhile having a perfect manifestation rather than an imperfect one. "Have to be left willingly" is a contradiction in terms. One keeps the body as long as one wills, with an illumined will, leaves it or changes it according to the same will. That is a very different thing from a body assailed constantly by desire and suffering and death brought on by decay or illness. Always assuming that the divine manifestation or any manifestation is worthwhile.

As for the second argument,[3] change and progress are not excluded from the supramental life. I do not see why the change of cells, supposing it continues in the supramentalised body, takes away from the value of the transformation, if it is a change to something equally or more conscious and luminous.

*

Well, don't you know that old men sometimes get a new or third set of teeth in their old age? And if monkey glands can renew

---

[2] *The correspondent asked, "What is the need of transformation if the body will have to be left willingly or unwillingly?" — Ed.*
[3] *The correspondent asked, "Since the body cells undergo changes from second to second, what value has the transformation of the body?" — Ed.*

functionings and forces and can make hair grow on a bald head, as Voronoff has proved by living examples, — well? And mark that Science is only at the beginning of these experiments [*to prolong life*]. If these possibilities are opening before Science, why should one declare their absolute impossibility by other means?

*

There is no ambiguity that I can see.[4] "*En fait*" and "*attachée*" do not convey any sense of inevitability. "*En fait*" means simply that in fact, actually, as things are at present all life (on earth) has death attached to it as its end; but it does not in the least convey the idea that it can never be otherwise or that this is the unalterable law of all existence. It is at present a fact for certain reasons which are stated, — due to certain mental and physical circumstances — if these are changed, death is not inevitable any longer. Obviously the alteration can only come "if" certain conditions are satisfied — all progress and change by evolution depends upon an "if" which gets satisfied. If the animal mind had not been pushed to develop speech and reason, mental man would never have come into existence, — but the "if", a stupendous and formidable one, was satisfied. So with the ifs that condition a farther progress.

The Conquest of Death

As for the conquest of death, it is only one of the sequelae of supramentalisation — and I am not aware that I have forsworn my views about the supramental descent. But I never said or thought that the supramental descent would automatically make everybody immortal. The supramental descent can only make the best conditions for anybody who can open to it then or thereafter attaining to the supramental consciousness and its

---

[4] *Sri Aurobindo is referring to the ambiguity seen by the correspondent in two statements of the Mother:* "If this belief [in the necessity of death] *could be cast out... death would no longer be inevitable*" *and* "*Death as a fact has been attached to all life upon earth....*" *(The Mother,* Questions and Answers 1929-1931, *2003 ed., p. 36) The correspondent read these statements in French. — Ed.*

Transformation and the Body

consequences. But it would not dispense with the necessity of sadhana. If it did, the logical consequence would be that the whole earth, men, dogs and worms, would suddenly wake up to find themselves supramental. There would be no need of an Asram or of Yoga.

What is vital is the supramental change of consciousness — conquest of death is something minor and, as I have always said, the last physical result of it, not the first result of all or the most important — a thing to be added to complete the whole, not the one thing needed and essential. To put it first is to reverse all spiritual values — it would mean that the seeker was actuated not by any high spiritual aim but by a vital clinging to life or a selfish and timid seeking for the security of the body — such a spirit could not bring the supramental change.

Certainly, everything depends on my success. The only thing that could prevent it, so far as I can see, would be my own death or the Mother's. But did you imagine that that [*my success*] would mean the cessation of death on this planet, and that sadhana would cease to be necessary for anybody?

*

There can be no immortality of the body without supramentalisation; the potentiality is there in the Yogic force and Yogis can live for 200 or 300 years or more, but there can be no real principle of it without the Supramental.

Even Science believes that one day death may be conquered by physical means and its reasonings are perfectly sound. There is no reason why the Supramental Force should not do it. Forms on earth do not last (they do in other planes) because these forms are too rigid to grow expressing the progress of the spirit. If they become plastic enough to do that, there is no reason why they should not last.

*

Death is there because the being in the body is not yet developed enough to go on growing in the same body without the need of change and the body itself is not sufficiently conscious. If the mind and vital and the body itself were more conscious and plastic, death would not be necessary.

*

As for immortality, it cannot come if there is attachment to the body, — for it is only by living in the immortal part of oneself which is unidentified with the body and bringing down its consciousness and force into the cells that it can come. I speak of course of Yogic means. The scientists now hold that it is (theoretically at least) possible to discover physical means by which death can be overcome, but that would mean only a prolongation of the present consciousness in the present body. Unless there is a change of consciousness and change of functioning, it would be a very small gain.

*

Immortality is one of the possible results of supramentalisation, but it is not an obligatory result and it does not mean that there will be an eternal or indefinite prolongation of life as it is. That is what many think it will be, that they will remain what they are with all their human desires and the only difference will be that they will satisfy them endlessly; but such an immortality would not be worth having and it would not be long before people are tired of it. To live in the Divine and have the divine consciousness is itself immortality and to be able to divinise the body also and make it a fit instrument for divine works and divine life would be its material expression only.

*

It depends on the consciousness [*whether one wants to live a long life*]. As it is, at present, most people do not get tired of life; they die because they must, not because they want to — at least, that is true of the vital; it is only a minority that tire of life and for many of these it is due to the discomforts of old age, continued ill-health, misfortune. Supposing a consciousness descended in the body that got rid of these discomforts, would people get tired of life in the same way merely because of its length or would they have some source of perpetual interest within as well as without that would keep them on — that is the question. Of course physical immortality would not mean that one is tied down to the body, but that one is not subject to disease and death, but can keep or leave the body at will. I don't know whether Ashwatthaman lives on because he cannot die or because he won't die — whether it is for him a doom or a privilege. There are by the way animals that live for many centuries, but as they have not the philosophic mind the question for them does not arise — probably they take it as a matter of course.

*

What you say about being tired of life, is true. Edison's family was very long lived but his grandfather after a century found it too long and died because he wanted to. On the other hand there are men who are strongly vital and do not get tired of life, like the Turk who died recently at 150, I think, but was still eager to live.

*

The ideal would be not to be subject to Death, but to change the body whenever it is necessary with full consciousness.

The Reproductive Method of the Supramental

The [*reproductive*] method of the supramental is more likely to be psychological than material. But these are things that we leave to the Supermind to arrange when it is there.

*

It is not at all certain that the hereditary method will be used for the reproduction of supermen. If it were used, the seed would have to be very different from what it is now — and the question would not arise.

Part Four

Problems of Philosophy, Science, Religion and Society

Section One

Thought, Philosophy, Science and Yoga

Chapter One

The Intellect and Yoga

Intellectual Truth and Spiritual Experience

Intellectual truths? Do you think that the intellectual truth of the Divine is its real truth? In that case there is no need of Yoga. Philosophy is enough.

*

Philosophy knows nothing about peace and silence or the inner and outer vital. These things are discovered only by Yoga.

*

Yoga is not a thing of ideas but of inner spiritual experience. Merely to be attracted to any set of religious or spiritual ideas does not bring with it any realisation. Yoga means a change of consciousness; a mere mental activity will not bring a change of consciousness, it can only bring a change of mind. And if your mind is sufficiently mobile, it will go on changing from one thing to another till the end without arriving at any sure way or any spiritual harbour. The mind can think and doubt and question and accept and withdraw its acceptance, make formations and unmake them, pass decisions and revoke them, judging always on the surface and by surface indications and therefore never coming to any deep and firm experience of Truth, but by itself it can do no more. There are only three ways by which it can make itself a channel or instrument of Truth. Either it must fall silent in the Self and give room for a wider and greater consciousness; or it must make itself passive to an inner Light and allow that Light to use it as a means of expression; or else it must itself change from the questioning intellectual superficial mind it now is to an intuitive intelligence, a mind of vision fit for the direct perception of the divine Truth.

If you want to do anything in the path of Yoga, you must fix once for all what way you mean to follow. It is no use setting your face towards the future and then always looking back towards the past; in this way you will arrive nowhere. If you are tied to your past, return to it and follow the way you then choose; but if you choose this way instead, you must give yourself to it single-mindedly and not look back at every moment.

*

My reason for wanting you to get rid of the mental concepts is that they are rigid and keep you tied to the idea and feeling of your incapacity and the impossibility of the sadhana. Get rid of that and a great obstacle disappears.

You would then see that there is no reason for the constant sense of grief and despair that reacts upon your effort and makes it sterile. I simply want you to put yourself, if it is possible, in that state of quietude and openness which is favourable to the higher consciousness and its action; if it is not possible at present, I have still said that I will do my utmost to help you to the experience. That does not mean that the utmost has been yet done or that it can be done in a few days. But (although people are not giving me the freedom of mind and disposal of time which I had asked for), it will be done.

*

The point about the intellect's misrepresentation of the "formless" (the result of a merely negative expression of something that is inexpressibly intimate and positive) is very well made and hits the truth in the centre. No one who has had the Ananda of the Brahman can do anything but smile at the charge of coldness; there is an absoluteness of immutable ecstasy in it, a concentrated intensity of silent and inalienable rapture that it is quite impossible even to suggest to anyone who has not had the experience. The eternal Reality is neither cold nor dry nor empty — you might just as well talk of the midsummer sunlight as cold or the ocean as dry or perfect fullness as empty. Even when you enter into it by elimination of form and everything else, it seizes as a miraculous fullness that is truly the Purnam — when it is entered affirmatively as well as by negation, there can obviously be no question of emptiness or dryness. All is there and more than one could ever dream of as the all. That is why one has to object to the intellect thrusting itself in as the *sabjāntā* judge — if it kept to its own limits, there would be no objection to it. But it makes constructions of words and ideas which have no application to the Truth, babbles foolish things in its ignorance and makes its constructions a wall which refuses to let in the Truth that surpasses its own capacities or scope.

*

You can tell him Mother does not discuss these mental problems [*such as the existence of evil in the world*] even with the disciples. It is quite useless trying to reconcile these things with the intellect. For there are two things: the Ignorance from which the struggle and discord come and the secret Light, Unity, Bliss and Harmony. The intellect belongs to the Ignorance. It is only by getting into another consciousness that one can live in the Light and Bliss and Unity and not be touched by the outward discord and struggle. That change of consciousness therefore is the only thing that matters; to reconcile with the intellect could make no difference.

*

Yes, you need not listen to the "common sense" of others at least; usually there is much that is common in it but very little that is sense. What your inner being feels is rather to be followed than the superficial reasonings of the outer intelligence.

*

How can Reason be the sole arbiter [*in the quest for Truth*]? Whose reason? The reason in different men comes to different, opposite or incompatible conclusions. We cannot say that Reason is infallible, any more than feeling is infallible or the senses are infallible.

*

Russell has the doubts because he has no spiritual experience, Rolland because he takes his emotional intellectuality for spirituality, Tagore —

If one is blind, it is quite natural — for the human intelligence which is rather an asinine thing at its best — to deny light; if one's highest natural vision is that of glimmering mists, it is equally natural to believe that all high vision is only a mist or a glimmer. But Light exists for all that — and for all that, spiritual Truth is more than a mist and a glimmer.

Intellectual Arguments against Spirituality

I have read Leonard Woolf's article,[1] but I do not propose to deal with it in my comments on Professor Sorley's letter[2] — for apart from the ignorant denunciation and cheap satire in which it deals, there is nothing much in its statement of the case against spiritual thought or experience; its reasoning is superficial and springs from an entire misunderstanding of the case for the mystic. There are four main arguments he sets against it and none of them have any value.

Argument number one. Mysticism and mystics have always risen in times of decadence, of the ebb of life and their loud quacking is a symptom of the decadence. This argument is absolutely untrue. In the East the great spiritual movements have arisen in the full flood of a people's life and culture or on a rising tide and they have themselves given a powerful impulse of expansion and richness to its thought and art and life; in Greece the mystics and the mysteries were there at the prehistoric beginning and in the middle (Pythagoras was one of the greatest of mystics) and not only in the ebb and decline; the mystic cults flourished in Rome too when its culture was at high tide; many great spiritual personalities of Italy, France, Spain sprang up

---

[1] Leonard Woolf, "Quack, Quack! or Having it Both Ways" [a review of C. E. M. Joad, Counterattack from the East: The Philosophy of Radhakrishnan (London: Allen and Unwin, 1932)]. "New Statesman and Nation", vol. 6, no. 145 (2 December 1933): pp. 702–4.
[2] See the letters on pages 357–68. — Ed.

in a life that was rich, vivid and not in the least touched with decadence. This hasty and inept generalisation has no truth in it and therefore no value.

Argument number two. A spiritual experience cannot be taken as a truth (it is a chimaera) unless it is proved just as the presence of a chair in the next room can be proved by showing it to the eye. Of course, a spiritual experience cannot be proved in that way, for it does not belong to the order of physical facts and is not physically visible or touchable. The writer's position would amount to this that only what is or can easily be made evident to everybody without any need of training, development, equipment or personal discovery, is to be taken as true. This is a position which, if accepted, would confine knowledge or truth within very narrow limits and get rid of a great deal of human culture. A spiritual peace, for example, — the peace that passeth all understanding — is a common experience of the mystics all over the world — it is a fact but a spiritual fact, a fact of the invisible; when one enters it or it enters into one, one knows that it is a truth of existence and is there all the time behind life and visible things. But how am I to "prove" these invisible facts to Mr. Leonard Woolf? he will turn away saying that this is the usual decadent quack quack and pass contemptuously on — perhaps to write another cleverly shallow article on some subject of which he has no personal knowledge or experience.

Argument number three. The generalisations based on spiritual experience are irrational as well as unproven. Irrational in what way? Are they merely foolish and inconceivable — infrarational — or do they belong to a suprarational order of experience to which the ordinary intellectual canons do not apply because these are founded on phenomena as they appear to the external mind and sense and not to an inner realisation which surpasses these phenomena? That is the contention of the mystics and it cannot be dismissed by merely saying that as they do not agree with ordinary experience, therefore they are nonsense and false. I would not undertake to defend as unimpeachable all that Joad or Radhakrishnan may have written — such as the formula that "the universe is good", — but for many or most of the statements marshalled for condemnation by the writer one can surely say that they are not irrational at all. "Integrating the personality" may have no meaning to him, it has a very clear meaning to many, for it is a truth of experience — and, if modern psychology is to be believed, it is not irrational since there is in our being not only a conscious but an unconscious or subconscious or concealed subliminal part and it is not impossible to become aware of both and make some kind of integration. To "transcend both consciousness and unconsciousness" gets at once a rational meaning if we admit that as there is a subconscious so there may be a superconscious part of our being. To reconcile disparate parts of our nature or our perception or experience of things is also not such a ridiculous or meaningless phrase. It is not absurd to say that the doctrine of Karma reconciles determinism and free-willism, since this doctrine supposes that our own past action and therefore our past will determined to a great extent the present results but not so as to exclude a present will modifying them and creating a fresh determinism of our existence yet to be. The phrase about the value of the world is quite intelligible once we see that it refers to a progressive value not determined by the good or bad experience of the moment, a value of existence developing through time and taken as a whole. As for the statement about God, it may have little or no meaning if it is taken in connection with the superficial idea of the Divine current in popular religion, but it is a perfectly logical result of the premiss that there is an Infinite and Eternal which is manifesting in itself Time and things that are phenomenally finite. One may accept or reject this complex idea of the Divine which is founded on a coordination of the data of long spiritual experience passed through by thousands of seekers in all times, but I fail to see why it should be considered unreasonable. If it is because that would mean "to have it not only in both ways but in every way", I do not see why this should be so reprehensible or a complex manifestation of a single Essence, Consciousness or Force should be considered *prima facie* inadmissible. There can be after all a synthetic and global view and consciousness of things which is not bound by the oppositions and divisions of a more analytical and selective or dissecting intelligence.

Argument number four. The plea of intuition is only a facile cover for an inability to explain or establish by the use of reason — Joad and Radhakrishnan reason, but take refuge in intuition because their reasoning fails. Can the issue be settled in so easy and trenchant a way? The fact is that the mystic stands on an inner knowledge, an inner experience — but if he philosophises, he must try to explain to the reason, though not necessarily always by the abstract reason alone, what he has seen to be the Truth. He cannot but say, "I am explaining a truth which is beyond outer phenomena and the intelligence which depends on phenomena; it is really the outcome of a certain kind of direct experience and the intuitive knowledge which arises from that experience, so it cannot be adequately communicated by symbols appropriate to the world of outer phenomena — yet I am obliged to do as well as I can with these to help me towards some statement which will be intellectually acceptable to you." There is no wickedness or deceitful cunning therefore in using metaphors and symbols with a cautionary "as it were", — so objected to by Mr. Woolf in the simile of the focus, which is surely not intended as an argument but as a suggestive image. I may observe that the writer himself takes refuge in metaphor, beginning with the famous "quack quack", and an adversary might well reply that he does so in order to damn the opposite side while avoiding the necessity of a sound philosophical reply to the ideas he dislikes and repudiates. An intensity of belief is not the measure of truth, but neither is an intensity of unbelief the right measure.

As to the real nature of intuition and its relation to the intellectual mind, that is quite another and very large and complex question which cannot be dealt with in a short space. I have confined myself to pointing out that this article is a quite inadequate and superficial criticism. A case can be made against spiritual experience and spiritual philosophy and its positions, but to deserve a serious reply it must be put forward by a better advocate and it must touch the real centre of the problem which lies here. As there is a category of facts to which our senses are our best available but very imperfect guide, as there is a category of truths which we seek by the keen but still imperfect light of our reason, so according to the mystic, there is a category of more subtle truths which surpass the reach both of the senses and the reason but can be ascertained by an inner direct knowledge and direct experience. These truths are supersensuous but not the less real for that — they have immense results upon the consciousness changing its substance and movement, bringing especially deep peace and abiding joy, a great light of vision and knowledge, a possibility of the overcoming of the lower animal nature, vistas of a spiritual self-development which without them do not exist. A new outlook on things arises which brings with it, if fully pursued into its consequences, a great liberation, inner harmony, unification — many other possibilities besides. These things have been experienced, it is true, by a small minority of the human race, but still there has been a host of independent witnesses to them in all times, climes and conditions and numbered among them are some of the greatest intelligences of the past, some of the world's most remarkable figures. Must these possibilities be immediately condemned as chimaeras because they are not only beyond the average man in the street but also not easily seizable even by many cultivated intellects or because their method is more difficult than that of the ordinary sense or reason? If there is any truth in them, is not this possibility opened by them worth pursuing as opening a highest range to self-discovery and world-discovery by the human soul? At its best, taken as true, it must be that — at its lowest, taken as only a possibility, as all things attained by man have been only a possibility in their earlier stages, it is a great and may well be a most fruitful adventure.

*

I know it is the Russian explanation of the recent trend to spirituality and mysticism that it is a phenomenon of capitalist society in its decadence. But to read an economic cause, conscious or unconscious, into all phenomena of man's history is part of the

Bolshevik gospel born of the fallacy of Karl Marx. Man's nature is not so simple and one-chorded as all that — it has many lines and each line produces a need of his life. The spiritual or mystic line is one of them and man tries to satisfy it in various ways, by superstitions of all kinds, by ignorant religionism, by spiritism, demonism and what not, in his more enlightened parts by spiritual philosophy, the higher occultism and the rest, at his highest by the union with the All, the Eternal or the Divine. The tendency towards the search for spirituality began in Europe with a recoil from the nineteenth century's scientific materialism, a dissatisfaction with the pretended all-sufficiency of the reason and the intellect and a feeling out for something deeper. That was a pre-war phenomenon, and began when there was no menace of Communism and the capitalistic world was at its height of insolent success and triumph, and it came rather as a revolt against the materialistic bourgeois life and its ideals, not as an attempt to serve or sanctify it. It has been at once served and opposed by the post-war disillusionment — opposed because the post-war world has fallen back either on cynicism and the life of the senses or on movements like Fascism and Communism; served because with the deeper minds the dissatisfaction with the ideals of the past or the present, with all mental or vital or material solutions of the problem of life has increased and only the spiritual path is left. It is true that the European mind having little light on these things dallies with vital will-o'-the-wisps like spiritism or theosophy or falls back upon the old religionism; but the deeper minds of which I speak either pass by them or pass through them in search of a greater Light. I have had contact with many and the above tendencies are very clear. They come from all countries and it was only a minority who hailed from England or America. Russia is different — unlike the others it had lingered in mediaeval religionism and not passed through any period of revolt — so when the revolt came it was naturally anti-religious and atheistic. It is only when this phase is exhausted that Russian mysticism can revive and take not a narrow religious but the spiritual direction. It is true that mysticism *à revers*, turned upside down, has made Bolshevism and its endeavour a creed rather than a political theme and a search for the paradisal secret millennium on earth rather than the building of a purely social structure. But for the most part Russia is trying to do on the communistic basis all that nineteenth-century idealism hoped to get at — and failed — in the midst of or against an industrial competitive environment. Whether it will really succeed any better is for the future to decide — for at present it only keeps what it has got by a tension and violent control which is not over.

The Valley of the False Glimmer

One feels here [*in the letters of Krishnaprem*] a stream from the direct sources of Truth that one does not meet so often as one could desire. Here is a mind that can not only think but see — and not merely see the surfaces of things with which most intellectual thought goes on wrestling without end or definite issue and as if there were nothing else, but look into the core. The Tantriks have a phrase *paśyantī vāk* to describe one level of the Vak-Shakti, the seeing Word; here is *paśyantī buddhi*, a seeing Intelligence. It might be because the seer within has passed beyond thought into experience, but there are many who have a considerable wealth of experience without its clarifying their eye of thought to this extent; the soul feels, but the mind goes on with mixed and imperfect transcriptions, blurs and confusions in the idea. There must have been the gift of right vision lying ready in this nature.

It is an achievement to have got rid so rapidly and decisively of the shimmering mists and fogs which modern intellectualism takes for Light of Truth. The modern mind has so long and persistently wandered — and we with it — in that Valley of the False Glimmer that it is not easy for anyone to disperse its mists with the sunlight of clear vision so soon and entirely as has here been done. All that is said here about modern humanism and humanitarianism, the vain efforts of the sentimental idealist and the ineffective intellectual, about synthetic eclecticism and other kindred things is admirably clear-minded, it hits the target. It is not by these means that humanity can get that radical change of its ways of life which is yet becoming so imperative, but only by reaching the bedrock of Reality behind, — not through mere ideas and mental formations, but by a change of the consciousness, an inner and spiritual conversion. But that is a truth for which it would be difficult to get a hearing in the present noise of all kinds of many-voiced clamour and confusion and catastrophe.

A distinction, the distinction very keenly made here, between the plane of phenomenal process, of externalised Prakriti, and the plane of Divine Reality ranks among the first words of the inner wisdom. The turn given to it in these pages is not merely an ingenious explanation; it expresses very soundly one of the clear certainties you meet when you step across the border and look at the outer world from the standing-ground of the inner spiritual experience. The more you go inward or upward, the more the view of things changes and the outer knowledge Science organises takes its real and very limited place. Science, like most mental and external knowledge, gives you only truth of process. I would add that it cannot give you even the whole truth of process; for you seize some of the ponderables, but miss the all-important imponderables; you get, hardly even the how, but the conditions under which things happen in Nature. After all the triumphs and marvels of Science the explaining principle, the rationale, the significance of the whole is left as dark, as mysterious and even more mysterious than ever. The scheme it has built up of the evolution not only of this rich and vast and variegated material world, but of life and consciousness and mind and their workings out of a brute mass of electrons, identical and varied only in arrangement and number, is an irrational magic more baffling than any the most mystic imagination could conceive. Science in the end lands us in a paradox effectuated, an organised and rigidly determined accident, an impossibility that has somehow happened, — it has shown us a new, a material Maya, *aghaṭana-ghaṭana-paṭīyasī*, very clever at bringing about the impossible, a miracle that cannot logically be and yet somehow is there actual, irresistibly organised, but still irrational and inexplicable. And this is evidently because Science has missed something essential; it has seen and scrutinised what has happened and in a way how it happened, but it has shut its eyes to something that made this impossible possible, something that it is there to express. There is no fundamental significance in things if you miss the Divine Reality; for you remain embedded in a huge surface crust of manageable and utilisable appearance. It is the magic of the Magician you are trying to analyse, but only when you enter into the consciousness of the Magician himself can you begin to experience the true origination, significance and circles of the Lila. I say "begin" because the Divine Reality is not so simple that at the first touch you can know all of it or put it into a single formula; it is Infinite and opens before you an Infinite Knowledge to which all Science put together is a bagatelle. But still you do touch the essential, the eternal behind things and in the light of That all begins to be profoundly luminous, intimately intelligible.

I have once before told you what I think of the ineffective peckings of certain well-intentioned scientific minds on the surface — or apparent surface — of the spiritual Reality behind things and I need not elaborate it. More important is the prognostic of a greater danger coming in the new attack by the adversary, the sceptics, against the validity of spiritual and supraphysical experience, their new strategy of destruction by admitting and explaining it in their own sense. There may well be a strong ground for the apprehension; but I doubt whether, if these things are once admitted to scrutiny, the mind of humanity will long remain satisfied with explanations so ineptly superficial and external, explanations that explain nothing. If the defenders of religion take up an unsound position, easily capturable, when they affirm only the subjective validity of spiritual experience, the opponents also seem to me to be giving away without knowing it the gates of the materialistic stronghold by their consent at all to admit and examine spiritual and supraphysical experience. Their entrenchment in the physical field, their refusal to admit or even examine supraphysical things was their tower of strong safety; once it is abandoned, the human mind pressing towards something less negative, more helpfully positive will pass to it over the dead bodies of their theories and the broken debris of their annulling explanations and ingenious psychological labels. Another danger may then arise, — not of a final denial of the Truth, but the repetition in old or new forms of a past mistake, on one side some revival of blind fanatical obscurantist sectarian religionism, on the other a stumbling into the pits and quagmires of the vitalistic occult and the pseudo-spiritual — mistakes that made the whole real strength of the materialistic attack on the past and its credos. But these are phantasms that meet us always on the border line or in the intervening country between the material darkness and the perfect Splendour. In spite of all, the victory of the supreme Light even in the darkened earth-consciousness stands firm beyond as the one ultimate certitude.

Art, poetry, music are not Yoga, not in themselves things spiritual any more than philosophy either is a thing spiritual or science. There lurks here another curious incapacity of the modern intellect — its inability to distinguish between mind and spirit, its readiness to mistake mental, moral and aesthetic idealisms for spirituality and their inferior degrees for spiritual values. It is mere truth that the mental intuitions of the metaphysician or the poet for the most part fall far short of a concrete spiritual experience; they are distant flickers, shadowy reflections, not rays from the centre of Light. It is not less true that, looked at from the peaks, there is not much difference between the high mental eminences and the lower climbings of this external existence. All the energies of the Lila are equal in the sight from above, all are disguises of the Divine. But one has to add that all can be turned into a first means towards the realisation of the Divine. A philosophic statement about the Atman is a mental formula, not knowledge, not experience: yet sometimes the Divine takes it as a channel of touch; strangely, a barrier in the mind breaks down, something is seen, a profound change operated in some inner part, there enters into the ground of the nature something calm, equal, ineffable. One stands upon a mountain ridge and glimpses or mentally feels a wideness, a pervasiveness, a nameless Vast in Nature; then suddenly there comes the touch, a revelation, a flooding, the mental loses itself in the spiritual, one bears the first invasion of the Infinite. Or you stand before a temple of Kali beside a sacred river and see what? — a sculpture, a gracious piece of architecture, but in a moment mysteriously, unexpectedly there is instead a Presence, a Power, a Face that looks into yours, an inner sight in you has regarded the World-Mother. Similar touches can come too through art, music, poetry to their creator or to one who feels the shock of the word, the hidden significance of a form, a message in the sound that carries more perhaps than was consciously meant by the composer. All things in the Lila can turn into windows that open on the hidden Reality. Still so long as one is satisfied with looking through windows, the gain is only initial; one day one will have to take up the pilgrim's staff and start out to journey there where the Reality is for ever manifest and present. Still less can it be spiritually satisfying to remain with shadowy reflections; a search imposes itself for the Light which they strive to figure. But since this Reality and this Light are in ourselves no less than in some high region above the mortal plane, we can in the seeking for it use many of the figures and activities of Life; as one offers a flower, a prayer, an act to the Divine, one can offer too a created form of beauty, a song, a poem, an image, a strain of music, and gain through it a contact, a response or an experience. And when that divine Consciousness has been entered or when it grows within, then too its expression in life through these things is not excluded from Yoga; these creative activities can still have their place, though not intrinsically a greater place than any other that can be put to divine use and service. Art, poetry, music, as they are in their ordinary functioning, create mental and vital, not spiritual values; but they can be turned to a higher end, and then, like all things that are capable of linking our consciousness to the Divine, they are transmuted and become spiritual and can be admitted as part of a life of Yoga. All takes new values not from itself, but from the consciousness that uses it; for there is only one thing essential, needful, indispensable, to grow conscious of the Divine Reality and live in it and live it always.

*

The Intellect and Yoga

It seems to me that Krishnaprem has seen very clearly with his usual accuracy and his mind of sight, *paśyantī buddhi*, the truth about yourself and your sadhana. I think that you could not do better than accept his diagnosis and follow entirely his suggested treatment. Especially you should accept his assurance about the final result and give no room in your mind to any doubt on that point or any disposition to give up your own case as hopeless. To my eyes you seem to have been making very good progress in several directions and I have no doubt about your emerging from your difficulties into the light.

I do not think there is any real impasse, I mean no inescapable hold-up on the road from which you cannot get out; it only seems to be to you like that because of the difficulties created for you by your intellect. It is because of its preconceptions and fixed judgments that you cannot make the equation he considers needful for you. The intellect is full of things like that and cannot by itself see truly the things that reveal their meaning fully only in the light of psychic or spiritual truth; the equation he speaks of belongs to that order. The intellect is of use for perceiving material facts and their relations but even these it cannot be relied on to see rightly in their total reality; it may see rightly, but as often wrongly and always only partly and imperfectly. Moreover, as the modern psychologists have discovered, it sees them coloured by the hues supplied from its own individual temperament, its own psychological personality and from its own peculiar angle. It thinks it is seeing quite objectively and impersonally but it does not so see and cannot so see; a dog might as well try to escape from its own pursuing tail: the human intellect's thought and sight cannot escape from its own subjectivity and colouring personality. The deeper and more accurate view of things can be more easily attained by the mind of sight which Krishnaprem has so much developed, *paśyantī buddhi*. You may say that you have got only your intellect to help you with its judgments and opinions: but mental judgments and opinions — well, they are always personal things and one can never be perfectly sure that one's own are correct and the judgments and opinions of others which differ widely or even diametrically from one's own are mistaken. But you need not be always solely dependent on this fallible and limited instrument; for, although you have not developed the mind of sight as Krishnaprem has done, it is certainly there. I have always seen that when you have been in a psychic condition with bhakti or the higher part of the mind and the vital uppermost in you this mind of sight has come out and your ideas, feelings and judgments have become remarkably clear, right and often luminous. This has only to develop, you will then be able to see more clearly what Krishnaprem sees and many of your difficulties will disappear and the equation you want to make may become clear to you.

As for surrender, you already have it initially in your will to serve for the sake of service without claiming reward or success and without attachment to wealth or fame. If you extend that attitude into your whole sadhana, then realisation is sure. In any case, you should throw away all obsession of the sense of failure or the impossibility of success in your sadhana. Krishnaprem is surely right in telling you, when the Grace is on you and what he names as the Radhashakti is there to give you its unseen help, that the success of your sadhana is sure and the realisation will come. The impasse is a temporary block; your trust will become complete and the road to realisation clear.

Chapter Two
Doubt and Faith

Doubt and Yoga

As to doubts and argumentative answers to them I have long given up the practice as I found it perfectly useless. Yoga is not a field for intellectual argument or dissertation. It is not by the exercise of the logical or the debating mind that one can arrive at a true understanding of Yoga or follow it. A doubting spirit, "honest doubt" and the claim that the intellect shall be satisfied and be made the judge on every point is all very well in the field of mental action outside. But Yoga is not a mental field, the consciousness which has to be established is not a mental, logical or debating consciousness — it is even laid down by Yoga that unless and until the mind is stilled, including the intellectual or logical mind, and opens itself in quietude or silence to a higher and deeper consciousness, vision and knowledge, sadhana cannot reach its goal. For the same reason an unquestioning openness to the Guru is demanded in the Indian spiritual tradition; as for blame, criticism and attack on the Guru, it was considered reprehensible and the surest possible obstacle to sadhana.

If the spirit of doubt could be overcome by meeting it with arguments, there might be something in the demand for its removal by satisfaction through logic. But the spirit of doubt doubts for its own sake, for the sake of doubt; it simply uses the mind as its instrument for its particular dharma and this not the least when that mind thinks it is seeking sincerely for a solution of its honest and irrepressible doubts. Mental positions always differ, moreover, and it is well known that people can argue for ever without one convincing the other. To go on perpetually answering persistent and always recurring doubts such as for long have filled this Asram and obstructed the sadhana, is merely to frustrate the aim of the Yoga and go against its central principle with no spiritual or other gain whatever. If anybody gets over his fundamental doubts, it is by the growth of the psychic in him or by an enlargement of his consciousness, not otherwise. Questions which arise from the spirit of enquiry, not aggressive or self-assertive, but as a part of a hunger for knowledge can be answered, but the "spirit of doubt" is insatiable and unappeasable.

*

I have started writing about Doubt, but even in doing so I am afflicted by the "doubt" whether any amount of writing or of anything else can ever persuade the eternal doubt in man which is the penalty of his native ignorance. In the first place, to write adequately would mean anything from 60 to 600 pages, but not even 6000 convincing pages would convince Doubt. For Doubt exists for its own sake; its very function is to doubt always and, even when convinced, to go on doubting still; it is only to persuade its entertainer to give it board and lodging that it pretends to be an honest truth-seeker. This is a lesson I have learnt from the experience both of my own mind and of the minds of others; the only way to get rid of Doubt is to take Discrimination as one's detector of truth and falsehood and under its guard to open the door freely and courageously to experience.

All the same I have started writing, but I will begin not with Doubt but with the demand for the Divine as a concrete certitude, quite as concrete as any physical phenomenon caught by the senses. Now, certainly, the Divine must be such a certitude not only as concrete but more concrete than anything sensed by ear or eye or touch in the world of Matter; but it is a certitude not of mental thought but of essential experience. When the Peace of God descends on you, when the Divine Presence is there within you, when the Ananda rushes on you like a sea, when you are driven like a leaf before the wind by the breath of the Divine Force, when Love flows out from you on all creation, when Divine Knowledge floods you with a Light which illumines and transforms in a moment all that was before dark, sorrowful and obscure, when all that is becomes part of the One Reality, when the Reality is all around you, you feel at once by the spiritual contact, by the inner vision, by the illumined and seeing thought, by the vital sensation and even by the very physical sense, everywhere you see, hear, touch only the Divine. Then you can much less doubt it or deny it than you can deny or doubt daylight or air or the sun in heaven — for of these physical things you cannot be sure that they are what your senses represent them to be; but in the concrete experience of the Divine, doubt is impossible.

As to permanence, you cannot expect permanence of the initial spiritual experiences from the beginning — only a few have that and even for them the high intensity is not always there; for most the experience comes and then draws back behind the veil waiting for the human parts to be prepared and made ready to bear and hold, first, its increase and then its permanence. But to doubt it on that account would be irrational in the extreme. One does not doubt the existence of air because a strong wind is not always blowing or of sunlight because night intervenes between dawn and dusk. The difficulty lies in the normal human consciousness to which spiritual experience comes as something abnormal and is in fact supernormal. This weak limited normality finds it difficult at first even to get any touch of that greater and intenser supernormal or it gets it diluted into its own duller stuff of mental or vital experience, and, when the spiritual does come in its own overwhelming power, very often it cannot bear or, if it bears, cannot hold and keep it. Still once a decisive breach has been made in the walls built by the mind against the Infinite, the breach widens, sometimes slowly, sometimes swiftly, until there is no wall any longer, and then there is the Permanence.

But the decisive experiences cannot be brought, the permanence of a new state of consciousness in which they will be normal cannot be secured if the mind is always interposing its own reservations, prejudgments, ignorant formulas or if it insists on arriving at the Divine certitude as it would at the quite relative truth of a mental conclusion, by reasoning, doubt, enquiry and all the other paraphernalia of Ignorance feeling and fumbling around after Knowledge; these greater things can only be brought by the progressive opening of a consciousness quieted and turned steadily towards spiritual experience. If you ask why the Divine has so disposed it on this highly inconvenient basis, it is a futile question, — for this is nothing else than a psychological necessity imposed by the very nature of things. It is so because these experiences of the Divine are not mental constructions, not vital movements; they are essential things, not things merely thought but realities, not mentally felt but felt in our very underlying substance and essence. No doubt, the mind is always there and can intervene; it can and does have its own type of mentalisings about the Divine, thoughts, beliefs, emotions, mental reflections of spiritual Truth, even a kind of mental realisation which repeats as well as it can some kind of figure of the higher Truth, and all this is not without value, but it is not concrete, intimate and indubitable. Mind by itself is incapable of ultimate certitude; whatever it believes, it can doubt; whatever it can affirm, it can deny; whatever it gets hold of, it can and does let go. That, if you like, is its freedom, noble right, privilege; it may be all you can say in its praise, but by these methods of mind you cannot hope (outside the realm of physical phenomena and hardly even there) to arrive at anything you can call an ultimate certitude. It is for this very compelling reason that mentalising or enquiring about the Divine cannot by its own right bring the Divine. If the consciousness is always busy with small mental movements, — especially accompanied, as they usually are, by a host of vital movements, desires, prepossessions and all else that vitiates human thinking, even apart from the native insufficiency of reason, — what room can there be for a new order of knowledge, for fundamental experiences or for those deep and stupendous upsurgings or descents of the Spirit? It is indeed possible for the mind in the midst of its activities to be suddenly taken by surprise, overwhelmed, swept aside while all is flooded with a sudden inrush of spiritual experience. But if afterwards it begins questioning, doubting, theorising, surmising what this might be and whether it is true or not, what else can the spiritual Power do but retire and wait for the bubbles of the mind to cease?

I would ask one simple question of those who would make

the intellectual mind the standard and judge of spiritual experience. Is the Divine something less than Mind or is It something greater? Is mental consciousness with its groping enquiry, endless argument, unquenchable doubt, stiff and unplastic logic something superior or even equal to the Divine Consciousness or is it something inferior in its action and status? If it is greater, then there is no reason to seek after the Divine. If it is equal, then spiritual experience is quite superfluous. But if it is inferior, how can it challenge, judge, make the Divine stand as an accused or a witness before its tribunal, summon It to appear as a candidate for admission before a Board of Examiners or pin It like an insect under its examining microscope? Can the vital animal hold up as infallible the standard of its vital instincts, associations and impulses and judge, interpret and fathom by it the mind of man? It cannot because man's mind is a greater power working in a wider, more complex way which the animal vital consciousness cannot follow. Is it so difficult to see similarly that the Divine Consciousness must be something infinitely wider, more complex than human mind, filled with greater powers and lights, moving in a way which mere Mind cannot judge, interpret or fathom by the standard of its fallible Reason and limited mental half-knowledge? The simple fact is there that spirit and mind are not the same thing and that it is the spiritual consciousness into which the Yogin has to enter (in all this I am not in the least speaking of the supermind) if he wants to be in permanent contact or union with the Divine. It is not then a freak of the Divine or a tyranny to insist on the mind recognising its limitations, quieting itself, giving up its demands and opening and surrendering to a greater Light than it can find on its own obscurer level.

This does not mean that the Mind has no place at all in the spiritual life; but it means that it cannot be even the main instrument, much less the authority to whose judgment all must submit itself, including the Divine. Mind must learn from the greater Consciousness it is approaching and not impose its own standards on it; it has to receive illumination, open to a higher Truth, admit a greater Power that does not work according to mental canons, surrender itself and allow its half-light half-darkness to be flooded from above till where it was blind it can see, where it was deaf it can hear, where it was insensible it can feel, and where it was baffled, uncertain, questioning, disappointed it can have joy, fulfilment, certitude and peace.

This is the position on which Yoga stands, a position based upon constant experience since men began to seek after the Divine. If it is not true, then there is no truth in Yoga and no necessity for Yoga. If it is true, then it is on that basis, from the standpoint of the necessity of this greater consciousness that we can see whether Doubt is of any utility for the spiritual life. To believe anything and everything is certainly not demanded of the spiritual seeker; such a promiscuous and imbecile credulity would be not only unintellectual, but in the last degree unspiritual. At every moment of the spiritual life until one has got fully into that higher Light, one has to be on one's guard and to be able to distinguish spiritual truth from pseudo-spiritual imitations of it or substitutes for it set up by the mind and by vital desire. A power to distinguish between truth of the Divine and the lies of the Asura is a cardinal necessity for Yoga. The question is whether that can best be done by the negative and destructive method of doubt, which often kills falsehood but rejects truth too with the same impartial blow, or a more positive, helpful and luminously searching power can be found which is not compelled by its inherent ignorance to meet truth and falsehood alike with the stiletto of doubt and the bludgeon of denial. An indiscriminateness of mental belief is not the teaching of spirituality or of Yoga; the faith of which it speaks is not a crude mental belief but the fidelity of the soul to the guiding light within it, a fidelity which has to remain firm till the light leads it into knowledge.

*

As for the doubts of which you have written, I cannot write much today for obvious reasons and in any case writing is not the remedy, though it may help and encourage — for these doubts rise not from the intellect but from the vital mind which sees things according to its condition and mood and needs something else than what the mind asks for to satisfy it. It is perfectly true that these reasonings have no force when the vital is in its true poise of love or joy or active and creative power, and when the vital is depressed then it is hard and seems sometimes impossible, so long as the depression is there, to surmount the trouble. But still the clouds do not last for ever — and even one has a certain power in the mind to shorten the period of these clouds, to reject and dissipate them and not to allow them to remain until they disappear in the course of nature.

By all means use the method of japa and bhakti. I have never insisted on your using the method of dry or hard tapasya — it was some idea or feeling in your own mind that made you lay so much stress on it. There are some to whom it is natural and necessary for a time, but each ought to move in his own way and there is no one rule for all — even if the objective is and must be the same, contact and union and opening to the Divine.

In the end these doubts and depressions and despairs must cease. Where the call of the soul perseveres, the response of the Divine must come.

Na hi kalyāṇakṛt kaścid durgatiṁ tāta gacchati.[1]

*

There is no reason why your present condition should be more than a passing phase, unless you yourself choose that it should be otherwise. If it is the "imposition" of the rule of Karmayoga on you that is the cause of your doubts, it is unjustified, because there is no imposition or compulsion, and you need only work if you wish to do so; if you think that by sitting in meditation only you will best progress, you are free to do it.

I did not answer to your statement of your doubts, because they seem to repose on certain statements and suppositions about myself (which are quite inaccurate) and I do not usually care to enter into personal matters. I do not know who gave you this information, e.g. that I have not done my sadhana in full

---

[1] *"Never does anyone who practises good, O beloved one, come to woe."* Gita 6.40. — Ed.

heat of work but have had to lead a very quiet and extremely retired life all the time. I am afraid, whoever he is, he knows nothing about either my past life or my present life or my Yoga. As for the ground put forward that there is no precedent for progress during work or for such a method, nor have people in the past been able to do it, it amounts to a statement that there has never been any such thing as Karmayoga or a Karmayogi, that the Gita was never written or was not founded on any truth of experience and that no Yogi ever did works as part of his sadhana. There seems to be some exaggeration in these statements from whatever quarter they may have been breathed into your mind. I have never said that the Supermind is working in the sadhaks here; I have said the contrary in many letters.

I say so much however only to indicate the quite gratuitous character of the affirmations on which these doubts are founded — from wherever they may come. But a detailed answer is hardly necessary; for meditation is not forbidden in this sadhana. Except for those who prefer to go through work alone, meditation and works and bhakti each in its place make up the foundations of the sadhana. But you are free to follow the way of meditation alone, as some others do, if you think that better.

*

I agree with most of what Krishnaprem says, though one or two things I would put from a different angle. Your reasonings about faith and doubt have been of a rather extravagant kind because they came to this that one must either doubt everything or believe everything however absurd that anybody says. I have repeatedly told you that there is not only room for discrimination in Yoga, but a need for it at every step — otherwise you will get lost in the jungle of things that are not spiritual — as for instance the tangle of what I call the intermediate zone. I have also told you that you are not asked to believe everything told you by anybody and that there is no call to put faith in all the miraculous things narrated about Bijoykrishna or another. That, I have said, is a question not of faith but of mental belief — and faith is not mental belief in outward facts, but an intuition of the inner being about spiritual things. Krishnaprem means the same thing when he says that faith is the light sent down by the higher to the lower personality. As for the epithet "blind" used by Ramakrishna, it means as I said, not ignorantly credulous, but untroubled by the questionings of the intellect and unshaken by outward appearances of fact. E.g. one has faith in the Divine even though the fact seems to be that the world here or at least the human world is driven by undivine forces. One has faith in the Guru even when he uses methods that your intellect cannot grasp or approves things as true of which you have yet no experience (for if his knowledge and experience are not greater than yours, why did you choose him as a Guru?). One has faith in the Path leading to the goal even when the goal is very far off and the way covered by mist and cloud and smitten repeatedly by the thunderbolt. And so on. Even in worldly things man can do nothing great if he has not faith — in the spiritual realm it is still more indispensable. But this faith depends not on ignorant credulity, but on a light that burns inside though not seen by the eyes of the outward mind, a knowledge within that has not yet taken the form of an outer knowledge.

One thing however — I make a distinction between doubt and discrimination. If doubt meant a discriminant questioning as to what might be truth of this or that matter, it would be a part of discrimination and quite admissible; but what is usually meant now by doubt is a negation positive and peremptory which does not stop to investigate, to consider in the light, to try, to inquire, but says at once, "Oh, no, I am never going to take that as possibly true." That kind of doubt may be very useful in ordinary life, it may be practically useful in battering down established things or established ideas or in certain kinds of external controversy to undermine a position that is too dogmatically positive; but I do not think it is of any positive use in matters even of intellectual inquiry. There is nothing it can do there that impartial discrimination cannot do much better. In spiritual matters discrimination has a huge place, but negating doubt simply stops the path to Truth with its placard "No entry" or its dogmatic "This far and no farther."

As for the intellect it is indispensable to man up to a certain point; after that it becomes an inferior instrument and often misleading and obstructive. It is what I meant when I wrote, "Reason was the helper; reason is the bar."[2] Intellect has done many things for man; it has helped to raise him high above the animal; at its best it has opened a first view on all great fields of knowledge. But it cannot go beyond that; it cannot get at Truth itself, only at some reflections, forms, representations of it. I myself cannot remember to have ever arrived at anything in the spiritual field by the power of the intellect — I have used it only to help the expression of what I have known and experienced, but even there it is only certain forms that it provided, they were used by another Light and a larger Mind than the intellect. When the intellect tried to decide things in this field, it always delayed matters. I suppose what it can do sometimes is to stir up the mind, plough it or prepare — but the knowledge comes only when one gets another higher than intellectual opening. Even in Mind itself there are things higher than the intellect, ranges of activity that exceed it. Spiritual knowledge is easier to those than to the reasoning intelligence.

*

The abnormal abounds in this physical world; the supernormal is there also. In these matters, apart from any question of faith, any truly rational man with a free mind (not tied up like the rationalist's or so-called freethinker's at every point with triple cords of *a priori* irrational disbelief) must not cry out at once, "Humbug! falsehood!", but suspend judgment until he has the necessary experience and knowledge. To deny in ignorance is no better than to affirm in ignorance.

*

As for the faith-doubt question you evidently give to the word faith a sense and a scope I do not attach to it. I will have to

---

[2] *Sri Aurobindo*, Essays in Philosophy and Yoga, *volume 13 of* THE COMPLETE WORKS OF SRI AUROBINDO, *p. 199.*

write not one but several letters to clear up the position. It seems to me that you mean by faith a mental belief in an alleged fact put before the mind and senses in the doubtful form of an unsupported asseveration. I mean by it a dynamic intuitive conviction in the inner being of the truth of supersensible things which cannot be proved by any physical evidence but which are a subject of experience. My point is that this faith is a most desirable preliminary (if not absolutely indispensable — for there can be cases of experience not preceded by faith) to the desired experience. If I insist so much on faith — but even less on positive faith than on the throwing away of *a priori* doubt and denial — it is because I find that this doubt and denial have become an instrument in the hands of the obstructive forces and clog your steps whenever I try to push you to an advance. If you can't or won't get rid of it, ("won't" out of respect for the reason and fear of being led into believing things that are not true, "can't" because of contrary experience) then I shall have to manage for you without it, only it makes a difficult instead of a straight and comparatively easy process.

Why I call the materialist's denial an *a priori* denial is because he refuses even to consider or examine what he denies, but *starts* by denying it, like Leonard Woolf with his "quack quack", on the ground that it contradicts his own theories, so it can't be true. On the other hand the belief in the Divine and the Grace and Yoga and the Guru etc. is not *a priori*, because it rests on a great mass of human experience which has been accumulating through the centuries and millenniums as well as the personal intuitive perception. Therefore it is an intuitive perception which has been confirmed by the experience of hundreds and thousands of those who have tested it before me.

*

Go on the path of Yoga without doubt of the ultimate success — surely you cannot fail! Doubts — they are nothing; keep the fire of aspiration burning, it is that that conquers.

Faith in Spiritual Things

I do not ask "undiscriminating faith" from anyone, all I ask is fundamental faith, safeguarded by a patient and quiet discrimination — because it is these that are proper to the consciousness of a spiritual seeker and it is these that I have myself used and found that they removed all necessity for the quite gratuitous dilemma of "either you must doubt everything supraphysical or be entirely credulous", which is the stock-in-trade of the materialist argument. Your doubt, I see, constantly returns to the charge with a repetition of this formula in spite of my denial — which supports my assertion that Doubt cannot be convinced, because by its very nature it does not want to be convinced; it keeps repeating the old ground always.

*

X upbraids you for losing your reason in blind faith, but what is his view of things except a reasoned faith; you believe according to your faith, which is quite natural, he believes according to his opinion, which is natural also but no better so far as the likelihood of getting at the true truth of things is in question.... Each reasons according to his view of things, his opinion, that is, his mental constitution and mental preference. So what's the use of running down faith which after all gives something to hold on to amidst the contradictions of an enigmatic universe? If one can get at a knowledge that knows, it is another matter; but so long as we have only an ignorance that argues, well, there is a place still left for faith — even, faith may be a glint from the knowledge that knows, however far off, and meanwhile there is not the slightest doubt that it helps to get things done. There's a bit of reasoning for you! just like all other reasoning too, convincing to the convinced, but not to the unconvincible, i.e., who don't agree with the ground upon which the reasoning dances. Logic after all is only a measured dance of the mind, nothing else.

*

Your dream was certainly not moonshine; it was an inner experience and can be given its full value. As for the other questions, they are full of complications and I do not feel armed to cut the Gordian knot with a sentence. Certainly, you are right to follow directly the truth for yourself and need not accept X's or anybody else's proposition or solution. Man needs both faith and reason so long as he has not reached a surer insight and greater knowledge. Without faith he cannot walk certainly on any road, and without reason he might very well be walking, even with the staff of faith to support him, in the darkness. X himself founds his faith, if not on reason, yet on reasons; and the rationalist, the rationaliser or the reasoner must have some faith even if it be faith only in reason itself as sufficient and authoritative, just as the believer has faith in his faith as sufficient and authoritative. Yet both are capable of error, as they must be since both are instruments of the human mind whose nature is to err, and they share that mind's limitations. Each must walk by the light he has even though there are dark spots in which he stumbles.

*

The faith in spiritual things that is asked of the sadhak is not an ignorant but a luminous faith, a faith in light and not in darkness. It is called blind by the sceptical intellect because it refuses to be guided by outer appearances or seeming facts, — for it looks to the truth behind, — and does not walk on the crutches of proof and evidence. It is an intuition, — an intuition not only waiting for experience to justify it, but leading towards experience. If I believe in self-healing, I shall after a time find out the way to heal myself — if I have faith in transformation, I can end by laying my hand on and unravelling the whole process of transformation. But if I begin with doubt and go on with more doubt, how far am I likely to go on the journey?

*

The faith is there, not in your mind, not in your vital, but in your psychic being. It was this faith that flung you out of the world and brought you to Pondicherry; it is this faith that keeps you to what the soul wills and refuses to go back on what it has decided. Even the mind's questionings have been a groping after some justification by which it can get an excuse for believing in spite of its difficulties. The vital's eagerness and its vairagya are shadows of this faith, forms which it has taken in order to keep the vital from giving up in spite of the pressure of despondency and struggle. Even in the mind and vital of the man of strongest mental and vital faith there are periods when the knowledge in the psychic gets covered up — but it persists behind the veil. In you the eclipse has been strong and long because, owing to certain mental and vital formations, the assent of the mind and vital got clouded over and could only take negative forms. But there is always the knowledge or intuition in the soul that started you on the way. I have been pressing on you the need of faith because the assent has again to take a positive form so as to give free way to the Divine Force; but the persistent drive in the soul (which is a hidden and externally suppressed faith) is itself sufficient to warrant the expectation of the Grace to come.

*

The sense of calm and light and divine guidance can never be an illusion. It is the dark state which is the state of Ignorance, of Maya — if faith fails then, it is because the darkness of the Ignorance shuts the mind to the Truth, obscuring the buddhi. What is thought when the buddhi is obscured cannot be the Truth; it is not darkness but the Light that brings Truth. Therefore you must take what you feel when you are in the light to be true, not what you feel when you are in the darkness.

Chapter Three

Philosophical Thought and Yoga

Metaphysical Thinkers, East and West

European metaphysical thought — even in those thinkers who try to prove or explain the existence and nature of God or of the Absolute — does not in its method and result go beyond the intellect. But the intellect is incapable of knowing the supreme Truth; it can only range about seeking for Truth and catching fragmentary representations of it, not the thing itself, and trying to piece them together. Mind cannot arrive at Truth; it can only make some constructed figure that tries to represent it or a combination of figures. At the end of European thought, therefore, there must always be Agnosticism, declared or implicit. Intellect, if it goes sincerely to its own end, has to return and give this report: "I cannot know; there is or at least it seems to me that there may be or even must be Something beyond, some ultimate Reality, but about its truth I can only speculate; it is either unknowable or cannot be known by me." Or, if it has received some light on the way from what is beyond it, it can say too: "There is perhaps a consciousness beyond Mind, for I seem to catch glimpses of it and even to get intimations from it. If that is in touch with the Beyond or if it is itself the consciousness of the Beyond and you can find some way to reach it, then this Something can be known but not otherwise."

Any seeking of the supreme Truth through intellect alone must end either in Agnosticism of this kind or else in some intellectual system or mind-constructed formula. There have been hundreds of these systems and formulas and there can be hundreds more, but none can be definitive. Each may have its value for the mind, and different systems with their contrary conclusions can have an equal appeal to intelligences of equal power and competence. All this labour of speculation has its utility in training the human mind and helping to keep before it the idea of Something beyond and Ultimate towards which it must turn. But the intellectual Reason can only point vaguely or feel gropingly towards it or try to indicate partial and even conflicting aspects of its manifestation here; it cannot enter into and know it. As long as we remain in the domain of the intellect only, an impartial pondering over all that has been thought and sought after, a constant throwing up of ideas, of all the possible ideas, and the formation of this or that philosophical belief, opinion or conclusion is all that can be done. This kind of disinterested search after Truth would be the only possible attitude for any wide and plastic intelligence. But any conclusion so arrived at would be only speculative; it could have no spiritual value; it would not give the decisive experience or the spiritual certitude for which the soul is seeking. If the intellect is our highest possible instrument and there is no other means of arriving at supraphysical Truth, then a wise and large Agnosticism must be our ultimate attitude. Things in the manifestation may be known to some degree, but the Supreme and all that is beyond the Mind must remain for ever unknowable.

It is only if there is a greater consciousness beyond Mind and that consciousness is accessible to us that we can know and enter into the ultimate Reality. Intellectual speculation, logical reasoning as to whether there is or is not such a greater consciousness cannot carry us very far. What we need is a way to get the experience of it, to reach it, enter into it, live in it. If we can get that, intellectual speculation and reasoning must fall necessarily into a very secondary place and even lose their reason for existence. Philosophy, intellectual expression of the Truth may remain, but mainly as a means of expressing this greater discovery and as much of its contents as can at all be expressed in mental terms to those who still live in the mental intelligence.

This, you will see, answers your point about the Western thinkers, Bradley and others, who have arrived through intellectual thinking at the idea of an "Other beyond Thought" or have even, like Bradley, tried to express their conclusions about it in terms that recall some of the expressions in the *Arya*. The idea in itself is not new; it is as old as the Vedas. It was repeated in other forms in Buddhism, Christian Gnosticism, Sufism. Originally, it was not discovered by intellectual speculation, but by the mystics following an inner spiritual discipline. When, somewhere between the seventh and fifth centuries B.C., men began both in the East and West to intellectualise knowledge, this Truth survived in the East; in the West, where the intellect began to be accepted as the sole or highest instrument for the discovery of Truth, it began to fade. But still it has there too tried constantly to return; the Neo-Platonists brought it back, and now, it appears, the Neo-Hegelians and others (e.g., the Russian Ouspensky and one or two German thinkers, I believe) seem to be reaching after it. But still there is a difference.

In the East, especially in India, the metaphysical thinkers have tried, as in the West, to determine the nature of the highest Truth by the intellect. But, in the first place, they have not given mental thinking the supreme rank as an instrument in the discovery of Truth, but only a secondary status. The first rank has always been given to spiritual intuition and illumination and spiritual experience; an intellectual conclusion that contradicts this supreme authority is held invalid. Secondly, each philosophy has armed itself with a practical way of reaching to the supreme state of consciousness, so that even when one begins with Thought, the aim is to arrive at a consciousness beyond mental thinking. Each philosophical founder (as also those who continued his work or school) has been a metaphysical thinker doubled with a Yogi. Those who were only philosophic intellectuals were respected for their learning but never took rank as truth discoverers. And the philosophies that lacked a sufficiently powerful means of spiritual experience died out and became things of the past because they were not dynamic for spiritual discovery and realisation.

In the West it was just the opposite that came to pass. Thought, intellect, the logical reason came to be regarded more and more as the highest means and even the highest end; in philosophy, Thought is the be-all and the end-all. It is by intellectual thinking and speculation that the truth is to be discovered; even spiritual experience has been summoned to pass the tests of the intellect, if it is to be held valid — just the reverse of the Indian position. Even those who see that mental Thought must be overpassed and admit a supramental "Other", do not seem to escape from the feeling that it must be through mental Thought, sublimating and transmuting itself, that this other Truth must be reached and made to take the place of the mental limitation and ignorance. And again Western thought has ceased to be dynamic; it has sought after a theory of things, not after realisation. It was still dynamic amongst the ancient Greeks, but for moral and aesthetic rather than spiritual ends. Later on, it became yet more purely intellectual and academic; it became intellectual speculation only without any practical ways and means for the attainment of the Truth by spiritual experiment, spiritual discovery, a spiritual transformation. If there were not this difference, there would be no reason for seekers like yourself to turn to the East for guidance; for in the purely intellectual field, the Western thinkers are as competent as any Eastern sage. It is the spiritual way, the road that leads beyond the intellectual levels, the passage from the outer being to the inmost Self, which has been lost by the over-intellectuality of the mind of Europe.

In the extracts you have sent me from Bradley and Joachim, it is still the intellect thinking about what is beyond itself and coming to an intellectual, a reasoned speculative conclusion about it. It is not dynamic for the change which it attempts to describe. If these writers were expressing in mental terms some realisation, even mental, some intuitive experience of this "Other than Thought", then one ready for it might feel it through the veil of the language they use and himself draw near to the same experience. Or if, having reached the intellectual conclusion, they had passed on to the spiritual realisation, finding the way or following one already found, then in pursuing their thought, one might be preparing oneself for the same transition. But there is nothing of the kind in all this strenuous thinking. It remains in the domain of the intellect and in that domain it is no doubt admirable; but it does not become dynamic for spiritual experience.

It is not by "thinking out" the entire reality, but by a change of consciousness that one can pass from the ignorance to the Knowledge — the Knowledge by which we become what we know. To pass from the external to a direct and intimate inner consciousness; to widen consciousness out of the limits of the ego and the body; to heighten it by an inner will and aspiration and opening to the Light till it passes in its ascent beyond Mind; to bring down a descent of the supramental Divine through self-giving and surrender with a consequent transformation of mind, life and body — this is the *integral* way to the Truth.[1] It is this that we call the Truth here and aim at in our Yoga.

World-Circumstances and the Divine

The whole world knows, spiritual thinker and materialist alike, that this world for the created or naturally evolved being in the ignorance or the inconscience of Nature is neither a bed of roses nor a path of joyous Light. It is a difficult journey, a battle and struggle, an often painful and chequered growth, a life besieged by obscurity, falsehood and suffering. It has its mental, vital, physical joys and pleasures, but these bring only a transient taste — which yet the vital self is unwilling to forego — and they end in distaste, fatigue or disillusionment. What then? To say the Divine does not exist is easy, but it leads nowhere — it leaves you where you are with no prospect or issue — neither Russell nor any materialist can tell you where you are going or even where you ought to go. The Divine does not manifest himself so as to be recognised in the external world-circumstances — admittedly so. These are not the works of an irresponsible autocrat somewhere — they are the circumstances of a working out of Forces according to a certain nature of being, one might say a certain proposition or problem of being into which we have all really consented to enter and cooperate. The work is painful,

---

[1] I have said that the idea of the Supermind was already in existence from ancient times. There was in India and elsewhere the attempt to reach it by rising to it; but what was missed was the way to make it integral for the life and to bring it down for transformation of the whole nature, even of the physical nature.

dubious, its vicissitudes impossible to forecast? There are either of two possibilities then, — to get out of it into Nirvana by the Buddhist or illusionist way or to get inside oneself and find the Divine there since he is not discoverable on the surface. For those who have made the attempt, and there were not a few but hundreds and thousands, have testified through the ages that he is there and that is why there exists the Yoga. It takes long? The Divine is concealed behind a thick veil of his Maya and does not answer at once or at any early stage to our call? Or he gives only a glimpse uncertain and passing and then withdraws and waits for us to be ready? But if the Divine has any value, is it not worth some trouble, time and labour to follow after him and must we insist on having him without any training or sacrifice or suffering or trouble? It is surely irrational to make a demand of such a nature. It is positive that we have to get inside, behind the veil, to find him, — it is only then that we can see him outside and the intellect be not so much convinced as forced to admit his presence by experience — just as when a man sees what he has denied and can no longer deny it. But for that the means must be accepted and the persistence in the will and patience in the labour.

*

I cannot very well answer the strictures of Russell or Vivekananda (in one of his moods), for the conception of the Divine as an external omnipotent Power who has created the world and governs it like an absolute and arbitrary monarch, the Christian or Semitic conception, the popular religious notion, has never been mine; it contradicts too much my seeing and experience during thirty years of sadhana. When I speak of the Divine Will I mean something different, — something that has descended here into an evolutionary world of Ignorance, standing at the back of things, pressing on the Darkness with its Light, leading things presently towards the best possible in the conditions of a world of Ignorance and leading it eventually towards a descent of a greater Power of the Divine which will be not an omnipotence held back and conditioned by the Law of the world as it is, but a full action and therefore bringing the reign of light, peace, harmony, joy, love, beauty and Ananda, for these are the Divine Nature. The Divine Grace is there, ready to act at every moment, but it manifests as one grows out of the Law of the Ignorance into the Law of Light and it is meant, not as an arbitrary caprice, however miraculous often its intervention, but as a help in that growth and a Light that leads and eventually delivers. If we take the facts of the world as they are and the facts of spiritual experience as a whole, neither of which can be denied or neglected, then I do not see what other Divine there can be. This Divine may lead us often through darkness, because the darkness is there in us and around us, but it is to the Light he is leading and not to anything else.

Intellectual Expression of Spiritual Experience

In reference to what Prof. Sorley has written on *The Riddle of This World*,[2] the book of course was not meant as a full or direct statement of my thought and, as it was written to sadhaks mostly, many things were taken for granted there. Most of the major ideas — e.g. Overmind — were left without elucidation. To make the ideas implied clear to the intellect, they must be put with precision in an intellectual form — so far as that is possible with supra-intellectual things. What is written in the book can be clear to those who have gone far enough in experience, but for most it can only be suggestive.

 I do not think, however, that the statement of supra-intellectual things necessarily involves a making of distinctions in the terms of the intellect. For, fundamentally, it is not an expression of ideas arrived at by speculative thinking. One has to arrive at spiritual knowledge through experience and a consciousness of things which arises directly out of that experience or else underlies or is involved in it. This kind of knowledge, then, is fundamentally a consciousness and not a

---

[2] *A small book of letters by Sri Aurobindo in which he discusses various questions of philosophy and spiritual experience. It was first published in 1933. — Ed.*

thought or formulated idea. For instance, my first major experience — radical and overwhelming, though not, as it turned out, final and exhaustive — came after and by the exclusion and silencing of all thought — there was, first, what might be called a spiritually substantial or concrete consciousness of stillness and silence, then the awareness of some sole and supreme Reality in whose presence things existed only as forms, but forms not at all substantial or real or concrete; but this was all apparent to a spiritual perception and essential and impersonal sense and there was not the least concept or idea of reality or unreality or any other notion, for all concept or idea was hushed or rather entirely absent in the absolute stillness. These things were known directly through the pure consciousness and not through the mind, so there was no need of concepts or words or names. At the same time this fundamental character of spiritual experience is not absolutely limitative; it can do without thought, but it can do with thought also. Of course, the first idea of the mind would be that the resort to thought brings one back at once to the domain of the intellect — and at first and for a long time it may be so; but it is not my experience that this is unavoidable. It happens so when one tries to make an intellectual statement of what one has experienced; but there is another kind of thought that springs out as if it were a body or form of the experience or of the consciousness involved in it — or of a part of that consciousness — and this does not seem to me to be intellectual in its character. It has another light, another power in it, a sense within the sense. It is very clearly so with those thoughts that come without the need of words to embody them, thoughts that are of the nature of a direct seeing in the consciousness, even a kind of intimate sense or contact formulating itself into a precise expression of its awareness (I hope this is not too mystic or unintelligible); but it might be said that directly the thoughts turn into words they belong to the kingdom of intellect — for words are a coinage of the intellect. But is it so really — or inevitably? It has always seemed to me that words came originally from somewhere else than the thinking mind, although the thinking mind secured hold

Philosophical Thought and Yoga

of them, turned them to its use and coined them freely for its purposes. But even otherwise, is it not possible to use words for the expression of something that is not intellectual? Housman contends that poetry is perfectly poetical only when it is non-intellectual, when it is nonsense. That is too paradoxical, but I suppose what he means is that if it is put to the strict test of the intellect it appears extravagant because it conveys something that expresses and is real to some other kind of seeing than that which intellectual thought brings to us. Is it not possible that words may spring from, that language may be used to express — at least up to a certain point and in a certain way — the supra-intellectual consciousness which is the essential power of spiritual experience? This however is by the way — when one tries to explain spiritual experience to the intellect itself, then it is a different matter.

The interpenetration of the planes is indeed for me a capital and fundamental part of spiritual experience without which Yoga as I practise it and its aim could not exist. For that aim is to manifest, reach or embody a higher consciousness upon earth and not to get away from earth into a higher world or some supreme Absolute. The old Yogas (not quite all of them) tended the other way — but that was, I think, because they found the earth as it is a rather impossible place for any spiritual being and the resistance to change too obstinate to be borne; earth-nature looked to them in Vivekananda's simile like the dog's tail which every time you straighten it goes back to its original curl. But the fundamental proposition in this matter was proclaimed very definitely in the Upanishads which went so far as to say that the Earth is the foundation and all the worlds are on the earth and to imagine a clean-cut or irreconcilable difference between them is ignorance: here and not elsewhere, not by going to some other world, the divine realisation must come. This statement was used to justify a purely individual realisation, but it can equally be the basis of a wider endeavour.

About polytheism, I certainly accept the truth of the many forms and personalities of the One which since the Vedic times has been the spiritual essence of Indian polytheism —

a secondary aspect in the seeking for the one and only Divine. But the passage referred to by Professor Sorley[3] is concerned with something else — the little godlings and Titans spoken of there are supraphysical beings of other planes. It is not meant to be suggested that they are real Godheads and entitled to worship — on the contrary it is indicated that to accept their influence is to move towards error and confusion or a deviation from the true spiritual way. No doubt they have some power to create, they are makers of forms in their own way and in their limited domain, but so are men too creators of outward and of inward things in their own domain and limits — and even man's creative powers can have a repercussion on the supraphysical levels.

I agree that asceticism can be overdone. It has its place as one means — not the only one — of self-mastery; but asceticism that cuts away life is an exaggeration, though one that had many remarkable results which perhaps could hardly have come otherwise. The play of forces in this world is enigmatic, escaping from any rigid rule of the reason, and even an exaggeration like that is often employed to bring about something needed for the full development of human achievement and knowledge and experience. But it was an exaggeration all the same and not, as it claimed to be, the indispensable path to the true goal.

*

I find nothing either to add or to object to in Prof. Sorley's comment on the still, bright and clear mind; it adequately indicates the process by which the mind makes itself ready for the reflection of the higher Truth in its undisturbed surface or substance. But one thing perhaps needs to be kept in view — that this pure stillness of the mind is indeed always the required condition, the desideratum, but for bringing it about there are more ways than one. It is not, for instance, only by an effort of the mind itself to get clear of all intrusive emotion or passion, to quiet its own

---

[3] *"for these intermediate planes are full of little Gods or strong Daityas..."*. The Riddle of This World *(1973), p. 38.*

characteristic vibrations, to resist the obscuring fumes of a physical inertia which brings about a sleep or a torpor of the mind instead of its wakeful silence, that the thing can be done. This is indeed an ordinary process of the Yogic path of knowledge; but the same end can be brought about or automatically happen by other processes — for instance, by the descent from above of a great spiritual stillness imposing silence on the mind and heart, on the life stimuli, on the physical reflexes. A sudden descent of this kind or a series of descents accumulative in force and efficacy is a well-known phenomenon of spiritual experience. Or again one may start a mental process of one kind or another for the purpose which would normally mean a long labour and yet may pull down or be seized midway, or even at the outset, by an overmind influx, a rapid intervention or manifestation of the higher Silence, with an effect sudden, instantaneous, out of all proportion to the means used at the beginning. One commences with a method, but the work is taken up by a Grace from above, by a response from That to which one aspires or by an irruption of the infinitudes of the Spirit. It was in this last way that I myself came by the mind's absolute silence, unimaginable to me before I had the actual experience.

There is another question of some importance — what is the exact nature of this brightness, clearness, stillness, of what is it constituted, more precisely, is it merely a psychological condition or something more? Professor Sorley says these epithets are after all metaphors and he wants to express and succeeds in expressing — though not without the use of metaphor — the same thing in a more abstract language. But I was not conscious of using metaphors when I wrote the phrase though I am aware that the words could to others have that appearance. I think even that they would seem to one who had gone through the same experience, not only a more vivid, but a more realistic and accurate description of this inner state than any abstract language could give. It is true that metaphors, symbols, images are constant auxiliaries summoned by the mystic for the expression of his vision or his experience. It is inevitable because he has to express in a language made or at least developed and manipulated by the mind the phenomena of a consciousness other than the mental and at once more complex and more subtly concrete. It is this subtly concrete, this supersensuously sensible reality of the phenomena of the spiritual — or the occult — consciousness to which the mystic arrives that justifies the use of metaphor and image as a more living and accurate transcription than the abstract terms which intellectual reflection employs for its own characteristic process. If the images used are misleading or not descriptively accurate, it is because the writer has a paucity, looseness or vagueness of language inadequate to the intensity of his experience. Apart from that, all new phenomenon, new discovery, new creation calls for the aid of metaphor and image. The scientist speaks of light waves or of sound waves and in doing so he uses a metaphor, but one which corresponds to the physical fact and is perfectly applicable — for there is no reason why there should not be a wave, a limited flowing movement of light or of sound as well as of water.

But still when I speak of the mind's brightness, clearness, stillness, I have no idea of calling metaphor to my aid; it is meant to be a description quite precise and positive — as precise, as positive as if I were describing in the same way an expanse of air or a sheet of water. For the mystic's experience of mind, especially when it falls still, is not that of an abstract condition or impalpable activity of the consciousness; it is rather an experience of a substance — an extended subtle substance in which there can be and are waves, currents, vibrations not physically material but still as definite, as perceptible, as tangible and controllable by an inner sense as any movement of material energy or substance by the physical senses. The stillness of the mind means, first, the falling to rest of the habitual thought movements, thought formations, thought currents which agitate this mind-substance. That repose, vacancy of movement, is for many a sufficient mental silence. But, even in this repose of all thought movements and all movements of feeling, one sees, when one looks more closely at it, that the mind-substance is still in a constant state of very subtle formless but potentially formative vibration — not at first easily observable, but afterwards quite

Philosophical Thought and Yoga

evident — and that state of constant vibration may be as harmful to the exact reflection or reception of the descending Truth as any formed thought movement or emotional movement; for these vibrations are the source of a mentalisation which can diminish or distort the authenticity of the higher Truth or break it up into mental refractions. When I speak of a still mind, I mean then one in which these subtler disturbances too are no longer there. As they fall quiet one can feel an increasing stillness which is not the lesser quietude of repose and also a resultant clearness as palpable as the stillness and clearness of a physical atmosphere.

This positiveness of experience is my justification for these epithets "still, clear"; but the other epithet, "bright", links itself to a still more sensible phenomenon of the subtly concrete. For in the brightness I describe there is another additional element that is connected with the phenomenon of Light well known and common to mystic experience. That inner Light of which the mystics speak is not a metaphor, as when Goethe called for more light in his last moments; it presents itself as a very positive illumination actually seen and felt by the inner sense. The brightness of the still and clear mind is a reflection of this Light that comes even before the Light itself manifests — and, even without any actual manifestation of the Light, is sufficient for the mind's openness to the greater consciousness beyond mind — just as we can see by the dawn-light before the sunrise; for it brings to the still mind, which might otherwise remain just still and at peace and nothing more, a capacity of penetrability to the Truth it has to receive and harbour. I have emphasised this point at a little length because it helps to bring out the difference between the abstract mental and the concrete mystic perception of supraphysical things which is the source of much misunderstanding between the spiritual seeker and the intellectual thinker. Even when they speak the same language it is a different order of perceptions to which the language refers. The same word in their mouths may denote the products of two different grades of consciousness. This ambiguity in the expression is a cause of much non-understanding and disagreement, while even a surface agreement may be a thin bridge or crust over a gulf of difference.

*

I come now to the question raised by Professor Sorley, what is the relation — or rather the position — of the intellect in regard to mystic or spiritual experience. Is it true as it is often contended that the mystic must, whether as to the validity of his experience itself or the validity of his expression of it, accept the intellect as the judge? It ought to be very plain that in the search, the discovery, the getting of the experience itself the intellect cannot claim to put its limits or its law on an endeavour whose very aim, first principle, constant method is to go beyond the domain of the ordinary earth-ruled and sense-ruled mental intelligence. It would be as if you were to ask me to climb a mountain with a rope around me attaching me to the terrestrial level — or as if I were permitted to fly but only on condition that I kept my feet on the earth or near enough to the safety of the ground while I do it. It may indeed be the securest thing to walk on earth, to be on the firm ground of terrestrial reason always; to attempt to ascend on wings to the Beyond-Mind ether may be to risk mental confusion and collapse and all possible accidents of error, illusion, extravagance, hallucination or what not — the usual charges of the positive earth-walking intellect against mystic experience; but I have to take the risk if I want to do it at all. The reasoning intellect bases itself on man's normal consciousness, it proceeds by the workings of a mental perception and conception of things; it is at its ease only when founded on a logical basis formed by terrestrial experience and its accumulated data. The mystic goes beyond into a region where the everyday mental basis falls away; the terrestrial data on which the reason founds itself are exceeded, there is even another law and canon of perception and knowledge. His entire business is to break out or upward or widen into a new consciousness which looks at things in a very different way, and if this new consciousness may include, though viewed with quite another vision, the data of the ordinary external intelligence, yet it cannot be limited by them, cannot bind itself to see from the intellectual standpoint or conform to its manner of conceiving, reasoning, its established interpretation of experience. A mystic entering the domain of the occult or of the spirit with the intellect as his only or his supreme light or guide would risk to see nothing, or see according to his preconceived mental idea of things or else he would arrive only at a subtly "positive" mental realisation of perceptions already laid down for him by the abstract speculations of the intellectual thinker.

There is a strain of spiritual thought in India which compromises with the modern intellectual demand and admits Reason as a supreme judge, — but it must be a Reason which in its turn is prepared to compromise and accept the data of spiritual experience as valid *per se*. That is to do what the Indian philosophers have always done; for they have tried to establish by the light of metaphysical reasoning generalisations drawn from spiritual experience; and it was always on the basis of that experience that they proceeded and with the evidence of the spiritual seekers as a supreme proof ranking higher than intellectual speculation or inference. In that way they preserved the freedom of spiritual and mystic experience and allowed the reasoning intellect to come in only on the second line as a judge of the generalised metaphysical statements drawn from the experience, but not of the experience itself. This is, I presume, something akin to Professor Sorley's own position — for he concedes that the experience itself is of the domain of the ineffable, but he suggests that as soon as I begin to interpret it, to state it, I fall back inevitably into the domain of the thinking mind; I am using its terms and ways of thought and expression and must accept the intellect as judge. If I do not, I knock away the ladder by which I have climbed — through mind to Beyond-Mind — and I am left unsupported in the air. It is not quite clear whether the truth of my experience itself is supposed to be invalidated by this unsustained position, but at any rate it remains something aloof and incommunicable without support or any consequences for thought or life. There are three propositions, I suppose, which I can take as laid down or admitted in this contention and joined together. First, the spiritual experience is itself of the Beyond-Mind, ineffable and, it should be presumed, unthinkable. Next, — in the expression, the interpretation of the experience, you are obliged to fall back into the domain of the consciousness you have left and so you must abide by its judgments, accept the terms and the canons of its law, submit to its verdict; for you have abandoned the freedom of the Ineffable and are no longer your own master. Last, spiritual truth may be true in itself, in its own self-experience, but any statement of it is liable to error and here the intellect is the sole possible arbiter.

I do not think I am prepared to accept any of these affirmations completely just as they are. It is true that spiritual and mystic experience carries one first into domains of Other-Mind or All-Mind (and also Other-Life and All-Life and I would add Other-Substance and All-Substance) and then emerges into the Beyond-Mind; it is true also that the ultimate Truth has been described as unthinkable, ineffable, unknowable — "speech cannot reach there, mind cannot arrive to it." But I may observe that it is so to human mind, but not to itself, since it is not an abstraction, but a superconscious (not unconscious) Existence, — for it is described as to itself self-evident and self-luminous, — therefore in some direct supramental or at least overmind way knowable and known, eternally self-aware. But here the question is not of an ultimate realisation of the ultimate Ineffable which according to many can only be reached in a supreme trance withdrawn from all outer mental or other awareness; we are speaking rather of an experience in a luminous silence of the mind and any such experience presupposes that before there is any last unspeakable experience of the Ultimate or disappearance into it, there is possible a reflection or descent of at least some Power or Presence of the identical Reality into the mind-substance. Along with it there is a modification of mind-substance, an illumination of it, — and of this experience an expression of some kind, a rendering into thought ought to be possible. Moreover an immense mass of well-established spiritual experience would have been impossible unless we suppose that the Ineffable and Unknowable has truths of itself, aspects, revealing presentations of it to our consciousness which are not utterly unthinkable and ineffable.

Philosophical Thought and Yoga

If it were not so, indeed, all account of spiritual truth and experience would be impossible. At most one could speculate about it, but that would be an activity very much indeed in the air and even a movement in a void, without support or data. At best, there could be a mere manipulation of all the possible ideas of what conceivably might be the Supreme and Ultimate. For we would have nothing before us to go upon other than the bare fact of a certain unaccountable translation by one way or another from consciousness to an incommunicable Supraconscience. That is indeed what much mystical seeking actually held up as the one thing essential both in Europe and India. Many Christian mystics spoke of a total darkness through which one must pass into the Ineffable Light and Rapture, a falling away of all mental lights and all that belongs to the ordinary activity of the nature; they aimed not only at a silence but a darkness of the mind protecting an inexpressible illumination. The Indian Sannyasins sought by silence, by concentration inwards, to shed mind altogether and pass into a thought-free trance from which, if one returns, no communication or expression could be brought back of what was there except a remembrance of ineffable existence and bliss. But still even here there were previous glimpses or contacts and results of contact of That which is Beyond; there were contacts of the Highest or of the occult universal Existence, which were held to be spiritual truths and on the basis of which the seers and mystics did not hesitate to formulate their experience and the thinkers to build on it numberless philosophies, theologies, books of exegesis or of creed and dogma. All then is not ineffable; there is a possibility of communication and expression, and the only question is of the nature of this transmission of the facts of a different order of consciousness to the mind and whether it is feasible for the intellect or must be left for something else than intellect to determine the validity of the expression or, even, of the original experience. If no valid account were possible there could be no question of the judgment of the intellect — only the violent contradiction of mind sitting down to judge a Beyond-Mind of which it can know nothing, starting to speak of the Ineffable, think of the Unthinkable, comprehend the Incommunicable.

Comments on Thoughts of J. M. E. McTaggart

I have heard of McTaggart as a philosopher but am totally unacquainted with his thought and his writings, so it is a little difficult for me to answer you with any certitude. Isolated thoughts or sentences may easily be misunderstood if they are not read against the background of the thinker's way of looking at things taken as a whole. There is always, too, the difference of standpoint and approach between the spiritual seeker or mystic who (sometimes) philosophises and the intellectual thinker who (sometimes or partly) mysticises. The one starts from a spiritual or mystic experience or at the least an intuitive realisation and tries to express it and its connection with other spiritual or intuitive truth in the inadequate and too abstract language of the mind; he looks behind thought and expression for some spiritual or intuitive experience to which it may point and, if he finds none, he is apt to feel the thought, however intellectually fine, or the expression, however intellectually significant, as something unsubstantial because without spiritual substance. The intellectual thinker starts from ideas and mentalised feelings and other mental or external phenomena and tries to reach the essential truth in or behind them; generally, he stops short at a mental abstraction or only a derivative mental realisation of something that is in its own nature other than mental. But if he has the true mystic somewhere in him, he will sometimes get beyond to at least flashes and glimpses. Is it not the compulsion of this approach (I mean the inadequacy of the method of intellectual philosophy, its fixation to the word and idea, while to the complete mystic word and idea are useful symbols only or significative flashlights) that kept McTaggart, as it keeps many, from the unfolding of the mystic within him? If the reviewer is right, that would be why he is abstract and dry, while what is beautiful and moving in his thought might be some light that shines through in spite of the inadequate means of expression to which philosophical thinking condemns us. However, subject to this rather lengthy caveat, I will try to deal with the extracted sentences or summarised thoughts you have placed before me in your letter.

"*Love the main occupation of the selves in absolute reality.*" This seems to me a little excessive. If instead of "the main occupation" it were said "an essential power", that might pass. I would myself say that bliss and oneness are the essential condition of the absolute reality and love as the most characteristic dynamic power of bliss and oneness must support fundamentally and colour their activities; but the activities themselves may be not of one main kind but manifold in character.

Benevolence and sympathy. In mental experience benevolence and sympathy have to be distinguished from love; but it seems to me that beyond the dividing mind, where the true sense of oneness begins, these become at a higher intensity of their movement characteristic values of love. Benevolence becomes an intense compulsion imposed by love to seek always the good of the loved, sympathy becomes the feeling out of love to contain, participate in and take as part of one's own existence all the movements of the loved and all that concerns him.

"*Love is authentic and justifies itself completely whether its cause be great or trivial.*" That is not often true in human practice; for there the destiny of love and its justification depend very much as a rule (though not always) on the nature of the cause or object. For if the object of love is trivial in the sense of his being an inadequate instrument for the dynamic realisation of the sense of oneness which McTaggart says is the essence of love, then love is likely to be baulked of its fulfilment. Unless, of course, it is satisfied with existing, with spending itself in its own fundamental way on the loved without expecting any return for its self-expenditure, any mutual unification. Still, of Love in its essence the statement may be true; but then it would point to the fact that Love at its origin is a self-existent force, an absolute, a transcendent (as I have put it), which does not depend upon the objects, — it depends only on itself or only on the Divine, — for it is a self-existent power of the Divine. If it were not self-existent, it would hardly be independent of the nature or reaction of its object. It is partly what I mean when I speak of transcendent Love — though this is only one aspect of its transcendence. That self-existent transcendent Love spreading itself over all, turning everywhere to contain, embrace, unite, help, upraise towards love and bliss and oneness, becomes cosmic divine Love; intensely fixing itself on one or others to find itself, to achieve a dynamic unification or to reach here towards the union of the soul with the Divine, it becomes the individual divine Love. But there are unhappily its diminutions in the human mind, human vital, human physical; there the divine essence of Love may easily become mixed with counterfeits, dimmed, concealed or lost in the twisted movements born of division and ignorance.

Love and self-reverence. It sounds very high, but also rather dry; this "emotion" in the lover does not seem to be very emotional, it is a hill-top syllogising far above the flow of any emotional urges. Self-reverence in this sense or in a deeper sense can come from Love, but it *can* come equally from a participation in Knowledge, in Power or anything else that one feels to be the highest good or else of the essence of the Highest. But the passion of love, the adoration of love, can bring in a quite different, even an opposite emotion. Especially in love for the Divine or for one whom one feels to be divine, the Bhakta feels an intense reverence for the Loved, a sense of something of immense greatness, beauty or value and for himself a strong impression of his own comparative unworthiness and a passionate desire to *grow* into likeness with that which one adores. What does come very often with the inrush of Love is an exaltation, a feeling of a greatening within, of new powers and high or beautiful possibilities in one's nature or of an intensification of the nature; but that is not exactly self-reverence. There is a deeper self-reverence possible, a true emotion, a sense of the value and even the sacredness of the soul, even the mind, life, body as an offering or itself the temple for the inner presence of the Beloved.

These reactions are intimately connected with the fact that Love, when it is worthy of the name, is always a seeking for union, for oneness, but also in its secret foundation it is a seeking, if sometimes only a dim groping for the Divine. Love in its depths is a contact of the Divine Possibility or Reality in oneself with the Divine Possibility or Reality in the loved. It is the inability to affirm or keep this character that makes human love either transient or baulked of its full significance or condemned to sink into a less exalted movement diminished to the capacity of the human receptacle. But there McTaggart brings in his saving clause, "When I love, I see the other not as he is now (and therefore really is not), but as he really is (that is, as he will be)." The rest of it, that "the other with all his faults is somehow infinitely good — at least for his friend", seems to me too mental to convey anything very definite from the standpoint of the spiritual inner values. But the formula quoted also is not overclear. It means, I suppose, something like Vivekananda's distinction between the apparent Man and the real Man; or it coincides up to a point with the saying of one of the early teachers of Vedanta, Yajnavalkya, "Not for the sake of the wife is the wife dear" (or, the friend — for the wife is only the first of a list), "but for the sake of the Self (the greater Self, the Spirit within) is she dear." But Yajnavalkya, a seeker of the one (not the plural) Absolute, would not have accepted the implication in McTaggart's phrase; he would have said that one must go beyond and eventually seek the Self not in the wife or friend — even though sought or glimpsed there for a time, but in its own self-existence. In any case there seems to be here an avowal that it is not the human being (what he now is), but the Divine or a portion of the Divine within (call it God if you will or call it Absolute) that is the object of the love. But the mystic would not be satisfied like McTaggart with that "will be", — would not consent to remain in love with the finite for the sake of an unrealised Infinite. He would insist on pushing on towards full realisation, towards finding the Divine in Itself or the Divine Manifest; he would not rest satisfied with the Divine unconscious of itself, unmanifested or only distantly *in posse.*

There is where the parallel with the Ishta Devata which you suggest would not hold; for the Ishta Devata on whom the seeker concentrates is a *conscious* Personality of the Divine answering to the needs of his own personality and showing to him as in a representative image what the Divine is or at least pointing him through itself to the Absolute. On the other side, when I spoke of the self-absorption of the Divine Force in its energising, I was trying to explain the possibility in a Divine or cosmic manifestation of this apparently inconscient Matter. I said that in the frontal movement there was something of the Divine that had thrown itself into material form with so much concentration that it became the motion and the form which the motion of Force creates and put all that was not that behind it, — even, but in a greater degree and more permanently, as a man can concentrate and forget his own existence in what he is doing, seeing or making. In man himself, who is not inconscient, this appears in a different way; his frontal being is unaware of what is behind the surface personality and action, like the part of the actor's being which becomes the role and forgets entirely the other more enduring self behind the actor. But in either case there is a larger self behind, "a Conscient in things inconscient", which is aware both of itself and of the self-forgetting frontal form seen as the creature. Does McTaggart recognise this conscious Divine within? He makes too little of this Absolute or Real Self which, as he yet sees, is within the unreal or less real appearance. His denial of the Divine comes from the insistence of his mind and vital temperament on the friend as he is, even though his higher mind may try to escape from that by the idea of what his friend will be; otherwise it is difficult to understand the stupendous exaggeration of his thesis that the love for friends is the *only* real thing in life and his unwillingness to give God a chance, lest that should take away the friend and leave the Divine in his place.

    I do not quite seize what is his conception of the Absolute. How can it be said that a society (?) of distinct selves are collectively the Absolute? If it is meant that where there is a union of conscious liberated selves there is the presence of the Divine and a certain manifestation is possible, — that is intelligible. Or if by society is meant only that the sum or totality of all distinct selves is the Divine and these distinct individual selves are portions of the Divine, that would be an intelligible (pantheistic) solution.

Only, it would be a Divine All or some kind of Cosmic Self or Spirit rather than the Absolute. For if there is an Absolute — which intellectually one is not bound to believe, except that something in the higher mind seems imperatively to ask for it or feel that it is there, — it must surely exist in its own absolute right, not constituted, not dependent for its being on a collectivity of distinct selves, but self-existent. To the intellect such an Absolute may seem an indefinable x which it cannot grasp; but mystic or spiritual experience pushed far enough ultimately leads to it, and whatever may be the gate of experience through which one gets the first glimpse of it, it is there even though not fully grasped in that opening experience.

Your own experience of it was, you say, that of an irruption of the Infinite into the finite — of a greater Power descending upon you or uplifting you to itself. That indeed is what it is always to the spiritual experience — and that is why I speak of it as the Transcendent. It reveals itself as such a descending and uplifting Power or a descending and uplifting Love — or Light, Peace, Bliss, Consciousness, Presence; it is not limited by its manifestation in the finite, — one feels it, the Peace, the Power, Love, Light or Bliss or the Presence in which all these are, to be a self-existent infinity, not something constituted by or limited to our first sight of it here. McTaggart's love of friends remained the *only* real thing for him; I must suppose that he had not this glimpse. But once this irruption has taken place, this descent and uplifting, that is bound to become in the end the one thing real, for by that alone can the rest find its own lasting greater reality. It is the descent of the Divine Consciousness and the ascent or uplifting into it of which we speak in our Yoga. All else can only hold, make good, fulfil itself if it can lift itself to be a part of this divine realisation or of its manifestation, and, to do that, it must accept a great transformation and perfection. But the central realisation must be the one central aim, and it is that realisation only which will make other things, all that is intended to be made part of it, divinely possible.

Comments on Terms Used by Henri Bergson[4]

I have not read him [*Bergson*] sufficiently to pronounce. So far as I know, he seems to have some perception of the dynamic creative intuition involved in Life, but none of the truly suprarational intuition above. If so, his Intuition which he takes to be the sole secret of things is only a secondary manifestation of something transcendent which is itself only the "rays of the Sun".

*

Instinct and intuition as described by him [*Bergson*] are vital, but it is possible to develop a corresponding mental intuition, and that is probably what he suggests — and which depends not on thought but a sort of mental direct contact with things. This is not exactly mysticism, though it is a first step towards it.

*

No, it [*Bergson's* élan vital] is not the Supramental. But Bergson's "intuition" seems to be a Life Intuition which is of course the Supramental fragmented and modified to act as a Knowledge in "Life-in-Matter". I can't say definitively yet, but that is the impression it gave me.

*

[*Bergson's* élan vital:] Not Sachchidananda but Chit-shakti in the disguise of Pranashakti. Bergson is, I believe, a vitalist (as opposed to a materialist on one side and an idealist on the other) with a strong perception of Time (in Upanishadic times they speculated whether Time was not the Brahman and some schools held that idea). So for him Brahman = Consciousness-Force = Time-Force = Life-Force. But the last two he sees vividly, while the first which is the real thing behind creation he sees very dimly.

*

---

[4] *The six replies in this group were written to a correspondent who quoted sentences from Bergson's writings, commented on them and then asked Sri Aurobindo for his views.* — Ed.

He [*Bergson*] sees Consciousness (Chit) not in its essential truth but as a creative Force = a sort of transcendent Life-Energy descending into Matter and acting there.

*

I suppose Bergson must already know what the "mystics" say about the matter and has put his own interpretation or value upon it. So he would not at all be impressed by your suggestion.[5] He would say, "I know all about that already."

Metaphysics, Science and Spiritual Experience

I do not find it easy to answer the few brief and casual sentences in X's letter, — precisely because they are so brief and casual.[6] Not knowing him or the turns of his mind, I do not exactly seize what is behind this passage in his letter. It would be easier to reply if I had some notion of the kind of thought or experience on which he takes his stand when he dismisses so cavalierly the statement of spiritual truth put forward in the *Arya*. As it is, I am obliged to answer to what *may* be behind his sentences and, as there is much that possibly stands behind them, the reply becomes long and elaborate and is in danger of seeming long and discursive. I could of course answer easily myself by a few brief and trenchant sentences of the same calibre, but in that kind of discussion there is no profit.

Let me say that he makes an initial mistake — quite natural for him, since he has not read the *Arya*, — when he describes the extract sent to him as a "theological fragment". I must insist that there is no theology in the *Arya*. Nothing there is written to support or to develop any kind of religious belief or dogma or to confirm or enunciate the credo of any old or new religion. No less does he miss the mark when he describes as a scholastic distinction the substance of the passage. The teaching there is not

---

[5] *The correspondent asked whether he should write to Bergson in order to explain the true meaning of intuition and how to develop it.* — Ed.

[6] *The paragraphs that follow are from the draft of a letter that was not revised or sent in this form to the correspondent.* — Ed.

taken from books, nor, although put in philosophic language, is it based upon abstract thought or any formal logic. It expresses a fundamental spiritual experience, dynamic for the growth of the being, confirmed and enlarged and filled with detail by almost thirty years of continuous sadhana, and, as such, it cannot be seriously challenged or invalidated by mere intellectual question or reasoning, but, if at all, then only by a greater and wider spiritual experience. Moreover, it coincides (not in expression, it may be, but in substance) with the experience of hundreds of spiritual seekers in many paths and in all parts of the world since the days of the Upanishads — and of Plotinus and the Gnostics and Sufis — to the present time. It is hardly admissible then to put it aside as the thought of a tyro or beginner in spiritual knowledge making his first clumsy potshots at a solution of the crossword enigma of the universe. That description seems to show that he has missed the point of the passage altogether and that also makes it difficult to reply; for where there is no meeting point of minds, discussion is likely to be sterile.

I was a little surprised at first by this entire lack of understanding, shown still more in his cavil at the two Divines — for I had somehow got the impression that X was a Christian and the recognition of "two Divines" — the Divine Transcendent and the Divine Immanent — is, I have read, perfectly familiar to Christian ideas and to Christian experience. The words themselves in fact — transcendent and cosmic — are taken from the West. I do not know that there is anything exactly corresponding to them in the language of Indian spiritual thinking, although the experiences on which the distinction rests are quite familiar. On another side, Christianity insists not only on a double but a triple Divine. It even strikes me that this triple Godhead or Trinity is not very far off at bottom from my trinity of the individual, cosmic and transcendent Divine — as far at least as one can judge who has not himself followed the Christian discipline. Christ, whether as the human Incarnation or the Christos in men or the Godhead proceeding from the Father, seems to me to be quite my individual Divine. The Father has very much the appearance of the One who overstands and is immanent in the cosmos. And although this is more obscure, yet if one can be guided by the indications in the Scripture, the Holy Ghost looks very much like a rather mysterious and inexpressible Transcendence and its descent very much like what I would call the descent of Light, Purity, Peace — that passeth all understanding — or Power of the supramental Spirit. In any case these Christian and Western ideas show surely that my affirmation of a double or a triple Divine is not anything new and ought not to be found startling or upsetting and I do not see why it should be treated as (in itself) obscure and unintelligible.

Again, are these or similar distinctions very positively made in the Christian, Sufi or other teachings mere theoretical abstractions, scholastic distinctions, theological cobwebs, or metaphysical puzzles? I had always supposed that they corresponded to very living, very dynamic, almost — for the paths to which they relate — indispensable experiences. No doubt, for those who follow other ways or no way at all or for those who have not yet had the illuminating and vivifying experience, they may seem at first a little difficult or unseizable. But that is true of most spiritual truth — and not of spiritual truth alone. There are many very highly intelligent and cultured people to whom a scientific explanation of even so patent and common a fact as electricity and electric light (this is a reminiscence of an article by Y. Y. in the *New Statesman and Nation*) seems equally difficult to seize by the mind or to fix either in the memory or the intelligence. And yet the distinction between positive and negative electricity, both necessary for the existence of the light, — like that of the passive and active Brahman (another scholastic distinction?) both necessary for the existence of the universe, — cannot be dismissed for that reason as something academic or scholastic, but is a very pertinent statement of things quite dynamic and real. No doubt the non-scientific man does not and perhaps need not trouble about these things and can be content to enjoy the electric light (when he is allowed to do so by the grace of the Pondicherry Municipality), without enquiring into the play of the forces behind it: but for the seeker after scientific truth or for the practical electrician it is a different matter. Now these distinctions in the spiritual field are a parallel case; they seem theoretical or abstract only so long as experience has not made them concrete, but once experienced they become living stuff of the consciousness and, after a certain stage, even the basis of action and growth in the spiritual life.

Here I am driven to a rather lengthy digression from the main theme — for I am met by X's rather baffling appeal to Whitham's History of Science. What has Whitham or Science to do with spiritual truth or spiritual experience? I can only suppose that he condemns all intrusion of anything like metaphysical thought into the spiritual field — a position excessive but not altogether untenable — and even perhaps proposes to bring the scientific method and the scientific mentality into spiritual experience as the sole true way of arriving at or judging the truth of things. I should like to make my view clear as to that point, because here much confusion has been created about it, and more is possible. And the first thing I would say is that if metaphysics has no right to intervene in spiritual experience, neither has Science. There are here three different domains of knowledge and experience each with its own instrumentation, its own way of approach and seeing, suited for its own task, but not to be imposed or substituted in these other fields of knowledge, — at least unless and until they meet by some kind of supreme reconciling transmutation in something that is at the source of all knowledge. For knowledge may be essentially one, but like the one Divine, it manifests differently in different fields of its play and to abolish their distinctions is not the way to arrive at true understanding of experience.

Science deals effectively with phenomena and process and the apparent play of forces which determine the process. It cannot deal even intellectually in any adequate way with ultimate truths, that is the province of the higher, less external mind — represented up till now by metaphysics, though metaphysics is not its only possible power. If Science tries to fix metaphysical truth by forcing on this domain its own generalisations in the physical field, as people have been doing for almost the last century, it makes a mess of thought by illegitimately extended conclusions and has in the end to retire from this usurpation as it is now beginning to retire. Its discoveries may be used by philosophy, but on the grounds proper to philosophy and not on the grounds proper to Science. The philosopher must judge the scientific conceptions of relativity or discontinuity or space-time, for instance, by his own processes and standards of evidence. So too, Science has no instrumentation or process of knowledge which can enable it to discover spiritual truth or to judge or determine the results of spiritual experience. There is a field of knowledge of process in the spiritual and the occult domain, in the discovery of a world of inner forces and their way of action and even of their objective dynamisation in the mind and life and the functioning of the body. But the mathematical exactitudes and rigid formulas of physical Science do not apply here and the mentality created by them would hamper spiritual experience.

Chapter Four
Science and Yoga

Science, Yoga and the Agnostic

I do not think anything can be said that would convince one who starts from exactly the opposite viewpoint to the spiritual, the way of looking at things of a Victorian agnostic. His points of doubt about the value — other than subjective and purely individual — of Yoga experience are that it does not aim at scientific truth and cannot be said to achieve ultimate truth because the experiences are coloured by the individuality of the seer. One might ask whether Science itself has arrived at any ultimate truth; on the contrary, ultimate truth even on the physical plane seems to recede as Science advances. Science started on the assumption that the ultimate truth must be physical and objective — and the objective Ultimate (or even less than that) would explain all subjective phenomena. Yoga proceeds on the opposite view that the ultimate Truth is spiritual and subjective and it is in that ultimate Light that we must view objective phenomena. It is the two opposite poles and the gulf is as wide as it can be.

Yoga, however, is scientific to this extent that it proceeds by subjective experiment and bases all its findings on experience; mental intuitions are admitted only as a first step and are not considered as realisation — they must be confirmed by being translated into and justified by experience. As to the value of the experience itself, it is doubted by the physical mind because it is subjective, not objective. But has the distinction much value? Is not all knowledge and experience subjective at bottom? Objective external physical things are seen very much in the same way by human beings because of the construction of the mind and senses; with another construction of mind and sense quite another account of the physical world would be given — Science itself has made that very clear. But your friend's point is that the Yoga experience is individual, coloured by the individuality of the seer. It may be true to a certain extent of the precise form or transcription given to the experience in certain domains; but even here the difference is superficial. It is a fact that Yogic experience runs everywhere on the same lines. Certainly, there are, not one line, but many; for, admittedly, we are dealing with a many-sided Infinite to which there are and must be many ways of approach; but yet the broad lines are the same everywhere and the intuitions, experiences, phenomena are the same in ages and countries far apart from each other and systems practised quite independently from each other. The experiences of the mediaeval European bhakta or mystic are precisely the same in substance, however differing in names, forms, religious colouring etc., as those of the mediaeval Indian bhakta or mystic — yet these people were not corresponding with one another or aware of each other's experiences and results as are modern scientists from New York to Yokohama. That would seem to show that there is something there identical, universal and presumably true — however the colour of the translation may differ because of the difference of mental language.

As for ultimate Truth, I suppose both the Victorian agnostic and, let us say, the Indian Vedantin may agree that it is veiled but there. Both speak of it as the Unknowable; the only difference is that the Vedantin says it is unknowable by the mind and inexpressible by speech, but still attainable by something deeper or higher than the mental perception, while even mind can reflect and speech express the thousand aspects it presents to the mind's outward and inward experience. The Victorian agnostic would, I suppose, cancel this qualification; he would pronounce for the doubtful existence and, if existent, for the absolute unknowableness of this Unknowable.

Science and Spirituality

I do not think the two questions you put are of much importance from the viewpoint of spiritual sadhana.

The question about science and spirituality would have been of some moment some twenty years ago and it filled the minds of men in the earlier years of the twentieth century, but it is now out of date. Science itself has come to the conclusion that it cannot, as it once hoped, determine what is the truth of things or their real nature or what is behind physical phenomena; it can only deal with the process of physical things and how they come about or on what lines men can deal with and make use of them. In other words, the field of physical science has been now definitely marked off and limited and questions about God or the ultimate reality or other metaphysical or spiritual problems are outside it. This is at least the case all over continental Europe and it is only in England and America that there is still some attempt to reason about these things on the basis of physical science. The so-called sciences which try to deal with the mind and men (psychology etc.) are so much dependent on physical science that they cannot go beyond narrow limits. If science is to turn her face towards the Divine it must be a new science not yet developed which deals directly with the forces of the Life-world and of Mind and so arrives at what is beyond Mind, but present-day science cannot do that.

From the spiritual point of view such temporary phenomena as the turn of educated Hindus towards materialism are of little importance. There have always been periods when the mind of nations, continents, cultures turned towards materialism and away from all spiritual belief. Such periods came in ancient Europe in the first century A.D., in western Europe in the nineteenth century, but they are usually of short duration. Western Europe has already lost its faith in materialism and is seeking for something else, either turning back to old religion or groping for something new. Russia and Asia are now going through the same materialistic wave. These waves come because of a certain necessity in human development—to destroy the bondage of old forms and leave a free field for new truth and new forms of truth and action in life as well as of what is behind life.

*

You ask me whether you have to give up your predilection for testing before accepting and to accept everything in Yoga *a priori*

— and by testing you mean testing by the ordinary reason. The only answer I can give to that is that the experiences of Yoga belong to an inner domain and go according to a law of their own, have their own method of perception, criteria and all the rest of it which are neither those of the domain of the physical senses nor of the domain of rational or scientific enquiry. Just as scientific enquiry passes beyond that of the physical senses and enters the domain of the infinite and the infinitesimal about which the senses can say nothing and test nothing — for one cannot see or touch an electron or know by the evidence of the sense-mind whether it exists or not or decide by that evidence whether the earth really turns round the sun and not rather the sun round the earth as our senses and all our physical experience daily tell us — so the spiritual search passes beyond the domain of scientific or rational enquiry and it is impossible by the aid of the ordinary positive reason to test the data of spiritual experience and decide whether those things exist or not or what is their law and nature. As in science, so here you have to accumulate experience on experience following faithfully the methods laid down by the Guru or by the systems of the past, you have to develop an intuitive discrimination which compares the experiences, see what they mean, how far and in what field each is valid, what is the place of each in the whole, how it can be reconciled or related with others that at first sight seem to contradict it, etc. etc. until you can move with a secure knowledge in the vast field of spiritual phenomena. That is the only way to test spiritual experience. I have myself tried the other method and found it absolutely incapable and inapplicable. On the other hand if you are not prepared to go through all that yourself — as few can do except those of extraordinary spiritual stature — you have to accept the leading of a Master, as in science you accept a teacher instead of going through the whole field of science and its experimentation all by yourself — at least until you have accumulated sufficient experience and knowledge. If that is accepting things *a priori*, well, you have to accept *a priori*. For I am unable to see by what valid tests you propose to make the ordinary reason the judge of what is beyond it.

You quote the sayings of Vivekananda and Kobiraj Gopinath. Is this Kobiraj the disciple of the Jewel Sannyasi or is he another? In any case, I would like to know before assigning a value to these utterances what they actually did for the testing of their spiritual perceptions and experiences. How did Vivekananda test the value of his spiritual experiences — some of them not more credible to the ordinary mind than the translation through the air of Bijoy Goswami's wife to Lake Manas or of Bijoy Goswami himself by a similar method to Benares? I know nothing of Kobiraj Gopinath, but what were his tests and how did he apply them? What were his methods? his criteria? It seems to me that no ordinary mind could accept the apparition of Buddha out of a wall or the half hour's talk with Hayagriva as valid facts by any kind of testing. It would either have to accept them *a priori* or on the sole evidence of Vivekananda which comes to the same thing or to reject them *a priori* as hallucinations or mere mental images accompanied in one case by an auditive hallucination. I fail to see how it could "test" them. Or how was I to test by the ordinary mind my experience of Nirvana? To what conclusion could I come about it by the aid of the ordinary positive reason? How could I test its validity? I am at a loss to imagine. I did the only thing I could — to accept it as a strong and valid truth of experience, let it have its full play and produce its full experiential consequences until I had sufficient Yogic knowledge to put it in its place. Finally, how without inner knowledge or experience can you or anyone else test the inner knowledge and experience of others?

I have often said that discrimination is not only perfectly admissible but indispensable in spiritual experience. But it must be a discrimination founded on knowledge, not a reasoning founded on ignorance. Otherwise you tie up your mind and hamper experience by preconceived ideas which are as much *a priori* as any acceptance of a spiritual truth or experience can be. Your idea that surrender can only come by love is a point in instance. It is perfectly true in Yogic experience that surrender by true love which means psychic and spiritual love is the most powerful, simple and effective of all, but one cannot, putting that forward as a dictum arrived at by the ordinary reason, shut up the whole of possible experience of true surrender into that formula or announce on its strength that one must wait till one loves perfectly before one can surrender. Yogic experience shows that surrender can also be made by the mind and will, a clear and sincere mind seeing the necessity of surrender and a clear and sincere will enforcing it on the recalcitrant members. Also experience shows that not only can surrender come by love, but love also can come by surrender or grow with it from an imperfect to a perfect love. One starts by an intense idea and will to know or reach the Divine and surrenders more and more one's ordinary personal ideas, desires, attachments, urges to action or habits of action so that the Divine may take up everything. Surrender means that, to give up our little mind and its mental ideas and preferences into a divine Light and a greater knowledge, our petty personal troubled blind stumbling will into a great calm tranquil luminous Will and Force, our little restless tormented feelings into a wide intense divine Love and Ananda, our small suffering personality into the one Person of which it is an obscure outcome. If one insists on one's own ideas and reasonings, the greater Light and Knowledge cannot come or else is marred and obstructed in the coming at every step by a lower interference; if one insists on one's own desires and fancies, that great luminous Will and Force cannot act in its own true power — for you ask it to be the servant of your desires; if one refuses to give up one's petty ways of feeling, eternal Love and supreme Ananda cannot descend or is mixed and is spilt from the effervescing crude emotional vessel. No amount of ordinary reasoning can get rid of that necessity of surmounting the lower in order that the higher may be there.

Science and the Supernormal

Scientific laws only give a schematic account of material processes of Nature — as a valid scheme they can be used for reproducing or extending at will a material process, but obviously they cannot give an account of the thing itself. Water for instance is not merely so much oxygen and hydrogen put together — the combination is simply a process or device for enabling the materialisation of a new thing called water; what that new thing really is is quite another matter. In fact there are different planes of substance, gross, subtle and more subtle going back to what is called causal (*kāraṇa*) substance. What is more gross can be reduced to the subtle state and the subtle brought into the gross state; that accounts for dematerialisation and materialisation and rematerialisation. These are occult processes and are vulgarly regarded as magic. Ordinarily the magician knows nothing of the why and wherefore of what he is doing, he has simply learned the formula or process or else controls elemental beings of the subtler states (planes or worlds) who do the thing for him. The Tibetans indulge widely in occult processes; if you see the books of Madame David-Neel who has lived in Tibet you will get an idea of their expertness in these things. But also the Tibetan Lamas know something of the laws of occult (mental and vital) energy and how it can be made to act on physical things. That is something which goes beyond mere magic. The direct power of mind-force or life-force upon Matter can be extended to an almost illimitable degree. It must be remembered that Energy is fundamentally one in all the planes, only taking more and more dense forms, so there is nothing *a priori* impossible in mind-energy or life-energy acting directly on material energy and substance; if they do they can make a material object do things or rather can do things with a material object which would be to that object in its ordinary poise or "law" unhabitual and therefore apparently impossible.

I do not see how cosmic rays can explain the origination of Matter; it is like Sir Oliver Lodge's explanation of life on earth that it comes from another planet; it only pushes the problem one step farther back — for how do the cosmic rays come into existence? But it is a fact that Agni is the basis of forms as the Sankhya pointed out long ago, i.e. the fiery principle in its three powers radiant, electric and gaseous (the Vedic trinity of Agni) is the agent in producing liquid and solid forms of what is called matter.

Obviously a layman can't do these things, unless he has a native "psychic" (that is, occult) faculty and even then he will have to learn the law of the thing before he can use it at will. It is always possible to use spiritual force or mind-power or will-power or a certain kind of vital energy to produce effects in men, things and happenings; but knowledge and much practice is needed before this possibility ceases to be occasional and haphazard and can be used quite consciously, at will or to perfection. Even then to have "a control over the whole material world" is too big a proposition; a local and partial control is more possible or, more widely, certain kinds of control over matter.

*

The desire [*of occultists and spiritists*] to satisfy the physical scientists is absurd and illogical. The physical scientists have their own field with its own instruments and standards. To apply the same tests to phenomena of a different kind is as foolish as to apply physical tests to spiritual truth. One can't dissect God or see the soul under a microscope. So also the subjection of disembodied spirits or even of psycho-physical phenomena to tests and standards valid only for material phenomena is a most false and unsatisfactory method. Moreover the physical scientist is for the most part resolved not to admit what cannot be neatly packed and labelled and docketed in his own system and its formulas. Dr. Jules Romains, himself a scientist as well as a great writer, makes experiments to prove that men can see and read with the eyes blindfolded, the scientists refuse even to admit or record the results. Khuda Baksh comes along and proves it patently, indubitably, under all legitimate tests, the scientists are quite unwilling to cede and record the fact even though his results are undeniable. He walks on fire unhurt and disproves all hitherto suggested explanations, — they simply cast about for another and still more silly explanation! What is the use of trying to convince people who are determined not to believe?

*

These theosophic and other modern attempts to square physical

Science with Yoga (Yogis formerly did not bother to differentiate spiritual functions from grey matter and white matter) make me always suspicious. It looks like manufacture of the mind, pseudo-science.

Science and Superstition

It is quite true that the word "superstition" has been habitually used as a convenient club to beat down any belief that does not agree with the ideas of the materialistic reason, that is to say, of the physical mind dealing with the apparent law of physical process and seeing no farther. It has also been used to dismiss ideas and beliefs not in agreement with one's own idea of what is the rational norm of supraphysical truths as well. For many ages man cherished beliefs that implied a force behind which acted on principles unknown to the physical mind and beyond the witness of the outward reason and the senses. Science came in with a method of knowledge which extended the evidence of this outer field of consciousness and thought that by this method all existence would become explicable. It swept away at once without examination all the ancient beliefs as so many "superstitions" — true, half true or false, all went into the dustbin in one impartial sweep, because they did not rely on the method of physical Science and lay outside its data or were or seemed incompatible with its standpoint. Even in the field of supraphysical experience only so much was admitted as could give a mentally rational explanation of itself according to a certain range of ideas — all the rest, everything that seemed to demand an occult, mystic or below-the-surface origin to explain it, was put aside as so much superstition. Popular beliefs that were the fruit sometimes of imagination but sometimes also of a traditional empirical knowledge or of a right instinct shared naturally the same fate. That all this was a hasty and illegitimate operation, itself based on the "superstition" of the all-sufficiency of the new method which really applies only to a limited field, is now becoming more and more evident. I agree with you that the word superstition is one which should be used either not at all or with great caution. It is evidently an anachronism to apply it to beliefs not accepted by the form of religion one happens oneself to follow or favour.

The growing reversal of opinion with regard to many things that were then condemned but are now coming into favour once more, is very striking. In addition to the instances you quote a hundred others might be added. One does not quite know why a belief in graphology should be condemned as irrational or superstitious; it seems to me quite rational to believe that a man's handwriting is the result of or consistent with his temperament and nature and, if so, it may very well prove on examination to be an index of character. It is now a known fact that each man is an individual by himself with his own peculiar formation different from others and made by minute variations in the general human plan, — this is true of small physical characteristics, it is evidently equally true of psychological characteristics; it is not unreasonable to suppose a correlation between the two. On that basis cheiromancy too may very well have a truth in it, for it is a known fact that the lines in an individual hand are different from the lines in others and that this as well as differences of physiognomy may carry in it psychological indications is not impossible. The difficulty for minds trained under rationalistic influences becomes greater when these lines or the data of astrology are interpreted as signs of destiny, because modern rationalism resolutely refused to admit that the future was determined or could be determinable. But this looks more and more like one of the "superstitions" of the modern mind, a belief curiously contradictory of the fundamental notions of Science. For Science has believed, at least until yesterday, that everything is determined in Nature and it attempts to find the law of that determination and to predict future physical happenings on that basis. If so, it is reasonable to suppose that there are unseen connections determining human events in the world and that future events may therefore be predictable. Whether it can be done on the lines of astrology or cheiromancy is a matter for enquiry and one does not get any farther by dismissing the possibility with a summary denial. The case for astrology is fairly strong; a case seems to exist for cheiromancy also.

On the other hand it is not safe to go too hastily in the other direction. There is the opposite tendency to believe everything in these fields and not keep one's eyes open to the element of limitation or error in these difficult branches of knowledge — it was this excess of belief that helped to discredit them, because their errors were patent. It does not seem to me established that the stars determine the future — though that is possible, but it does look as if they indicate it — or rather some certitudes and many potentialities of the future. Even the astrologers admit that there is another element of determination in man himself which limits the field of astrological prediction and may even alter many of its ascertained results. There is a very tangled and difficult complex of forces making up any determination of things in the world and when we have disentangled one thread of the skein and follow it we may get many striking results, but we cannot rely on it as the one wholly reliable clue. The mind's methods are too rigid and conveniently simple to unravel the true or whole truth whether of the Reality or of its separate phenomena.

I would accept your statement about the possibility of knowing much about a man from an observation of a small part of his being, physical or psychological, but I think it is to go too far to say that one can reconstruct a whole man from one minute particle of a hair. I should say from my knowledge of the complexity and multiplicity of elements in the human being that such a procedure would be hazardous and would leave a large part of the Unknown overshadowing the excessive certitude of this inferential structure.

I suppose we cannot go so far as to deny that there is such a thing as superstition — a fixed blind belief without any ground in something that is quite unsound and does not hang together. The human mind readily claps on such beliefs to things which can be or are in themselves true, and this is a mixture which very badly confuses the search for knowledge. But precisely because of that mixture, because somewhere behind the superstition or not far off from it there is very usually some real truth, one ought to be cautious in using the word or sweeping away with it as a convenient broom the true, the partly true and the unfounded together and claiming that the bare ground left is the only truth of the matter.

*

When I wrote that sentence [*about a "fixed blind belief"*] I was not thinking really of religious beliefs, but of common popular ideas and beliefs. Your feeling about the matter, in any case, is quite sound. One can and ought to believe and follow one's own path without condemning or looking down on others for having beliefs different from those one thinks or sees to be the best or the largest in truth. The spiritual field is many-sided and full of complexities and there is room for an immense variety of experiences. Besides, all mental egoism, — and spiritual egoism — has to be surmounted and this sense of superiority should therefore not be cherished.

P. S. A sincere, whole-hearted and one-pointed following of this Yoga should lead to a level where these rigid mental divisions do not exist for they are mental walls put round one part of Truth and Knowledge so as to cut it off from the rest, but this view from above the mind is comprehensive and everything falls into its place in the whole.

The Limitations of Science

I think what you write is unexceptionable as a statement of the necessary limitations of physical Science to its own field. It is only in the occult sciences that one can find the necessary connection or bridge between the spiritual and material which X is demanding from the physical sciences. X's attitude is a sort of reaction against the old error of the materialism which used science to discredit not only the mistakes of religion, but all spiritual truth — but that phase is now over and one can be content with recording its passing without trying to reverse the process by using science to support or establish spiritual truth — spiritual truth can exist in itself and needs no such buttressing from outside.

*

I think X bases his ideas on the attempt of Jeans, Eddington and other English scientists to thrust metaphysical conclusions into scientific facts; it is necessary that he should appreciate fully the objections of more austerely scientific minds to such a mixture. Moreover, spiritual seeking has its own accumulated knowledge which does not depend in the least on the theories or discoveries of science in the purely physical sphere. X's attempt like that of Jeans and others is a reaction against the illegitimate attempts of some scientific minds in the nineteenth century and of many others who took advantage of the march of scientific discovery to discredit or abolish as far as possible the religious spirit and to discredit also metaphysics as a cloudy verbiage, exalting science as the only clue to the truth of the universe. But I think that attitude is now dead or moribund; the scientists recognise, as you point out, the limits of their sphere. I may observe that the conflict between religion and science never arose in India (until the days of European education) because religion did not interfere with scientific discovery and scientists did not question religious or spiritual truth because the two things were kept on separate but not opposing lines.

*

The defect in what X writes about Science seems to be that he is insisting vehemently on the idea that Science is still materialistic or at least that scientists, Jeans and Eddington excepted, are still fundamentally materialists. This is not the fact. Most continental scientists have now renounced the idea that Science can explain the fundamentals of existence. They hold that Science is only concerned with process and not with fundamentals. They declare that it is not the business of Science nor is it within its means to decide anything about the great questions which concern philosophy and religion. This is the enormous change which the latest developments of Science have brought about. Science itself nowadays is neither materialistic nor idealistic. The rock on which materialism was built and which in the 19th century seemed unshakeable has now been shattered. Materialism has now become a philosophical speculation just like any other theory; it cannot claim to found itself on a sort of infallible Biblical authority, based on the facts and conclusions of Science. This change can be felt by one like myself who grew up in the heyday of absolute rule of scientific materialism in the 19th century. The way which had been almost entirely barred except by rebellion now lies wide open to spiritual truths, spiritual ideas, spiritual experiences. That is the real revolution. Mentalism is only a halfway house but mentalism and vitalism are now perfectly possible as hypotheses based on the facts of existence, scientific facts as well as any others. The facts of Science do not compel anyone to take any particular philosophical direction. They are now neutral and can even be used on one side or another though most scientists do not consider such a use as admissible. Nobody here ever said that the new discoveries of physics supported the ideas of religion or churches; they merely contended that Science had lost its old materialistic dogmatism and moved away by a revolutionary change from its old moorings.

It is this change which I expected and prophesied in my poems in the first *Ahana* volume, "A Vision of Science" and "In the Moonlight".[1]

*

Psychologists of course having to deal with mental movements more easily recognise that there can be no real equation between them and physiological processes and at the most mind and body react on each other as is inevitable since they are lodging together. But even a great physical scientist like Huxley recognised that mind was something quite different from matter and could not possibly be explained in the terms of matter. Only since then physical Science became very arrogant and presumptuous and tried to subject everything to itself and its processes. Now in theory it has begun to recognise its limitations in a general way, but the old mentality is still too habitual in most scientists to shake off yet.

*

[1] *These two poems are currently published in* Collected Poems, *volume 2 of* THE COMPLETE WORKS OF SRI AUROBINDO, *pp. 204–6 and 237–44.— Ed.*

The minds of these people [*scientists*] are too much accustomed to deal with physical things and things measurable by instruments and figures to be much good for any other provinces. Einstein's views outside his domain are crude and childish, a sort of unsubstantial commonplace idealism without grasp on realities. As a man can be a great scholar and yet simple and foolish, so a man can be a great scientist but his mind and ideas negligible in other things.

*

There is nothing superior in the scientist's brain except a faculty of observing and analysing and drawing conclusions. It is the intellectual plane.

*

The scientific mind refuses to leave anything unclassed. Has it not classified the Divine also?

*

How does Sir James Jeans or any other scientist know that it was by a "mere accident" that life came into existence or that there is no life anywhere else in the universe or that life elsewhere must either be exactly the same as life here under the same conditions or not existent at all? These are mere mental speculations without any conclusiveness in them. Life can be an accident only if the whole world also is an accident — a thing created by Chance and governed by Chance. It is not worth while to waste time on this kind of speculation, for it is only the bubble of a moment.

The material universe is only the façade of an immense building which has other structures behind it and it is only if one knows the whole that one can have some knowledge of the truth of the material universe. There are vital, mental and spiritual ranges behind which give the material its significance. If the earth is the only field of the spiritual evolution in Matter — (assuming that) — then it must be as part of the total design. The idea that all the rest must be a waste is a human idea which would not trouble the vast Cosmic Spirit — whose consciousness and life are everywhere, in the slime and dust as much as in the human intelligence. But this is a speculative question which is quite alien to our practical purpose. For us it is the development of the spiritual consciousness in the human body that matters.

In this development there are stages — the whole truth cannot be known till all are passed and the final stage is there. The stage in which you are is one in which the Self is beginning to be realised, the Self free from all embodiment and not depending on embodiment for its perpetual existence. It is therefore natural that you should feel the embodiment to be something quite subordinate and like the earth-life of Jeans almost accidental. It is because of this stage that the Mayavadins, taking it for final, thought the world to be an illusion. But this is only a stage of the journey. Beyond this Self which is static, separate, formless, there is a greater consciousness in which the Silence and the Cosmic Activity are united but in another knowledge than the walled-in ignorance of the embodied human being. This Self is only one aspect of the Divine Reality. It is when one gets to that greater Consciousness that cosmic existence and form and life and mind no longer appear to be an accident but find their significance. Even there there are two stages, the overmental and the supramental, and it is not till one gets to the last that the full truth of existence can become entirely real to the consciousness. Observe what you experience and know that it has its value and is indispensable as a stage, but do not take the experience as the final knowledge.

Physics and Metaphysics

The difficulty is that you are a non-scientist trying to impose your ideas on the most difficult because most material field of science — physics. It is only if you were a scientist yourself basing your ideas on universally acknowledged scientific facts or else your own discoveries — though even then with much difficulty — that you could get a hearing or your opinion have any weight. Otherwise you open yourself to the accusation of pronouncing in a field where you have no authority, just as the scientist himself does when he pronounces on the strength of his discoveries that there is no God. When the scientist says that "scientifically speaking God is a hypothesis which is no longer necessary" he is talking arrant nonsense — for the existence of God is not and cannot be and never was a scientific hypothesis or problem at all, it is and always has been a spiritual or a metaphysical problem. You cannot speak scientifically about it at all either pro or con. The metaphysician or the spiritual seeker has a right to point out that it is nonsense; but if you lay down the law to the scientist in the field of science, you run the risk of having the same objection turned against you.

As to the unity of all knowledge, that is a thing *in posse*, not yet *in esse*. The mechanical method of knowledge leads to certain results, the higher method leads to certain others, and they at many points fundamentally disagree. How is the difference to be bridged — for each seems valid in its own field: it is a problem to be solved, but you cannot solve it in the way you propose. Least of all in the field of physics. In psychology one can say that the mechanical or physiological approach takes hold of the thing by the blind end and is the least fruitful of all — for psychology is not primarily a thing of mechanism and measure, it opens to a vast field beyond the physical instrumentalities of the body consciousness. In biology one can get a glimpse of something beyond mechanism, because there is from the beginning a stir of consciousness progressing and organising itself more and more for self-expression. But in physics you are in the very domain of the mechanical law where process is everything and the driving consciousness has chosen to conceal itself with the greatest thoroughness — so that, "scientifically speaking", it does not exist there. One can discover it there only by occultism and Yoga, but the methods of occult science and of Yoga are not measurable or followable by the means of physical science — so the gulf remains still in existence. It may be bridged one day, but the physicist is not likely to be the bridge builder, so it is no use asking him to try what is beyond his province.

*

Science and Yoga

The Isha Upanishad passage[2] is of course a much larger statement of the nature of universal existence than the Einstein theory which is confined to the physical universe. You can deduce too a much larger law of relativity from the statement in the verse. What it means from this point of view — for it contains much more in it — is that the absolute Reality exists but it is immovable and always the same, the universal movement is a motion of consciousness in this Reality of which only the Transcendent itself can seize the truth, which is self-evident to It, while the apprehension of it by the Gods (the mind, senses etc.) must necessarily be imperfect and relative since they can try to follow but none can really overtake (apprehend or seize) that Truth, each being limited by its own view-point,[3] lesser instrumentality or capacity of consciousness etc. This is the familiar attitude of the Indian or at least the Vedantic mind which held that our knowledge, perception and experience of things in the world and of the world itself must be *vyāvahārika*, relative, practical or pragmatic only, — so declared Shankara, — it is in fact an illusory knowledge, the real Truth of things lying beyond our mental and sensory consciousness. Einstein's relativity is a scientific, not a metaphysical statement. The form and field of it are different — but, I suppose, if one goes back from it and beyond it to its essential significance, the real reason for its being so, one can connect it with the Vedantic conclusion. But to justify that to the intellect, you would have to go through a whole process to show how the connection comes — it does not self-evidently follow.

As for Jeans, many would say that his conclusions are not at all legitimate. Einstein's law is a scientific generalisation based upon certain relations proper to the domain of physics and, if valid, valid there in the limits of that domain, or, if you like, in the general domain of scientific observation and measurement of physical processes and motions; but how can you transform

---

[2] "*One unmoving that is swifter than Mind, That the Gods reach not, for It progresses ever in front. That, standing, passes beyond others as they run.*" Isha Upanishad, *verse 4. Sri Aurobindo's translation. See Isha Upanishad, volume 17 of* THE COMPLETE WORKS OF SRI AUROBINDO, *p. 6.*

[3] The Gods besides are in and subject to Space and Time, part of the motion in Space and Time, not superior to it.

that at once into a metaphysical generalisation? It is a jump over a considerable gulf — or a forceful transformation of one thing into another, of a limited physical result into an unlimited all-embracing formula. I don't quite know what Einstein's law really amounts to, but does it amount to more than this that our scientific measurements of time and other things are, in the conditions under which they have to be made, relative because subject to the unavoidable drawback of these conditions? What metaphysically follows from that — if anything at all does follow — it is for the metaphysicians, not the scientists to determine. The Vedantic position was that the Mind itself (as well as the senses) is a limited power making its own representations, constructions, formations and imposing them on the Reality. That is a much bigger and more intricate affair shooting down into the very roots of our existence. I think myself there are many positions taken by modern Science which tend to be helpful to that view — though in the nature of things they cannot be sufficient to prove it.

I state the objections only; I myself see certain fundamental truths underlying all the domains and the one Reality everywhere. But there is a great difference in the instruments used and the ways of research followed by the seekers in these different ways (the physical, the occult and the spiritual) and for the intellect at least the bridge between them has still to be built. One can point out analogies but it can be maintained very well that Science cannot be used for yielding or buttressing results of spiritual knowledge. The other side can be maintained also and it is best that both should be stated — so this is not meant to discourage your thesis.

*

The article [*on metaphysics and science*] reads as if it had been written by a professor rather than a philosopher. What you speak of [4] is, I suppose, a survival of the nineteenth-century scientific contempt for metaphysics; all thinking must be based on

---

[4] The correspondent said that the author of the article assumed that metaphysics is *"one among the experimental sciences and has a darkened* séance *room for its laboratory"*. — Ed.

scientific *facts* and the generalisations of science, often so faulty and ephemeral, must be made the basis for any sound metaphysical thinking. That is to make philosophy the handmaid of science, metaphysics the camp-follower of physics and to deny her her sovereign rights in her own city. It ignores the fact that the philosopher has his own domain and his own instruments; he may use scientific discoveries as material just as he may use any other facts of existence, but whatever generalisations science offers he must judge by his own standards — whether they are valid for transference to the metaphysical plane and, if so, how far. Still in the heyday of physical science before it discovered its own limitations and the shakiness of its scheme of things floating precariously in a huge infinity or boundless Finite of the Unknown, there was perhaps some excuse for such an attitude. But spiritualism glorified under the name of psychical research? That is not a science; it is a mass of obscure and ambiguous documents from which you can draw only a few meagre and doubtful generalisations. Moreover, so far as it belongs to the occult, it touches only the inferior regions of the occult — what we would call the lowest vital worlds — where there is as much falsehood and fake and confused error as upon the earth and even more. What is a philosopher to do with all that obscure and troubled matter? I do not catch the point of many of his remarks. Why should a prediction of a future event alter our conception — at least any philosophic conception — of Time? It can alter one's ideas of the relation of events to each other or of the working out of forces or of the possibilities of consciousness, but Time remains the same as before.

The dream[5] is, of course, the rendering of an attempt at

---

[5] *A dream in which the correspondent had a long-distance telephone conversation. He commented: "Is there not something very symbolic about the emergence of telephony and cinematography just at an epoch when human behaviour and relationship is breaking down? Owing to falsehood and callousness and self-centred indifference to others, each person is to every other more and more a meaningless shadow and a deceptive voice." He also spoke about the decline of nobility and tenderness in art: "I fail to see any further need for human beings either as creators or enjoyers of such 'art'; perhaps in an Asuric civilisation, men are anyhow superfluous and only 'incarnated Asuras' are required?" — Ed.*

communication on the subtle plane. As for the telephone and cinema, there is something of what you say, but it seems to me that these and other modern things could have taken on a different character if they had been accepted and used in a different spirit. Mankind was not ready for these discoveries, in the spiritual sense, nor even, if the present confusions are a sign, intellectually ready. The aesthetic downfall is perhaps due to other causes, a disappointed idealism in its recoil generating its opposite, a dry and cynical intellectualism which refuses to be duped by the ideal, the romantic or the emotional or anything that is higher than the reason walking by the light of the senses. The Asuras of the past were after all often rather big beings; the trouble about the present ones is that they are not really Asuras, but beings of the lower vital world, violent, brutal and ignoble, but above all narrow-minded, ignorant and obscure. But this kind of cynical narrow intellectualism that is rampant now, does not last — it prepares its own end by increasing dryness — men begin to feel the need of new springs of life.

*

I am afraid I have lost all interest in these speculations [*about subjectivism in modern physics*]; things are getting too serious for me to waste time on these inconclusive intellectualities. I do not at all mind your driving your point triumphantly home and replacing a dogmatism from materialistic Science on its throne of half a century ago from which it could victoriously ban all thought surpassing its own narrow bounds as mere wordy metaphysics and mysticism and moonshine. Obviously, if material energies alone can exist in the material world, there can be no possibility of a life divine on the earth. A mere metaphysical "sleight of mind", as one might call it, could not justify it against the objections of scientific negation and concrete common sense. I had thought that even many scientific minds on the Continent had come to admit that Science could no longer claim to decide what was the reality of things, that it had no means of deciding it and could only discover and describe the how and process of the operations of material Force in the physical front of things.

That left the field open to higher thought and speculation, spiritual experience and even to mysticism, occultism and all those greater things which almost everybody had come to disbelieve as impossible nonsense. That was the condition of things when I was in England. If that is to return or if Russia and her dialectical materialism are to lead the world, well, fate must be obeyed and life divine must remain content to wait perhaps for another millennium. But I do not like the idea of one of our periodicals[6] being the arena for a wrestle of that kind. That is all. I am writing under the impression of your earlier article on this subject, as I have not gone carefully through the later ones; I dare say these later ones may be entirely convincing and I would find after reading them that my own position was wrong and that only an obstinate mystic could still believe in such a conquest of Matter by the Spirit as I had dared to think possible. But I am just such an obstinate mystic; so, if I allowed your exposition of the matter to be published in one of our own periodicals, I would be under the obligation of returning to the subject in which I have lost interest and therefore the inclination to write, so as to reestablish my position and would have to combat the claim of materialistic Science to pronounce anything on these matters on which it has no means of enquiry nor any possibility of arriving at a valid decision. Perhaps I would have practically to rewrite *The Life Divine* as an answer to the victorious "negation of the materialist"! This is the only explanation which I can give, apart from sheer want of time to tackle the subject, for my long and disappointing silence.

Space and Time

You are reasoning on the analogy of our own very cabined and limited sense-consciousness and its rather clumsy relations with the happenings in material space. What is space after all but an extension of conscious being in which Consciousness-Force builds its own surroundings? In the subtle physical plane there

---

[6] *Mother India, a journal published in Mumbai at that time.* — Ed.

are not one, but many layers of consciousness and each moves in its own being, that is to say, in its own space. I have said that each subtle plane is a conglomeration or series of worlds. Each space may at any point meet, penetrate or coincide with another; accordingly at one point of meeting or coincidence there might be several subtle objects occupying what we might rather arbitrarily call the same space, and yet they may not be in any actual relation with each other. If there is a relation created, it is the multiple consciousness of the seer in which the meeting-place becomes apparent that creates it.

On the other hand, there may be a relation between objects in different regions of space correlated to each other as in the case of the gross physical object and its subtle counterpart. There you can more easily reason of relations between one space and another.

*

The objection[7] is founded on human three-dimensional ideas of Space and division in spaces, which are again founded upon the limited nature of the human senses. To some beings space is one-dimensional, to others two-dimensional, to others three-dimensional — but there are other dimensions also. It is well recognised in metaphysics that the Infinite can be in a point and not only in extension of space — just as there is an eternity of extension in Time but also an Eternity which is independent of Time so that it can be felt in the moment — one has not to think of millions and millions of years in order to realise it. So too the rigid distinction of One against Many, a One that cannot be many or of an All that is made up by addition and not self-existent are crude mental notions of the outer finite mind that cannot be applied to the Infinite. If the All were of this material and unspiritual character, tied down to a primary arithmetic and geometry, the realisation of the universe in oneself, of the

---

[7] *The correspondent asked: "How can the Divine, who is All or Omnipresent, incarnate in the small space of a human body? I believe it is because this seems impossible to the mind that the Arya Samajists do not accept the possibility of incarnation." — Ed.*

all in each and each in all, of the universe in the Bindu would be impossible. Your Arya Samajists are evidently innocent of the elements of metaphysical thinking or they would not make such objections.

*

Time and Space are not limited, they are infinite — they are the terms of an extension of consciousness in which things take place or are arranged in a certain relation, succession, order. There are again different orders of Time and Space; that too depends on the consciousness. The Eternal is extended in Time and Space, but he is also beyond all Time and Space. Timelessness and Time are two terms of the eternal existence. The Spaceless Eternal is not one indivisible infinity of Space, there is in it no near or far, no here or there — the Timeless Eternal is not measurable by years or hours or aeons, the experience of it has been described as the eternal moment. But for the mind this state cannot be described except by negatives, — one has to go beyond and to realise it.

*

Time is to the Intuition an extension of consciousness in which happenings are arranged and has not the same rigidity that it has to the intellect.

*

The idea of time may be a mental construction, but the sense of it may not be. Savages have the idea of time but it is in connection with the sun and stars and the lapse of day and night and the seasons, not perhaps a separate construction — but one is not sure for they have metaphysical conceptions of their own. Animals are not, I think, so limited in their consciousness — they have not only sensations, but an acute memory of certain things, observation, clear associations, an intelligence that plans, a very accurate sense of place and memory of place, an initial power of reasoning (not reflectively as the human mind does, but practically as any vital mind can do). I have seen a young kitten observing, arriving at a correct conclusion, proceeding to do what was necessary for her purpose, a necessity imposed by that conclusion, just as a human child might do. We cannot therefore say that animals have no ideas. No clear measure of yesterday and tomorrow, perhaps, but the perception of past and future needs is there and of right times and seasons also — all vital, practical, not reflectively mental in the human way.

But it is true that when one gets beyond the mind, this sense of time changes into timelessness, into the eternal present.

*

No doubt, the physical regulated time consciousness belongs mainly to the waking state but it can be subliminal as well as of the mental waking consciousness. E.g. sometimes one wills at night to get up at a fixed time in the morning and wakes exactly at that hour and minute — it is something in the subliminal being that recorded the time and vigilantly executed it.

*

When one begins to feel the inner being and live in it (the result of the experience of peace and silence) the ordinary time sense disappears or becomes purely external.

*

The present is a convention or only a constant movement out of the past into the future.

Matter

As for what you write about your experience and your ideas, it looks as if it were simply the old thoughts and movements rising, as they often do, to interfere with the straight course of the sadhana. Mental realisations and ideas of this kind are at best only half-truths and not always even that; once one has taken up a sadhana that goes beyond the mind, it is a mistake to give them too much importance. They can easily become by misapplication a fruitful ground for error.

If you examine the ideas that have come to you, you will see that they are quite inadequate. For example:

1. Matter is *jaḍa* only in appearance. As even modern Science admits, Matter is only energy in action, and, as we know in India, energy is force of consciousness in action.

2. Prakriti in the material world seems to be *jaḍa*, but this too is only an appearance. Prakriti is in reality the conscious power of the Spirit.

3. A bringing down of the Spirit into Matter cannot lead to a *laya* in *jaḍa prakṛti*. A descent of the Spirit could only mean a descent of light, consciousness and power, not a growth of unconsciousness and inertia which is what is meant by the *jaḍa laya*.

4. The Spirit is there already in Matter as everywhere else; it is only a surface apparent unconsciousness or involved consciousness which veils its presence. What we have to do is to awake Matter to the spiritual consciousness concealed in it.

5. What we aim at bringing down into the material world is the supramental consciousness, light and energy, because it is this alone that can truly transform it.

If there is at any time a growth of unconsciousness and inertia, it is because of the resistance of the ordinary nature to the spiritual change. But this is usually raised up in order to be dealt with and eliminated. If it is allowed to remain concealed and not raised up, the difficulty will never be grappled with and no real transformation will take place.

*

If there were no creative power in the material energy, there would be no material universe. Matter is not unconscious or without dynamism—only it is an involved Force and Consciousness that work in it. It is what the psychologists call the Inconscient from which all comes—but it is not really Inconscient.

Animals

The satisfaction of their emotions and desires and their bodily needs [*is what animals desire*] — mostly. Animals are predominantly the vital creation on earth — the mind in them also is a vital mind — they act according to the push of the forces and have a vital but not a mental will.

*

Even the animal is more in touch with a certain harmony in things than man. Man's only superiority is a more complex consciousness and capacity (but terribly perverted and twisted by misuse of Mind) and the ability (not much used as yet) of reaching towards higher things.

*

Human life and mind are neither in tune with Nature like the animals nor with Spirit — it [*human nature*] is disturbed, incoherent, conflicting with itself, without harmony and balance. We can then regard it as diseased, if not itself a disease.

*

Yes, it is a more simple and honest consciousness — that of the animal. Of course it expects something, but even if it does not get, the affection remains. Many animals, even if ill-treated, do not lose their love which means a remarkable psychic development in the vital.

*

The emotional being of animals is often much more psychic than that of men who can be very insensitive. There were recently pictures of the tame tigress kept by a family and afterwards given by them to a Zoo. The look of sorrow on the face of the tigress in her cage at once gentle and tragically poignant is so intense as to be heartbreaking.

*

A very strong time sense [*in animals*] — at least some of them — but usually it works only in connection with strong desires or habits, e.g. food.

*

Cats have a very sure vital perception.

*

Most animals do not usually attack unless they are menaced or frightened or somehow made angry — and they can feel the atmosphere of people.

*

There are people who can move the ears without doing Yoga at all or calling upon the resources of the Kundalini. I suppose it is simply a movement that man has lost through disuse, not having had like the animals to prick up his ear at every moment to listen to sounds that might indicate danger. I suppose he could revive the faculty if it were of any use.

*

Yes — to watch the animals with the right perception of their consciousness helps to get out of the human mental limitations and see the Cosmic Consciousness on earth individualising itself in all forms — plant, animal, man and growing towards what is beyond man.

Plants

It is true that the plant world — even the animals if one takes them the right way — can be much better than human beings. It is the mental distortion that makes men worse.

*

The plants are very psychic, but they can express it only by silence and beauty.

*

Form, colour, scent + something else which is indefinable [*constitute the beauty of flowers*].

*

The rose is not the only beautiful flower, there are hundreds of others; most flowers are beautiful. The rose is among the first of flowers because of the richness of its colour, the intensity of sweetness of its scent and the grace and magnificence of its form.

Life on Other Planets

As for the other question, there is no reason to suppose that there is not life in any part of the material cosmic system except earth. No doubt the suns and nebulae cannot harbour material life because there is not the necessary basis, but wherever there is a formed world, Life can exist. It used formerly to be supposed that life could not exist except in conditions identical with the earth, but it is now being discovered that even man and the animals can adapt themselves to atmospheric conditions deficient in oxygen such as exist in the stratosphere — this proves that all depends on adaptation. There are animals that can exist only in the sea, yet sea-animals have become amphibious or turned into land animals — so animals on earth can by habit of the adaptation live only in a certain range of atmosphere and need oxygen, but they could adapt themselves to other conditions — it is a law of habit of Nature, not a law of inevitable necessity of Nature. It is therefore quite possible for life to exist on other planets in our and other systems, though the beings there may not be quite like earthly humanity or life quite the same.

Section Two

Religion, Idealism, Morality and Yoga

Chapter One
Religion and Yoga

Religion and the Truth

The Divine Truth is greater than any religion or creed or scripture or idea or philosophy — so you must not tie yourself to any of these things.

*

I regard the spiritual history of mankind and especially of India as a constant development of a divine purpose, not a book that is closed, the lines of which have to be constantly repeated. Even the Upanishads and the Gita were not final though everything may be there in seed. In this development the recent spiritual history of India is a very important stage and the names I mentioned [*Ramakrishna and Vivekananda*] had a special prominence in my thought at the time — they seemed to me to indicate the lines from which the future spiritual development had most directly to proceed, not staying but passing on. I do not know that I would put my meaning exactly in the language you suggest. I may say that it is far from my purpose to propagate any religion new or old for humanity in the future. A way to be opened that is still blocked, not a religion to be founded, is my conception of the matter.

*

It is news to me that I have excluded Mahomedans from the Yoga. I have not done it any more than I have excluded Europeans or Christians. As for giving up one's past, if that means giving up the outer forms of the old religions, it is done as much by the Hindus here as by the Mahomedans. The Hindus here — even those who were once orthodox Brahmins and have grown old in it, — give up all observance of caste, take food from Pariahs and are served by them, associate and eat with Mahomedans, Christians, Europeans, cease to practise temple worship or

Sandhya (daily prayer and mantras), accept a non-Hindu from Europe as their spiritual director. These are things people who have Hinduism as their aim and object would not do — they do it because they are obliged here to look to a higher ideal in which these things have no value. What is kept of Hinduism is Vedanta and Yoga, in which Hinduism is one with Sufism of Islam and with the Christian mystics. But even here it is not Vedanta and Yoga in their traditional limits (their past), but widened and rid of many ideas that are peculiar to the Hindus. If I have used Sanskrit terms and figures, it is because I know them and do not know Persian and Arabic. I have not the slightest objection to anyone here drawing inspiration from Islamic sources if they agree with the Truth as Sufism agrees with it. On the other hand I have not the slightest objection to Hinduism being broken to pieces and disappearing from the face of the earth, if that is the Divine Will. I have no attachment to past forms; what is Truth will always remain; the Truth alone matters.

Religion in India

Religion is always imperfect because it is a mixture of man's spirituality with the errors that come in trying to sublimate ignorantly his lower nature. Hindu religion appears to me as a cathedral temple half in ruins, noble in the mass, often fantastic in detail, but always fantastic with a significance — crumbled and overgrown in many places, but a cathedral temple in which service is still done to the Unseen and its real presence can be felt by those who enter with the right spirit. The outer social structure which it built for its approach is another matter.

*

If it is meant by the statement [*of Mahatma Gandhi*][1] that the

---

[1] "*But religion is not like a house or a cloak, which can be changed at will. It is more an integral part of one's self than of one's body. Religion is the tie that binds one to one's Creator and whilst the body perishes, as it has to, religion persists even after death.*" M. K. Gandhi, on a statement by B. R. Ambedkar concerning change of religion, in The Collected Works of Mahatma Gandhi, vol. 62 (New Delhi: The Publications Division, 1975), p. 37. — Ed.

form of religion is something permanent and unchangeable, then that cannot be accepted. But if religion here means one's way of communion with the Divine, then it is true that that is something belonging to the inner being and cannot be changed like a house or a cloak for the sake of some personal, social or worldly convenience. If a change is to be made, it can only be for an inner spiritual reason, because of some development from within. No one can be bound to any form of religion or any particular creed or system, but if he changes the one he has accepted for another, for external reasons, that means he has inwardly no religion at all and both his old and his new religion are only an empty formula. At bottom that is, I suppose, what the statement drives at. Preference for a different approach to the Truth or the desire of inner spiritual self-expression are not the motives of the recommendation of change to which objection is made by the Mahatma here; the object proposed is an enhancement of social status and consideration which is no more a spiritual motive than conversion for the sake of money or marriage. If a man has no religion in himself, he can change his credal profession for any motive; if he has, he cannot; he can only change it in response to an inner spiritual need. If a man has a bhakti for the Divine in the form of Krishna, he can't very well say, "I will swap Krishna for Christ so that I may become socially respectable."

*

You can write to him not to be depressed by his failures but to go on aspiring and trust in the Divine Grace. He should not allow himself to be impeded by narrow caste ideas. Always in India the Brahmins have bowed down before a man of spiritual realisation, who becomes by that very fact of realisation above caste. He should open himself more to the help from here. Man is a mass of imperfections — it is only by the divine Grace that he reaches the Divine.

Religious Ceremonies

It is correct, religions at best modify only the surface of the nature. Moreover they degenerate very soon into a routine of ceremonial habitual worship and fixed dogmas.

*

If you feel no enthusiasm for the *śrāddha* it is better definitely to stop it. Once on this path there is no meaning in it any longer, — for the reason you yourself give.[2] The *śrāddha* is, besides, entirely on the vital plane and if help has to be given to those who have passed into other worlds of consciousness, there are better ways of doing it.

*

Replace the *śrāddha* by a long meditation with X on the father praying that he may have all the rest and illumination that the departed can have.

*

I only said what was originally *meant* by the ceremonies — the rites. I was not referring to the feeding of the caste or the Brahmins which is not a rite or ceremony. Whether the *śrāddha* as performed is actually effective is another matter — for those who perform it have not either the knowledge or the occult power.

*

The old traditions [*stotras, homas, aradhanas, recitations, etc.*] are still strong with many — let them satisfy this tendency in this way so long as it does not drop from them.

*

Useless and therefore inadvisable [*to sacrifice animals to Kali*]. External sacrifices of this kind have no longer any meaning — as so many saints have said, sacrifice ego, anger, lust etc. to Kali, not goats or cocks.

---

[2] *The correspondent said that a sadhak is expected to forget all conventional family relationships and live only for the Divine. — Ed.*

Religious Fanaticism

There is nothing noble in fanaticism — there is no nobility of motive though there may be a fierce enthusiasm of motive. Religious fanaticism is something psychologically low-born and ignorant — and usually in its action fierce, cruel and base. Religious ardour like that of the martyr who sacrifices himself only is a different thing.

Chapter Two
Idealism and Spirituality

Human Perfection and Spirituality

I would not describe the perfections you describe in your letter, fine though they are, as spiritual in the proper sense of the word — for they lack the essential condition of spirituality. Perfection of all kinds is indeed good, as it is the sign of the pressure of the consciousness in the material world towards full self-expression in this or that limit, on this or that level. In a certain sense it is an urge of the Divine itself hidden in forms that tends in the lesser degrees of consciousness towards its own increasing self-revelation. Perfection of an object or a scene in inanimate Nature, animate perfection of strength, speed, physical beauty, courage or animal fidelity, affection, intelligence, perfection of art, music, poetry, literature, — perfection of the intellect in any kind of mental activity, the perfect statesman, warrior, artist, craftsman, — perfection in vital force and capacity, perfection in ethical qualities, character, temperament, — all have their high value, their place as rungs in the ladder of evolution, the seried steps of the spirit's emergence. If one likes to call that spiritual because of this hidden urge behind it one can do so; it can at least be regarded as a preparation for the secret spirit's emergence. But thought and knowledge can only proceed by making the necessary distinctions. Much confusion is created by neglecting them. This mental idealism, ethical development, religious piety and fervour, occult powers and feats have all been taken as spirituality and the spiritual evolution kept tied to the moorings of the planes of lesser consciousness which do indeed prepare the soul by experience for the spiritual consciousness but are not themselves that. For perfection can only become truly spiritual when it is founded on the awakened spiritual consciousness and takes on its peculiar essence. We are told by Europeans that the lined and ravaged face of the Greek bust of Homer is far more spiritual than the empty ecstatic smile of the Buddha. We are told often nowadays that to earn for one's family and carry out our domestic duties, to be a good and moral man, a perfect citizen, patriot, worker for the country, is far more spiritual than to sit in idle meditation seeking for a remote and invisible Deity. Philanthropy, altruism, service to mankind are represented as the true spiritual things. Mental idealisms, ethical strivings, aesthetic finenesses are put forward by the modern mind as things spiritual. All this is represented as the best and highest we can achieve — though an increasing disillusionment, dissatisfaction, feeling of emptiness in them is also growing at the same time. All this has had its use, for everything has its own value in its own place and those who are satisfied with them are entitled to give them their full value and hold them as the great good and the thing to be done, kartavyam karma. But spirituality stands on its own basis and does not depend on these things nor does it even include them so long as they are based on some other than the spiritual consciousness and not transformed on the inner spiritual basis. So also people speak of religious men as spiritual, but one may be a very religious man yet not spiritual. The popular idea confuses great feats of occult power, ascetic feats, miracles, astonishing performances like those of your Jewel Sannyasi as the works of a spiritual achievement and the signs of a great Yogi. But one may be a powerful occultist or do marvels of asceticism and yet be not spiritual at all — for in any true sense of the word, in its proper and native significance it means one who has attained to the spiritual consciousness, the realisation of the inner or higher Self, the contact or union with the Divine or that which is eternal or is striving after and approaching these things. Spiritual perfection can only come by a life based on that search and that achievement.[1]

The Collapse of Twentieth-Century Idealism

Tagore, of course, belonged to an age which had faith in its

---

[1] *This is the draft of a letter reproduced in a thoroughly rewritten form on pages 424–27.* — Ed.

ideas and whose very denials were creative affirmations. That makes an immense difference. Your strictures on his later development may or may not be correct, but this mixture even was the note of the day and it expressed a tangible hope of a fusion into something new and true — therefore it could create. Now all that idealism has been smashed to pieces by the immense adverse Event and everybody is busy exposing its weakness, but nobody knows what to put in its place. A mixture of scepticism and slogans, "Heil Hitler" and the Fascist salute and Five-Year Plan and the beating of everybody into one amorphous shape, a disabused denial of all ideals on one side and on the other a blind shut-my-eyes and shut-everybody's-eyes plunge into the bog in the hope of finding some firm foundation there, will not carry us very far. And what else is there? Until new spiritual values are discovered, no great enduring creation is possible.

*

It is queer these intellectuals go on talking of creation while all they stand for is collapsing into the *Néant* without their being able to raise a finger to save it. What the devil are they going to create and from what material? and of what use if a Hitler with his cudgel or a Mussolini with his castor oil can come and wash it out or beat it into dust in a moment?

*

If there are such great spiritual men in Europe [*as a book reviewer claimed*], they seem to have the gift of invisibility. Or perhaps he means intellectuals like Romain Rolland or else Roman Catholic priests and cardinals or the Reverend Holmes or pacifists like Lord Robert Cecil or in the past Tolstoy who spent his whole life trying in vain to live according to his ideals. Idealising intellectualism and religionism are all that is left of spirituality in Europe.

Chapter Three

Morality and Yoga

The Spiritual Life and the Ordinary Life

The spiritual life (*adhyātma jīvana*), the religious life (*dharma jīvana*) and the ordinary human life of which morality is a part are three quite different things and one must know which one desires and not confuse the three together. The ordinary life is that of the average human consciousness separated from its own true self and from the Divine and led by the common habits of the mind, life and body which are the laws of the Ignorance. The religious life is a movement of the same ignorant human consciousness, turning or trying to turn away from the earth towards the Divine but as yet without knowledge and led by the dogmatic tenets and rules of some sect or creed which claims to have found the way out of the bonds of the earth-consciousness into some beatific Beyond. The religious life may be the first approach to the spiritual, but very often it is only a turning about in a round of rites, ceremonies and practices or set ideas and forms without any issue. The spiritual life, on the contrary, proceeds directly by a change of consciousness, a change from the ordinary consciousness, ignorant and separated from its true self and from God, to a greater consciousness in which one finds one's true being and comes first into direct and living contact and then into union with the Divine. For the spiritual seeker this change of consciousness is the one thing he seeks and nothing else matters.

Morality is a part of the ordinary life; it is an attempt to govern the outward conduct by certain mental rules or to form the character by these rules in the image of a certain mental ideal. The spiritual life goes beyond the mind; it enters into the deeper consciousness of the Spirit and acts out of the truth of the Spirit. As for the question about the ethical life and the need to realise God, it depends on what is meant by fulfilment of the objects of life. If an entry into the spiritual consciousness is part of it, then mere morality will not give it to you.

Politics as such has nothing to do with the spiritual life. If the spiritual man does anything for his country, it is in order to do the will of the Divine and as part of a divinely appointed work and not from any other common human motive. In none of his acts does he proceed from the common mental and vital motives which move ordinary men but acts out of the truth of the Spirit and from an inner command of which he knows the source.

The kind of worship (*pūjā*) spoken of in the letter belongs to the religious life. It can, if rightly done in the deepest religious spirit, prepare the mind and heart to some extent but no more. But if worship is done as part of meditation or with a true aspiration to the spiritual reality and the spiritual consciousness and with the yearning for contact and union with the Divine, then it can be spiritually effective.

If you have a sincere aspiration to the spiritual change in your heart and soul, then you will find the way and the Guide. A mere mental seeking and questioning are not enough to open the doors of the Spirit.

*

In the ordinary life, people accept the vital movements, anger, desire, greed, sex etc. as natural, allowable and legitimate things, part of the human nature. Only so far as society discourages them or wishes to keep them within fixed limits or subject to a decent restraint or measure, people try to control them so as to conform to the social standard of morality or rule of conduct. Here on the contrary as in all spiritual life, the conquest and complete mastery of these things is demanded. That is why the struggle is more felt, not because these things rise more strongly in sadhaks than in ordinary men, but because of the intensity of the struggle between the spiritual mind which demands control and the vital movements which rebel and wish to continue in the new as they did in the old life. As for the idea that the sadhana raises up things of the kind, the only truth in that is this that, first, there are many things in the ordinary man of which he is not conscious because the vital hides them from the mind and gratifies them without the mind realising what is the force that is moving the action — thus things that are done under the plea of altruism, philanthropy, service etc. are largely moved by ego which hides itself behind these justifications; in Yoga the secret motive has to be pulled out from behind the veil, exposed and got rid of. Secondly, some things are suppressed in the ordinary life and remain lying in the nature, suppressed but not eliminated; they may rise up any day or they may express themselves in nervous forms or other disorders of the mind or vital or body without it being evident what is their real cause. This has been recently discovered by European psychologists and much emphasised, even exaggerated in a new science called psychoanalysis. Here again in sadhana one has to become conscious of these suppressed impulses and eliminate them — this may be called raising up, but that does not mean that they have to be raised up into action but only raised up before the consciousness so as to be cleared out of the being.

As for some men being able to control themselves and others being swept away, that is due to difference of temperament. Some men are sattwic and control comes easy to them, up to a certain point at least; others are more rajasic and find control difficult and often impossible. Some have a strong mind and mental will and others are vital men in whom the vital passions are stronger or more on the surface. Some do not think control necessary and let themselves go. In sadhana the mental or moral control has to be replaced by the spiritual mastery — for the mental control is only partial and it controls but does not liberate; it is only the psychic and spiritual that can do that. That is the main difference in this respect between the ordinary and the spiritual life.

*

Everything depends upon the aim you put before you. If for the realisation of one's spiritual aim it is necessary to give up the ordinary life of the Ignorance (*saṁsāra*), it must be done; the claim of the ordinary life cannot stand against that of the spirit.

If a Yoga of works alone is chosen as the path, then one may remain in the *saṁsāra*, but it will be freely, as a field of action and not from any sense of obligation; for the Yogin must be free inwardly from all ties and attachments. On the other hand there is no necessity to live the family life — one can leave it and take any kind of works as a field of action.

In the Yoga practised here the aim is to rise to a higher consciousness and to live out of the higher consciousness alone, not with the ordinary motives. This means a change of life as well as a change of consciousness. But all are not so circumstanced that they can cut loose from the ordinary life; they accept it therefore as a field of experience and self-training in the earlier stages of the sadhana. But they must take care to look at it as a field of experience only and to get free from the ordinary desires, attachments and ideas which usually go with it; otherwise it becomes a drag and hindrance on their sadhana. When one is not compelled by circumstances there is no necessity to continue the ordinary life.

One becomes tamasic by leaving the ordinary actions and life only if the vital is so accustomed to draw its motives of energy from the ordinary consciousness and its desires and activities that if it loses them, it loses all joy and charm and energy of existence. But if one has a spiritual aim and an inner life and the vital part accepts them, then it draws its energies from within and there is no danger of one's being tamasic.

Morality

The principle of life which I seek to establish is spiritual. Morality is a question of man's mind and vital, it belongs to a lower plane of consciousness. A spiritual life therefore cannot be founded on a moral basis, it must be founded on a spiritual basis. This does not mean that the spiritual man must be immoral — as if there were no other law of conduct than the moral. The law of action of the spiritual consciousness is higher, not lower than the moral — it is founded on union with the Divine and living in the Divine Consciousness and its action is founded on obedience to the Divine Will.

*

The beliefs you speak of with regard to right and wrong, beauty and ugliness etc. are necessary for the human being and for the guidance of his life. He cannot do without the distinctions they involve. But in a higher consciousness when he enters into the Light or is touched by it, these distinctions disappear, for he is then approaching the eternal and infinite good and right which he reaches perfectly when he is able to enter into the Truth Consciousness or Supermind. The belief in the guidance of God is also justified by spiritual experience and is very necessary for the sadhana; this also rises to its highest and completest truth when one enters into the Light.

*

It [*the reason people remain calm and self-controlled in ordinary life*] is social pressure accompanied by a certain habit of mental control born of the social pressure. It is not from peace at all. Remove the social pressure even partly and as in England and America recently people let themselves go and do according to the vital impulses instead of controlling them — except of course those who stick to the religious and moral ideas of the past even when society drifts away from these ideas.

Vice and Virtue

Vice and virtue have nothing to do with darkness or light, truth and falsehood. The spiritual man rises above vice and virtue, he does not rise above truth and light, unless you mean by truth and light, human truth and mental light. They have to be transcended, just as virtue and vice have to be transcended.

*

Are you in a position to make a judgment as to what will or will not help God's work? You seem to have very elementary ideas in these matters. What is your idea of divinisation, — to be a virtuous man, a good husband, son, father, a good citizen etc.? In that case I myself am most undivine, — for I have never been these things. Men like X or Y would then be the great Transformed Divine Men.

*

Many sinners are people who are preparing to turn to the Divine and many virtuous people have a long run of lives yet to go through before they will think of it.

*

Vices are simply an overflow of energy in unregulated channels.

The Sattwic Man and the Spiritual Man

The passage through sattwa is the ordinary idea of Yoga, it is the preparation and purification by the yama-niyama of Patanjali or by other means in other Yogas, e.g., saintliness in the bhakti schools, the eightfold path in Buddhism etc., etc. In our Yoga the evolution through sattwa is replaced by the cultivation of equanimity, *samatā*, and by the psychic transformation.

*

It is a very beautiful character that you describe in your letter, a perfect type of the sattwic man, a fine and harmonised ethical nature supported and vivified by a fine and developed psychic being. But still, although it may be regarded as an excellent preparation for the spiritual life, it cannot by itself be called spirituality — unless indeed we reduce the meaning of the word to the connotation ordinarily given to it in the West where mental ideation, ethical striving, a flowering of fine character, altruism, self-sacrifice, self-denial, philanthropy, service to men or mankind are considered the height of spiritual aspiration or spiritual attainment. Obviously if that is to be the last word of earthly achievement, there is no need for anything farther; the close and vivid discovery of soul or self, the straining towards that which is behind life and above mind, the passion for the Eternal or the Infinite, the hunger for a freedom and wideness of consciousness and existence not limited by the narrow moulds of intellect, character and the past life-aims of humanity, the thirst for union with the Divine or for the pure bliss and beauty of spiritual existence not tied down to mental and vital values must be dismissed as a superfluous dream for which there is neither place nor necessity here. Yet these things have been not only dreamed of and hungered after but reached and tasted by beings born in a mortal and human body. Spirituality lies there; its essence consists in a bursting of the human mental, moral, aesthetic, vital moulds in order to reach beyond them and enter into a consciousness of which these things are the very stuff, to which these experiences are native. Anything less than that, than a striving after it or at least a partial realisation of it is not spirituality. The spiritual man is one who has realised something of it even if only in one aspect out of many; one who is striving after it is the spiritual seeker. All else however magnificently intellectual, ethical, aesthetically beautiful and harmonious, vitally splendid, great and forceful or physically perfect is a valuable achievement on the way, but not yet that, for one has not passed the Rubicon of mind into a new empire.

Owing to the nature of the past evolution of consciousness and of spirituality itself, there has been much confusion on this point and there is still more today because of the present domination of the Western ideal. On one side or another mental idealism, ethical development, altruistic character and action, religious piety and fervour, occult powers, feats of ascetic endurance have been put forward as the essence of spirituality or the test or proof of achievement or the signposts of the journey to spiritual perfection. It is ignored that any of these things may be there and yet there need not be any spiritual life behind it, any rebirth into a new consciousness or any remoulding of either the inner or the outer consciousness no longer in a higher or richer power of mind and life and body only, the instruments, but in the direct light and force of the hitherto veiled user of the instrument, the now revealed and directly active soul, self, spirit or of the

Divine or Eternal whose representatives or aspects they are.

This confusion meets us at every point and in all sorts of forms whose common error is to ignore the essence and core of the matter. The Western intellect presents us with the strivings of the mind, life, emotions, passions, moral will and tells us these are the real spiritual things, man's highest aim and endeavour and all else is vain mysticism, asceticism, evasion of life. It appears that the lined and ravaged face of a Greek bust of Homer is a thousand times more spiritual than the empty calm or the ecstatic smile of the Buddha! We are told by others that to care for the family and carry out our social and domestic duties, to be a good man, a perfect citizen, patriot, worker for the community, to serve mankind are the real things far more spiritual than to sit in idle meditation seeking for some remote and invisible transcendental Reality — or unreality. Philanthropy, altruism, service, selfless labour for humankind, these are the spiritual summits. True selflessness lies there, to sacrifice or offer one's life to the good of others, to the community, to the race. To seek one's own inner spiritual growth, to draw back from ordinary life in order to reach something beyond, to search after the Divine above humanity is mere egoism, not true spirituality, but an aberration, a misdirection of the will and life.

All that might be admirable and true — as certainly all the things thus eulogised have their place in the human evolution, if the premise on which it were founded were true — that the seeking for something behind, something beyond, something of which the evolution of mind, life and body was only a veil or a preparation is an illusion and a chimaera. But if these things are real, if the seeking is a lasting and major drive in Nature, then all these objections and recommendations are futile. For this drive will fulfil itself, this hidden reality will draw and draw us till we achieve it. Those who feel its call, cannot do otherwise than follow and strive, even if need be leave all else for it, hold all other greatness, splendour, nobility, beauty as cheaper minor things compared with this other Light and Greatness and Beauty of which they have had the vision, the intimation, the formless attraction or else the passing touch or glimpse. Ever since Mind itself reached a certain development, there has been at first dimly and gropingly, then more and more clearly and intimately this drive in man towards something behind and beyond Man, towards the discovery or the expression of something hidden in his being and a world existence which is more real than his surface self even at its best, greater, fuller, truer, more divine. To arrive at that can come only by a change of consciousness, a reversal of consciousness, a new basis of consciousness which is not the lower instrumental consciousness of mind, life and body.

At each step of evolution we have this change, reversal, new base. Matter is bound in an involved consciousness which is in practice an inconscience; life in the plant in a still involved consciousness struggling for growth, expansion, persistence, seeking after movement and sensation and conscious living without yet reaching them; life in the animal in a vital consciousness possessed of these things, already emotional, possessed of a mind, but a mind still involved in life-movement, not reflective, not subjective and turning upon life to understand, master and control it. Mind is based on a consciousness that has attained this emergence, this reflective and controlling power, this growing understanding, mastery, self-awareness. But mind is still aware only of life and of itself, it is not aware of the person, the reality behind, the user of the instrument; it is seeking for these things and it is this search that constitutes the drive for a new evolution; for mind is a twilight preparing for light, an ignorance seeking after knowledge, a bondage to Nature groping after freedom and mastery over Nature. It is not on mind, on its self-modifying ignorance and bondage or even on its half-light, half-mastery, half-knowledge that the next step can base itself. It must base itself on soul consciousness, consciousness of the spirit and self — for so only can there be the full light, the spontaneous mastery, the intimate and real knowledge.

*

Obviously [*in sadhana*] the rajasic movements are likely to create more trouble than the sattwic ones. The greatest difficulty of the sattwic man is the snare of virtue and self-righteousness, the ties of philanthropy, mental idealisms, family affections etc., but except the first, these are, though difficult, still not so difficult to overpass or else transform. Sometimes however these things are as sticky as the rajasic difficulties.

Selfishness and Unselfishness

Selfishness and the reaction of unselfishness of which you speak are both of them things that have to be put aside — both are obstacles or movements leading off from the true and straight path. For both these things belong to the mind and vital, they are different forms of the ego. The mind in its attempt to get away from the rajasic selfish ego tries to do just the opposite of what selfishness usually does and serve others, sacrifice itself for others, but in doing so it is only constructing another kind of egoism that prides itself on its own unselfishness and altruism and makes human service its mental ideal instead of spiritual service of the Divine. That it is a misguiding movement you saw yourself; for it wanted to sacrifice your sadhana, that is, your seeking for the Divine to this new ego of altruistic self-righteousness; it was prepared to do things without permission of the Mother or rather avoiding asking for permission. One has to get rid of selfishness and ego, not in this way, but by selfless service of the Divine and by merging the ego in the Divine Consciousness, submitting the personal will to the Divine Will, calling into the being the Divine Peace, Purity, Oneness, Knowledge, Light, Ananda, replacing the ego by the psychic being devoted and surrendered to the Divine. It is the love of the Divine that saves, not a love turned towards human beings. When the Divine Consciousness is there, then there comes based on the love of the Divine a true love and oneness for all beings. But that does not act separately from the Divine but only according to the Divine Mother's will and in her service.

*

Unselfishness is not the only thing to be aimed at — by itself it would be only a moral, not a spiritual attainment.

Humility

A spiritual humility within is very necessary, but I do not think an outward one is very advisable (absence of pride or arrogance or vanity is indispensable of course in one's outer dealings with others) — it often creates pride, becomes formal or becomes ineffective after a time. I have seen people doing it to cure their pride, but I have not found it producing a lasting result.

*

It [*to feel like doing namaskar to everyone*] is a feeling which some have who either want to cultivate humility (X used to do it, but I never saw that it got rid of his innate self-esteem) or who have or are trying to have the realisation of Narayan in all with a Vaishnava turn in it. To feel the One in all is right, but to bow down to the individual who lives still in his ego is good neither for him nor for the one who does it. Especially in this Yoga it tends to diffuse what should be concentrated and turned towards a higher realisation than that of the cosmic feeling which is only a step on the way.

*

It is only this habit of the nature — self-worrying and harping on the sense of deficiency — that prevents you from being quiet. If you threw that out, it would be easy to be quiet. Humility is needful, but constant self-depreciation does not help; excessive self-esteem and self-depreciation are both wrong attitudes. To recognise any defects without exaggerating them is useful but, once recognised, it is no good dwelling on them always; you must have the confidence that the Divine Force can change everything and you must let the Force work.

*

The view taken by the Mahatma in these matters [*of caste*] is Christian rather than Hindu — for the Christian, self-abasement, humility, the acceptance of a low status to serve humanity or the Divine are things which are highly spiritual and the noblest privilege of the soul. This view does not admit any hierarchy of castes; the Mahatma accepts castes but on the basis that all are equal before the Divine; a Bhangi doing his dharma is as good as the Brahmin doing his, there is division of function but no hierarchy of functions. That is one view of things and the hierarchic view is another, both having a standpoint and logic of their own which the mind takes as wholly valid but which only corresponds to a part of the reality. All kinds of work are equal before the Divine and all men have the same Brahman within them, is one truth, but that development is not equal in all is another. The idea that it needs special punya to be born as a Bhangi is of course one of those forceful exaggerations of an idea which are common with the Mahatma and impress greatly the mind of his hearers. The idea behind is that his function is an indispensable service to the society, quite as much as the Brahmin's, but that being disagreeable it would need a special moral heroism to choose it voluntarily and he thinks as if the soul freely chose it as such a heroic service and as a reward of righteous acts — that is hardly likely. The service of the scavenger is indispensable under certain conditions of society, it is one of those primary necessities without which society can hardly exist and the cultural development of which the Brahmin life is part could not have taken place. But obviously the cultural development is more valuable than the service of the physical needs for the progress of humanity as opposed to its first static condition and that development can even lead to the minimising and perhaps the eventual disappearance by scientific inventions of the need for the functions of the scavenger. But that I suppose the Mahatma would not approve of as it is machinery and a departure from the simple life. In any case it is not true that the Bhangi life is superior to the Brahmin life and the reward of especial righteousness. On the other hand the traditional conception that a man is superior to others because he is born a Brahmin is not rational or justifiable. A spiritual or cultured man of Pariah birth is superior in the divine values to an unspiritual and worldly-minded or a crude and uncultured Brahmin. Birth counts, but the basic value is in the man himself, the soul behind, and the degree to which it manifests itself in his nature.

*

As for the sense of superiority, that too is a little difficult to avoid when greater horizons open before the consciousness, unless one is already of a saintly and humble disposition. There are men like Nag Mahashoy in whom spiritual experience creates more and more humility, there are others like Vivekananda in whom it erects a giant sense of strength and superiority—European critics have taxed him with it rather severely; there are others in whom it fixes a sense of superiority to men and humility to the Divine. Each position has its value. Take Vivekananda's famous answer to the Madras Pundit who objected to one of his assertions, "But Shankara does not say so." To which Vivekananda replied, "No, Shankara does not say so, but I, Vivekananda, say so", and the Pundit sank back amazed and speechless. That "I, Vivekananda" stands up to the ordinary eye like a Himalaya of self-confident egoism. But there was nothing false or unsound in Vivekananda's spiritual experience. This was not mere egoism, but the sense of what he stood for and the attitude of the fighter who, as the representative of something very great, could not allow himself to be put down or belittled. This is not to deny the necessity of non-egoism and of spiritual humility, but to show that the question is not so easy as it appears at first sight. For if I have to express my spiritual experiences, I must do it with truth — I must record them, their *bhāva*, the thoughts, feelings, extensions of consciousness which accompany them. What can I do with the experience in which one feels the whole world in oneself or the force of the Divine flowing in one's being and nature or the certitude of one's faith against all doubts and doubters or one's oneness with the Divine or the smallness of human thought and life compared with this greater knowledge and existence? And I have to use the word "I" — I cannot take refuge in saying "this body" or "this appearance", — especially as I am not a Mayavadin. Shall I not inevitably fall into expressions which will make X shake his head at my assertions as full of pride and ego? I imagine it would be difficult to avoid it.

Another thing, it seems to me that you identify faith very much with mental belief — but real faith is something spiritual, a knowledge of the soul. The assertions you quote in your letter are the hard assertions of a mental belief leading to a great vehement assertion of one's creed and god because they are one's own and must therefore be greater than those of others — an attitude which is universal in human nature. Even the atheist is not tolerant, but declares his credo of Nature and Matter as the only truth and on all who disbelieve it or believe in other things he pours scorn as unenlightened morons and superstitious half-wits. I bear him no grudge for thinking me that; but I note that this attitude is not confined to religious faith but is equally natural to those who are free from religious faith and do not believe in Gods or Gurus.

*

Perhaps one could say that it [*spiritual humility*] is to be aware of the relativity of what has been done compared with what is still to be done — and also to be conscious of one's being nothing without the Divine Grace.

Sacrifice

Sacrifice has a moral and psychological value always. This value is the same no matter what may be the cause for which the sacrifice is made, provided the one who makes it believes in the truth or justice or other worthiness of his cause. If one makes the sacrifice for a cause one knows to be wrong or unworthy, all depends on the motive and spirit of the sacrifice. Bhishma accepting death in a cause he knew to be unjust, obeyed the call of loyalty to what he felt to be his personal duty. Many have done that in the past, and the moral and psychic value of their act lies, irrespective of the nature of the cause, in the nobility of the motive.

As to the other question, in this sense of the word sacrifice there is none for the man who gives up something which he does not value, except in so far as he undergoes loss, defies social ban or obloquy or otherwise pays a price for his liberation. I may say, however, that without being cold and unloving a man may be so seized by a spiritual call or the call of a great human cause that the family or other ties count for nothing beside it, and he leaves all joyfully, without a pang, to follow the summoning Voice.

In the spiritual sense, however, sacrifice has a different meaning — it does not so much indicate giving up what is held dear as an offering of oneself, one's being, one's mind, heart, will, body, life, actions to the Divine. It has the original sense of "making sacred" and is used as an equivalent of the word Yajna. When the Gita speaks of the "sacrifice of knowledge", it does not mean a giving up of anything, but a turning of the mind towards the Divine in the search for knowledge and an offering of oneself through it. It is in this sense, too, that one speaks of the offering or sacrifice of works. The Mother has written somewhere that the spiritual sacrifice is joyful and not painful in its nature. On the spiritual path, very commonly, if a seeker still feels the old ties and responsibilities strongly, he is not asked to sever or leave them, but to let the call in him grow till all within is ready. Many, indeed, come away earlier because they feel that to cut loose is their only chance, and these have to go sometimes through a struggle. But the pain, the struggle, is not the essential character of the spiritual self-offering.

*

It [*pain and struggle in offering oneself to the Divine*] simply means that your sacrifice is still mental and has not yet become spiritual in its character. When your vital being consents to give up its desires and enjoyments, when it offers itself to the Divine, then the yajna will have begun. What I meant was that the European sense of the word is not the sense of the word "yajna" or the sense of "sacrifice" in such phrases as "the sacrifice of works". It does not mean that you give up all works for the sake of the Divine — for then there would be no sacrifice of works at all. Similarly the sacrifice of knowledge does not mean that you painfully and resolutely make yourself a fool for the sake of the

Lord. Sacrifice means an inner offering to the Divine and the real spiritual sacrifice is a very joyful thing. Otherwise, one is only trying to make oneself fit and has not yet begun the real yajna. It is because your mind is struggling with your vital, the unwilling animal, and asking it to allow itself to be immolated that there is the pain and struggle. If the spiritual will (or psychic) were more in the front then you would not be lamenting over the loss of the ghee and butter and curds thrown into the Fire or trying to have a last lick at it before casting it. The only difficulty would be about bringing down the gods fully enough (a progressive labour), not about lamentations over the ghee. By the way, do you think that the Mother or myself or others who have taken up the spiritual life had not enjoyed life and that it is therefore that the Mother was able to speak of a joyous sacrifice to the Divine as the true spirit of spiritual sacrifice? Or do you think we spent the preliminary stages in longings for the lost fleshpots of Egypt and that it was only later on we felt the joy of the spiritual sacrifice? Of course we did not; we and many others had no difficulty on the score of giving up anything we thought necessary to give up and no hankerings afterwards. Your rule is as usual a stiff rule that does not at all apply generally.

*

Sacrifice depends on the inner attitude. If one has nothing outward to sacrifice, one has always oneself to give.

Ahimsa, Destruction and Violence

The doctrines of Ahimsa and non-violence and altruism are early steps on the road to spiritual knowledge — but once advanced on the road what is true behind them takes its place, as a thread in the complex weft of spiritual truth and feeling, not as a rigid ethical rule or all-swallowing dogma. The Manifestation here is too complex in its concealed Unity for such mental or emotional formulas to be unerring guides.

*

The impersonal Truth, precisely because it is impersonal, can contain quite opposite things. There is a truth in Ahimsa, there is a truth in Destruction also. I do not teach that you should go on killing everybody every day as a spiritual dharma. I say that destruction can be done when it is part of the Divine work commanded by the Divine. Non-violence is better than violence as a rule, and still sometimes violence may be the right thing. I consider dharma as relative; unity with the Divine and action from the Divine Will the highest way. Buddha did not aim at action in the world, but at cessation from the world-existence. For that he found the eightfold Path a necessary preparatory discipline and so proclaimed it.

It [Ahimsa] had nothing to do with the Yuga [*at the time of Buddha*], but with the path towards liberation found by Buddha. There are many paths and all need not be one and the same in their teaching.

*

Destruction in itself is neither good nor evil. It is a fact of Nature, a necessity in the play of forces as things are in this world. The Light destroys the Darkness and the Powers of Darkness, and that is not a movement of Ignorance!

It all depends on the character of the destruction and the forces that enter into it. All dread of fire or other violent forces should be overcome. For dread shows a weakness — the free spirit can stand fearless before even the biggest forces of Nature.

*

This world is so arranged that it is not possible to live without some destruction of life — so for this there need be no remorse. Only one should not destroy life wantonly or inflict needless suffering on animals or any living things.

*

I feel inclined to back out of the arena[1] or take refuge in the

---

[1] *The correspondent asked whether the violence done to animals by medical researchers was justifiable; their experiments with animals, he said, sometimes led to the saving of human lives. — Ed.*

usual saving formula, "There is much to be said on both sides." Your view is no doubt correct from the common-sense or what might be called the "human" point of view. Krishnaprem takes the standpoint that we must not only consider the temporary good to humanity, but certain inner laws. He thinks the harm, violence or cruelty to other beings is not compensated and cannot be justified by some physical good to a section of humanity or even to humanity as a whole; such methods awake, in his opinion, a sort of Karmic reaction apart from the moral harm to the men who do these things. He is also of the opinion that the cause of disease is psychic, that is to say, subjective and the direction should be towards curing the inner causes much more than patching up by physical means. These are ideas that have their truth also. I fully recognise the psychic law and methods and their preferability, but the ordinary run of humanity is not ready for that rule and, while it is so, doctors and their physical methods will be there. I have also supported justifiable violence on justifiable occasions, e.g., Kurukshetra and the war against Hitler and all he means. The question then, from this middle point of view, about the immediate question is whether this violence is justifiable and the occasion justifiable. I back out.

War and Conquest

War and conquest are part of the economy of vital Nature, it is no use blaming this or that people for doing it — everybody does it who has the power and the chance. China who now complains was herself an imperialist and colonising country through all the centuries in which Japan kept religiously within her own borders. If it were not profitable, I suppose nobody would do it. England has grown rich on the plundered wealth of India. France depends for many things on her African colonies. Japan needs an outlet for her overabundant population and safe economic markets nearby. Each is pushed by forces that use the minds of rulers and peoples to fulfil themselves — unless human nature changes no amount of moralising will prevent it.

*

There has been almost continuous war in the world — it is as in the history of the Roman Republic when the gates of the temple of Janus were closed only once or twice in its many centuries — a sign that the Republic was at peace with all the world. There have been in modern times long intervals between long wars, but small ones have been generally going on somewhere or another. Man is a quarrelling and fighting animal and so long as he is so how can there be peace?

Poverty

It is a world which has emerged from the Inconscient and these things [*poverty and misery*] are results of the imperfect working of the human mind which, being born into the ignorant life and matter, has to learn by effort and experience. Ignorance and ego have to be outgrown before there can be a true utilisation of the resources of Nature.

Natural Calamities

Why should earthquakes occur by some wrong movement of man? When man was not there, did not earthquakes occur? If he were blotted out by poison gas or otherwise, would they cease? Earthquakes are a perturbation in Nature due to some pressure of forces; frequency of earthquakes may coincide with a violence of upheavals in human life but the upheavals of earth and human life are both results of a general clash or pressure of forces, one is not the cause of the other.

Chapter Four
Social Duties and the Divine

Family, Society, Country and the Divine

Family, society, country are a larger ego — they are not the Divine. One can work for them and say that one is working for the Divine only if one is conscious of the Divine Adesh to act for that purpose or of the Divine Force working within one. Otherwise it is only an idea of the mind identifying country etc. with the Divine.

*

I suppose each man makes or tries to make his own organisation of life out of the mass of possibilities the forces present to him. Self (physical self) and family are the building most make — to earn, to create a family and maintain it, perhaps to get some position in the present means of life one chooses, in business, the profession etc., etc. Country or humanity are usually added to that by a minority. A few take up some ideal and follow it as the mainstay of their life. It is only the very religious who try to make God the centre of their life — that too rather imperfectly, except for a few. None of these things are secure or certain, even the last being certain only if it is followed with an absoluteness which only a few are willing to give. The life of the Ignorance is a play of forces through which man seeks his way and all depends on his growth through experience to the point at which he can grow out of it into something else. That something else is in fact a new consciousness — whether a new consciousness beyond the earthly life or a new consciousness within it.

*

I don't remember the context; but I suppose he [*the writer of Yogic Sadhan*] means that when one has to escape from the lower dharma, one has often to break it so as to arrive at a larger one. E.g. social duties, paying debts, looking after family, helping to serve your country, etc. etc. The man who turns to the spiritual life, has to leave all that behind him often and he is reproached by lots of people for his Adharma. But if he does not do this Adharma, he is bound for ever to the lower life — for there is always some duty there to be done — and cannot take up the spiritual dharma or can do it only when he is old and his faculties impaired.

*

Idealising is a pastime of the mind — except for the few who are passionately determined to make the ideal real. Buddha is in Nirvana and his wife and child are there too perhaps, so it is easy to praise his spiritual greatness and courage — but for living people with living relatives a similar action is monstrous. They ought to be satisfied with praising Buddha and take care not to follow his example.

*

The tendency you speak of, to leave the family and social life for the spiritual life, has been traditional in India for the last 2000 years and more — chiefly among men, it touches only a very small number of women. It must be remembered that Indian social life has subordinated almost entirely the individual to the family. Men and women do not marry according to their free will; their marriages are mostly arranged for them while they are still children. Not only so, but the mould of society has been long of an almost iron fixity putting each individual in his place and expecting him to conform to it. You speak of issues and a courageous solution, but in this life there are no problems and issues and no call for a solution — a courageous solution is only possible where there is freedom of the personal will; but where the only solution (if one remains in this life) is submission to the family will, there can be nothing of that kind. It is a secure life and can be happy if one accommodates oneself to it and has no unusual aspirations beyond it or is fortunate in one's environment; but it has no remedy for or escape from incompatibilities or any kind of individual frustration; it leaves little room for initiative or free movement or any individualism. The only outlet for the individual is his inner spiritual or religious life and the recognised escape is the abandonment of the *saṁsāra*, the family life, by some kind of Sannyasa. The Sannyasi, the Vaishnava Vairagi or the Brahmachari are free; they are dead to the family and can live according to the dictates of the inner spirit. Only if they enter into an order or asram, they have to abide by the rules of the order, but that is their own choice, not a responsibility which has been laid on them without their choice. Society recognised this door of escape from itself; religion sanctioned the idea that distaste for the social or worldly life was a legitimate ground for taking up that of the recluse or religious wanderer. But this was mainly for men; women, except in old times among the Buddhists who had their convents and in later times among the Vaishnavas, had little chance of such an escape unless a very strong spiritual impulse drove them which would take no denial. As for the wife and children left behind by the Sannyasi, there was little difficulty, for the joint family was there to take up or rather to continue their maintenance.

At present what has happened is that the old framework remains, but modern ideas have brought a condition of inadaptation, of unrest, the old family system is breaking up and women are seeking in more numbers the same freedom of escape as men have always had in the past. That would account for the cases you have come across — but I don't think the number of such cases can be as yet at all considerable, it is quite a new phenomenon; the admission of women to Asrams is itself a novelty. The extreme unhappiness of a mental and vital growth which does not fit in with the surroundings, of marriages imposed that are unsuitable and where there is no meeting-point between husband and wife, of an environment hostile and intolerant of one's inner life and on the other hand the innate tendency of the Indian mind to seek a refuge in the spiritual or religious escape will sufficiently account for the new development. If society wants to prevent it, it must itself change. As to individuals, each case must be judged on its own merits; there is too much complexity in the problem and too much variation of nature, position, motives for a general rule.

Philanthropy

Whatever one does must be from the highest spontaneous inner urge in oneself. So long as the urge is towards philanthropy, Gandhism etc., he has to follow that — to follow the way of spiritual endeavour he must have the need, the distinct call in himself — not merely a mental recognition but the soul's call.

*

Perhaps you could write (in Bengali)[1] something to him about the true object of the Yoga — especially on two points:

(1) The object is not philanthropy but to find the Divine, to enter into the Divine Consciousness and find one's true being (which is not the ego) in the Divine. (2) The *ripus* cannot be conquered by *damana*; even if it succeeds to some extent, it only keeps them down but does not destroy them, often compression only increases their force. It is by purification through the Divine Consciousness entering into the egoistic nature and changing it that the thing can be done.

As for accepting him, it depends on his capacity to open himself to the Influence and receive it. If he likes to try, he can, but he will not succeed unless he is entirely in earnest. There is something in him that can turn to the Divine, but there is also much in his nature that may resist. It is only if he gives himself from deep within and is absolutely persevering in the Way that he can succeed.

Give him some idea of the central process of the Yoga, especially opening to the working of the Divine Power and rejection of all that is of the lower nature.

Humanitarianism

The idea of usefulness to humanity is the old confusion due

---

[1] *Sri Aurobindo wrote this reply to his secretary, Nolini Kanta Gupta, who replied to the correspondent. — Ed.*

to secondhand ideas imported from the West. Obviously, to be "useful" to humanity there is no need of Yoga; everyone who leads the human life is useful to humanity in one way or another. Yoga is directed towards God, not towards man. If a divine supramental consciousness and power can be brought down and established in the material world, that obviously would mean an immense change for the earth including humanity and its life. But the effect on humanity would only be one result of the change; it cannot be the object of the sadhana. The object of the sadhana can only be to live in the divine consciousness and to manifest it in life.

*

As to the extract about Vivekananda, the point I make there[2] does not seem to me humanitarian. You will see that I emphasise there the last sentences of the passage quoted from Vivekananda, not the words about God the poor and sinner and criminal. The point is about the Divine in the World, the All, *sarva-bhūtāni* of the Gita. That is not merely humanity, still less only the poor or the wicked; surely even the rich or the good are part of the All and those also who are neither good nor bad nor rich nor poor. Nor is there any question (I mean in my own remarks) of philanthropic service; so neither *daridra* nor *sevā* is the point. I had formerly not the humanitarian but the humanity view — and something of it may have stuck to my expressions in the *Arya*. But I had already altered my viewpoint from the "Our Yoga for the sake of humanity" to "Our Yoga for the sake of the Divine". The Divine includes not only the supracosmic but the cosmic and the individual — not only Nirvana or the Beyond but Life and the All. It is that I stress everywhere. But I shall keep the extracts for a day or two and see what there is, if anything, that smacks too much of a too narrow humanistic standpoint. I stop here for today.

*

---

[2] *In* The Synthesis of Yoga *Sri Aurobindo wrote: "Often, we see this desire of personal salvation overcome by another attraction which also belongs to the higher turn of our nature and which indicates the essential character of the action the liberated soul*

Social Duties and the Divine

Today a Kanchenjunga of correspondence has fallen on my head, so I could not write about humanity and its progress. Were not the later views of Lowes Dickinson greyed over by the sickly cast of a disappointed idealism? I have not myself an exaggerated respect for humanity and what it is — but to say that there has been no progress is as much an exaggerated pessimism as the rapturous hallelujahs of the nineteenth century to a progressive humanity were an exaggerated optimism.

I shall manage to read through the chapter you sent me, though how I manage to find time for these things is a standing miracle and a signal proof of a Divine Providence.

Yes, the "progress" you are making is of the genuine kind — the signs are recognisable. And after all the best way to make humanity progress is to move on oneself — that may sound either individualistic or egoistic, but it isn't; it is only common sense.

Yad yad ācarati śreṣṭhas tat tad evetaro janaḥ.[3]

*

It is no use entertaining these feelings. One has to see what the world is without becoming bitter — for the bitterness comes from one's own ego and its disappointed expectations. If one wants the victory of the Divine, one must achieve it in oneself first.

---

must pursue.... It is that which inspires a remarkable passage in a letter of Swami Vivekananda. 'I have lost all wish for my salvation,' wrote the great Vedantin, 'may I be born again and again and suffer thousands of miseries so that I may worship the only God that exists, the only God I believe in, the sum-total of all souls, — and above all, my God the wicked, my God the miserable, my God the poor of all races, of all species is the special object of my worship. He who is the high and low, the saint and the sinner, the god and the worm, Him worship, the visible, the knowable, the real, the omnipresent; break all other idols. In whom there is neither past life nor future birth, nor death nor going nor coming, in whom we always have been and always will be one, Him worship; break all other idols.'
  "The last two sentences contain indeed the whole gist of the matter." The Synthesis of Yoga, *volume 23 of* THE COMPLETE WORKS OF SRI AUROBINDO, *pp. 269 – 70.*
  [3] *"Whatsoever the Best doeth, that the lower kind of man puts into practice." Gita 3.21. Sri Aurobindo's translation.* Essays on the Gita, *volume 19 of* THE COMPLETE WORKS OF SRI AUROBINDO, *p. 135.*

Social and Political Activism

All this insistence upon action is absurd if one has not the light by which to act. Yoga must include life and not exclude it does not mean that we are bound to accept life as it is with all its stumbling ignorance and misery and the obscure confusion of human will and reason and impulse and instinct which it expresses. The advocates of action think that by human intellect and energy making an always new rush everything can be put right; the present state of the world after a development of the intellect and a stupendous output of energy for which there is no historical parallel is a signal proof of the illusion under which they labour. Yoga takes the stand that it is only by a change of consciousness that the true basis of life can be discovered; from within outward is indeed the rule. But within does not mean some quarter inch behind the surface. One must go deep and find the soul, the self, the Divine Reality within us and only then can life become a true expression of what we can be instead of a blind and always repeated confused blur of the inadequate and imperfect thing we were. The choice is between remaining in the old jumble and groping about in the hope of stumbling on some discovery or standing back and seeking the Light within till we discover and can build the godhead within and without us.

*

I had never a very great confidence in X's yoga-turn getting the better of his activism — he has two strong ties that prevent it, ambition and need to act and lead in the vital and in the mind a mental idealism — these two things are the great fosterers of illusion. The spiritual path needs a certain amount of realism — one has to see the real value of the things that are — which is very little, except as steps in evolution. Then one can either follow the spiritual static path of rest and release or the spiritual dynamic path of a greater truth to be brought down into life. But otherwise —

Part Five

Questions of Spiritual and Occult Knowledge

Section One

The Divine and the Hostile Powers

Chapter One

Terminology

The Dynamic Divine, the Gods, the Asuras

The dynamic aspect of the Divine is the Supreme Brahman, not the Gods. The Gods are Personalities and Powers of the dynamic Divine. You speak as if the evolution were the sole creation; the creation or manifestation is very vast and contains many planes and worlds that existed before the evolution, all different in character and with different kinds of beings. The fact of being prior to the evolution does not make them undifferentiated. The world of the Asuras is prior to the evolution, so are the worlds of the mental, vital or subtle physical Devas — but these beings are all different from each other. The great Gods belong to the Overmind plane; in the Supermind they are unified as aspects of the Divine, in the Overmind they appear as separate personalities. Any godhead can descend by emanation to the physical plane and associate himself with the evolution of a human being with whose line of manifestation he is in affinity. But these are things which cannot be very easily understood by the mind, because the mind has too rigid an idea of personality — the difficulty only disappears when one enters into a more flexible consciousness above where one is nearer to the experience of One in all and All in one.

The Soul, the Divine, the Gods, the Asuras

The word soul has various meanings according to the context; it may mean the Purusha supporting the formation of Prakriti which we call a being, though the proper word would be rather a becoming; it may mean on the other hand specifically the psychic being in an evolutionary creature like man; it may mean the spark of the Divine which has been put into Matter by the descent of the Divine into the material world and which upholds all evolving formations here. There is and can be no psychic being in a non-evolutionary creature like the Asura; there can be none in a God who does not need one for his existence. But what the God has is a Purusha and a Prakriti or Energy of nature of that Purusha. If any being of the typal worlds wants to evolve he has to come down to earth and take a human body and accept to share in the evolution. It is because they do not want to do this that the vital beings try to possess men so that they may enjoy the materialities of physical life without bearing the burden of the evolution or the process of conversion in which it culminates. I hope this is clear and solves the difficulty.

*

The three stages you speak of [1] are stages not of evolution but of the involution of the Divine in Matter. The Devas and Asuras are not evolved in Matter; for the typal being only a Purusha with its Prakriti is necessary — this Purusha may put out a mental and vital Purusha to represent it and according as it is centred in one or another it belongs to the mental or vital world. That is all.

There is no essential difference anywhere, for all is fundamentally the essential Divine; the difference is in the manifestation. Practically, we may say that the Jivatman is one of the divine Many and dependent on the One; the Atman is the One supporting the Many. The psychic being does not merge in the Jivatman, it becomes united with it so that there is no difference between the central being supporting the manifestation from above and the same being supporting the manifestation from within it, because the psychic being has become fully aware of the play of the Divine through it. What is called merging takes place in the Divine Consciousness when the Jivatman feels itself so one with the Divine that there is nothing else.

---

[1] *The correspondent's letter is not available to determine these stages.* — Ed.

Terms in *The Mother*

(1) Falsehood and Ignorance

Ignorance means Avidya, the separative consciousness and the egoistic mind and life that flows from it and all that is natural to the separative consciousness and the egoistic mind and life. This Ignorance is the result of a movement by which the cosmic Intelligence separated itself from the light of Supermind (the divine Gnosis) and lost the Truth, — truth of being, truth of divine consciousness, truth of force and action, truth of Ananda. As a result instead of a world of integral truth and divine harmony created in the light of the divine Gnosis, we have a world founded on the part truths of an inferior cosmic Intelligence in which all is half truth, half error. It is this that some of the ancient thinkers like Shankara, not perceiving the greater Truth-Force behind, stigmatised as Maya and thought to be the highest creative power of the Divine. All in the consciousness of this creation is either limited or else perverted by separation from the integral Light; even the Truth it perceives is only a half knowledge. Therefore it is called the Ignorance.

Falsehood, on the other hand, is not this Avidya, but an extreme result of it. It is created by an Asuric power which intervenes in this creation and is not only separated from the Truth and therefore limited in knowledge and open to error, but in revolt against the Truth or in the habit of seizing the Truth only to pervert it. This Power, the dark Asuric Shakti or Rakshasic Maya, puts forward its own perverted consciousness as true knowledge and its wilful distortions or reversals of the Truth as the verity of things. It is the powers and personalities of this perverted and perverting consciousness that we call hostile beings, hostile forces. Whenever these perversions created by them out of the stuff of the Ignorance are put forward as the truth of things, that is the Falsehood, in the Yogic sense, *mithyā*, *moha*.

(2) Powers and Appearances

These are the forces and beings that are interested in maintaining the falsehoods they have created in the world of the Ignorance and in putting them forward as the Truth which men must follow. In India they are termed Asuras, Rakshasas, Pisachas (beings respectively of the mentalised vital, middle vital and lower vital planes) who are in opposition to the Gods, the Powers of Light. These too are Powers, for they too have their cosmic field in which they exercise their function and authority and some of them were once divine Powers (the former gods, *pūrve devāḥ*, as they are called somewhere in the Mahabharata) who have fallen towards the Darkness by revolt against the divine Will behind the cosmos. The word "Appearances" refers to the forms they take in order to rule the world, forms often false and always incarnating falsehood, sometimes pseudo-divine.

(3) Powers and Personalities

The use of the word Power has already been explained — it can be applied to whatever or whoever exercises a conscious power in the cosmic field and has authority over the world-movement or some part of it or some movement in it. But the Four of whom you speak are also Shaktis, manifestations of different powers of the supreme Consciousness and Force, the Divine Mother, by which she rules or acts in the universe. And they are at the same time divine Personalities; for each is a being who manifests different qualities and personal consciousness-forms of her Godhead. All the greater Gods are in this way personalities of the Divine — one Consciousness playing in many personalities, *ekaṁ sat bahudhā*. Even in the human being there are many personalities and not only one, as used formerly to be imagined; for all consciousness can be at once one and multiple. "Powers and Personalities" simply describe different aspects of the same being; a Power is not necessarily impersonal and certainly it is not *avyaktam*, as you suggest, — on the contrary it is a manifestation acting in the worlds of the divine manifestation.

(4) Emanations

Emanations correspond to your description of the Matrikas of whom you speak in your letter. An emanation of the Mother is something of her consciousness and power put forth from her, which so long as it is in play is held in close connection with her and, when its play is no longer required, is withdrawn back into its source, but can always be put out and brought into play once more. But also the detaining thread of connection can be severed or loosened and that which came forth as an emanation can proceed on its way as an independent divine being with its own play in the world. All the Gods can put forth such emanations from their being, identical with them in essence of consciousness and power though not commensurate. In a certain sense the universe itself can be said to be an emanation from the Supreme. In the consciousness of the sadhaka an emanation of the Mother will ordinarily wear the appearance, form and characteristics with which he is familiar.

In a sense the four Powers of the Mother may be called, because of their origin, her Emanations, just as the Gods may be called Emanations of the Divine, but they have a more permanent and fixed character; they are at once independent beings allowed their play by the Adyā Shakti and yet portions of the Mother, the Mahashakti, and she can always either manifest through them as separate beings or draw them together as her own various Personalities and hold them in herself, sometimes drawn back, sometimes at play, according to her will. In the supramental plane they are always in her and do not act independently but as intimate portions of the original Mahashakti and in close union and harmony with each other.

(5) Gods

These four Powers are the Mother's cosmic godheads, permanent in the world-play; they stand among the greater cosmic Godheads to whom allusion is made when it is said the Mother as the Mahashakti of this triple world "stands there (in the

Overmind plane) above the Gods".[2] The Gods, as has been already said, are in origin and essence permanent Emanations of the Divine put forth from the Supreme by the Transcendent Mother, the Adyā Shakti; in their cosmic action they are Powers and Personalities of the Divine each with his independent cosmic standing, function and work in the universe. They are not impersonal entities but cosmic Personalities, although they can and do ordinarily veil themselves behind the movement of impersonal forces. But while in the Overmind and the triple world they appear as independent beings, they return in the Supermind into the One and stand there united in a single harmonious action as multiple personalities of the one Person, the divine Purushottama.

(6) Presence

It is intended by the word Presence to indicate the sense and perception of the Divine as a Being, felt as present in one's existence and consciousness or in relation with it, without the necessity of any farther qualification or description. Thus of the "ineffable Presence"[3] it can only be said that it is there and nothing more can or need be said about it, although at the same time one knows that all is there, personality and impersonality, Power and Light and Ananda and everything else, and that all these flow from that indescribable Presence. The word may be used sometimes in a less absolute sense, but that is always the fundamental significance, — the essential perception of the essential presence supporting everything else.

---

[2] *"Determining all that shall be in this universe and in the terrestrial evolution by what she sees and feels and pours from her, she stands there above the Gods and all her Powers and Personalities are put out in front of her for the action...."* Sri Aurobindo, The Mother with Letters on the Mother, *volume 32 of* THE COMPLETE WORKS OF SRI AUROBINDO, *p. 16.*

[3] *"Alone, she harbours the absolute Power and the ineffable Presence."* Sri Aurobindo, The Mother with Letters on the Mother, *p. 14.*

(7) The Transcendent Mother

This is what is termed the Adyā Shakti; she is the supreme Consciousness and Power above the universe and it is by her that all the Gods are manifested, and even the supramental Ishwara comes into manifestation through her — the supramental Purushottama of whom the Gods are Powers and Personalities.

Chapter Two

The Gods

The Gods or Divine Powers

The Gods are Personalities or Powers put forth by the Divine — they are therefore in front limited Emanations, although the full Divine is behind each of them.

*

Of course, the gods exist — that is to say, there are Powers that stand above the world and transmit the divine workings. It is the physical mind which believes only in what is physical that denies them. There are also beings of other worlds — gods and Asuras etc.

*

There are Gods everywhere on all the planes.

*

The Gods are in the universal Self — if identified with the universal Self one can feel their presence there.

*

While the Gods cannot be transformed, for they are typal and not evolutionary beings, they can come for conversion — that is to say, to give up their own ideas and outlook on things and conform themselves to the higher Will and supramental Truth of the Divine.

*

The higher beings are not likely to be in disharmony with each other as they are not subject to the lower ignorance.

*

The Gods have their own enjoyments, though they may not be of a material character.

*

There are no planes of manifestation without forms — for without form creation or manifestation cannot be complete. But the supraphysical planes are not bound to the forms like the physical. The forms there are expressive, not determinative. What is important on the vital plane is the force or feeling and the form expresses it. A vital being has a characteristic form but he can vary it or mask his true form under others. What is primary on the mental plane is the perception, the idea, the mental significance and the form expresses that and these mental forms too can vary — there can be many forms expressing an idea in different ways or on different sides of the idea. Form exists but it is more plastic and variable than in physical nature.

As to the Gods, man can build forms which they will accept; but these forms too are inspired into man's mind from the planes to which the God belongs. All creation has the two sides, the formed and the formless; the Gods too are formless and yet have forms, but a Godhead can take many forms, here Maheshwari, there Pallas Athene. Maheshwari herself has many forms in her lesser manifestations, Durga, Uma, Parvati, Chandi etc. The Gods are not limited to human forms — man also has not always seen them in human forms only.

The Gods and the Overmind

The natives of the Overmind are Gods. Naturally the Gods rule the cosmos.

*

The Overmind is the world of the Gods and the Gods are not merely Powers, but have Forms also.

*

In the Overmind the Gods are still separated existences.

*

Beyond the Overmind (in the supramental nearest the Overmind for instance) the Gods are eternal in their principle, but not in their forms and separate activities; they are there simply aspects of the One. If you meet a Godhead there, it is not as a separate Person; you feel only the Divine having a particular face, as it were, and relation with you for a certain purpose.

*

The Formateurs of the Overmind have shaped nothing evil — it is the lower forces that receive from the Overmind and distort its forces.

Vedic Gods of the Indian Tradition

There are many forms of Agni, — the solar fire, the vaidyuta fire and the nether fire are one Trinity — the fivefold fire is part of the Vedic symbolism of sacrifice.

*

Vayu and Indra are cosmic godheads presiding over the action of cosmic principles — they are not the manomaya purusha or pranamaya purusha in each man. You have a mental being or purusha in you and a vital being or purusha, but you cannot say that you are in your mind Indra or in your vital Vayu. The Purusha is an essential being supporting the play of Prakriti — the Godhead (Indra, Vayu) is a dynamic being manifested in Prakriti for the works of the plane to which he belongs. There is an immense difference.

*

Yes, Mitra is rather a combination of the two powers [*Mahalakshmi and Mahasaraswati*].

*

I indicate the psychological powers which they [*six Vedic Gods*] bring with them:
Mitra — Harmony.
Varuna — Wideness.
Aryaman — Power, Tapasya.
Brihaspati — Wisdom (Word and Knowledge).
Vishnu — Cosmic Consciousness.
Vayu — Life.

Post-Vedic Gods of the Indian Tradition

Brahma, Vishnu, Shiva are only three Powers and Personalities of the One Cosmic Godhead.

*

Brahma is the Power of the Divine that stands behind formation and creation.

*

As for Vishnu being the creator, all the three Gods are often spoken of as creating the universe — even Shiva who is by tradition the Destroyer.

*

There is no particular connection between Shiva and the Overmind — the Overmind is the higher station of all the Gods.

*

Mahashiva means a greater manifestation than that ordinarily worshipped as Shiva — the creative dance of a greater Divine manifesting Power.

*

At X's conscientious hesitations between Krishna and Shakti and Shiva I could not help indulging in a smile. If a man is attracted by one form or two forms only of the Divine, it is all right, — but if he is drawn to several at a time he need not torment himself over it. A man of some development has necessarily several sides in his nature and it is quite natural that different aspects should draw or govern different personalities in him — he can very well accept them all and harmonise them in the One Divine and the One Adya Shakti of whom all are the manifestations.

*

Shiva is the Lord of Tapas. The power is the power of Tapas.

Krishna as a godhead is the Lord of Ananda, Love and Bhakti; as an incarnation, he manifests the union of wisdom (Jnana) and works and leads the earth-evolution through this towards union with the Divine by Ananda, Love and Bhakti.

The Devi is the Divine Shakti — the Consciousness and Power of the Divine, the Mother and Energy of the worlds. All powers are hers. Sometimes Devi-power may mean the power of the universal World-Force; but this is only one side of the Shakti.

*

Mahakali and Kali are not the same, Kali is a lesser form. Mahakali in the higher planes appears usually with the golden colour.

*

Ganesh is the Power that removes obstacles by the force of Knowledge — Kartikeya represents victory over the hostile Powers. Of course the names given are human, but the Gods exist.

*

Ganesh (among other things) is the devata of spiritual Knowledge — so as you are getting this knowledge, you saw yourself in this form, identified with Ganesh.

Chapter Three

The Hostile Forces and Hostile Beings

The Existence of the Hostile Forces

The hostile forces exist and have been known to Yogic experience ever since the days of the Veda and Zoroaster in Asia (and the mysteries of Egypt and Chaldea and the Cabbala) and in Europe also from old times. These things of course cannot be felt or known so long as one lives in the ordinary mind and its ideas and perceptions — for there there are only two categories of influences recognisable, the ideas and feelings and actions of oneself and others and the play of environment and physical forces. But once one begins to get the inner view of things, it is different. One begins to experience that all is an action of forces, forces of Prakriti psychological as well as physical which play upon our nature — and these are conscious forces or are supported by a consciousness or consciousnesses behind. One is in the midst of a big universal working and it is impossible any longer to explain everything as the result of one's own sole and independent personality. You yourself have at one time written that your crises of despair etc. came upon you as if thrown on you and worked themselves out without your being able to determine or put an end to them. That means an action of universal forces and not merely an independent action of your own personality, though it is something in your nature of which they make use. But you are not conscious, and others also, of this intervention and pressure at its source for the reason I state. Those in the Asram who have developed the inner view of things on the vital plane[1] have plenty of experience of the hostile forces.

---

[1] One may have the experiences on the mental plane without this knowledge coming — for there Mind and Idea predominate and one does not feel the play of Forces —

However, you need not personally concern yourself with them so long as they remain incognito.

*

It is true that all comes from the Divine and it is true also that a Divine Presence and a Divine Will is behind all that happens and leads the world towards a divine goal.

At the same time it is also taught in the Gita that this world is a world of obscurity and ignorance and to attain to the Divine one must overcome certain forces of Nature, such as Desire, which the Gita calls the enemy difficult to overcome. It is in this sense that we speak of hostile forces — those which stand in the way of coming out of the Ignorance and attaining to the consciousness of the Divine.

It is again true that those who have a complete and living faith in the Divine and a perfect sincerity in their vision of the Divine everywhere and a pure sattwic nature need not trouble themselves about the hostile forces — for from them the forces of the Ignorance fall back and cannot take possession of their nature.

The teaching about the hostile forces (Asuri Rakshasi forces) is necessary for those who have a divided consciousness or a more rajasic temperament — for if they are not on their guard they may fall into the control of undesirable forces of Desire and Ego —

rākṣasīm āsurīṁ caiva prakṛtiṁ mohinīṁ śritāḥ[2]

*

Yes, they [*the hostile forces*] have their own world and, if they kept to it, there could be no objection to their existence. There is a world that is natural to them and has its own rhythm, its own

---

it is only in the vital that that becomes clear. In the mind plane they manifest at most as mental suggestions and not as concrete Powers. Also if one looks at things with the Mind only (even though it be the Inner Mind), one may see the subtle play of Nature-Forces but without recognising the conscious intention which we call hostile.

[2] "Dwelling in the deluding Asuric and Rakshasic nature." Gita 9.12. — Ed.

dharma — just as the lesser gods have theirs. But, they want to dominate the evolution and for that purpose they have taken their station in the vital worlds which influence the earth nature and give it its materials for life.

They were created or rather manifested like other orders of being as a type or several types expressing some cosmic stress, some possibility in the Infinite, the expression of a certain kind of consciousness and force. When the work that they are permitted to do on earth, the work of negation, perversion, miscreation is finished they will be destroyed here, but there is no reason to suppose that they may not exist in their own universe, as it were, outside the system here. For here their presence is an Adharma, a disturbance of the true harmony and natural evolution there should be on the earth plane; it is an intrusion and not a natural presence.

How did the Ignorance come into being out of Sachchidananda? Or ego? The Hostile Forces in their own world embody ego self-fulfilled and having its own free play — ego on earth is not self-fulfilled and not meant to be, it is in conflict with a cosmic Force greater than itself and is only a temporary expedient for bringing forth individuality out of the indeterminateness of just conscient life and inconscient Matter.

*

If there were no hostile forces and there were still the evolutionary world, there could be ignorance still but not perversity in the ignorance. All would be a partial truth acting through imperfect instruments but for the best purposes of this or that stage in a progressive manifestation.

The Nature of the Hostile Forces

The mere intensity of the force does not show that it is a bad power; the Divine Force often works with a great intensity. Everything depends on the nature of the force and its working; what does it do, what seems to be its purpose? If it works to purify or open the system, or brings with it light or peace or prepares the change of the thought, ideas, feelings, character in the sense of a turning towards a higher consciousness, then it is the right force. If it is dark or obscure or perturbs the being with rajasic or egoistic suggestions or excites the lower nature, then it is an adverse Force.

*

The hostiles have themselves bodies though not of a gross physical kind — they see, but with a subtle seeing that includes not only bodies, but movements of forces, thoughts, feelings.

*

Very great [*are the occult powers of the hostile beings*] — it is their occult powers and knowledge of occult processes that make them so strong and effective.

*

The lesser forces of Light are usually too much insistent on seeking for Truth to make effectivity their logic or their rule — the hostiles are too pragmatic to care for Truth, they want only success. As for the greater Forces (e.g. Overmind) they are dynamic and try always to make consciousness effective, but they insist on consciousness, while the hostiles care nothing for that — the more unconscious you are and their automatic tool, the better they are pleased — for it is unconsciousness that gives them their chance.

The Conquest of the Hostile Forces

The universe is certainly or has been up to now in appearance a rough and wasteful game with the dice of chance loaded in favour of the Powers of darkness, the Lords of obscurity, falsehood, death and suffering. But we have to take it as it is and find out — if we reject the way out of the old sages — the way to conquer. Spiritual experience shows that there is behind it all a wide terrain of equality, peace, calm, freedom, and it is only by getting into it that we can have the eye that sees and hope to gain the power that conquers.

*

It [*the adverse force*] is the Power that keeps up ignorance and darkness in the world — it can only be destroyed when mankind is no longer in love with ignorance and darkness. Each sadhak has to push it out of contact with his being. When it has gone from him, then there will be no longer any serious difficulties in his sadhana.

*

The hostile Forces are Powers of Darkness who are in revolt against the Light and the Truth and want to keep this world under their rule in darkness and ignorance. Whenever anyone wants to reach the Truth, to realise the Divine, they stand in the way as much as possible. But what they are specially against is the work the Mother and myself are doing, to bring down the Light here into the earth and establish the Truth — that would mean their own expulsion. So they always try to destroy the work as a whole and to spoil the sadhana of each sadhak. It is not only you who are attacked: all are attacked more or less — especially when there is a great progress, these forces try to interfere. The only way to avoid it is to be entirely turned towards the Mother and to refuse any opportunity to these Forces.

*

The evil forces are perversions of the Truth by the Ignorance — in any complete transformation they must disappear and the Truth behind them be delivered. In this way they can be said to be transformed by destruction.

Asuras, Rakshasas and Other Vital Beings

The Asuras and Rakshasas etc. do not belong to the earth, but to supraphysical worlds; but they act upon the earth life and dispute the control of human life and character and action with the Gods. They are the Powers of Darkness combating the Powers of Light.

Sometimes they possess men in order to act through them, sometimes they take birth in a human body. When their use in the play is over, they will either change or disappear or no longer seek to intervene in the earth-play.

*

These things [*such as temptation by Apsaras*] are possible but they do not usually happen — because it is difficult for beings of the subtle worlds to materialise to such an extent or for a long time. They prefer to act by influencing human beings, using them as instruments or taking possession of a human mind and body.

*

There are two kinds of Asuras — one kind were divine in their origin but have fallen from their divinity by self-will and opposition to the intention of the Divine: they are spoken of in the Hindu scriptures as the former or earlier gods; these can be converted and their conversion is indeed necessary for the ultimate purposes of the universe. But the ordinary Asura is not of this character, is not an evolutionary but a typal being and represents a fixed principle of the creation which does not evolve or change and is not intended to do so. These Asuras, as also the other hostile beings, Rakshasas, Pisachas and others resemble the devils of the Christian tradition and oppose the divine intention and the evolutionary purpose in the human being; they don't change the purpose in them for which they exist which is evil, but have to be destroyed like the evil. The Asura has no soul, no psychic being which has to evolve to a higher state; he has only an ego and usually a very powerful ego; he has a mind, sometimes even a highly intellectualised mind; but the basis of his thinking and feeling is vital and not mental, at the service of his desire and not of truth. He is a formation assumed by the life-principle for a particular kind of work and not a divine formation or a soul.

*

Yes. Some kinds of Asuras are very religious, very fanatical about

The Hostile Forces and Hostile Beings

their religion, very strict about rules of ethical conduct. Others of course are just the opposite. There are others who use spiritual ideas without believing in them to give them a perverted twist and delude the sadhaka. It is what Shakespeare described as the Devil quoting Scripture for his own purpose.

At present what they are most doing is to try to raise up the obscurity and weakness of the most physical mind, vital, material parts to prevent the progress or fulfilment of the sadhana.

*

As to Asuras, not many of them have shown signs of repentance or possibility of conversion up to now. It is not surprising that they should be powerful in a world of Ignorance, for they have only to persuade people to follow the established bent of their lower nature, while the Divine calls always for a change of nature. It is not to be wondered at that the Asura has an easier task and more momentary success in his combinations. But that temporary success does not bind the future.

*

It is the movements of the lower nature that get purified. The Asuras themselves are not so easily transformed.

*

The Asuras are really the dark side of the mental, or more strictly, of the vital mind plane. This mind is the very field of the Asuras. Their main characteristic is egoistic strength and struggle, which refuse the higher law. The Asura has self-control, *tapas* and intelligence, but all that for the sake of his ego. On the lower vital plane the corresponding forces we call the Rakshasas which represent violent passions and influences. There are also other kinds of beings on the vital plane which are called the Pisachas and Pramathas. They manifest more or less in the physico-vital.

On the physical plane the corresponding forces are obscure beings, more forces than beings, what the Theosophists call the elementals. They are not strongly individualised beings like the Rakshasas and Asuras, but ignorant and obscure forces working in the subtle physical plane. What we in Sanskrit call the Bhutas mostly come under this class. But there are two kinds of elementals, the one mischievous and the other not.

There are no Asuras on the higher planes where the Truth prevails, except in the Vedic sense — "the Divine in its strength". The mental and vital Asuras are only a deviation of that power.

*

The Gandharvas are of the vital plane but they are vital Gods, not Asuras. Many Asuras are beautiful in appearance and can carry even a splendour or light with them. It is the Rakshasas, Pisachas, etc. who are ugly or evil in appearance.

*

Some of the vital beings are very intelligent — but they do not make friends with the Light — they only try to avoid destruction and wait their time.

*

Very few [*vital beings*] come upon earth — they prefer to get hold of human beings and make them their instruments. They do not evolve. They have no evolved or evolving psychic being and they dread to incarnate just because they would then be obliged to progress and evolve the psychic.

*

There is no particular number [*of vital beings that surround a person*] — but sometimes there are particular vital beings that attach themselves to a man if he accepts them.

Section Two

The Avatar and the Vibhuti

Chapter One

The Meaning and Purpose of Avatarhood

The Avatar or Incarnation

Surely for the earth consciousness it is so [*the very fact that the Divine manifests himself is the greatest of all splendours*]. Consider the obscurity here and what it would be if the Divine did not directly intervene and the Light of Lights did not break out of the obscurity — for that is the meaning of the manifestation.

*

An Incarnation is the Divine Consciousness and Being manifesting through a physical body. It is possible from any plane.

*

It is the omnipresent cosmic Divine who supports the action of the universe; if there is an Incarnation, it does not in the least diminish the cosmic Presence and the cosmic action in the three or thirty million universes.

*

The descending Power chooses its own place, body, time for the manifestation; something of that is foreseen by those who have vision but not the whole.

*

An Avatar is supposed to be from birth. Each soul at its birth takes from the cosmic mind, life and matter to shape a new external personality for himself. What prevents the Divine from doing the same? What is continued from birth to birth is the inner being.

*

Each being in a new birth prepares a new mind, life and body — otherwise John Smith would always be John Smith and would have no chance of being Piyush Kanti Ghose. Of course inside there are old personalities contributing to the new lila — but I am speaking of the new visible personality, the outer man, mental, vital, physical. It is the psychic being that keeps the link from birth to birth and makes all the manifestations of the same person. It is therefore to be expected that the Avatar should take on a new personality each time, a personality suited for the new times, work, surroundings. In my own view of things, however, the new personality has a series of non-Avatar births behind him, births in which the intermediate evolution has been followed and assisted from age to age.

*

If they [*the difficulties and struggles of the Avatar*] are shams, they have no value for others or for any true effect. If they have no value for others or for any true effect, they are perfectly irrational and unreal and meaningless. The Divine does not need to suffer or struggle for himself; if he takes on these things it is in order to bear the world-burden and help the world and men; and if the sufferings and struggles are to be of any help, they must be real. A sham or falsehood cannot help. They must be as real as the struggles and sufferings of men themselves — the Divine bears them and at the same time shows the way out of them. Otherwise his assumption of human nature has no meaning and no utility and no value. It is strange that you cannot understand or refuse to admit so simple and crucial a point. What is the use of admitting Avatarhood if you take all the meaning out of it?

The Divine and Human Sides of the Avatar

There are two sides of the phenomenon of Avatarhood, the Divine Consciousness behind and the instrumental personality. The Divine Consciousness is omnipotent but it has put forth the instrumental personality in Nature, under the conditions of Nature, and it uses it according to the rules of the game

— though also sometimes to change the rules of the game. If Avatarhood is only a flashing miracle, then I have no use for it. If it is a coherent part of the arrangement of the omnipresent Divine in Nature, then I can understand and accept it.

*

As for the Divine and human, that also is a mind-made difficulty. The Divine is there in the human, and the human fulfilling and exceeding its highest aspirations and tendencies becomes the Divine. That is what your silly X could not understand — that when the Divine descends, he takes upon himself the burden of humanity in order to exceed it — he becomes human in order to show humanity how to become Divine. But that cannot be if there is only a weakling without any divine Presence within or divine Force behind him — he has to be strong in order to put his strength into all who are willing to receive it. There is therefore in him a double element — human in front, divine behind — and it is that which gives the impression of unfathomableness of which X complained. If you look upon the human alone, looking with the external eye only and are not willing or ready to see anything else, you will see a human being only — if you look for the Divine, you will find the Divine.

*

The Avatar is not supposed to act in a non-human way — he takes up human action and uses human methods with the human consciousness in front and the Divine behind. If he did not his taking a human body would have no meaning and would be of no use to anybody. He could just as well have stayed above and done things from there.

*

What do you mean by lust? Avatars can be married and have children and that is not possible without sex; they can have friendships, enmities, family feelings etc. etc. — these are vital things. I think you are under the impression that an Avatar must be a saint or a Yogi.

*

One can be the head of a spiritual organisation or the Messiah of a religion or an Avatar without in this life reaching the Supermind and beyond.

Human Judgments of the Divine

It is true that it is impossible for the limited human reason to judge the way or purpose of the Divine, which is the way of the Infinite dealing with the finite.

*

It is not by your mind that you can hope to understand the Divine and its action, but by the growth of the true and divine consciousness within you. If the Divine were to unveil and reveal itself in all its glory, the mind might feel a Presence, but it would not understand its action or its nature. It is in the measure of your own realisation and by the birth and growth of that greater consciousness in yourself that you will see the Divine and understand its action even behind its terrestrial disguises.

*

Men's way of doing things is a mental convention; they see things and do things with the mind and what they want is a mental and human perfection. When they think of a manifestation of Divinity, they think it must be an extraordinary perfection in doing the ordinary human things — an extraordinary business faculty, political, poetic or artistic faculty, an accurate memory, not making any mental mistakes, not undergoing any defeat or failure. Or else they think of things which they call superhuman like the people who expected me not to eat food at all or wanted me to know and tell them what will be the value of the cotton shares in Bombay from day to day, or like those who think great Yogis are those who sleep on nails or eat them. All that has nothing to do with manifesting the Divine.

At that rate Rama would be undivine because he followed the Mayamriga as if it were a natural deer and Krishna would be undivine because he was forced by Jarasandha to take refuge in distant Dwaraka. These human ideas are false.

The Divinity acts according to another consciousness — the consciousness of the Truth above and the Lila below and it acts according to the need of the Lila, not according to men's ideas of what it should or should not do. This is the first thing one must grasp, otherwise one can understand nothing about the manifestation of the Divine.

*

I do not know why you should be suddenly bewildered by what I wrote[1] — it is nothing new and we have been saying it since a whole eternity. I wrote this short answer in reference to a question which supposed that certain "perfections" must be demanded of the Divine Manifestation which seemed to me quite irrelevant to the reality. I put forward two propositions which appear to me indisputable unless we are to revise all spiritual knowledge in favour of modern European ideas about things.

First, the Divine Manifestation even when it manifests in mental and human ways has behind it a consciousness greater than the mind and not bound by the petty mental and moral conventions of this very ignorant human race — so that to impose these standards on the Divine is to try to do what is irrational and impossible. Secondly, this Divine Consciousness behind the apparent personality is concerned with only two things in a fundamental way — the Truth above and here below the Lila and the purpose of the incarnation or manifestation and it does what is necessary for that in the way its greater than human consciousness sees to be the necessary and intended way. I shall try if I can develop that when I write about it — perhaps I shall take your remarks about Rama and Krishna as the starting-point — but that I shall see hereafter.

But I do not understand how all that can prevent me from answering mental questions. On my own showing, if it is necessary for the divine purpose, it has to be done. Ramakrishna himself whom you quote for the futility of asking questions

---

[1] *See the letter beginning "I would not describe" on pages 416–17.— Ed.*

answered thousands of questions, I believe. But the answers must be such as Ramakrishna gave and such as I try to give, answers from a higher spiritual experience, from a deeper source of knowledge and not lucubrations of the logical intellect trying to coordinate its ignorance; still less can they be a placing of the Divine or the Divine Truth before the judgment of the intellect to be condemned or acquitted by that authority — for the authority here has no sufficient jurisdiction or competence.

The Work of the Avatar

I have said that the Avatar is one who comes to open the Way for humanity to a higher consciousness — if nobody can follow the Way, then either our conception of the thing, which is also that of Christ and Krishna and Buddha, is all wrong or the whole life and action of the Avatar is quite futile. X seems to say that there is no way and no possibility of following, that the struggles and sufferings of the Avatar are unreal and all humbug, — there is no possibility of struggle for one who represents the Divine. Such a conception makes nonsense of the whole idea of Avatarhood — there is then no reason in it, no necessity for it, no meaning in it. The Divine being all-powerful can lift people up without bothering to come down on earth. It is only if it is part of the world-arrangement that he should take upon himself the burden of humanity and open the Way that Avatarhood has any meaning.

*

If the Divine were not in essence omnipotent, he could not be omnipotent anywhere — whether in the supramental or anywhere else. Because he chooses to limit or determine his action by conditions, it does not make him less omnipotent. His self-limitation is itself an act of omnipotence.

*

Why the immortal Hell should the Divine be tied down to succeed in all his operations? What if failure suits him better and serves better the ultimate purpose? What if the gentleman in question had to be given his chance as Duryodhan was given his chance when Krishna went to him as ambassador in a last effort to avoid the massacre of Kurukshetra? What rigid primitive notions are these about the Divine! And what about my explanation of how the Divine acts through the Avatar?[2] It seems all to have gone into water.

By the way about the ass becoming an elephant — what I meant to say was that the only reason why it can't be done is because there is no recognisable process for it. But if a process can be discovered whether by a scientist (let us say transformation or redistribution of the said ass's atoms or molecules — or what not) or by an occultist or by a Yogi, then there is no reason why it should not be done. In other words certain conditions have been established for the game and so long as those conditions remain unchanged certain things are not done — so we say they are impossible, can't be done. If the conditions are changed, then the same things are done or at least become licit — allowable, legal, according to the so-called laws of Nature, — and then we say they can be done. The Divine also acts according to the conditions of the game. He may change them, but he has to change them first, not proceed while maintaining the conditions to act by a series of miracles.

*

If your argument is that the life, actions, struggles of the Avatar (e.g. Rama's, Krishna's) are unreal because the Divine is there and knows it is all a Maya, in man also there is a self, a spirit that is immortal, untouched, divine, you can say that man's sufferings and ignorance are only put on, shams, unreal. But if man feels them as real and if the Avatar feels his work and the difficulties to be serious and real?

If the existence of the Divinity is of no practical effect, what is the use of a theoretical admission? The manifestation of the

---

[2] *The "explanation" Sri Aurobindo refers to here is probably the one presented in* Essays on the Gita, *First Series, Chapters XV to XVII. — Ed.*

Divinity in the Avatar is of help to man because it helps him to discover his own divinity, find the way to realise it. If the difference is so great that the humanity by its very nature prevents all possibility of following the way opened by the Avatar, it merely means that there is no divinity in man that can respond to the Divinity in the Avatar.

*

I repeat, the Divine when he takes on the burden of terrestrial nature, takes it fully, sincerely and without any conjuring tricks or pretence. If he has something behind him which emerges always out of the coverings, it is the same thing in essence, even if greater in degree, that there is behind others — and it is to awaken that that he is there.

The psychic being does the same for all who are intended for the spiritual way — men need not be extraordinary beings to follow Yoga. That is the mistake you are making — to harp on greatness as if only the great can be spiritual.

*

An Avatar or Vibhuti have the knowledge that is necessary for their work, they need not have more. There was absolutely no reason why Buddha should know what was going on in Rome. An Avatar even does not manifest all the Divine omniscience and omnipotence; he has not come for any such unnecessary display; all that is behind him but not in the front of his consciousness. As for the Vibhuti, the Vibhuti need not even know that he is a power of the Divine. Some Vibhutis, like Julius Caesar for instance, have been atheists. Buddha himself did not believe in a personal God, only in some impersonal and indescribable Permanent.

The Avatar: Historicity and Symbols

Then as to the Avatar and the symbols. There is, it seems to me, a cardinal error in the modern insistence on the biographical and historical, that is to say, the external factuality of the Avatar, the incidents of his outward life. What matters is the spiritual Reality, the Power, the Influence that came with him or that he brought down by his action and his existence. First of all what matters in a spiritual man's life is not what he did or what he was outside to the view of the men of his time (that is what historicity or biography comes to, does it not?) but what he was and did within; it is only that that gives any value to his outer life at all. It is the inner life that gives to the outer any power it may have, and the inner life of a spiritual man is something vast and full and, at least in the great figures, so crowded and teeming with significant things that no biographer or historian could ever hope to seize it all or tell it. Whatever is significant in the outward life is so because it is a symbol of what has been realised within himself and one may go on and say that the inner life also is only significant as an expression, a living representation of the movement of the Divinity behind it. That is why we need not enquire whether the stories about Krishna were transcripts, however loose, of his acts on earth or are symbol-representations of what Krishna was and is for men, of the Divinity expressing itself in the figure of Krishna. Buddha's renunciation, his temptation by Mara, his enlightenment under the Bo-Tree are such symbols, so too the virgin birth, the temptation in the desert, the crucifixion of Christ are such symbols true by what they signify, even if they are not scrupulously recorded historical events. The outward facts as related of Christ or Buddha come to not much more than what has happened in many other lives — what is it that gives Buddha or Christ their enormous place in the spiritual world? It was because something manifested through them that was more than any outward event or any teaching. The verifiable historicity gives us very little of that, yet it is that only that matters. So it seems to me that Krishnaprem is fundamentally right in what he says of the symbols. To the physical mind only the words and facts and acts of a man matter; to the inner mind it is the spiritual happenings in him that matter. Even the teachings of Christ and Buddha are spiritually true not as mere mental teachings but as the expression of spiritual states or happenings in them which by their life on earth they made possible (or at any rate more dynamically potential) in others. Also evidently sectarian walls are a mistake, an accretion, a mental limiting of the Truth which may serve a mental, but not a spiritual purpose. The Avatar, the Guru have no meaning if they do not stand for the Eternal; it is that that makes them what they are for the worshipper or the disciple.

It is also a fact that nobody can give you any spiritual revelation which does not come from something in one's own true Self, it is always the Divine who reveals himself and the Divine is within you; so He who reveals must be felt in your own heart. Your query here simply suggests that this is a truth which can be misinterpreted or misused, but so can every spiritual truth if it is taken hold of in the wrong way — and the human mind has a great penchant for taking Truth by the wrong end and arriving at falsehood. All statements about these things are, after all, mental statements and at the mercy of any mind that interprets them. There is a snag in every such statement created not by the Truth that it expresses but by the mind's interpretation. The snag here (what you call the slip) lies not in the statement itself which is quite correct, but in the deflected sense in which it may be taken by ignorant or self-sufficient minds enamoured of their ego. Many have put forward the "own self" gospel without taking the trouble to see whether it is the true Self, have pitted the ignorance of their "own self" — in fact, their ego — against the knowledge of the Guru or made their ego or something that flattered and fostered it the Ishta Devata. The snag in the worship of Guru or Avatar is a sectarian bias which insists on the Representative or the Manifestation but loses sight of the Manifested; the snag in the emphasis on the other side is the ignoring of the need or belittling of the value of the Representative or Manifestation and the substitution not of the true Self one in all but of one's "own self" as the guide and light. How many have done that here and lost the way through the pull of the magnified ego which is one of the great perils on the way! However that does not lessen the truth of the things said by Krishnaprem — only in looking at the many sides of Truth one must put each thing in its place in the harmony of the All which

The Meaning and Purpose of Avatarhood

is for us the expression of the Supreme.

*

The answer to the question [*whether the Krishna of Brindavan and the stories of his lila are literally true or merely symbols of deep spiritual realities*] depends on what value one attaches to spiritual experience and to mystic and occult experience, that is to say, to the data of other planes of consciousness than the physical, as also on the nature of the relations between the cosmic consciousness and the individual and collective consciousness of man. From the point of view of spiritual and occult Truth, what takes shape in the consciousness of man is a reflection and particular kind of formation, in a difficult medium, of things much greater in their light, power and beauty or in their force and range which come to it from the cosmic consciousness of which man is a limited and, in his present state of evolution, a still ignorant part. All this explanation about the genius of the race, of the consciousness of a nation creating the Gods and their forms is a very partial, somewhat superficial and in itself a misleading truth. Man's mind is not an original creator, it is an intermediary; to start creating it must receive an initiating "inspiration", a transmission or a suggestion from the cosmic consciousness, and with that it does what it can. God is, but man's conceptions of God are reflections in his own mentality, sometimes of the Divine, sometimes of other Beings and Powers and they are what his mentality can make of the suggestions that come to him, generally very partial and imperfect so long as they are still mental, so long as he has not arrived at a higher and truer, a spiritual or mystic knowledge. The Gods already exist, they are not created by man even though he does seem to conceive them in his own image; fundamentally, he formulates as best he can what truth about them he receives from the cosmic Reality. An artist or a bhakta may have a vision of the Gods and it may get stabilised and generalised in the consciousness of the race and in that sense it may be true that man gives their forms to the Gods; but he does not invent these forms, he records what he sees; the forms that he gives are given to him. In the "conventional" form of Krishna men have embodied what they could see of his eternal beauty and what they have seen may be true as well as beautiful, it conveys something of the form, but it is fairly certain that if there is an eternal form of that eternal beauty it is a thousand times more beautiful than what man had as yet been able to see of it. Mother India is not a piece of earth; she is a Power, a Godhead, for all nations have such a Devi supporting their separate existence and keeping it in being. Such Beings are as real and more permanently real than the men they influence, but they belong to a higher plane, are part of the cosmic consciousness and being and act here on earth by shaping the human consciousness on which they exercise their influence. It is natural for man who only sees his own consciousness individual, national or racial at work and does not see what works upon it and shapes it, to think that all is created by him and there is nothing cosmic and greater behind it. The Krishna consciousness is a reality, but if there were no Krishna, there could be no Krishna consciousness: except in arbitrary metaphysical abstractions there can be no consciousness without a Being who is conscious. It is the person who gives value and reality to the personality, he expresses himself in it and is not constituted by it. Krishna is a being, a person and it is as the Divine Person that we meet him, hear his voice, speak with him and feel his presence. To speak of the consciousness of Krishna as something separate from Krishna is an error of the mind, which is always separating the inseparable and which also tends to regard the impersonal, because it is abstract, as greater, more real and more enduring than the person. Such divisions may be useful to the mind for its own purposes, but it is not the real truth; in the real truth the being or person and its impersonality or state of being are one reality.

The historicity of Krishna is of less spiritual importance and is not essential, but it has still a considerable value. It does not seem to me that there can be any reasonable doubt that Krishna the man was not a legend or a poetic invention but actually existed upon earth and played a part in the Indian past. Two facts emerge clearly, that he was regarded as an important

The Meaning and Purpose of Avatarhood

spiritual figure, one whose spiritual illumination was recorded in one of the Upanishads, and that he was traditionally regarded as a divine man, one worshipped after his death as a deity; this is apart from the story in the Mahabharata and the Puranas. There is no reason to suppose that the connection of his name with the development of the Bhagavata religion, an important current in the stream of Indian spirituality, was founded on a mere legend or poetic invention. The Mahabharata is a poem and not history, but it is clearly a poem founded on a great historical event, traditionally preserved in memory; some of the figures connected with it, Dhritarashtra, Parikshit, for instance, certainly existed and the story of the part played by Krishna as leader, warrior and statesman can be accepted as probable in itself and to all appearance founded on a tradition which can be given a historical value and has not the air of a myth or a sheer poetical invention. That is as much as can be positively said from the point of view of the theoretical reason as to the historical figure of the man Krishna; but in my view there is much more than that in it and I have always regarded the incarnation as a fact and accepted the historicity of Krishna as I accept the historicity of Christ.

The story of Brindavan is another matter; it does not enter into the main story of the Mahabharata and has a Puranic origin and it could be maintained that it was intended all along to have a symbolic character. At one time I accepted that explanation, but I had to abandon it afterwards; there is nothing in the Puranas that betrays any such intention. It seems to me that it is related as something that actually occurred or occurs somewhere; the Gopis are to them realities and not symbols. It was for them at the least an occult truth, and occult and symbolic are not the same thing; the symbol may be only a significant mental construction or only a fanciful invention, but the occult is a reality which is actual somewhere, behind the material scene as it were and can have its truth for the terrestrial life and its influence upon it, may even embody itself there. The lila of the Gopis seems to be conceived as something which is always going on in a divine Gokul and which projected itself in an earthly Brindavan and can always be realised and its meaning made actual in the soul. It is to be presumed that the writers of the Puranas took it as having been actually projected on earth in the life of the incarnate Krishna and it has always been so accepted by the religious mind of India.

These questions and the speculations to which they have given rise have no indispensable connection with the spiritual life. There what matters is the contact with Krishna and the growth towards the Krishna consciousness, the presence, the spiritual relation, the union in the soul and, till that is reached, the aspiration, the growth in bhakti and whatever illumination one can get on the way. To one who has had these things, lived in the presence, heard the voice, known Krishna as Friend or Lover, Guide, Teacher, Master or, still more, has had his whole consciousness changed by the contact, or felt the presence within him, all such questions have only an outer and superficial interest. So also, to one who has had contact with the inner Brindavan and the lila of the Gopis, made the surrender and undergone the spell of the joy and the beauty or even only turned to the sound of the flute, the rest hardly matters. But from another point of view, if one can accept the historical reality of the incarnation, there is this great spiritual gain that one has a *point d'appui* for a more concrete realisation in the conviction that once at least the Divine has visibly touched the earth, made the complete manifestation possible, made it possible for the divine supernature to descend into this evolving but still very imperfect terrestrial nature.

*

What he [*Krishnaprem*] says[3] — the central thing — is very correct as always, the position of all who have any notion of spirituality, though the religionists seem to find it difficult to get to it. But though Christ and Krishna are the same, they are the same in difference; that is indeed the utility of so many manifestations

---

[3] *In his letter to the correspondent, Krishnaprem observed that "Christ and Krishna are the same." He also said: "Why is Christianity tottering? Primarily because the Christians have pinned their faith on historical events and a historical person." — Ed.*

instead of there being only one as these missionaries would have it. But is it really because the historical Christ has been made too much the foundation-stone of the faith that Christianity is failing? It may be something inadequate in the religion itself — perhaps in religion itself; for all religions are a little off-colour now. The need of a larger opening of the soul into the Light is being felt, an opening through which the expanding human mind and heart can follow.

The Avatar and the Vibhuti

The Avatar is necessary when a special work is to be done and in crises of the evolution. The Avatar is a special manifestation, while for the rest of the time it is the Divine working within the ordinary human limits as a Vibhuti.

*

An Avatar, roughly speaking, is one who is conscious of the presence and power of the Divine born in him or descended into him and governing from within his will and life and action; he feels identified inwardly with this divine power and presence. A Vibhuti is supposed to embody some power of the Divine and is enabled by it to act with great force in the world but that is all that is necessary to make him a Vibhuti: the power may be very great but the consciousness is not that of an inborn or indwelling Divinity. This is the distinction we can gather from the Gita which is the main authority on this subject. If we follow this distinction, we can confidently say from what is related of them that Rama and Krishna can be accepted as Avatars; Buddha figures as such although with a more impersonal consciousness of the Power within him; Ramakrishna voiced the same consciousness when he spoke of him who was Rama and who was Krishna being within him. But Chaitanya's case is peculiar; for according to the accounts he ordinarily felt and declared himself a bhakta of Krishna and nothing more, but in great moments he manifested Krishna, grew luminous in mind and body and was Krishna himself and spoke and acted as the Lord. His contemporaries saw in him an Avatar of Krishna, a manifestation of the divine love. Shankara and Vivekananda were certainly Vibhutis; they cannot be reckoned as more, though as Vibhutis they were very great.

*

It was not my intention to question in any degree Chaitanya's position as an Avatar of Krishna and the divine love. That character of the manifestation appears very clearly from all the accounts about him and even, if what is related about the appearance of Krishna in him from time to time is accepted, these outbursts of the splendour of the Divine Being are among the most remarkable in the story of the Avatar. As for Ramakrishna, the manifestation in him was not so intense but more many-sided and fortunately there can be no doubt about the authenticity of the details of his talk and actions since they have been recorded from day to day by so competent an observer as Mahendranath Gupta. I would not care to enter into any comparison as between these two great spiritual personalities; both exercised an extraordinary influence and did something supreme in their own sphere.

Chapter Two

Specific Avatars and Vibhutis

The Ten Avatars as a Parable of Evolution

Avatarhood would have little meaning if it were not connected with the evolution. The Hindu procession of the ten Avatars is itself, as it were, a parable of evolution. First the Fish Avatar, then the amphibious animal between land and water, then the land animal, then the Man-Lion Avatar, bridging man and animal, then man as dwarf, small and undeveloped and physical but containing in himself the godhead and taking possession of existence, then the rajasic, sattwic, nirguna Avatars, leading the human development from the vital rajasic to the sattwic mental man and again the overmental superman. Krishna, Buddha and Kalki depict the last three stages, the stages of the spiritual development — Krishna opens the possibility of Overmind, Buddha tries to shoot beyond to the supreme liberation but that liberation is still negative, not returning upon earth to complete positively the evolution; Kalki is to correct this by bringing the Kingdom of the Divine upon earth, destroying the opposing Asura forces. The progression is striking and unmistakable.

As for the lives in between the Avatar lives, it must be remembered that Krishna speaks of many lives in the past, not only a few supreme ones, and secondly that while he speaks of himself as the Divine, in one passage he describes himself as a Vibhuti, *vṛṣṇīnāṁ vāsudevaḥ*. We may therefore fairly assume that in many lives he manifested as the Vibhuti veiling the fuller Divine Consciousness. If we admit that the object of Avatarhood is to lead the evolution, this is quite reasonable, the Divine appearing as Avatar in the great transitional stages and as Vibhutis to aid the lesser transitions.

*

In speaking of supreme liberation [*in the previous letter*] I was simply taking the Buddhist, Adwaita view for granted and correcting it by saying that this Nirvana view is too negative. Krishna opened the possibility of Overmind with its two sides of realisation, static and dynamic. Buddha tried to shoot from mind to Nirvana in the Supreme, just as Shankara did in another way after him. Both agree in overleaping the other stages and trying to get at a nameless and featureless Absolute. Krishna on the other hand was leading by the normal course of evolution. The next normal step is not a featureless Absolute, but the Supermind. I consider that in trying to overshoot, Buddha like Shankara made a mistake, cutting away the dynamic side of the liberation. Therefore there has to be a correction by Kalki.

I was of course dealing with the Ten Avatars as a "parable of the evolution", and only explaining the interpretation we can put on it from that point of view. It was not my own view of the thing that I was giving.

*

I only took the Puranic list of Avatars and interpreted it as a parable of evolution, so as to show that the idea of evolution is implicit behind the theory of Avatarhood. As to whether one accepts Buddha as an Avatar or prefers to put others in his place (in some lists Balaram replaces Buddha), is a matter of individual feeling. The Buddhist Jatakas are legends about the past incarnations of the Buddha, often with a teaching implied in them, and are not a part of the Hindu system. To the Buddhists Buddha was not an Avatar at all, he was the soul climbing up the ladder of spiritual evolution till it reached the final stage of emancipation — although Hindu influence did make Buddhism develop the idea of an eternal Buddha above, that was not a universal or fundamental Buddhistic idea. Whether the Divine in manifesting his Avatarhood could choose to follow the line of evolution from the lowest scale, manifesting on each scale as a Vibhuti, is a question again to which the answer is not inevitably in the negative. If we accept the evolutionary idea, such a thing may have its place.

If Buddha taught something different from Krishna, that

does not prevent his advent from being necessary in the spiritual evolution. The only question is whether the attempt to scale the heights of an absolute Nirvana through negation of cosmic existence was a necessary step or not, having a view to the fact that one can make the attempt to reach the Highest on the *neti neti* as well as the *iti iti* line.

*

Too much importance need not be attached to the details about Kalki — they are rather symbolic than an attempt to prophesy details of future history. What is expressed is something that has to come, but it is symbolically indicated, no more.

So too, too much weight need not be put on the exact figures about the Yugas in the Purana. Here again the Kala and the Yugas indicate successive periods in the cyclic wheel of evolution, the perfect state, decline and disintegration of successive ages of humanity followed by a new birth — the mathematical calculations are not the important element. The argument of the end of the Kali Yuga already come or coming and a new Satya Yuga coming is a very familiar one and there have been many who have upheld it.

Rama as an Avatar

I have no intention of entering into a supreme defence of Rama — I only entered into the points about Bali etc. because these are usually employed nowadays to belittle him as a great personality on the usual level. But from the point of view of Avatarhood I would no more think of defending his moral perfection according to modern standards than I would think of defending Napoleon or Caesar against the moralists or the democratic critics or the debunkers in order to prove that they were Vibhutis. Vibhuti, Avatar are terms which have their own meaning and scope, and they are not concerned with morality or immorality, perfection or imperfection according to small human standards or setting an example to men or showing new moral attitudes or giving new spiritual teachings. These things may or may not be done, but they are not at all the essence of the matter.

Also, I do not consider your method of dealing with Rama's personality to be the right one. It has to be taken as a whole in the setting that Valmiki gave it (not treated as if it were the story of a modern man) and with the significance that he gave to his hero's personality, deeds and works. If it is pulled out of its setting and analysed under the dissecting knife of a modern ethical mind, it loses all its significance at once. Krishna so treated becomes a mere debauchee and trickster who no doubt did great things in politics — but so did Rama in war. Achilles and Odysseus pulled out of their setting become, one a furious egoistic savage, and the other a cruel and cunning savage. I consider myself under an obligation to enter into the spirit, significance, atmosphere of the Mahabharata, Iliad, Ramayana and identify myself with their time-spirit before I can feel what their heroes were in themselves apart from the details of their outer action.

As for the Avatarhood, I accept it for Rama first because he fills a place in the scheme and seems to me to fill it rightly — and because when I read the Ramayana I feel a great afflatus which I recognise and which makes of its story — mere faery-tale though it seems — a parable of a great critical transitional event that happened in the terrestrial evolution and gives to the main character's personality and actions a significance of the large typical cosmic kind which these actions would not have had if they had been done by another man in another scheme of events. The Avatar is not bound to do extraordinary actions, but he is bound to give his acts or his work or what he is — any of these or all — a significance and an effective power that are part of something essential to be done in the history of the earth and its races.

All the same, if anybody does not see as I do and wants to eject Rama from his place, I have no objection — I have no particular partiality for Rama — provided somebody is put in who can more worthily fill up the gap his absence leaves. There *was* somebody there, Valmiki's Rama or another Rama or somebody else not Rama.

Also I do not mean that I admit the validity of your remarks about Rama, even taken as a piecemeal criticism; but that I have no time for today. I maintain my position about the killing of Bali and the banishment of Sita in spite of Bali's preliminary objection to the procedure, afterwards retracted, and in spite of the opinions of Rama's relatives. Necessarily from the point of view of the antique dharma — not from that of any universal moral standard — which besides does not exist, since the standard changes according to clime or age.

*

No, certainly not — an Avatar is not at all bound to be a spiritual prophet — he is never in fact merely a prophet, he is a realiser, an establisher — not of outward things only, though he does realise something in the outward also, but, as I have said, of something essential and radical needed for the terrestrial evolution which is the evolution of the embodied spirit through successive stages towards the Divine. It was not at all Rama's business to establish the spiritual stage of that evolution — so he did not at all concern himself with that. His business was to destroy Ravana and to establish the Ramarajya — in other words, to fix for the future the possibility of an order proper to the sattwic civilised human being who governs his life by the reason, the finer emotions, morality or at least moral ideals, such as truth, obedience, cooperation and harmony, the sense of humour, the sense of domestic and public order, to establish this in a world still occupied by anarchic forces, the Animal Mind and the powers of the vital Ego making its own satisfaction the rule of life, in other words, the Vanara and the Rakshasa. This is the meaning of Rama and his life-work and it is according as he fulfilled it or not that he must be judged as Avatar or no Avatar. It was not his business to play the comedy of the chivalrous Kshatriya with the formidable brute beast that was Bali, it was his business to kill him and get the Animal Mind under his control. It was his business to be not necessarily a perfect, but a largely representative sattwic Man, a faithful husband and lover, a loving and obedient son, a tender and perfect brother, father, friend — he is friend of all kinds of people, friend of the outcaste Guhaka, friend of the Animal leaders, Sugriva, Hanuman, friend of the vulture Jatayu, friend even of the Rakshasa Vibhishan. All that he was in a brilliant, striking but above all spontaneous and inevitable way, not with a forcing of this note or that like Harishchandra or Shivi, but with a certain harmonious completeness. But most of all, it was his business to typify and establish the things on which the social idea and its stability depend, truth and honour, the sense of the Dharma, public spirit and the sense of order. To the first, to truth and honour, much more even than to his filial love and obedience to his father — though to that also — he sacrificed his personal rights as the elect of the King and the Assembly and fourteen of the best years of his life and went into exile in the forests. To his public spirit and his sense of public order (the great and supreme civic virtue in the eyes of the ancient Indians, Greeks, Romans, for at that time the maintenance of the ordered community, not the separate development and satisfaction of the individual was the pressing need of human evolution) he sacrificed his own happiness and domestic life and the happiness of Sita. In that he was at one with the moral sense of all the antique races, though at variance with the later romantic individualistic sentimental morality of the modern man who can afford to have that less stern morality just because the ancients sacrificed the individual in order to make the world safe for the spirit of social order. Finally it was Rama's business to make the world safe for the ideal of the sattwic human being by destroying the sovereignty of Ravana, the Rakshasa menace. All this he did with such a divine afflatus in his personality and action that his figure has been stamped for more than two millenniums on the mind of Indian culture and what he stood for has dominated the reason and idealising mind of man in all countries — and in spite of the constant revolt of the human vital is likely to continue to do so until a greater Ideal arises. And you say in spite of all this that he was no Avatar? If you like — but at any rate he stands among the few greatest of the great Vibhutis. You may dethrone him now — for man is no longer satisfied with the sattwic ideal and is seeking for something more — but his work and meaning remain stamped on the past of the earth's evolving race.

When I spoke of the gap that would be left by his absence, I did not mean a gap among the prophets and intellectuals, but a gap in the scheme of Avatarhood — there was somebody who was the Avatar of the sattwic Human as Krishna was the Avatar of the overmental Superhuman — I see no one but Rama who can fill the place. Spiritual teachers and prophets (as also intellectuals, scientists, artists, poets, etc.) — these are at the greatest Vibhutis, but they are not Avatars. For at that rate all religious founders would be Avatars — Joseph Smith (I think that is his name) of the Mormons, St. Francis of Assisi, Calvin, Loyola and a host of others as well as Christ, Chaitanya or Ramakrishna.

For faith, miracles, Bijoy Goswami, another occasion. I wanted to say this much more about Rama — which is still only a hint and is not the thing I was going to write about the general principle of Avatarhood.[1]

*

I am rather perplexed by your strictures on Rama. Cowardice is the last thing that can be charged against Valmiki's Rama; he has always been considered as a warrior and it is the "martial races" of India who have made him their god. Valmiki everywhere paints him as a great warrior. His employment of ruse against an infrahuman enemy does not prove the opposite — for that is always how the human (even great warriors and hunters) has dealt with the infrahuman. I think it is Madhusudan who has darkened Valmiki's hero in Bengali eyes and turned him into a poor puppet, but that is not the authentic Rama who, say what one will, was a great epic figure, — Avatar or no Avatar. As

---

[1] Nor, I may add, is it a complete or supreme defence of Rama. For that I would have to write about what the story of the Ramayana meant, appreciate Valmiki's presentation of his chief characters (they are none of them copy-book examples, but great men and women with the defects and merits of human nature, as all men, even the greatest, are), and show also how the Godhead, which was behind the frontal and instrumental personality we call Rama, worked out every incident of his life as a necessary step in what had to be done. As to the weeping of Rama, I had answered that in my other yet unfinished letter. You are imposing the colder and harder Nordic ideal on the Southern temperament which regarded the expression of emotion, not its suppression, as a virtue. Witness the weeping and lamentations of Achilles, Ulysses and other Greek, Persian and Indian heroes — the latter especially as lovers.

for conventional morality, all morality is a convention — man cannot live without conventions, mental and moral, otherwise he feels himself lost in the rolling sea of the anarchic forces of vital Nature. Even the Russells and Bernard Shaws can only end by setting up another set of conventions in the place of those they have skittled over. Only by rising above mind can one really get beyond conventions — Krishna was able to do it because he was not a mental human being but an overmental godhead acting freely out of a greater consciousness than man's. Rama was not that, he was the Avatar of the sattwic human mind — mental, emotional, moral — and he followed the Dharma of the age and race. That may make him temperamentally congenial to Gandhi and the reverse to you; but just as Gandhi's temperamental recoil from Krishna does not prove Krishna to be no Avatar, so your temperamental recoil from Rama does not establish that he was not an Avatar. However, my main point will be that Avatarhood does not depend upon these questions at all, but has another basis, meaning and purpose.

*

No time for a full answer to your renewed remarks on Rama tonight. You are intrigued only because you stick to the standard modern measuring rods of moral and spiritual perfection (introduced by Seeley and Bankim) for the Avatar — while I start from another standpoint altogether and resolutely refuse these standard human measures. The ancient Avatars except Buddha were *not* either standards of perfection or spiritual teachers — in spite of the Gita which was spoken, says Krishna, in a moment of supernormal consciousness which he lost immediately afterwards. They were, if I may say so, representative cosmic men who were instruments of a divine Intervention for fixing certain things in the evolution of the earth-race. I stick to that and refuse to submit myself in this argument to any other standard whatever.

I did not admit that Rama was a blind Avatar, but offered you two alternatives of which the latter represents my real view founded on the impression made on me by the Ramayana that

Rama knew very well but refused to be talkative about it — his business being not to disclose the Divine, but to fix mental, moral and emotional man (not to originate him for he was there already) on the earth as against the Animal and the Rakshasa forces. My argument from Chaitanya (who was for most of the time, first a pandit and then a bhakta, but only occasionally the Divine himself) is perfectly rational and logical, if you follow my line and don't insist on a high specifically spiritual consciousness for the Avatar. I shall point out what I mean in my next.

By sattwic man I do not mean a moral or an always self-controlled one, but a predominantly mental (as opposed to a vital or merely physical man) who has rajasic emotions and passions, but lives predominantly according to his mind and its will and ideas. There is no such thing, I suppose, as a purely sattwic man — since the three gunas go always together in a state of unstable equilibrium, but a predominantly sattwic man is what I have described. My impression of Rama from Valmiki is such — it is quite different from yours. I am afraid your picture of him is quite out of focus — you efface the main lines of the character, belittle and brush out all the lights to which Valmiki gave so much value and prominence and hammer always at some details and some parts of shadow which you turn into the larger part of Rama. That is what the debunkers do — but a debunked figure is not the true figure.

By the way, a sattwic man can have strong passion and strong anger — and when he lets the latter loose, the normally violent fellow is simply nowhere. Witness the outbursts of anger of Christ, the indignation of Chaitanya — and the general evidence of experience and psychology on that point. All this however by the way — I shall try to develop later.

P. S. The trait of Rama which you give as that of an undeveloped man, viz., his decisive spontaneous action according to the will and the idea that came to him, is a trait of the cosmic man and many Vibhutis, men of action of the large Caesarian or Napoleonic type. That also I hope to develop sometime.

*

Why should Rama not have *kāma* as well as *prema*? — they were supposed to go together as between husband and wife in ancient India. The performances of Rama in the *viraha* of Sita are due to Valmiki's poetic idea which was also Kalidasa's and everybody else's in those far-off times about how a complete lover should behave in such a quandary. Whether the actual Rama bothered himself to do all that is another matter.

As for the unconscious Avatar, why not? Chaitanya is supposed to be an Avatar by the Vaishnavas, yet he was conscious of the Godhead behind only when that Godhead came in front and possessed him on rare occasions. Christ said "I and my Father are one", but yet he always spoke and behaved as if there were a difference. Ramakrishna's earlier period was that of one seeking God, not aware from the first of his identity. These are the reputed religious Avatars who ought to be more conscious than a man of action like Rama. And supposing the full and permanent consciousness, why should the Avatar proclaim himself except on rare occasions to an Arjuna or to a few bhaktas or disciples? It is for others to find out what he is; though he does not deny when others speak of him as That, he is not always saying and perhaps never may say or only in moments like that of the Gita, "I am He."

*

When I said, "Why not an unconscious Avatar?" I was taking *your* statement (not mine) that Rama was unconscious and how could there be an unconscious Avatar. My own view is that Rama was not blind, not unconscious of his Avatarhood, only uncommunicative about it. But I said that even taking your statement to be correct, the objection was not insuperable. I instanced the case of Chaitanya and the others, because there the facts are hardly disputable. Chaitanya for the first part of his life was simply Nimai Pandit and had no consciousness of being anything else. Then he had his conversion and became the bhakta, Chaitanya. This bhakta at times seemed to be possessed by the presence of Krishna, knew himself to be Krishna, spoke, moved and appeared with the light of the Godhead — none around him could think of or see him as anything else when he was in this glorified and transfigured condition. But from that he fell back to the ordinary consciousness of the bhakta and, as I have read in his biography, refused then to consider himself as anything more. These, I think, are the facts. Well then, what do they signify? Was he only Nimai Pandit at first? It is quite conceivable that he was so and the descent of the Godhead into him only took place after his conversion and spiritual change. But also afterwards when he was in his normal bhakta-consciousness, was he then no longer the Avatar? An intermittent Avatarhood? Krishna coming down for an afternoon call into Chaitanya and then going up again till the time came for the next visit? I find it difficult to believe in this phenomenon. The rational explanation is that in the phenomenon of Avatarhood there is a Consciousness behind, at first veiled or sometimes perhaps only half-veiled, which is that of the Godhead and a frontal consciousness, human or apparently human or at any rate with all the appearance of terrestriality, which is the instrumental Personality. In that case, it is possible that the secret Consciousness was all along there, but waited to manifest until after the conversion; and it manifested intermittently because the main work of Chaitanya was to establish the type of a spiritual and psychic bhakti and love in the emotional vital part of man, preparing the vital in us in that way to turn towards the Divine — at any rate, to fix that possibility in the earth-nature. It was not that there had not been the emotional type of bhakti before; but the completeness of it, the *élan*, the vital's rapture in it had never manifested as it manifested in Chaitanya. But for that work it would never have done if he had always been in the Krishna consciousness; he would have been the Lord to whom all gave bhakti, but not the supreme example of the divine ecstatic bhakta. At the same time the occasional manifestation showed who he was and at the same time evidenced the mystic law of the Immanence.

Voilà — for Chaitanya. But, if Chaitanya, the frontal consciousness, the instrumental Personality, was all the time the Avatar, yet except in his highest moments was unconscious of it and even denied it, that pushed a little farther would establish the possibility of what you call an unconscious Avatar — that is to say, of one in which the veiled consciousness might not come in front but always move the instrumental Personality from behind. The frontal consciousness might be aware in the inner parts of its being that it was only an instrument of Something Divine which was its real Self, but outwardly would think, speak and behave as if it were only the human being doing a given work with a peculiar power and splendour. Whether there was such an Avatar or not is another matter, but logically it is quite possible.

*

What is all this obsession of greater or less? In our Yoga we do not strive after greatness.

It is not a question of Sri Krishna's disciples, but of the earth consciousness — Rama was a mental man, there is no touch of the overmind consciousness (direct) in anything he said or did, but what he did was done with the greatness of the Avatar. But there have since been men who did live in touch with the planes above mind — higher mind, illumined mind, Intuition. There is no question of asking whether they were "greater" than Rama; they might have been less "great", but they were able to live from a new plane of consciousness. And Krishna's opening the overmind certainly made it possible for the attempt at bringing Supermind to the earth to be made.

*

About greater and less, one point. Is Captain John Higgins of S.S. *Mauretania* a greater man than Christopher Columbus because he can reach America without trouble in a few days? Is a university graduate in philosophy greater than Plato because he can reason about problems and systems which had never even occurred to Plato? No, only humanity has acquired greater scientific power which any good navigator can use or a wider intellectual knowledge which anyone with a philosophic training can use. You will say greater scientific power and wider knowledge is not a change of consciousness. Very well, but there are Rama and Ramakrishna. Rama spoke always from the thinking intelligence, the common property of developed men; Ramakrishna spoke constantly from a swift and luminous spiritual intuition. Can you tell me which is the greater? the Avatar recognised by all India? or the saint and Yogi recognised as an Avatar only by his disciples and some others who follow them?

Krishna as an Avatar

Krishna is not the supramental light. The descent of Krishna would mean the descent of the Overmind Godhead preparing, though not itself actually bringing, the descent of Supermind and Ananda. Krishna is the Anandamaya, he supports the evolution through the Overmind leading it towards his Ananda.

*

What Krishna worked for was the Overmind consciousness acting in the mind and vital.

*

What was said[2] was that Krishna as a manifestation on earth opened the possibility of the Overmind consciousness here to men and stood for that, as Rama was the incarnation in mental Man. If Krishna was *an* overmind "God", that means he was not an Incarnation, not the Divine, but somebody else who claimed to be the Divine — i.e. he was a god who somehow thought he was God.

*

I suppose very few recognised him [*Krishna*] as an Avatar; certainly it was not at all a general recognition. Among the few those nearest him do not seem to have counted — it was less prominent people like Vidura etc.

*

---

[2] The correspondent asked, "Why is it said that Krishna is an Overmind God?" — Ed.

Those who were with Krishna were in all appearance men like other men. They spoke and acted with each other as men with men and were not thought of by those around them as gods. Krishna himself was known by most as a man — only a few worshipped him as the Divine.

*

Yuge yuge[3] may be used in a general sense, as in English "from age to age" and not refer technically to the *yuga* proper according to the Puranic computation. But the *bahūni* has an air of referring to very numerous lives especially when coupled with *tava ca*. In that case all these many births could not be full incarnations, — many may have been merely Vibhuti births carrying on the thread from incarnation to incarnation. About Arjuna's accompanying him in each and every birth, nothing is said, but it would not be likely — many, of course.

Buddha as an Avatar

He [*Buddha*] affirmed practically something unknowable that was Permanent and Unmanifested. Adwaita does the same. Buddha never said he was an Avatar of a Personal God but that he was the Buddha. It is the Hindus who made him an Avatar. If Buddha had looked upon himself as an Avatar at all, it would have been as an Avatar of the impersonal Truth.

*

If a Divine Consciousness and Force descended and through the personality we call Buddha did a great work for the world, then Buddha can be called an Avatar — the tapasya and arriving at knowledge are only an incident of the manifestation.

If on the other hand Buddha was only a human being like many others who arrived at some knowledge and preached it,

---

[3] *In the Gita, Krishna tells Arjuna, "Many are my lives that are past" (4.5) and again, "I am born from age to age." (4.8) The correspondent asked how Krishna's past lives could be many* (bahūni) *if he was born only from age to age* (yuge yuge). *— Ed.*

then he was not an Avatar—for of that kind there have been thousands and they cannot be all Avatars.

*

I don't know that historically there could have been any other Buddha. It is the Vaishnava Puranas, I think, that settled the list of Avatars, for they are all Avatars of Vishnu according to the Purana. The final acceptance by all may have come later than Shankara, after the Buddhist-Brahminic controversy had ceased to be an actuality. For some time there was a tendency to substitute Balarama's name for Buddha's or to say that Buddha was an Avatar of Vishnu, but that he came to mislead the Asuras. He is evidently aimed at in the story of Mayamoha in the Vishnu Purana.

*

He [*Buddha*] had a more powerful vital than Ramakrishna, a stupendous will and an invincible mind of thought. If he had led the ordinary life, he would have been a great organiser, conqueror and creator.

Mahomed and Christ

Mahomed would himself have rejected the idea of being an Avatara, so we have to regard him only as the prophet, the instrument, the Vibhuti. Christ realised himself as the Son who is one with the Father—he must therefore be an *aṁśa avatāra*, a partial incarnation.

Ramakrishna

He [*Ramakrishna*] never wrote an autobiography. What he said was in conversation with his disciples and others. He was certainly quite as much an Avatar as Christ or Chaitanya.

Augustus Caesar and Leonardo da Vinci

Augustus Caesar organised the life of the Roman Empire and it was this that made the framework of the first transmission of the Graeco-Roman civilisation to Europe — he came for that work and the writings of Virgil and Horace and others helped greatly towards the success of his mission. After the interlude of the Middle Ages, this civilisation was reborn in a new mould in what is called the Renaissance, not in its life-aspects but in its intellectual aspects. It was therefore a supreme intellectual, Leonardo da Vinci, who took up again the work and summarised in himself the seeds of modern Europe.

*

Never heard before of my declaring or anybody declaring such a thing [*that a divine descent was attempted during the Renaissance with Leonardo da Vinci as its centre*]. What Leonardo da Vinci held in himself was all the new age of Europe on its many sides. But there was no question of Avatarhood or consciousness of a descent or pressure of spiritual planes. Mysticism was no part of what he had to manifest.

Napoleon

I don't think it can be said that Napoleon had little of ego. He was exceedingly ego-centric. He made himself a dictator from Brumaire, and as a dictator he should always have acted — but he felt the need of support and made the error of seeking it in the democratic way — a way for which he was utterly unfit. He had the capacities of a ruler but not of a politician — as a politician he would have been an entire failure. His hesitations were due to this defect — if it can be called one. He could not have dealt successfully with parties or a parliamentary assembly.

*

I never heard that Napoleon failed at Waterloo for want of self-confidence. I have always read that he failed because he was, owing to his recent malady, no longer so quick and self-confident in decision and so supple in mental resource as before. Please don't rewrite history unless you have data for your novel version.

Chapter Three

Human Greatness

Greatness

Why should the Divine not care for the outer greatness? He cares for everything in the universe. All greatness is the Vibhuti of the Divine, says the Gita.

*

Obviously outer greatness is not the aim of Yoga. But that is no reason why one should not recognise the part played by greatness in the order of the universe or the place of great men of action, great poets and artists etc.

*

People have begun to try to prove that great men were not great, which is a very big mistake. If greatness is not appreciated by men, the world will become mean, small, dull, narrow and tamasic.

*

By greatness is meant an exceptional capacity of one kind or another which makes a man eminent among his fellows.

*

That kind of greatness [*scientific, literary, political*] has nothing to do with the psychic. It consists in a special mental capacity (Raman, Tagore) or in a great vital force which enables them to lead men and dominate them. These faculties are often but not always accompanied by something in the personality Daivic or Asuric which supports their action and gives to men an impression of greatness apart even from the special capacity — the sense of a great personality.

*

Most great men know perfectly well that they are great.

*

It is the power in them [*great men*] that is great and that power comes from the Divine — by their actions and greatness they help the world and aid the cosmic purpose. It does not matter whether they have ego or not — they are not doing Yoga.

*

If a man rises to a higher plane of consciousness, it does not necessarily follow that he will be a greater man of action or a greater creator. One may rise to spiritual planes of inspiration undreamed of by Shakespeare and yet not be as great a poetic creator as Shakespeare. "Greatness" is not the object of spiritual realisation any more than fame or success in the world — how are these things the standard of spiritual realisation?

*

Of course you can [*do Yoga without being great*] — there is no need of being great. On the contrary humility is the first necessity, for one who has ego and pride cannot realise the Highest.

*

Each one can be truly great only in the measure in which he feels and opens to the source of all greatness, the Divine.

Greatness and Vices

It is not only the very very very big people who are of importance to the Divine. All energy, strong capacity, power of effectuation are of importance.

As for Napoleon, Caesar and Shakespeare, not one of them was a virtuous man, but they were great men — and that was your contention, that only virtuous men are great men and those who have vices are not great, which is an absurd contention. All of them went after women — two were ambitious, unscrupulous. Napoleon was most arrogant and violent.

Shakespeare stole deer, Napoleon lied freely, Caesar was without scruples.

*

But do you really believe that men like Napoleon, Caesar, Shakespeare were not great men and did nothing for the world or for the cosmic purpose? that God was deterred from using them for His purpose because they had defects of character and vices? What a singular idea!

*

Why should he [*the Divine*] care [*about the vices of great men*]? Is he a policeman? So long as one is in the ordinary nature, one has qualities and defects, virtues and vices. When one goes beyond, there are no virtues and vices, — for these things do not belong to the Divine Nature.

*

Yes, certainly. Many great men even have often very great vices and many of them. Great men are not usually model characters.

*

They [*great men*] have more energy and the energy comes out in what men call vices as well as in what men call virtues.

*

Men with great capacities or a powerful mind or a powerful vital have very often more glaring defects of character than ordinary men — or at least the defects of the latter do not show so much, being like themselves, smaller in scale.

*

Great or dazzling, or small in their field, ambition is ambition and it is necessary for most for an energetic action. What is the use of calling a thing a vice when it is small and glorifying it when it is big?

Section Three

Destiny, Karma, Death and Rebirth

Chapter One
Fate, Free Will and Prediction

Destiny

Each follows in the world his own line of destiny which is determined by his own nature and actions — the meaning and necessity of what happens in a particular life cannot be understood except in the light of the whole course of many lives. But this can be seen by those who can get beyond the ordinary mind and feelings and see things as a whole, that even errors, misfortunes, calamities are steps in the journey, the soul gathering experience as it passes through and beyond them until it is ripe for the transition which will carry it beyond these things to a higher consciousness and higher life. When one comes to that line of crossing one has to leave behind one the old mind and feelings. One looks then on those who are still fixed in the pleasures and sorrows of the ordinary world with sympathy and wherever it is possible with spiritual helpfulness, but no longer with attachment. One learns that they are being led through all their stumblings and trusts to the universal Power that is watching and supporting their existence to do for them whatever for them is the best. But the one thing that is really important for us is to get into the greater Light and the Divine Union — to turn to the Divine alone, to put our trust there alone whether for ourselves or for others.

*

Destiny in the rigid sense applies only to the outer being so long as it lives in the Ignorance. What we call destiny is only in fact the result of the present condition of the being and the nature and energies it has accumulated in the past acting on each other and determining the present attempts and their future results. But as soon as one enters the path of spiritual life, this old predetermined destiny begins to recede. There comes in a new factor, the

Divine Grace, the help of a higher Divine Force other than the force of Karma which can lift the sadhak beyond the present possibilities of his nature. One's spiritual destiny is then the divine election which ensures the future. The only doubt is about the vicissitudes of the path and the time to be taken by the passage. It is here that the hostile forces playing on the weaknesses of the past nature strive to prevent the rapidity of the progress and to postpone the fulfilment. Those who fell, fell not because of the attacks of the vital forces, but because they put themselves on the side of the hostile Force and preferred a vital ambition or desire (ambition, vanity, lust, etc.) to the spiritual siddhi.

*

Each has his own destiny which he brings with him into the world.

*

Each has his own destiny and his entering into a particular family in one life is only an incident.

*

Obviously, neither Nature nor Destiny nor the Divine work in the mental way or by the law of the mind or according to its standards — that is why even to the scientist and the philosopher Nature, Destiny, the way of the Divine, all remain a mystery.

*

Nature is very largely what you make of her — or can make of her.

*

Destiny is not an absolute, it is a relative. One can alter it for the better or the worse.

Free Will and Determinism

It is difficult indeed to make out what Planck means in these pages[1] — what is his conclusion and how he arrives at it; he has probably so condensed his arguments that the necessary explanatory links are missing. The free will affair, I see by glancing through the previous pages, arises only incidentally from his position that the new discoveries grouped round the quantum theory do not make a radical difference in physics. If there is a tendency to regard laws as statistical — in which case there is no "strict causality" and no determinism — still there is nothing to prove that they cannot be treated and may not be advantageously treated as dynamical also — in which case determinism can stand; the uncertainty of individual behaviour (electrons, quanta) does not really undermine determinism, but only brings a new feature into it. That seems from a hasty glance to be his position. Certain scientific thinkers consider this uncertainty of individual behaviour to be a physical factor correspondent to the element of free will in individual human beings. It is here that Planck brings in the question of free will to refute the conclusion that it affects strict causality and the law of determinism. His argument, as far as I can make it out, is this:

(1) The law of strict causality stands because any given action or inner happening of the individual human being is an effect determined completely by two causes, (a) the previous state of his mind taken as a whole, (b) external influences.

(2) The will is a mental process completely determined by these two factors; therefore it is not free, it is part of the chain of strict causality — as are also the results of the free will.

(3) What is important is not the actual freedom of the will, but the man's consciousness of freedom. This creates an inner experience of conscious motive which again creates fresh motives and so on indefinitely. For this reason it is impossible for a man to predict his future action — for at any moment a fresh motive may arise. But when we look back at the past, then the concatenation of cause and effect becomes apparent.

(4) The fact of strict causality (or at least the theory of it)

---

[1] *Max Planck,* The Universe in the Light of Modern Physics *(London: George Allen and Unwin, 1931), pp. 84–87.*

stands therefore unshaken by the consciousness of free will of the individual. It is only obscured by the fact that a man cannot predict his own actions or grasp the causes of his present state; but that is because here the subject and object are the same and this subject-object is in a state of constant alterative motion unlike an object outside, which is supposed not to change as a result of the inner movements of the knower.

There is a reference to causal law and ethical law which baffles me. Is the "ethical law" something outside the strict chain of effects and causes? Is there such a thing at all? If "strict causality" rules all, what is such an ethical law doing there?

That is the argument so far as I can follow it, but it does not seem to me very conclusive. If a man's conduct cannot be predicted by himself, neither can it be predicted by anyone else, though here the subject and object are not the same; if not predictable, then it must be for the same reason, the element of free will and the mobility created by the possible indefinite intrusion of fresh motives. If that is so, strict causality cannot be affirmed, though a plastic causality in which the power of choice called by us free will is an element (either as one among many contributory causes or as an instrument of a cause beyond itself) can still be asserted as possible.

The statement that the action of the individual is strictly determined by his total mental state + external influences is doubtful and does not lead very far. It is possible to undermine the whole idea of inevitable causality by holding that the total existing state before a happening is only the condition under which it happens — there are a mass of antecedents and there is a sequent, if it may be so called, or a mass of sequences, but nothing proves that the latter are inevitable consequences of the mass of antecedents. Possibly this total existing state is a matrix into which some seed of happening is thrown or becomes active, so that there may be many possible results, and in the case of human action it is conceivable that free will is *the* or at least *a* determining factor.

I do not think therefore that these arguments of Planck carry us very far. There is also of course the question raised in the book itself whether, granting determinism, a local state of things is an independent field of causality or all is so bound together that it is the whole that determines the local result. A man's action then would be determined by universal forces and his state of mind and apparent choice would be only part of the instrumentation of Universal Force.

*

In the case of Socrates and that of the habitual drunkard raised by you, the difference you make is correct. The weak-willed man is governed by his vital and physical impulsions, his mental being is not dynamic enough to make its will prevail over them. His will is not "free" because it is not strong enough to be free, it is the slave of the forces that act on or in his vital and physical nature. In the case of Socrates the will is so far free that it stands above the play of these forces and he determines by his mental idea and resolve what he shall or shall not do. The question remains whether the will of Socrates is only free in this sense, itself being actually determined by something larger than the mentality of Socrates, something of which it is the instrument, whether Universal Force or a Being in him of which his daemon was the voice and which not only gave his mind that decisive awareness of the mental ideal but imposed on it the drive to act in obedience to the awareness. Or it may be subject to a nexus between the inner Purusha and the Universal Force. In the latter case there would be an unstable balance between determinism of Nature and a self-determination from within. If we start from the Sankhya view of things, that Being would be the soul or Purusha and both in the strong-willed Socrates and in the weak-willed slave of vital impulse, the action and its results would be determined by the assent or refusal of the Purusha. In the latter the Purusha gives its assent to and undergoes the play of the forces of Nature, the habit of the vital impulse, through a vital submission while the mind looks on helpless. In Socrates the Purusha has begun to emancipate itself and decide what it shall accept or shall not accept — the conscious being has begun to impose itself on the forces that act on it. This mastery has become so complete that he can largely determine his own actions and can even within certain limits not only forecast but fix the results — so that what he wants shall happen sooner or later.

As for the Superman, that is the conscious being whose emancipation is complete by his rising to a station beyond the limits of mind. He can determine his action in complete accord with an awareness which perceives all the forces acting in and on and around him and is able, instead of undergoing, to use them and even to determine.

*

After reading Krishnaprem's exposition [*on free will and determinism*], I saw what might be said from the intellectual point of view on this question so as to link the reality of the supreme Freedom with the phenomenon of the determinism of Nature — in a different way from his but to the same purpose. In reality, the freedom and the determination are only two sides of the same thing — for the fundamental truth is self-determination, a self-determination of the cosmos and in it a secret self-determination of the individual. The difficulty arises from the fact that we live in the surface mind of ignorance, do not know what is going on behind and see only the phenomenal process of Nature. There the apparent fact is an overwhelming determinism of Nature and as our surface consciousness is part of that process we are unable to see the other term of the biune reality. For practical purposes, on the surface there is an entire determinism in Matter — though this is now disputed by the latest school of Science. As Life emerges a certain plasticity sets in, so that it is difficult to predict anything exactly as one predicts material things that obey a rigid law. The plasticity increases with the growth of Mind so that man can have at least a sense of free will, of a choice of his action, of a self-movement which at least helps to determine circumstances. But this freedom is dubious because it can be declared to be an illusion, a device of Nature, part of its machinery of determination, only a seeming freedom or at most a restricted, relative and subject independence. It is only when one goes behind away from Prakriti to Purusha and upward away from Mind to spiritual Self that the side of freedom comes to be first evident and then, by unison with the Will which is above Nature, complete.

*

Well, the determination of human life and events is a mysterious thing. Can't help that, you know. Fate is composed of many things — Cosmic Will + individual self-determination + play of forces + Karma + x + y + z + a + b + c ad infinitum.

Predictions and Prophecy

I am afraid I have no great confidence in Cheiro's ideas and prophecies — some prophecies are fulfilled but most have gone wrong. The idea about the Jews is an old Jewish and Christian belief; not much faith can be put in it. As for the numbers it is true that according to occult science numbers have a mystic meaning. It is also true that there are periods and cycles in life as well as in world-life. But too exact a meaning cannot always be put in these things.

*

Mother says Cheiro has always missed his predictions. They are (at best) half truths which you have to turn this way or that to get something out of them corresponding with the fact.

*

Your extracts taken by themselves are very impressive, but when one reads the book, the impression made diminishes and fades away. You have quoted Cheiro's successes, but what about his failures? I have looked at the book and was rather staggered by the number of prophecies that have failed to come off. You can't deduce from a small number of predictions, however accurate, that all is predestined down to your putting the questions in the letter and my answer. It may be, but the evidence is not sufficient to prove it. What is evident is that there is an element of the predictable, predictable accurately and in detail as well as in large points, in the course of events. But that was already known; it leaves the question still unsolved whether all is so predictable, whether destiny is the sole factor in existence or there are other factors also that can modify destiny, — or, destiny being given, there are not different sources or powers or planes of destiny and we can modify the one with which we started by calling in another destiny source, power or plane and making it active in our life. Metaphysical questions are not so simple that they can be trenchantly solved either in one sense or in another contradictory to it — that is the popular way of settling things, but it is quite summary and inconclusive. All is free will or else all is destiny — it is not so simple as that. This question of free will or determination is the most knotty of all metaphysical questions and nobody has been able to solve it — for a good reason, that both destiny and will exist and even a free will exists somewhere — the difficulty is only how to get at it and make it effective.

Astrology? Many astrological predictions come true, quite a mass of them, if one takes all together. But it does not follow that the stars rule our destiny; the stars merely record a destiny that has been already formed, they are a hieroglyph, not a Force, — or if their action constitutes a force, it is a transmitting energy, not an originating Power. Someone is there who has determined or something is there which is Fate, let us say; the stars are only indicators. The astrologers themselves say that there are two forces, *daiva* and *puruṣārtha*, fate and individual energy, and the individual energy can modify and even frustrate fate. Moreover the stars often indicate several fate-possibilities; for example that one may die in mid-age, but that if that determination can be overcome, one can live to a predictable old age. Finally, cases are seen in which the predictions of the horoscope fulfil themselves with great accuracy up to a certain age, then apply no more. This often happens when the subject turns away from the ordinary to the spiritual life. If the turn is very radical the cessation of predictability may be immediate; otherwise certain results may still last on for a time, but there is no longer the same inevitability. This would seem to show that there is or can be a higher-power or higher-plane or higher-source spiritual destiny which can, if its hour has come, override the lower-power, lower-plane or lower-source vital and material fate of which the stars are indicators. I say vital because character can also be indicated from the horoscope much more completely and satisfactorily than the events of the life.

The Indian explanation of fate is Karma. We ourselves are our own fate through our actions, but the fate created by us binds us; for what we have sown, we must reap in this life or another. Still we are creating new fate for the future even while undergoing old fate from the past in the present. That gives a meaning to our will and action and does not, as European critics wrongly believe, constitute a rigid and sterilising fatalism. But again our will and action can often annul or modify even the past Karma, it is only certain strong effects, called *utkaṭa karma*, that are non-modifiable. Here too the achievement of the spiritual consciousness and life is supposed to annul or give the power to annul Karma. For we enter into union with the Will Divine, cosmic or transcendent, which can annul what it had sanctioned for certain conditions, new-create what it had created; the narrow fixed lines disappear, there is a more plastic freedom and wideness. Neither Karma nor Astrology therefore points to a rigid and for ever immutable fate.

As for prophecy, I have never met or known of a prophet, however reputed, who was infallible. Some of their predictions come true to the letter, others do not, — they half-fulfil or misfire entirely. It does not follow that the power of prophecy is unreal or the accurate predictions can be all explained by probability, chance or coincidence. The nature and number of those that cannot is too great. The variability of fulfilment may be explained either by an imperfect power in the prophet sometimes active, sometimes failing or by the fact that things are predictable in part only, they are determined in part only or else by different factors or lines of power, different series of potentials and actuals. So long as one is in touch with one line, one predicts accurately, otherwise not — or if the line of power changes, one's prophecy also goes off the rails. All the same, one may say, there must be, if things are predictable at all, some power or plane through which or on which all is foreseeable; if there is a divine Omniscience and Omnipotence it must be so. Even then what is foreseen has to be worked out, actually is worked out by a play of forces, — spiritual, mental, vital, physical forces — and in that plane of forces there is no absolute rigidity discoverable. Personal will or endeavour is one of those forces — Napoleon when asked why he believed in Fate, yet was always planning and acting, answered, "Because it is fated that I should work and plan" — in other words, his planning and acting were part of Fate, contributed to the results Fate had in view. Even if I foresee an adverse result, I must work for the one that I consider should be; for it keeps alive the force, the principle of Truth which I serve and gives it a possibility to triumph hereafter, so that it becomes part of the working of a future favourable Fate, even if the fate of the hour is adverse. Men do not abandon a cause because they have seen it fail or foresee its failure; and they are spiritually right in their stubborn perseverance. Moreover, we do not live for material result alone, — far more the object of life is the growth of the soul, not outward success of the hour or even of the near future. The soul can grow against or even by a material destiny that is adverse.

Finally, even if all is determined, why say that Life is, in Shakespeare's phrase or rather Macbeth's, "a tale told by an idiot, full of sound and fury, signifying nothing"? Life would rather be that if it were all chance and random incertitude. But if it is something foreseen, planned in every detail, does it not rather mean that life does signify something, that there must be a secret Purpose that is being worked up to, powerfully, persistently through the ages, and ourselves are a part of it and fellow-workers in the fulfilment of that invincible Purpose?

*

Well, one of the greatest ecstasies possible is to feel oneself carried by the Divine, — not by the stars or Karma, for the latter is a bad business, dry and uncomfortable — like being turned on a machine, "*yantrārūḍhāni māyayā*".

Astrology and Yoga

Astrology is an occult science — it is not a part of the Yoga except as anything can be made part of the Yoga — if done in the right spirit.

*

That is not the question.[2] The question is what influence has the sadhak on the stars at his birth?

---

[2] *The correspondent asked, "Can astrological truths have any influence on a sadhak?"* — Ed.

Chapter Two
Karma and Heredity

Karma

Karma is not luck, it is the transmission of past energies into the present with their results.

*

All energies put into activity — thought, speech, feeling, act — go to constitute Karma. These things help to develop the nature in one direction or another, and the nature and its actions and reactions produce their consequences inward and outward: they also act on others and create movements in the general sum of forces which can return upon oneself sooner or later. Thoughts unexpressed can also go out as forces and produce their effects. It is a mistake to think that a thought or will can have effect only when it is expressed in speech or act: the unspoken thought, the unexpressed will are also active energies and can produce their own vibrations, effects or reactions.

*

If it [*the soul*] goes on with its Karma, then it does not get liberation. If it wants only farther experience, it can just stay there in the ordinary nature. The aim of Yoga is to transcend Karma. Karma means subjection to lower Nature; through Yoga the soul goes towards freedom.

*

The bondage to the effects of Karma remains so long as one has not passed out of the ordinary human consciousness which is its field to the higher spiritual consciousness where all bonds are untied. As for peace one can gain it by an entire reliance on the Divine and surrender to the Divine Will.

*

In life all sorts of things offer themselves. One cannot take anything that comes with the idea that it is sent by the Divine. There is a choice and a wrong choice produces its consequence.

Karma and Heredity

Karma and heredity are the two main causes [*of one's temperament*]. According to some heredity is also subject to Karma, but that may be only in a general way, not in all the details.

*

Many things in the body and some in the mind and vital are inherited from the father and mother or other ancestors — that everybody is supposed to know. There are other things that are not inherited, but peculiar to one's own nature or developed by the happenings of this life.

*

You must realise that all human beings are made partly of what is given them by their ancestors (not only father and mother but all the ancestors), partly of what they bring with them. The part they get from the ancestors is called hereditary — it is part (not the whole) of the physical and lower vital consciousness, sometimes a little of the external mind also — it is a small portion of the external being, but although small, it is sometimes very persistent and active. The rest of the being, inner and a great part too of the external, is brought from past lives. This hereditary part has to be got rid of and replaced by the true individuality spreading itself to the whole external nature.

*

A very big stamp in most cases[1] — it is in the physical vital and physical material that the stamp chiefly exists — and it is increased by education and upbringing.

*

---

[1] *The correspondent asked whether the influence of heredity, race, caste and family leaves a stamp on one's lower nature.* — Ed.

There is always a hereditary part of the nature which is a large portion of the outward nature — there is also the educational influence of the father which has put a stamp on you.

*

Hereditary influence[2] creates an affinity and affinity is a living thing. It is only when the hereditary part is changed that the affinity ceases.

*

It is your own being that seeks for the Divine. The hereditary part is not your true being, but something you have taken up as part of this birth. It can be got rid of or changed.

Evolution, Karma and Ethics

The question as put in your letter seems to me to be too rigidly phrased and not to take into sufficient account the plasticity of the facts and forces of existence. It sounds like the problem which one might raise on the strength of the most recent scientific theories — if all is made up of protons and electrons, all exactly similar to each other (except for the group numbers, and why should a difference of quantity make such an extraordinary difference or any difference of quality?) how does their action result in such stupendous differences of degree, kind, power, everything? But why should we assume that the psychic seeds or sparks all started in a race at the same time, equal in conditions, equal in power and nature? Granted that the One Divine is the source of all and the Self is the same in all; but in manifestation why should not the Infinite throw itself out in infinite variety, why must it be in an innumerable sameness? How many of these psychic seeds started long before others and have a great past of development behind them and how many are young and raw and half-grown only? And even among those who started together,

---

[2] *The correspondent asked whether the hereditary influence created by his father had come to an end in him.* — Ed.

why should not there be some who ran at a great speed and others who loitered and grew with difficulty or went about in circles? And then there is an evolution, and it is only at a certain stage in the evolution that the animal belt is past and there is a human beginning; what constitutes the human beginning, which represents a very considerable revolution or turnover? Up to the animal line it is the vital and physical that have been developing — for the human to begin is it not necessary that there should be the descent of a mental being to take up the vital and physical evolution? And may it not well be that the mental beings who descend are not all of the same power and stature and, besides, do not take up equally developed vital and physical consciousness-material? There is also the occult tradition of a hierarchy of beings who stand above the present manifestation and put themselves into it with results which will obviously be just such a stupendous difference of degrees, and even intervene by descending into the play through the gates of birth in human Nature. There are many complexities and the problem cannot be put with the rigidity of a mathematical formula.

A great part of the difficulty of these problems, I mean especially the appearance of inexplicable contradiction, arises from the problem itself being badly put. Take the popular account of reincarnation and Karma — it is based on the mere mental assumption that the workings of Nature ought to be moral and proceed according to an exact morality of equal justice — a scrupulous, even mathematical law of reward and punishment or, at any rate, of results according to a human idea of right correspondences. But Nature is non-moral — she uses forces and processes moral, immoral and amoral pell-mell for working out her business. Nature in her outward aspect seems to care for nothing except to get things done — or else to make conditions for an ingenious variety of the play of life. Nature in her deeper aspect as a conscious spiritual Power is concerned with the growth, by experience, the spiritual development of the souls she has in her charge — and these souls themselves have a say in the matter. All these good people lament and wonder that unaccountably they and other good people are visited with such meaningless sufferings and misfortunes. But are they really visited with them by an outside Power or by a mechanical Law of Karma? Is it not possible that the soul itself — not the outward mind, but the spirit within — has accepted and chosen these things as part of its development in order to get through the necessary experience at a rapid rate, to hew through, *durchhauen*, even at the risk or the cost of much damage to the outward life and the body? To the growing soul, to the spirit within us, may not difficulties, obstacles, attacks be a means of growth, added strength, enlarged experience, training for spiritual victory? The arrangement of things may be that and not a mere question of the pounds, shillings and pence of a distribution of rewards and retributory misfortunes!

It is the same with the problem of the taking of animal life under the circumstances put forward by your friend in the letter. It is put on the basis of an invariable ethical right and wrong to be applied to all cases — is it right to take animal life at all, under any circumstances, is it right to allow an animal to suffer under your eyes when you can relieve it by an euthanasia? There can be no indubitable answer to a question put like that, because the answer depends on data which the mind has not before it. In fact there are many other factors which make people incline to this short and merciful way out of the difficulty — the nervous inability to bear the sight and hearing of so much suffering, the unavailing trouble, the disgust and inconvenience — all tend to give force to the idea that the animal itself would want to be out of it. But what does the animal really feel about it — may it not be clinging to life in spite of the pain? Or may not the soul have accepted these things for a quicker evolution into a higher state of life? If so, the mercy dealt out may conceivably interfere with the animal's Karma. In fact the right decision might vary in each case and depend on a knowledge which the human mind has not — and it might very well be said that until it has it, it has not the right to take life. It was some dim perception of this truth that made religion and ethics develop the law of Ahimsa — and yet that too becomes a mental rule which it is found impossible to apply in practice. And perhaps the moral of it all is that we must act for the best according to our lights in each case, as things are, but that the solution of these problems can only come by pressing forward towards a greater light, a greater consciousness in which the problems themselves, as now stated by the human mind, will not arise because we shall have a vision which will see the world in a different way and a guidance which at present is not ours. The mental or moral rule is a stop-gap which men are obliged to use, very uncertainly and stumblingly, until they can see things whole in the light of the spirit.

Chapter Three
Death

Death and Karma

It [*death*] is a universal force — the happening or change called death is simply one result of the working of the force.

*

Most people die before the vitality of the body is exhausted. It is due to many causes of which one is the destiny prepared by past lives; another the inner purpose or utility of the present life being completed — but these are subtle and secret reasons — others, accident, violence or other causes, are only an exterior machinery.

*

X had reached a stage of her development marked by a predominance of the sattwic nature, but not a strong vital (which works towards a successful or fortunate life) or the opening to a higher light, — her mental upbringing and surroundings stood against that and she herself was not ready. Her early death with much suffering may have been the result of past (prenatal) influences or they may have been chosen by her own psychic being as a passage towards a higher state for which she was not yet prepared but towards which she was moving. This and the non-fulfilment of her capacities would be a final tragedy if there were this life alone. As it is she has passed towards the psychic sleep to prepare for her life to come.

*

You can explain[1] to X that the death of his nephew had nothing

---

[1] *Written by Sri Aurobindo to his secretary, who replied to the enquirer.* — Ed.

to do with their [*his family members'*] obscurities and imperfections — it was part of his own Karma — each person has his own destiny and follows its line; to be in a certain family and with certain relations is only a temporary incident in its course. The sadhak should be free from these attachments and regard these happenings as ordeals to be passed through with equality and faith in the Divine — doing his best for those who are in his charge but not disturbed by results.

*

It is a very intricate and difficult question to tackle[2] and it can hardly be answered in a few words. Moreover it is impossible to give a general rule as to why there are these close inner contacts followed by a physical separation through death — in each case there is a difference and one would have to know the persons and be familiar with their soul history to tell what was behind their meeting and separation. In a general way, a life is only one brief episode in a long history of spiritual evolution in which the soul follows the curve of the line set for the earth, passing through many lives to complete it. It is an evolution out of material inconscience to consciousness and on towards the divine Consciousness, from ignorance to divine Knowledge, from darkness through half-lights to Light, from death to Immortality, from suffering to the Divine Bliss. Suffering is due first to the Ignorance, secondly to the separation of the individual consciousness from the Divine Consciousness and Being, a separation created by the Ignorance — when that ceases, when one lives completely in the Divine and no more in one's separated smaller self, then only suffering can altogether cease. Each soul follows its own line and these lines meet, journey together for a space, then part to meet again perhaps hereafter — often they meet to help each other on the journey in one way or another. As for the after-death period, the soul passes into other planes of existence, staying there for a while till it reaches its place of rest where it

---

[2] *A mother whose sixteen-year-old son had died wrote to ask why his death had taken place. Her letter was referred to Sri Aurobindo. — Ed.*

remains until it is ready for another terrestrial existence. This is the general law, but for the connections of embodied soul with embodied soul, that is a matter of personal evolution on which nothing general can be said as it is intimate to the soul stories of the two and needs a personal knowledge. That is all I can say, but I don't know that it will be of much help to her, as these things are helpful usually only when one enters into the consciousness in which they become not mere ideas but realities. Then one grieves no longer because one has entered into the Truth and the Truth brings calm and peace.

Death and Grieving

I can understand the shock your wife's catastrophic death must have been to you. But you are now a seeker and sadhak of the Truth and must set your mind above the normal reactions of the human being and see things in a larger greater light. Regard your lost wife as a soul that was progressing through the vicissitudes of the life of Ignorance — like all others here — in that progress things happen that seem unfortunate to the human mind and a sudden accidental or violent death cutting short prematurely this always brief spell of terrestrial experience we call life seems to it especially painful and unfortunate. But one who gets behind the outward view knows that all that happens in the progress of the soul has its meaning, its necessity, its place in the series of experiences which are leading it towards the turning point where one can pass from the Ignorance to the Light. He knows that whatever happens in the Divine Providence is for the best even though it may seem to the mind otherwise. Look on your wife as a soul that has passed the barrier between two states of existence. Help her journey towards her place of rest by calm thoughts and the call to the Divine Help to aid her upon it. Grief too long continued does not help but delays the journey of the departed soul. Do not brood on your loss, but think only of her spiritual welfare.

*

The telegram announces the passing away of your husband. All has been done that could be done to keep him in life. What has happened must now be accepted calmly as the thing decreed and best for his soul's progress from life to life though not the best in human eyes which look only at the present and at outside appearance. For the spiritual seeker death is only a passage from one form of life to another, and none is dead but only departed. Look at it as that and shaking from you all reactions of vital grief — they cannot help him in his journey, — pursue steadfastly the path to the Divine.

*

There is nothing to grieve about as death means only passing over to another country — to which you probably go very often when you are asleep.

That is, so long as one has attachment — one ought to look at it like that. But all attachment to past ties should be overcome.

*

Of course, that is the real fact — death is only a shedding of the body, not a cessation of the personal existence. A man is not dead because he goes into another country and changes his clothes to suit that climate.

The After-Death Sojourn

There is after death a period in which one passes through the vital world and lives there for a time. It is only the first part of this transit that can be dangerous or painful; in the rest one works out, under certain surroundings, a remnant of the vital desires and instincts which one had in the body. As soon as one is tired of these and able to go beyond, the vital sheath is dropped and the soul, after a little time needed to get rid of some mental survivals, passes into a state of rest in the psychic world and remains there till the next life on earth.

One can help the departed soul by one's good will or by occult means if one has the knowledge. The one thing that one should not do is to hold them back by sorrow for them or longings or anything else that would pull them nearer to earth or delay their journey to their place of rest.

*

It may happen to some not to realise for a little time that they are dead, especially if the death has been unforeseen and sudden, but it cannot be said that it happens to all or to most — some may enter into a state of semi-unconsciousness or obsession by a dark inner condition, created by their state of mind at death, in which they realise nothing of where they are etc., others are quite conscious of the passage. It is true that the departing being in the vital body lingers for some time near the body or the scene of life very often for as many as eight days and in the ancient religions mantras and other means were used for the severance. Even after the severance from the body a very earthbound nature or one full of strong physical desires may linger long in the earth-atmosphere up to a maximum period extended to three years. Afterwards it passes to the vital worlds, proceeding on its journey which must sooner or later bring it to the psychic rest till the next life. It is true also that sorrow and mourning for the dead impedes its progress by keeping it tied to the earth-atmosphere and pulling it back from its passage.

*

After death the soul passes in a little while or at once from the earth atmosphere and goes into the vital worlds where it remains for a time until it is ready to leave it. Thus it passes on its way till it is ready to pass into the psychic world where it rests until it is ready for a new birth.

*

After death one passes through various vital and mental planes till the psychic being drops its vital and mental sheaths and enters into rest on the psychic plane till the time comes for rebirth.

*

At the time of death the being goes out of the body through the head; it goes out in the subtle body and goes to different planes of existence for a short time until it has gone through certain experiences which are the result of its earthly existence. Afterwards it reaches the psychic world where it rests in a kind of sleep until it is time for it to start a new life on earth. That is what happens usually — but there are some beings who are more developed and do not follow this course.

*

That is a superstition [*that people have to live in* naraka (*hell*) *due to their bad actions*]. People after death pass through certain vital and mental worlds or through certain psychological states which are the results of their nature and action in life, afterwards they go to the psychic world and return to birth at a later time.

*

When the Mother spoke of the continuance of the same trouble after death, she did not mean another life. At death you go out of this physical frame in another kind of body, not physical, and are the same person with the same consciousness. That is why to talk of dying as going to rest is an ignorance and why it is useless. The only real thing is to get rid of the old lower self and be reborn to the new higher one, which can only be done by a change within you. That is what the Mother wants of you.

Chapter Four

Rebirth

The Psychic's Choice at the Time of Death

The psychic being at the time of death chooses what it will work out in the next birth and determines the character and conditions of the new personality. Life is for the evolutionary growth by experience in the conditions of the Ignorance till one is ready for the higher light.

*

The dying wish of the man is only something on the surface — it may be determined by the psychic and so help to shape the future but it does not determine the psychic's choice. That is something behind the veil. It is not the outer consciousness's action that determines the inner process, but the other way round. Sometimes, however, there are signs or fragments of the inner action that come up on the surface, e.g. some people have a vision or remembrance of the circumstances of their past in a panoramic flash at the time of death, that is the psychic's review of the life before departing.

*

The psychic being's choice at the time of death doesn't work out the next formation of personality, it fixes it. When it enters the psychic world, it begins to assimilate the essence of its experience and by that assimilation is formed the future psychic personality in accordance with the fixation already made. When this assimilation is over, it is ready for a new birth — but the less developed beings do not work out the whole thing for themselves, there are beings and forces of the higher world who have that work. Also when it comes to birth, it is not sure that the forces of the physical world will not come across the working out of what it wanted — its own new instrumentation may not be strong enough for that purpose; for there is the interaction of its own energies and the cosmic forces here. There may be frustration, diversion, a partial working out — many things may happen. All that is not a rigid machinery, it is a working out of complex forces. It may be added however that a developed psychic being is much more conscious in this transition and works much of it out itself. The time depends also on the development and on a certain rhythm of the being — for some there is practically immediate rebirth, for others it takes longer, for some it may take centuries; but here again, once the psychic being is sufficiently developed, it is free to choose its own rhythm and its own intervals. The ordinary theories are too mechanical — and that is the case also with the idea of *puṇya* and *pāpa* and their results in the next life. There are certainly results of the energies put forth in a past life, but not on that rather infantile principle. A good man's sufferings in this life would be a proof according to the orthodox theory that he had been a very great villain in his past life, a bad man's prospering would be a proof that he had been quite angelic in his last visit to earth and sown a large crop of virtues and meritorious actions to reap this bumper crop of good fortune. Too symmetrical to be true. The object of birth being growth by experience, whatever reactions come to past deeds must be for the being to learn and grow, not as lollipops for the good boys of the class (in the past) and canings for the bad ones. The real sanction for good and ill is not good fortune for the one and bad fortune for the other, but this that good leads us towards a higher nature which is eventually lifted above suffering and ill pulls us towards the lower nature which remains always in the circle of suffering and evil.

Assimilation in the Psychic World

The soul after it leaves the body travels through several states or planes until the psychic being has shed its temporary sheaths, then it reaches the psychic world where it rests in a kind of sleep till it is ready for reincarnation. What it keeps with it of the human experience in the end is only the essence of all that it has gone through, what it can use for its development. This is the general rule, but it does not apply to exceptional cases or to very developed beings who have achieved a greater consciousness than the ordinary human level.

It is not the soul (the psychic being) that takes a lesser form [*in its next birth*], it is some part of the manifested being, usually some part of the vital that does it, owing to some desire, affinity, need of particular experience. This happens fairly often to the ordinary man.

*

After leaving the body, the soul, after certain experiences in other worlds, throws off its mental and vital personality and goes into rest to assimilate the essence of its past and prepare for a new life. It is this preparation that determines the circumstances of the new birth and guides it in its reconstitution of a new personality and the choice of its materials.

The departed soul retains the memory of its past experiences only in their essence, not in their form or detail. It is only if the soul brings back some past personality or personalities as part of its present manifestation that it is likely to remember the details of the past life. Otherwise, it is only by Yogadrishti that the memory comes.

There may be what seem to be retrograde movements [*in the evolution of the soul*], but these are only like zigzag movements, not a real falling back, but a return on something not worked out so as to go on better afterwards.

The soul does not go back to the animal condition; but part of the vital personality may disjoin itself and join an animal birth to work out its animal propensities there.

There is no truth in the popular belief about the avaricious man becoming a serpent. These are popular romantic superstitions.

*

The soul takes birth each time, and each time a mind, life and body are formed out of the materials of universal Nature, according to the soul's past evolution and its need for the future.

When the body is dissolved, the vital goes into the vital plane and remains there for a time, but after a time the vital sheath disappears. The last to dissolve is the mental sheath. Finally the soul or psychic being retires into the psychic world to rest there till a new birth is due.

This is the general course for ordinarily developed human beings. There are variations according to the nature of the individual and his development. For example, if the mental is strongly developed, then the mental being can remain; so also can the vital, provided they are organised by and centred around the true psychic being; they share the immortality of the psychic.

The soul gathers the essential element of its experiences in life and makes that its basis of growth in the evolution; when it returns to birth it takes up with its mental, vital, physical sheaths so much of its Karma as is useful to it in the new life for farther experience.

It is really for the vital part of the being that *śrāddha* and rites are done — to help the being to get rid of the vital vibrations which still attach it to the earth or to the vital worlds, so that it may pass quickly to its rest in the psychic peace.

*

The movement of the psychic being dropping its outer, its vital and mental sheaths on its way to the psychic plane, is its normal movement after death. But there can be any number of variations; one can return directly from the vital plane without passing on to farther and higher states, and there are cases of an almost immediate rebirth, sometimes even attended with a detailed memory of the events of the past life.

Hell and heaven are often imaginary states of the soul, or rather of the vital being, which it constructs about it after its passing. What is meant by hell is a painful passage through some vital world or a dolorous lingering there, as for instance in many cases of suicide where one remains surrounded by the forces of suffering and turmoil created by this unnatural and violent exit. There are also, of course, real worlds of mind and vital worlds which are penetrated with joyful or dark experiences, and one may pass through these as the result of things formed in the nature which create the necessary affinities. But the idea of reward or retribution is a crude and vulgar conception and we can disregard it as a mere popular error.

There is no rule of complete forgetfulness in the return of the soul to rebirth. There are, especially in childhood, many impressions of the past life which can be strong and vivid enough, but a materialising education and the overpowering influences of the environment must often, but not quite always, prevent their true nature from being recognised. There are even a number of people who have definite recollections of a past life. But these things are discouraged by education and the atmosphere and cannot remain or develop; in most cases they are stifled out of existence. At the same time it must be noted that what the psychic being mainly carries away with it and brings back is ordinarily the essence and effect of the experiences it had in former lives, and not the details, so that you cannot expect the same coherent memory as one has of past happenings in the present existence.

A soul can go straight to the psychic world but that depends on the state of consciousness at the time of departure. If the psychic is in front at the time, this immediate transition is possible. It does not depend on the acquisition of a mental and vital as well as a psychic immortality — those who have acquired that would rather have the power to move about in the different planes and even act on the physical world without being bound to it. On the whole it may be said that there is no one rigid rule for these things; manifold variations are possible depending upon the consciousness, its energies, tendencies and formations, although there is a general framework and design into which all fit and take their place.

The Psychic Being and the Progression from Life to Life

It is necessary to understand clearly the difference between the evolving soul (psychic being) and the pure Atman, self or spirit. The pure self is unborn, does not pass through death or birth, is independent of birth or body, mind or life or this manifested Nature. It is not bound by these things, not limited, not affected, even though it assumes and supports them. The soul, on the contrary, is something that comes down into birth and passes through death — although it does not itself die, for it is immortal — from one state to another, from the earth-plane to other planes and back again to the earth-existence. It goes on with this progression from life to life through an evolution which leads it up to the human state and evolves through it all a being of itself which we call the psychic being. This being supports the evolution and develops a physical, a vital, a mental human consciousness as its instruments of world-experience and of a disguised, imperfect, but growing self-expression. All this it does from behind a veil, showing something of its divine self only in so far as the imperfection of the instrumental being will allow it. But a time comes when it is able to prepare to come out from behind the veil, to take command and turn all the instrumental nature towards a divine fulfilment. This is the beginning of the true spiritual life. The soul is able now to make itself ready for a higher evolution of manifested consciousness than the mental human — it can pass from the mental to the spiritual and through degrees of the spiritual to the supramental state. Till then, till it has reached the spiritual realisation, there is no reason why it should cease from birth, it cannot in fact so cease. If having reached the spiritual state, it wills to pass out of the terrestrial manifestation, it may indeed make such an exit, — but there is also possible a higher manifestation, in the Knowledge and not in the Ignorance.

Your question therefore does not arise. It is not the naked spirit, but the psychic being that goes to the psychic plane to rest till it is called again to another life. There is therefore no need of a Force to compel it to take birth anew. It is in its nature something that is put forth from the Divine to support the evolution and it must do so till the Divine's purpose in its evolution is accomplished. Karma is only a machinery, it is not the fundamental cause of terrestrial existence — it cannot be, for when the soul first entered this existence, it had no Karma.

What again do you mean by "the all-veiling Maya" or by "losing all consciousness"? The soul cannot lose all consciousness, for its very nature is consciousness though not of the mental kind to which we give the name. The consciousness is merely covered, not lost or abolished by the so-called Inconscience of material Nature and then by the half-conscious ignorance of mind, life and body. It manifests, as the individual mind and life and body grow, as much as may be of the consciousness which it holds in potentiality, manifests it in the outward instrumental nature as far as and in the way that is possible through these instruments and through the outer personality that has been prepared for it and by it — for both are true — for the present life.

I know nothing about any terrible suffering endured by the soul in the process of rebirth; popular beliefs even when they have some foundation are seldom enlightened and accurate.

*

1. The psychic being stands behind mind, life and body, supporting them; so also the psychic world is not one world in the scale like the mental, vital or physical worlds, but stands behind all these and it is there that the souls evolving here retire for the time between life and life. If the psychic were only one principle in the rising order of body, life and mind on a par with the others and placed somewhere in the scale on the same footing as the others, it could not be the soul of all the rest, the divine element making the evolution of the others possible and using them as instruments for a growth through cosmic experience towards the Divine. So also the psychic world cannot be one among the other worlds to which the evolutionary being goes for supraphysical experience, it is a plane where it retires into itself for rest, for a spiritual assimilation of what it has experienced and for a replunging into its own fundamental consciousness and psychic nature.

2. For the few who go out of the Ignorance and enter into Nirvana, there is no question of their going straight up into higher worlds of manifestation. Nirvana or Moksha is a liberated condition of the being, not a world — it is a withdrawal

from the worlds and the manifestation. The analogy of Pitriyana and Devayana can hardly be mentioned in this connection.

3. The condition of the souls that retire into the psychic world is entirely static; each withdraws into himself and is not interacting with the others. When they come out of their trance, they are ready to go down into a new life, but meanwhile they do not act upon the earth life. There are other beings, guardians of the psychic world, but they are concerned only with the psychic world itself and the return of the souls to reincarnation, not with the earth.

4. A being of the psychic world cannot get fused into the soul of a human being on earth. What happens sometimes is that a very advanced psychic being sometimes sends down an emanation which resides in a human being and prepares it until it is ready for the psychic being itself to enter into the life. This happens when some special work has to be done and the human vehicle prepared. Such a descent produces a remarkable change of a sudden character in the personality and the nature.

5. Usually, a soul follows continuously the same line of sex. If there are shiftings of sex, it is as a rule a matter of parts of the personality which are not central.

6. As regards the stage at which the soul returning for rebirth enters the new body no rule can be laid down, for the circumstances vary with the individual. Some psychic beings get into relation with the birth-environment and the parents from the time of inception and determine the preparation of the personality and future in the embryo, others join only at the time of delivery, others even later on in the life and in these cases it is some emanation of the psychic being which upholds the life. It should be noted that the conditions of the future birth are determined fundamentally not during the stay in the psychic world but at the time of death — the psychic being then chooses what it should work out in the next terrestrial appearance and the conditions arrange themselves accordingly.

Note that the idea of rebirth and the circumstances of the new life as a reward or punishment for *puṇya* or *pāpa* is a crude human idea of "justice" which is quite unphilosophical and unspiritual and distorts the true intention of life. Life here is an evolution and the soul grows by experience, working out by it this or that in the nature, and if there is suffering, it is for the purpose of that working out, not as a judgment inflicted by God or Cosmic Law on the errors or stumblings which are inevitable in the Ignorance.

*

It is difficult to give a positive answer to these questions, because no general rule can be laid down applicable to all. The mind makes rigid rules or one rigid rule, but the Manifestation is in reality very plastic and various and many-sided. My answers therefore must not be taken as exhaustive of the subject or complete.

1. He [*a Jivanmukta*] can go wherever his aim was fixed, into a state of Nirvana or one of the divine worlds and stay there or remain, wherever he may go, in contact with the earth-movement and return to it if his will is to help that movement.

This is doubtful [*whether a Jivanmukta can go direct from the world of the soul's present highest achievement to a still higher world*]. If originally he is not a being of the evolution but of some higher world, he could go back to that world. If he wants to go higher, it is logical that he should return to the field of evolution so long as he has not evolved the consciousness proper to that higher plane. The orthodox idea that even the gods have to come to earth if they want salvation may be applied to this ascension also. If he is originally an evolutionary being (Ramakrishna's distinction of the Jivakoti and Ishwarakoti may be extended to this also), he must proceed by the evolutionary path to either the negative withdrawal through Nirvana or some positive divine fulfilment in the increasing manifestation of Sachchidananda.

As to the impossibility of return [*to the earth*], that is a knotty question. A divine being can always return — as Ramakrishna said, the Ishwarakoti can at will ascend or descend the stair between Birth and Immortality. For the others, it is probable that they may rest for a relative infinity of time, *śāśvatīḥ samāḥ*, if that is the will in them, but a return cannot be barred out unless they have reached their highest possible status.

No [*a Jivanmukta does not take rest in the psychic world before taking birth again on earth*]. That is part of the evolutionary line only, not obligatory for divine returns.

2. An advanced psychic being may mean here [*in the preceding letter*] one who has arrived at the soul's freedom and is immersed in the Divine — immersed does not mean abolished. Such a being does not sleep in the psychic world, but may remain in his state of blissful immersion or come back for some purpose.

The word "descend" has various meanings according to the context — I used it here in the sense of the psychic being "coming down" into the human consciousness and body ready for it; that descent might be at the time of birth or before or it may come down later and occupy the personality it has prepared for itself. I do not quite understand what are these personalities from above[1] — it is the psychic being itself that takes up a body.

3. No, the psychic being cannot take up more than one body. There is only one psychic being for each human being, but the Beings of the higher planes, e.g. the Gods of the Overmind can manifest in more than one human body at a time by sending different emanations into different bodies. These would be called Vibhutis of these Devatas.

4. These [*guardians of the psychic world*] are not human souls nor is this an office to which they are appointed nor are they functionaries — these are beings of the psychic plane pursuing their own natural activity in that plane. My word "guardians" [*in the preceding letter*] was simply a phrase meant to indicate by an image or metaphor the nature of their action.

The New Birth

When there is a new birth one brings all that is necessary from

---

[1] *The correspondent asked whether the "personalities" of an advanced being "move about in the higher planes". — Ed.*

past lives but also one gathers what is necessary from the earth consciousness and so too brings in new elements as one develops.

*

It is a little difficult to explain. When one gets a new body, the nature which inhabits it, nature of mind, nature of vital, nature of physical, is made up of many personalities, not one simple personality as is supposed — although there is one central being. This complex personality is formed partly by bringing together personalities of past lives, but also by gathering experiences, tendencies, influences from the earth atmosphere — which are taken up by one of the constituent personalities as suitable to his own nature. Such an influence left behind by Vivekananda or one of his disciples may have been taken up by you without your being an incarnation of either.

*

The being as it passes through the series of its lives takes on personalities of various kinds and passes through various types of experiences, but it does not carry these on to the next life, as a rule. It takes on a new mind, vital and body. The mental capacities, occupations, interests, idiosyncrasies of the past mind and vital are not taken over by the new mind and vital, except to the extent that is useful for the new life. One may have the power of poetic expression in one life, but in the next have no such power nor any interest in poetry. On the other hand tendencies suppressed or missed or imperfectly developed in one life may come out in the next. There would be therefore nothing surprising in the contrast which you noted. The essence of past experiences is kept by the psychic being but the forms of experience or of personality are not, except such as are needed for the new stage in the soul's progress.

The being in its long course of experience may permit for a time the search after sensual pleasure and afterwards discard it and turn to higher things. This can happen even in the course of a lifetime, *a fortiori* in a second life where the old personalities would not be carried over.

Reincarnation and Soul Evolution

You must avoid a common popular blunder about reincarnation. The popular idea is that Titus Balbus is reborn again as John Smith, a man with the same personality, character, attainments as he had in his former life with the sole difference that he wears coat and trousers instead of a toga and speaks in cockney English instead of popular Latin. That is not the case. What would be the earthly use of repeating the same personality or character a million times from the beginning of time till its end! The soul comes into birth for experience, for growth, for evolution till it can bring the Divine into matter. It is the central being that incarnates, not the outer personality — the personality is simply a mould that it creates for its figures of experience in that one life. In another birth it will create for itself a different personality, different capacities, a different life and career. Supposing Virgil is born again, he may take up poetry in one or two other lives, but he will certainly not write an epic but rather perhaps slight but elegant and beautiful lyrics such as he wanted to write, but did not succeed, in Rome. In another birth he is likely to be no poet at all, but a philosopher and a Yogin seeking to attain and to express the highest truth — for that too was an unrealised trend of his consciousness in that life. Perhaps before he had been a warrior or ruler doing deeds like Aeneas or Augustus before he sang them. And so on — on this side or that the central being develops a new character, a new personality, grows, develops, passes through all kinds of terrestrial experience.

As the evolving being develops still more and becomes more rich and complex, it accumulates its personalities, as it were. Sometimes they stand behind the active elements, throwing in some colour, some trait, some capacity here and there, — or they stand in front and there is a multiple personality, a many-sided character or a many-sided, sometimes what looks like a universal capacity. But if a former personality, a former capacity is brought fully forward, it will not be to repeat what was already done, but to cast the same capacity into new forms and new shapes and fuse it into a new harmony of the being which will not be a reproduction of what it was before. Thus you must not expect to be what the warrior and the poet were — something of the outer characteristics may reappear but very much changed and new-cast in a new combination. It is in a new direction that the energies will be guided to do what was not done before.

Another thing. It is not the personality, the character that is of the first importance in rebirth — it is the psychic being who stands behind the evolution of the nature and evolves with it. The psychic when it departs from the body, shedding even the mental and vital on its way to its resting place, carries with it the heart of its experiences, — not the physical events, not the vital movements, not the mental buildings, not the capacities or characters, but something essential that it gathered from them, what might be called the divine element for the sake of which the rest existed. That is the permanent addition, it is that that helps in the growth towards the Divine. That is why there is usually no memory of the outward events and circumstances of past lives — for this memory there must be a strong development towards unbroken continuance of the mind, the vital, even the subtle physical; for though it all remains in a kind of seed memory, it does not ordinarily emerge. What was the divine element in the magnanimity of the warrior, that which expressed itself in his loyalty, nobility, high courage, what was the divine element behind the harmonious mentality and generous vitality of the poet and expressed itself in them, that remains and in a new harmony of character may find a new expression or, if the life is turned towards the Divine, be taken up as powers for the realisation or for the work that has to be done for the Divine.

What Survives and What Does Not

Nothing in the nature is carried over [*in the next incarnation*] except the essence of the past experiences and energies as much as is necessary for the new life. The rest is held in reserve, but things so held in reserve can be brought forward in a new form and under new conditions.

*

If all is centred consciously around the psychic then they [*the mental and vital parts of the being*] survive, otherwise they separate. The vital for instance survives for a time, then breaks up and dissolves into desires and fragmentary bits of vital personality. The mental is usually more lasting — but that too dissolves. It all depends on the person, how far he has developed his mind or vital or connected them with the psychic.

*

If one has had a strong spiritual development, that makes it easier to retain the developed mental or vital after death. But it is not absolutely necessary that the person should have been a Bhakta or a Jnani. One like Shelley or like Plato for instance could be said to have a developed mental being centred round the psychic — of the vital the same can hardly be said. Napoleon had a strong vital but not one organised round the psychic being.

*

What you suggest [*that certain forces from a past life or lives may "stick" to a person in the present life*] is true — that is to say when it is some past personality which or part of which is strongly carried over into the present life. It is, I believe, true that you were a revolutionary in a past life or if not a revolutionary, engaged in a violent political action. I can't put a name or a precise form on it. But it was not only the sudden angers and violences, but probably also the desire to help, to reform, to purify and other intensities and vehemences that came from there. When a personality is carried over like that it is not only the undesirable sides that are carried over but things that purified and chastened can be useful.

*

There is no such thing as an insuperable difficulty from past lives. There are formations that help and formations that hamper; the latter have to be dismissed and dissolved, not to be allowed to repeat themselves. The Mother told you that to explain the origin of this tendency and the necessity of getting rid of it —

there was no hint of any insuperable difficulty, quite the contrary.

*

For most people [*when they die*] the vital dissolves after a time as it is not sufficiently formed to be immortal. The soul descending makes a new vital formation suitable for the new life.

*

The physical always dissolves and in each new life one gets a new physical formation. To preserve the same physical would mean physical immortality.

*

Not *as* they are.[2] What remains and to what degree depends on the development in each case. Of course the centres themselves remain — for they are in the subtle body and it is from there that they act on the corresponding physical centres.

*

No, the subconscient is an instrument for the physical life and disappears [*after death*]. It is too incoherent to be an organised enduring existence.

Lines of Force and Consciousness

What is exactly your theory? There is one thing — influences — everybody undergoes influences, absorbs them or rejects, makes them disappear in one's own developed [*poetic*] style or else keeps them as constituent strands. There is another thing — lines of Force. In the universe there are many lines of Force on which various personalities or various achievements and formations spring up — e.g. the line Pericles – Caesar – Napoleon or the line Alexander – Jenghiz – Tamerlane – Napoleon — meeting together there — so it may be too in poetry, lines of poetic force prolonging themselves from one poet to another, meeting and

---

[2] *The disciple asked, "Do the centres remain as they are after death?"* — Ed.

diverging. Yours seems to be a third — a daemon or individual Spirit of Poetry migrating from one individual to another, several perhaps meeting together in one poet who gives them all a combined full expression. Is that it? If so, it is an interesting idea and arguable.

*

But after all it is a line of consciousness and not a personality that reincarnates; the personality is only for the one life, so it does not bind though it may influence at certain points the present life.

Beings of the Higher Planes

It is always possible for a being of the higher planes to take birth on earth — in that case they create a mind or vital for themselves or else they join a mind, vital and body which has already been prepared under their influence — there are indeed many ways and not one only in which they can manifest here.

*

As there are many personalities in a man in his various ordinary planes of consciousness, so also several beings can associate themselves with his consciousness as it develops afterwards — descending into his higher mind or other higher planes of being and connecting themselves with his personality. That is for the principle. But as for the particular information [*about a certain person*], it is inaccurate. It has probably reference to the period when Mother was bringing down beings to aid in the work.

Fragments of a Dead Person that Reincarnate

All human incarnations or births have naturally a psychic being. It is only other types like the vital beings that have not, and that is precisely the reason why they want to possess men and enjoy physical life without being themselves born here, for so they escape the psychic law of evolution and spiritual progress and change. But these formations [*the vital fragments of a dead person*] are different, they are things that do not leave the earth and do not possess but simply attach themselves to some human rebirth (of course with a psychic in it) which has some affinity and therefore does not object to or resist their inclusion.

*

The fragments [*of a dead person*] are not of the inner being (who goes on his way to the psychic world) but of his vital sheath which falls away after death. These can join for birth the vital of some other Jiva who is being born or they can be used by a vital being to enter a body in process of birth and partly possess it for the satisfaction of its propensities. The junction can also take place after birth.

Connections from Life to Life

There is a vital connection generally — the psychic is comparatively rare. It is something in past lives usually that determines these connections in this one, but the connection in this life is seldom the same as that of the past which determined it.

Lines of Sex in Rebirth

As far as I know, the births follow usually one line [*of sex*] or the other and do not alternate — that, I think, is the Indian tradition also, though there are purposeful exceptions like Shikhandi's. If there is a change of sex, it is only part of the being that associates itself with the change, not the central being.

*

Not sex exactly [*is present in the psychic being*], but what might be called the masculine and feminine principle. It is a difficult question [*whether a man can be reborn as a woman or a woman as a man*]. There are certain lines the reincarnation follows and so far as my experience goes and general experience goes, one follows usually a single line. But the alteration of sex cannot be declared impossible. There may be some who do alternate. The presence of feminine traits in a male does not necessarily indicate a past feminine birth — they may come in the general play of forces and their formations. There are besides qualities common to both sexes. Also a fragment of the psychological personality may have been associated with a birth not one's own. One can say of a certain person of the past, "That was not myself, but a fragment of my psychological personality was present in him." Rebirth is a complex affair and not so simple in its mechanism as in the popular idea.

*

All the instances I have heard of in the popular accounts of rebirth are of man becoming man and woman becoming woman in the next life — except when they become animal, but even then I think the male becomes a male animal and the female a female animal. There are only stray cases quoted like Shikhandi's in the Mahabharata for variations of sex. The Theosophist conception is full of raw imagination, one Theosophist even going so far as to say that if you are a man in this birth you are obliged to be a woman in the next and so on.

Asuric Births

Āsurīṣu[3] can't possibly mean "animal". The Gita uses precise terms and if it had meant animal it would have said animal and not Asuric. As for the punishment, it is that they [*Asuric men*] go down in their nature to more depths of Asurism till they touch bottom as it were. But that is a natural result of their uncontrolled tendencies which they freely indulge without any effort to rise out of them while by the cultivation of the higher side of personality one naturally rises and develops towards godhead or the Divine. In the Gita the Divine is regarded as the controller of the whole cosmic action through Nature, so the "I cast" is in

---

[3] Kṣipāmyajasram aśubhān āsurīṣveva yoniṣu. "*I cast down them continually into more and more Asuric births.*" Gita 16.19.

harmony with its ideas. The world is a mechanism of Nature, but a mechanism regulated by the presence of the Divine.

Animals and the Process of Rebirth

The soul in the animal evolves its manifestation to a point at which it can pass from the expression in animal to the expression in human consciousness.

*

It is when the vital gets broken up, some strong movements of it, desires, greeds, may precipitate themselves into animal forms, e.g., sexual desire with the part of the vital consciousness under its control into a dog or some habitual movement of excessive greed may carry part of the vital consciousness into a pig. The animals represent the vital consciousness with mind involved in the vital, so that it is naturally there that such things would gravitate for satisfaction.

*

Mūḍhayoniṣu or *adho gacchanti* [*in the Gita*] does not necessarily refer to animal birth, but it is true that there has been a general belief of that kind [*that a man may be born as an animal in his next birth*] not only in India but wherever "transmigration" or "metempsychosis" was believed in. Shakespeare is referring to Pythagoras' belief in transmigration when he speaks of the passage of somebody's grandmother into an animal. But the soul, the psychic being, once having reached the human consciousness cannot go back to the inferior animal consciousness any more than it can go back into a tree or an ephemeral insect. What is true is that some part of the vital energy or the formed instrumental consciousness or nature can and very frequently does so, if it is strongly attached to anything in the earth life. This may account for some cases of immediate rebirth with full memory in human forms also. Ordinarily it is only by Yogic development or by clairvoyance that the exact memory of past lives can be brought back.

Remembering Past Lives

Certainly, the subconscient is formed for this life only and is not carried with it by the soul from one life to another. The memory of past lives is not something that is active anywhere in the being — if by memory is meant the memory of details. That memory of details is quiescent and untraceable except in so far as certain constituent personalities taken over from the past retain the memories of the particular life in which they were manifest. E.g. if some personality that was put forth by one in Venice or Rome remembers from time to time a detail or details of what happened then. But usually it is only the essence of past lives that is activised in the being, not any particular memories. So it is impossible to say that the memory is located in a particular part of the consciousness or in a particular plane.

*

These ideas of past lives are not experiences, they are mental formations trying to give a name and form to something that is true, but you must not attach any importance to the forms the mind gives it. The truth is that there was a connection in past lives, but the forms given by the mind are likely to be mistaken.

*

It is not the ego, but the inner being that remembers the past lives — and the inner being as a rule is perfectly detached about them.

*

The different and contrasting phases through which you pass are obviously due to the emergence of different personalities in you created by past lives. One is full of the zest of life and its ardour, the other has the Nirvanic tendency and a certain incapacity for mastery over the physical existence. This is very self-evident and the putting of a name or a frame to the past lives in which these personalities were formed could hardly add anything of importance. If you yourself remembered the essence of them (not the details), then it might be of some use for your own consciousness in determining the limits of each influence in you and its place — but that can also be done well enough even without that remembrance.

Unimportance of Past-Life Experience in Yoga

These things (events etc.) [*of past lives*] are not known usually unless they come in some concentrated state of vision of themselves. The Mother nowadays seldom has these states because the whole concentration is on bringing down the supramental principle here. When that work is done then these things may come.

*

The Mother only speaks to people about their past births when she sees definitely some scene or memory of their past in concentration; but this happens rarely nowadays.

What is remembered mainly from past lives is the nature of the personality and the subtle results of the life-experience. Names, events, physical details are remembered only under exceptional circumstances and are of a very minor importance. When people try to remember these outward things, they usually build up a number of romantic imaginations which are not true.

I think you should dismiss this idea about the past lives. If the memory of past personalities comes of itself (without a name or mere outward details) that is sometimes important as giving a clue to something in the present development, but to know the nature of that personality and its share in the present constitution of the character is quite enough. The rest is of little use.

*

It is not of course indispensable to know [*about past lives*]. It is sometimes a matter of interest for knowing the lines of one's past development and how one has come to what one is now. But to overpass this outward development is of course the main aim of the Yoga. We are not to be tied by our past lives.

*

Too much importance must not be given to past lives. For the purpose of this Yoga one is what one is and, still more, what one will be. What one was has a minor importance.

Speculating about Past Lives

It is not necessary to attach any entire belief to these ideas of past births. X's idea of Y's rebirth is evidently a mere idea — nothing else.

When there is any truth in these things, it is most often a perception that some Force once represented in a certain person has also some part in one's own nature — not that the same personality is here.

Of course, there is rebirth, but to establish that one is such a one reborn, a deeper experience is necessary, not a mere mental intuition which may easily be an error.

*

Ideas of this kind about Vivekananda and Ramakrishna are ideas of the mind to which the vital strongly attaches itself — the truth of the past lives cannot be discovered in that way. These mental ideas are not true. You must wait for direct knowledge in a liberated nature before you can know who in past lives you were.

*

It is better not to think of past lives just now. The mind and vital would probably become active and weave things that are not true.

*

Seriously, these historical identifications are a perilous game and open a hundred doors to the play of imagination. Some may, in the nature of things must be true; but once people begin, they don't know where to stop. What is important is the lines, rather than the lives, the incarnation of Forces that explain what one now is — and, as for particular lives or rather personalities, those alone matter which are very definite in one and have powerfully contributed to what one is developing now. But it is not always possible to put a name upon these; for not one hundred-thousandth part of what has been has still a name preserved by human Time.

Traditional Indian Ideas about Rebirth and Other Worlds

The general Divine Will in the universe is for the progressive manifestation in the universe. But that is the general will — it admits the withdrawal of individual souls who are not ready to persevere in the world.

*

The escape from birth was a universal ideal at that time [*the time of the Gita*] except with one or two sects of the Shaivas, I believe. It is not at all consistent with the Divine taking many births, for the Gita speaks of the highest condition not as a *laya*, but as a dwelling in the Divine. If so there seems to be no reason why the *mukta* and *siddha* who has reached that dwelling in the consciousness of the Divine should fear rebirth and its troubles any more than the Divine does.

*

The Pitriyan is supposed to lead to inferior worlds attained by the Fathers who still belong to the evolution in the Ignorance. By the Devayan one gets beyond the Ignorance into the light. The difficulty about the Pitris is that in the Puranas they are taken as the Ancestors to whom the tarpan is given — it is an old Ancestor worship such as still exists in Japan, but in the Veda they seem to be the Fathers who have gone before and discovered the supraphysical worlds.

European Resistance to the Idea of Reincarnation

But that [*the idea of reincarnation*] is just what is disputed by the Western scientific mind or was up till yesterday and is still considered as unverifiable today. It is contended that the idea of self is an illusion — apart from the body. It is the experiences of the body that create the idea of a self and the desire to live prolongs itself illusorily in the notion that the self outlasts the body. The West is accustomed besides to the Christian idea that the self is created with the body — an idea which the Christians took over from the Jews who believed in God but not in immortality — so the Western mind is dead set against any idea of reincarnation. Even the religious used to believe that the soul was born in the body, God first making the body then breathing the soul into it (Prana?). It is difficult for Europeans to get over this past mental inheritance.

Section Four

Occult Knowledge and Powers

Chapter One
Occult Knowledge

Occultism and the Supraphysical

[*Occultism:*] The knowledge and right use of the hidden forces of Nature.

*

What did he himself [*Ramakrishna*] say about it—that it was the sins of his disciples which constituted the cancer. There is a physical aspect to things and there is an occult supraphysical aspect—one need not get in the way of the other. All physical things are the expression of the supraphysical. The existence of a body with physical instruments and processes does not, as the 19th century wrongly imagined, disprove the existence of a soul which uses the body even if it is also conditioned by it. Laws of Nature do not disprove the existence of God. The fact of a material world to which our instruments are accorded does not disprove the existence of less material worlds which certain subtler instruments can show to us.

Occult Forces

[*Occult forces:*] The forces that can only be known by going behind the veil of apparent phenomena—especially the forces of the subtle physical and supraphysical planes.

*

Nature-forces are conscious forces—they can very well combine all that is necessary for an action or a purpose and when one means fails, take another.

*

They [*general forces and impulses in the atmosphere*] are able to act with a greater force if they can make a special formation than by a general psychological action common to all human nature.

*

The forces are conscious. There are besides individualised beings who represent the forces or use them. The wall between consciousness and force, impersonality and personality becomes much thinner when one goes behind the veil of matter. If one looks at a working from the side of impersonal force one sees a force or energy at work acting for a purpose or with a result, if one looks from the side of being one sees a being possessing, guiding and using or else representative of and used by a conscious force as its instrument of specialised action and expression. You speak of the wave, but in modern science it has been found that if you look at the movement of energy, it appears on one side to be a wave and act as a wave, on the other as a mass of particles and to act as a mass of particles each acting in its own way. It is somewhat the same principle here.

*

The experience you had of something going out from the head like an arrow probably indicates something going out of the mental consciousness towards some aim or object. Sometimes it is a part of the mind-consciousness itself that goes like that either upward to a higher plane or somewhere in the world around — and afterwards returns. Sometimes it is a thought-force or a will-force. Forces are always going out from us without our knowing it even, and often they have some effect there. If we think of a person or a place and things happening there, something can go out like that to that person or place. If we have a will or strong mental desire that something should happen, a will-force may go out and try to make that happen. But also forces can go out from the inner mind without any conscious cause on the surface.

The Play of Forces

My experience shows me that human beings are less deliberate and responsible for their acts than the moralists, novelists and dramatists make them and I look rather to see what forces drove them than what the man himself may have seemed by inference to have intended or purposed — our inferences are often wrong and even when they are right touch only the surface of the matter.

*

All life is the play of universal forces. The individual gives a personal form to these universal forces. But he can choose whether he shall respond or not to the action of a particular force. Only most people do not really choose — they undergo the play of the forces. Your illnesses, depressions etc. are the repeated play of such forces. It is only when one can make oneself free of them that one can be the true person and have a true life — but one can be free only by living in the Divine.

*

Predestination and chance are words — words that obscure the truth by their extreme rigidity of definition. All is done through a play of forces which seems to be a play of different possibles, but there is Something that looks and selects and uses without being either blindly arbitrary (predestination) or capriciously decisive (chance).

*

There is no question of responsibility.[1] The "Something" does not act arbitrarily, paying no heed to the play of forces or the man's nature. "Selects" does not mean "selects at random". If a man puts himself on the side of or into the hands of the hostile influences and says, "This way I will go and no other. I want my ego, my greatness, my field of power and action", has not the Something the right to say, "I agree. Go and find it — if you can"? On the other hand, if the balance of forces is otherwise,

---

[1] *The correspondent wrote, in regard to the preceding letter: "If there is Something that looks, selects and uses our actions, then it is not the play of forces that is responsible for any action; the ultimate responsibility lies with this Something."*

less on one side, the selection may be the other way, the saving element being present, and determine another orientation. But to understand the working of this Cosmic Something one must see not only the few outward factors observed by the human eye, but the whole working with all its multitudinous details — that one cannot do unless one is oneself in the cosmic consciousness and with some opening at least to the Overmind.

There is no such thing as "free" will, but there is the power of the Purusha to say "yes" or "no" to any particular pressure of Prakriti and there is the power of the mind, vital etc. to echo feebly or strongly the Purusha's "yes" or "no" or to resist it. A constant (not a momentary) Yes or No has its effect in the play of the forces and the selection by the Something.

*

No, of course not [*helpful synchronicities are not just accidents*]. But they seem so to all who live in the outward vision only. "Coincidence the scientists do them call." But anyone with some intelligence and power of observation who lives more in an inward consciousness can see the play of invisible forces at every step which act on men and bring about events without their knowing about the instrumentation. The difference created by Yoga or by an inner consciousness — for there are people like Socrates who develop or have some inner awareness without Yoga — is that one becomes conscious of these invisible forces and can also consciously profit by them or use and direct them. That is all.

*

I have not said [*in the preceding letter*] that everything is rigidly predetermined. Play of forces does not mean that. What I said was that behind visible events in the world there is always a mass of invisible forces at work unknown to the outward minds of men and by Yoga (by going inward and establishing a conscious connection with the cosmic Self and Force and forces) one can become conscious of these forces, intervene consciously in the play, to some extent at least determine things in the result of the play. All that has nothing to do with predetermination. On the contrary one watches how things develop and gives a push here and a push there when possible or when needed. There is nothing in all that to contradict the dictum of the great scientist Sir C. V. Raman. Raman said once that all these scientific discoveries are only games of chance. Only, when he says these things are games of chance, he is merely saying that human beings don't know how it works out. It is not a rigid predetermination, but it is not a blind inconscient Chance either. It is a play in which there is a working out of possibilities in Time.

*

What X said is true, the play of the forces is very complex and one has to be conscious of them and, as it were, see and watch how they work before one can really understand why things happen as they do. All action is surrounded by a complexity of forces and if one puts a force for one of them to succeed, one must be careful to do it thoroughly and maintain it and not leave doors open for the other contrary ones to find their way in. I left at least two doors open and the forces that wanted him [*a sadhak*] here pushed in through them. As for what they were, it can only be said that it was probably a mixture. Each man is himself a field of many forces — some were working for his sadhana, some were working for his ego and desires. There are besides powers which seek to make a man an instrument for purposes not his own without his knowing it. All of these may combine to bring about a particular result. These forces work each for the fulfilment of its own drive — they need not be at all what we call hostile forces, — they are simply forces of Nature. It is not a fact however that hostile forces cannot bring a man here — e.g. when Y came back and wanted to enter the Asram, there was clearly a hostile force working that wanted to create trouble, but it was not strong enough to do it.

*

X's new consciousness makes him feel more strongly the opposite forces that one contacts when one moves in the world and has to do affairs and meet with others and he is afraid of a response in his vital which will upset his sadhana or create difficulties. Evidently he is a man who is psychically sensitive or has become so to that thing which you blindly refuse to recognise even when you are in the midst of it — the play of forces. You can feel your friend's atmosphere through the letter "so beautiful, so strengthening, so refreshing" and it has an immediate effect on you. But your mind stares like an owl and wonders, "What the hell can this be?" — I suppose, because your medical books never told you about it and how can things be true which are not known either to the ordinary mind or science? It is by an incursion of an opposite kind of forces that you fall into the Old Man's clutches, but you can only groan and cry, "What's this?" and when they are swept aside in a moment by other forces blink and mutter, "Well, that's funny!" Your friend can feel and know at once when he is being threatened by the opposite forces — and so he can be on his guard and resist Old Nick, because he can detect at once one of his principal means of attack.

*

It is this play of forces that is trying to bring about your removal to Burdwan and, if it succeeds, you have not to be troubled or shaken or disappointed, but to accept and make use of all that happens for your sadhana and progress. For the play of cosmic forces, the will in the cosmos — as one might say — does not always work apparently in favour of a smooth and direct line for the work or the sadhana, it often brings in what seem to be upheavals, sudden turns which break or deflect the line, opposing or upsetting circumstances or perplexing departures from what had been temporarily settled and established. The one thing is to preserve equanimity and make an opportunity and means of progress out of all that happens in the course of the life and the sadhana. There is a higher secret Will transcendent behind the play and will of the cosmic forces — a play which is always a mixture of things favourable and things adverse — and it is that Will which one must wait upon and have faith in; but you must not expect to be able always to understand its workings. The mind wants this or that to be done, the line once taken to be maintained, but what the mind wants is not at all always what is intended in a larger purpose. One has to follow indeed a fixed central aim in the sadhana and not deviate from it, but not to build on outward circumstances, conditions etc. as if they were fundamental things.

*

One can not only receive a force, but an impulse, thought or sensation. One may receive it from others, from beings in Nature or from Nature herself if she chooses to give her Force a ready-made form of that kind.

*

The force "created" is not yours — it is Prakriti's — your will sets it in motion, it does not really create it; but once set in motion, it tends to fulfil itself so far as the play of other forces will allow it. So, naturally, if you want to stop it, you have to set a contrary force in motion which will be strong enough to prevail against its momentum.

*

There is one cosmic Force working in all and a vibration of that Force or any one of its movements can awake (it does not always) the same vibration in another.

*

The play of forces can lead to nothing, if the One Force does not take them up and change them.

The Place of Occult Knowledge in Yoga

To know and use the subtle forces of the supraphysical planes is part of the Yoga.

*

You take a very utilitarian view of spiritual things. Whatever develops in the sadhana, provided it is genuine, has its place in the total experience and knowledge. A knowledge of the occult worlds and occult forces and phenomena has its place also. Visions and voices are only a small part of that vast realm of occult experience. As for utility, for one who has intelligence and discrimination, visions etc. have many uses — but very little use for those who have no discrimination or understanding.

*

Because a great number of people don't know how to use these [occult] faculties or misuse them or give them excessive value or nourish their ego by them, does it follow that the faculties themselves have no Yogic use or value?

*

Even by itself it [*the development of the occult faculties*] is a progress in the development of the consciousness though it may not carry with it any spiritualisation of the nature.

*

I do not know what you mean by practical sadhana. If one develops the occult faculty and the occult experience and knowledge, these things can be of great use, therefore practical. In themselves they are a proof of opening of the inner consciousness and also help to open it farther — though they are not indispensable for that.

*

He [*Ramana Maharshi*] discouraged his disciples [*from having any occult dealings*] because his aim was the realisation of the inner Self and the intuition — in other words the fullness of the spiritual Mind — visions and voices belong to the inner occult sense, therefore he did not want them to lay stress on it. I also discourage some from having any dealing with visions and voices because I see that they are being misled or in danger of being misled by false visions and false voices. That does not mean that visions and voices have no value.

*

People who have the occult faculty always tend to give too large a place to it.

Spiritism

About spiritism I think I can say this much for the present. It is quite possible for the dead or rather the departed — for they are not dead — who are still in regions near the earth to have communication with the living. Sometimes it happens automatically, sometimes by an effort at communication on one side of the curtain or the other. There is no impossibility of such communication by the means used by the spiritists; usually however genuine communications or a contact can only be with those who are yet in a world which is a sort of idealised replica of the earth-consciousness in which the same personality, ideas, memories persist that the person had here. But all that pretends to be communication with departed souls is not genuine, — especially when it is done through a paid professional medium. There is there an enormous amount of mixture of a very undesirable kind — for apart from the great mass of unconscious suggestions from the sitters or the contributions of the medium's subliminal consciousness one gets into contact with a world of beings which is of a very deceptive or self-deceptive illusory nature. Many of these come and claim to be the departed souls of relatives, acquaintances, well-known men, famous personalities etc. There are also beings who pick up the discarded feelings and memories of the dead and masquerade with them. There are a great number of beings who come to such séances only to play with the consciousness of men or exercise their powers through this contact with the earth and who dupe the mediums and sitters with their falsehoods, tricks and illusions. (I am supposing of course the case of mediums who are not themselves tricksters.) A contact with such a plane of spirits can be harmful (most mediums become nervously or morally unbalanced) and spiritually dangerous. Of course, all pretended communications with the famous dead of long-past times are in their very nature deceptive and most of those with the recent ones also — that is evident from the character of these communications. Through conscientious mediums one may get sound results (in the matter of the dead) but even these are very ignorant of the nature of the forces they are handling and have no discrimination which can guard them against trickery from the other side of the veil. Very little genuine knowledge of the nature of the after-life can be gathered from these séances; a true knowledge is more often gained by the experience of individuals who make serious contact or are able in one way or another to cross the border.

*

They [*mediums and clairvoyants*] are most of them in contact with the vital-physical or subtle physical worlds and do not receive anything higher at all.

*

Not much confidence can be placed in all that [*communications from spirit guides on other planes*]. If examined closely it will be seen that these spirit guides only suggest to their subjects what is in the mind of the sitter or sitters or in the air and it comes to very little. Influences from the other worlds there are of course and any number of them, but the central guidance is not of this kind except in very rare cases.

Séances

Automatic writings and spiritualistic séances are a very mixed affair. Part comes from the subconscious mind of the medium and part from that of the sitters. But it is not true that all can be accounted for by a dramatising imagination and memory. Sometimes there are things none present could know or remember; sometimes even, though that is rare, glimpses of the future. But usually these séances etc. put one into rapport with a very low world of vital beings and forces, themselves obscure, incoherent or tricky and it is dangerous to associate with them or to undergo any influence. Ouspensky and others must have gone through these experiments with too "mathematical" a mind, which was no doubt their safeguard but prevented them from coming to anything more than a surface intellectual view of their significance.

*

The psychic does not give up the mental and other sheaths (apart from the physical) immediately at death. It is said that it takes three years on the whole to get clear away from the zone of communicability with the earth — though there may be cases of slower or quicker passage. The psychic world does not communicate with earth — at any rate not in that way. And the ghost or spirit who turns up at séances is not the psychic being. What comes through the medium is a mixture of the medium's subconscient mind (using subconscient in the ordinary, not in the Yogic sense), that of the sitters, vital sheaths left by the departed or perhaps occupied or used by some "spirit", i.e. some vital being, the departed himself in his vital sheath or else something assumed for the occasion (but it is the vital part that communicates), elementals, spirits of the lowest vital physical world near earth, etc. etc. A horrible confusion for the most part — a hotch-potch of all sorts of things coming through a medium of "astral" grey light and shadow. Many communicants seem to be people who have just gone across into some subtle world where they feel surrounded by an improved edition of the earthly life and think that is the real and definitive other world after earth — but it is a mere optimistic prolongation of the ideas and images and associations of the human plane. Hence the next world as depicted by the spiritualist "guides" and other séance communicants.

Ghosts

What do you mean by a ghost? The word "ghost" as used in popular parlance covers an enormous number of distinct phenomena which have no necessary connection with each other. To name a few only —

(1) An actual contact with the soul of a departed human being housed in its subtle body and transcribed to our mind by the appearance of an image or the hearing of a voice.

(2) A mental formation stamped by the thoughts and feelings of a departed human being on the atmosphere of a place or locality, wandering about there or repeating itself — till that formation either exhausts itself or is dissolved by one means or another. This is the explanation of such phenomena as the haunted house in which the scenes attending or surrounding or preceding a murder are repeated over and over again and many similar phenomena.

(3) A being of the lower vital planes who has assumed the discarded vital sheath of a departed human being or a fragment of his vital personality and appears and acts in the form and perhaps with the surface thoughts and memories of that person.

(4) A being of the lower vital plane who by the medium of a living human being or by some other means or agency is able to materialise itself sufficiently so as to appear and act in a visible form or speak with an audible voice or, without so appearing, to move about material things, e.g. furniture or to materialise objects or to shift them from place to place. This accounts for what are called *poltergeists*, phenomena of stone-throwing, tree-inhabiting *bhūtas* and other well-known phenomena.

(5) Apparitions which are the formations of one's own mind but take to the senses an objective appearance.

(6) Temporary possession of people by vital beings who sometimes pretend to be departed relatives etc.

(7) Thought-images of themselves projected, often by people at the moment of death, which appear at that time or a few hours afterwards to their friends or relatives.

You will see that in only one of these cases, the first, can a soul be posited and there no difficulty arises.

Chapter Two
Occult Powers or Siddhis

General Remarks

The *aṣṭasiddhis* as obtained in the ordinary Yoga are vital powers or, as in the Rajayoga, mental siddhis. Usually they are uncertain in their application and precarious depending on the maintenance of the process by which they were attained.

*

It is certainly possible to have consciousness of things going on at a distance and to intervene.

The idea that true Yogins do not or ought not to use such powers, I regard as an ascetic superstition. I believe that all Yogins who have these powers do use them whenever they find that they are called on from within to do so. They may refrain if they think the use in a particular case is contrary to the Divine Will or see that preventing one evil may be opening the door to worse or for any other valid reason, or simply because it is outside the scope of their action, but not from any general prohibitory rule. What is forbidden to anyone with a strong spiritual sense is to be a miracle-monger, performing extraordinary things for show, for gain, for fame, out of vanity or pride. It is forbidden to use powers from mere vital motives, to make an Asuric ostentation of them or to turn them into a support for arrogance, conceit, ambition — or any other of the amiable weaknesses to which human nature is prone. It is because half-baked Yogins so often fall into these traps of the hostile forces that the use of Yogic powers is sometimes discouraged as harmful to the user. But it is mostly people who live much in the vital that so fall; with a strong and free and calm mind and a psychic awake and alive, such pettinesses are not likely to occur. As for those who can live in the true divine consciousness, certain powers are not "powers" at all in that sense, not, that is to say, supernatural or abnormal, but rather their normal way of seeing and acting, part of the consciousness — and how can they be forbidden or refuse to act according to their consciousness and its nature?

I suppose I have had myself an even more completely European education than you and I have had too my period of agnostic denial, but from the moment I looked at these things I could never take the attitude of doubt and disbelief which was for so long fashionable in Europe. Abnormal, otherwise supraphysical experiences and powers, occult or Yogic, have always seemed to me something perfectly natural and credible. Consciousness in its very nature could not be limited by the ordinary physical human-animal consciousness; it must have other ranges. Yogic or occult powers are no more supernatural or incredible than is supernatural or incredible the power to write a great poem or compose great music. Few people can do it, as things are, — not even one in a million; for poetry and music come from the inner being and to write or to compose true and great things one has to have the passage clear between the outer mind and something in the inner being. That is why you got the poetic power as soon as you began Yoga — Yoga-force made the passage clear. It is the same with Yogic consciousness and its powers; the thing is to get the passage clear, — for they are already there within you. Of course the first thing is to believe, aspire and, with the true urge within, make the endeavour.

*

It is not possible to put any credence in the stories about this Swami and Mahabhutan. It is possible that he has practised some kind of Tantric Yoga and obtained a few occult powers, but in all that you have said about him and in the printed papers there is no trace of any spiritual realisation or experience. All that he seems to think about is occult powers and feats of thaumaturgy. Those who take their stand on occult powers divorced from spiritual experience are not Yogis of a high plane of achievement. There are Yogis who behave as if they had no control over themselves — the theory is that they separate the spirit from the nature and live in the inner realisation leaving the nature to a disordered action "like a child, mad man, pisacha or inert object". There are others who deliberately use rough or violent speech to keep people at a distance or to test them. But the outbreak of rage of this Swami which you recount seems to have been simply an outburst of fury due to offended egoism. His judgment about Ramana Maharshi is absurd in the extreme.[1] As to his asking for the nail, hair etc. and his presenting of clothes or jumper, it was probably to establish a physical means of establishing an occult influence on you and your wife possibly by some Tantric or magic kriya — in Tibet such magic processes are well known and in common use.

*

There are many Yogins of the Vedantic school who follow both siddhis and the final emancipation — they would say, I suppose, that they take the siddhis on the way to Nirvana. The harmonisation is in the supermind — the Divine Truth at once static and dynamic, a withdrawal and extinction of the Ignorance, a re-creation in the Divine Knowledge.

*

I am unable to see why you should give up Yoga, because you cannot believe in the action of occult laws and forces or in siddhis. The object of Yoga is realisation of the Divine; these other things are side-matters which need be no part of spiritual experience, nor is belief in them necessary for realisation. Everyone has the right of private judgment in these matters; so you need not worry.

Occult Powers Not the Object of Our Yoga

Yes, the object of our Yoga is to establish direct contact with the Divine above and bring down the divine consciousness from above into all the centres. Occult powers belonging to the

---

[1] Absurd because the greatness of a Yogi does not depend at all on how long he lives or his state of health, but on the height or the depth of his spiritual realisation and experience.

mental, vital and subtle physical planes are not our object. One can have contact with various Divine Forms and Personalities on the way, but there is no need to establish them in the centres, though sometimes that happens automatically (as with the four Personalities of the Mother) for a time in the course of the sadhana. But it is not a rule to do so. Our Yoga is meant to be plastic and to allow all necessary workings of the Divine Power according to the nature, but these in the details may vary with each individual.

*

All these "experiments" of yours are founded upon the vital nature and the mind in connection with it; working on this foundation, there is no security against falsehood and fundamental error. No amount of powers (small or great) developing can be a surety against wandering from the Truth; and, if you allow pride and arrogance and ostentation of power to creep in and hold you, you will surely fall into error and into the power of rajasic Maya and Avidya. Our object is not to get powers, but to ascend towards the divine Truth-consciousness and bring its Truth down into the lower members. With the Truth all the necessary powers will come, not as one's own, but as the Divine's. The contact with the Truth cannot grow through rajasic mental and vital self-assertion, but only through psychic purity and surrender.

*

An activity on the astral plane in contact with the astral Forces attended by a leaving of the body is not a spiritual aim but belongs to the province of occultism. It is not a part of the aim of Yoga. Also fasting is not permissible in the Asram, as its practice is more often harmful than helpful to the spiritual endeavour.

This aim suggested to you seems to be part of a seeking for occult powers; such a seeking is looked on with disfavour for the most part by spiritual teachers in India because it belongs to the inferior planes and usually pushes the seeker on a path which may lead him very far from the Divine. Especially, a contact with the forces and beings of the astral (or, as we term it, the vital) plane is attended with great dangers. The beings of this plane are often hostile to the true aim of spiritual life and establish contact with the seeker and offer him powers and occult experiences only in order that they may lead him away from the spiritual path or else that they may establish their own control over him or take possession of him for their own purpose. Often, representing themselves as divine powers, they mislead, give erring suggestions and impulsions and pervert the inner life. Many are those who, attracted by these powers and beings of the vital plane, have ended in a definitive spiritual fall or in mental and physical perversion and disorder. One comes inevitably into contact with the vital plane and enters into it in the expansion of consciousness which results from an inner opening, but one ought never to put oneself into the hands of these beings and forces or allow oneself to be led by their suggestions and impulsions. This is one of the chief dangers of the spiritual life and to be on one's guard against it is a necessity for the seeker if he wishes to arrive at his goal. It is true that many supraphysical or supernormal powers come with the expansion of the consciousness in Yoga; to rise out of the body consciousness, to act by subtle means on the supraphysical planes etc. are natural activities for the Yogi. But these powers are not sought after, they come naturally, and they have not the astral character. Also, they have to be used on purely spiritual lines, that is by the Divine Will and the Divine Force, as an instrument, but never as an instrumentation of the forces and beings of the vital plane. To seek their aid for such powers is a great error.

Prolonged fasting may lead to an excitation of the nervous being which often brings vivid imaginations and hallucinations that are taken for true experiences; such fasting is frequently suggested by the vital Entities because it puts the consciousness into an unbalanced state which favours their designs. It is therefore discouraged here. The rule to be followed is that laid down by the Gita which says that "Yoga is not for one who eats too much or who does not eat"; a moderate use of food sufficient for the maintenance and health and strength of the body. There is no brotherhood of the kind you describe in India. There are Yogis who seek to acquire and practise occult powers but it is as individuals learning from an individual Master. Occult associations, lodges, brotherhoods for such a purpose as described by European occultists are not known in Asia.

As regards secrecy, a certain discretion or silence about the instructions of the Guru and one's own experiences is always advisable, but an absolute secrecy or making a mystery of these things is not. Once a Guru is chosen, nothing must be concealed from him. The suggestion of absolute secrecy is often a trick of the astral Powers to prevent the seeking for enlightenment and succour.

*

Ordinarily, all the more inward and all the abnormal psychological experiences are called psychic. I use the word psychic for the soul as distinguished from the mind and vital. All movements and experiences of the soul would in that sense be called psychic, those which rise from or directly touch the psychic being; where mind and vital predominate, the experience would be called psychological (surface or occult). "Spiritual" has nothing to do with the Absolute, except that the experience of the Absolute is spiritual. All contacts with self, the higher consciousness, the Divine above are spiritual. There are others that could not be so sharply classified and set off against each other.

The spiritual realisation is of primary importance and indispensable. I would consider it best to have the spiritual and psychic development first and have it with the same fullness before entering the occult regions. Those who enter the latter first may find their spiritual realisation much delayed — others fall into the mazy traps of the occult and do not come out in this life. Some no doubt can carry on both together, the occult and the spiritual, and make them help each other; but the process I suggest is the safer.

The governing factors for us must be the spirit and the psychic being united with the Divine — the occult laws and phenomena have to be known but only as an instrumentation, not as the governing principles. The occult is a vast field and complicated and not without its dangers. It need not be abandoned but it should not be given the first place.

*

You need not think about the occult Power. Let the Mother's consciousness grow in you and her Force work; occult powers are not indispensable, but if they are needed they will come in their proper time.

*

A sincere heart is worth all the extraordinary powers in the world.

Ethical Rules for the Use of Occult Powers

There are a number of rules, really of an ethical, not a spiritual nature, which are necessary for the very safety of the society itself — those, for instance, against an egoistic use of occult secrets; for if that were disregarded, there would be inevitably a clash with other formations on the same plane and consequent disaster.

Thought Reception and Thought Reading

About X's faculty of receiving the thoughts of others, — if this had been of the nature of thought reading, that is to say looking at the minds of others and seeing what is there, the remedy would have been simple; refusal to look would be enough and even the faculty might disappear by atrophy through long discontinuance. But if the thoughts of others come to her of themselves, it may be the psychic opening in her inner mind which it would be difficult to get rid of. If she could remain indifferent or push away these unwelcome visitors behind her and not think of them again, that would be one remedy; it might even be discouraged from coming after a time by this lack of reception. As for why it comes, it is not something that comes but something that is there, a faculty or a psychic habit of the nature — I use the word psychic in the popular sense, it has nothing to do with what I call the psychic being. If she practises Yoga and is able to make some considerable progress, then it would be possible for her to bar the door to these visitors. At the same time I might say that this power need not be a mere source of trouble; it can be helpful even: for it can give one who has acquired mastery over his own nature the knowledge of the thoughts and feelings around her and she can then help, guide, change what has to be changed in their minds so that they can become more effective for the divine work. I shall await what further you have to tell me about X's experiences before saying anything further about her entry into the field of Yoga.

Occult Powers and Health

Your generalisation cannot stand because it is contradicted by other numerous instances which go to prove the opposite. In my own experience I have found that those who possessed well developed and well organised "psychic" and occult powers were healthy and well poised; indeed they said that in ill health or physical weakness they could do nothing — it impaired their power. These certainly had no lack or deficiency of the red aura.

The woman you speak of was evidently under a vital Influence. A vital Influence always acts by disorganising the system and by disturbing the mental, vital or physical balance. But such cases of phenomena in the vital mind due to a possession or influence have no relation to the true mastery of psychic or occult powers (clairvoyance, clair-audience etc.).

Visions and experiences need not at all depend upon physical weakness or a pathological taint. It is not safe to judge from individual cases. The majority of those who have developed the faculty do not suffer from these defects. Those on the other hand who cannot keep their psychic experiences when in a robust state of health, lose them because then they get into a very external consciousness and feel at ease in it; but the true psychic does not depend for his experiences on disease.

The Power of Healing

I don't know whether I can throw any positive light on X's mystic experiences. The description, at any rate the latter part, is not very easy to follow as it is very allusive in its expressions and not always precise enough to be clear. The first part of the experience indicates a native power of healing of whose action she herself does not know the process. It seems from her account to come from something in herself which should be, from the terms she uses, a larger and higher and brighter and more powerful consciousness with which she is in occasional communion but in which she does not constantly live. On the other hand another sentence seems to point to a Godhead or Divine Presence and it would then be not so much within as above. The language later on would seem to indicate such a Presence giving commands to her to guide others so that they might grow in consciousness. But she distinctly speaks of it as a greater "me" standing behind a blue diamond force. We must fall back then on the idea of a greater consciousness very high up with a feeling of divinity, a sense of considerable light and spiritual authority — perhaps in one of those higher spiritual mental planes of which I speak in *The Life Divine* and the letters. The diamond light could well be native to these planes; it is usually white, but there it might well be blue: it is a light that dispels or drives away all impure things, especially a demoniac possession or the influence of some evil force. Evidently, the use of a power like this should be carefully guarded from the intrusion of any wrong element such as personal love of power, but that need not cause any apprehension as a keen inlook into oneself would be sufficient to reject it or keep it aloof. I think that is all I can say upon the data given in her letter.

*

It is difficult to say [*why Christ healed people*] — it looks from the Bible account as if he did it as a sign that he was one sent by the Divine with power.

Miracles

What do you mean by a miracle? What people call a miracle is only something done in a striking way by a process unknown to them which their minds cannot follow.

*

I have explained that there is no such thing as a miracle. If a higher consciousness opens a higher power in him, the sadhak has to use it as part of the new consciousness but in the right way, without egoism, selfishness, vanity or pride.

Magic

Jādu (magic) is a special practice which is done by professional magicians or those who learn the art of the magician, but it is no part of Yoga. What happens in Yoga is that sometimes or even very commonly certain powers develop in the sadhak by which he can influence others or make them do things or make things happen that he wants. This and other Yogic powers should never be used by the sadhak for egoistic purposes or to satisfy his vital desires. They can only be used when they become part of the realised divine consciousness by the Mother herself or at her command for good and unselfish purposes. There is no harm in Yogic powers that come naturally as a part of the new consciousness and are not used for a wrong personal purpose. For instance you see something in vision or dream and that happens afterwards in the waking state. Well, that is a Yogic power of prevision, knowing future things which often occurs as the consciousness grows; there is nothing wrong in its happening; it is part of the growth in sadhana. So with other powers. Only one must not get proud or boast or misuse the powers for the sake of desire, pride, power or the satisfaction of the ego.

*

By black magic is meant the occultism of the adverse powers — the occultism of the divine Powers is quite different. One is based on unity, the other on division.

Note on the Texts

Note on the Texts

LETTERS ON YOGA — I, the first of four volumes, contains letters in which Sri Aurobindo speaks about the foundations of his spiritual teaching and method of Yogic practice. The letters have been arranged in five parts dealing with five broad subject areas:

1. The Divine, the Cosmos and the Individual
2. The Parts of the Being and the Planes of Consciousness
3. The Evolutionary Process and the Supermind
4. Problems of Philosophy, Science, Religion and Society
5. Questions of Spiritual and Occult Knowledge

The letters in this volume have been selected from the extensive correspondence Sri Aurobindo carried on with his disciples and others between 1927 and 1950. Letters from this corpus appear in seven volumes of THE COMPLETE WORKS OF SRI AUROBINDO: *Letters on Poetry and Art* (Volume 27), *Letters on Yoga* (Volumes 28–31), *The Mother with Letters on the Mother* (Volume 32), and *Letters on Himself and the Ashram* (Volume 35). The titles of these works specify the nature of the letters included in the volumes, but there is some overlap. For example, a number of letters in the present volume are also published in *Letters on Himself and the Ashram*.

The Writing of the Letters

Between 1927 and 1950, Sri Aurobindo replied to hundreds of correspondents in tens of thousands of letters, some of them many pages in length, others only a few words long. Most of his replies, however, were sent to just a few dozen disciples, almost all of them resident members of his Ashram; of these disciples, about a dozen received more than half the replies. Sri Aurobindo wrote most of these letters between 1931 and 1937, the prime period of his correspondence. Letters before and after this period were written on a more restricted scale and confined to a few persons for special reasons.

Disciples in the Ashram wrote to Sri Aurobindo on loose sheets or sent him the notebooks in which they kept diaries as a record of their spiritual endeavour and a means of communicating with him. These notebooks and loose sheets reached Sri Aurobindo via an internal "post" once or twice a day. Letters from outside which his secretary thought he might like to see were sent at the same time. Correspondents wrote in English if they knew the language well enough, but a good number wrote in Bengali, Gujarati, Hindi or French, all of which Sri Aurobindo read fluently, or in other languages that were translated into English for him. The disciples usually addressed their letters to the Mother, since Sri Aurobindo had asked them to do so, but most assumed that he would answer them. He generally replied in the notebook or on the sheets sent by the correspondent, writing beneath the correspondent's remarks or in the margin or between the lines; sometimes, however, he wrote his reply on a separate sheet of paper. In some cases he had his secretary prepare a typed copy of his letter, which he revised before it was sent. For correspondents living outside the Ashram, Sri Aurobindo sometimes addressed his reply not to the correspondent but to his secretary, who quoted, paraphrased or translated the reply and signed the letter himself. In these indirect replies, Sri Aurobindo often referred to himself in the third person.

While going through Sri Aurobindo's letters, the reader should keep in mind that each letter was written to a specific person at a specific time, in specific circumstances and for a specific purpose. The subjects taken up arose in regard to the needs of the person. Sri Aurobindo varied the style and tone of his replies according to his relationship with the correspondent; to those with whom he was close, he sometimes employed humour, irony and even sarcasm.

Although written to specific recipients, these letters contain much of general interest, which justifies their inclusion in a volume destined for the general public. For the reasons mentioned above, however, the advice in them does not always apply equally to everyone. Aware of this, Sri Aurobindo himself made some cautionary remarks about the proper use of his letters:

I should like to say, in passing, that it is not always safe to apply practically to oneself what has been written for another. Each sadhak is a case by himself and one cannot always or often take a mental rule and apply it rigidly to all who are practising the Yoga.

The tendency to take what I lay down for one and apply it without discrimination to another is responsible for much misunderstanding. A general statement, too, true in itself, cannot be applied to everyone alike or applied now and immediately without consideration of condition or circumstance or person or time.

It is not a fact that all I write is meant equally for everybody. That assumes that everybody is alike and there is no difference between sadhak and sadhak. If it were so everybody would advance alike and have the same experiences and take the same time to progress by the same steps and stages. It is not so at all.[1]

The Typing and Revision of the Letters

Most of the shorter items in this volume, and many of the longer ones, were not typed or revised during Sri Aurobindo's lifetime and are reproduced here directly from his handwritten manuscripts. A good number of the letters, however, as mentioned above, were typed for Sri Aurobindo and revised by him before sending. Other letters were typed by the recipients for their own use or for circulation within the Ashram. At first, circulation of the letters was restricted to members of the Ashram and others whom Sri Aurobindo had accepted as disciples. When these letters were circulated, personal references were removed. Persons mentioned by Sri Aurobindo were indicated by their initials or by the letters X, Y, Z, etc. Copies of these typed letters were kept by Sri Aurobindo's secretary and sometimes presented to Sri Aurobindo for revision before publication. These typed copies sometimes contained errors, most of which were corrected by him while revising.

---

[1] First and third passages: *Letters on Himself and the Ashram*, volume 35 of THE COMPLETE WORKS OF SRI AUROBINDO, pp. 473 and 475. Second passage: *The Mother with Letters on the Mother*, volume 32, p. 349.

Sri Aurobindo's revision sometimes amounted merely to making minor changes here and there, sometimes to a complete rewriting of the letter. He generally removed personal references if this had not already been done by the typist. When necessary, he also rewrote the openings or other parts of the replies in order to free them from dependence on the correspondent's question. As a result, some of these letters have an impersonal tone and read more like brief essays than personal communications.

The Publication of the Letters

Around 1933, Sri Aurobindo's secretary Nolini Kanta Gupta began to compile selections from the growing body of letters in order to publish them. During Sri Aurobindo's lifetime, four small books of letters were published: *The Riddle of This World* (1933), *Lights on Yoga* (1935), *Bases of Yoga* (1936) and *More Lights on Yoga* (1948). Sri Aurobindo revised the typescripts of most of the letters in these books. During this revision, he continued the process of removing personal references. A letter he wrote in August 1937 alludes to his approach to the revision:

> I had no idea of the book being published as a collection of personal letters — if that were done, they would have to be published whole as such without a word of alteration. I understood the book was meant like the others [*i.e., like* Bases of Yoga, *etc.*] where only what was helpful for an understanding of things Yogic was kept with necessary alterations and modifications.... With that idea I have been not only omitting but recasting and adding freely. Otherwise as a book it would be too scrappy and random for public interest. In the other books things too personal were omitted — it seems to me the same rule must hold here — except very sparingly where unavoidable.

A number of letters not included in the four books mentioned above were published in the mid and late 1940s in several journals associated with the Ashram: *Sri Aurobindo Circle*, *Sri Aurobindo Mandir Annual*, *The Advent* and *Mother India*. Many letters in these journals were revised by Sri Aurobindo before publication.

Note on the Texts

By the mid-1940s a significant body of letters had been collected, typed and revised. In 1945 plans were made, with Sri Aurobindo's approval, to publish a collection of his letters. The work of compiling and editing these letters was done under his guidance. At that time, many typed or printed copies of letters, some revised, some not, were presented to Sri Aurobindo for approval or revision. The resulting material was arranged and published in a four-volume series entitled *Letters of Sri Aurobindo*. Series One appeared in 1947, Series Two and Three in 1949 and Series Four in 1951. The first, third and fourth series contained letters on Yoga, the third letters on poetry and literature. In 1958, most of these letters on Yoga, along with many additional ones, were published under the titles *On Yoga II: Tome One* and *On Yoga II: Tome Two*, as Volumes VI and VII of the Sri Aurobindo International Centre of Education collection. The first tome, with further additions, was reissued in 1969. In 1970 a new edition of the letters was published under the title *Letters on Yoga*; this edition contained many new letters not included in *On Yoga II*. The three volumes of the enlarged edition constituted volumes 22, 23 and 24 of the Sri Aurobindo Birth Centenary Library.

The present edition, also titled *Letters on Yoga*, incorporates the Centenary Library letters, but also contains a large number of letters that have come to light in the four decades between the two editions. One source of new letters is the correspondences of several disciples which were published in books after the Centenary Library edition had been issued. Govindbhai Patel's correspondence was published in 1974 in a book entitled *My Pilgrimage to the Spirit*; an enlarged edition appeared in 1977. Nagin Doshi's correspondence, *Guidance from Sri Aurobindo: Letters to a Young Disciple*, was brought out in three volumes in 1974, 1976 and 1987. *Nirodbaran's Correspondence with Sri Aurobindo* came out in two volumes in 1983 and 1984. Sahana Devi's correspondence came out in 1985 in a book entitled *At the Feet of Sri Aurobindo and the Mother*. Prithwi Singh's correspondence came out in 1988 as *Sri Aurobindo and the Mother to Prithwi Singh*. Dilip Kumar Roy's correspondence was issued in four volumes in 2003, 2005, 2007 and 2011 under the title *Sri Aurobindo to Dilip*. A second source of new material is individual letters and small collections of letters published in Ashram journals and elsewhere after the Centenary

Library had been issued. A third source is letters transcribed from manuscripts or from early typed copies. Many unpublished letters were discovered while reviewing correspondences long held by the Ashram; some of these had never been assessed to find letters for publication; others had been assessed, but relatively few letters were selected at the time. Additional letters were received by the Ashram upon the passing away of disciples. From the three sources mentioned above, many letters have been found that are worthy of publication. The present edition contains about one-third more letters than appear in the Centenary Library.

The Selection, Arrangement and Editing of the Letters

In compiling the present edition, all known manuscripts, typed copies or photographic copies of manuscripts and printed texts of letters were checked. From these sources, letters that seemed to be of general interest were selected. Electronic texts of the letters were then made and carefully checked at least twice against the handwritten, typed, photocopied, and printed versions of the texts.

The selected letters have been arranged according to subject and placed in the four volumes of the present edition. Each volume is divided and subdivided into parts, sections, chapters and groups with descriptive headings; each group, the lowest unit of division, contains one or more letters devoted to the specific subject of the group.

The present volume consists of about 1150 separate items, an "item" being defined as what is published between one heading or asterisk and another heading or asterisk. Many items correspond exactly to individual letters; a good number, however, contain only part of the individual letters; a small number consist of two or more letters (or parts of them) that were joined together by early typists or editors and then revised in that form by Sri Aurobindo.

Whenever possible, the letters are reproduced to their full extent. In some cases, however, portions of the letters have been omitted because they are not of general interest. A number of letters, for example, begin with personal remarks by Sri Aurobindo unrelated to the more substantial remarks which follow; these personal openings have often been removed. In some letters, Sri Aurobindo marked the transition from one part of a letter to another with a phrase such as "As to"; these transitional phrases have often been retained and stand at the beginning of abbreviated letters — that is, letters in which the first part of the letter has been omitted or placed elsewhere.

A number of letters, or portions of them, have been published in more than one volume of THE COMPLETE WORKS OF SRI AUROBINDO. Most of this doubling of letters occurs between *Letters on Yoga* and *Letters on Himself and the Ashram*. The form of these letters is not always the same in both places. In *Letters on Himself and the Ashram*, the manuscript version of a given letter has often been used because it contains Sri Aurobindo's remarks on himself or the Mother or members of the Ashram. These personal remarks, as noted above, were usually removed by Sri Aurobindo when he revised the letter for publication as a letter on Yoga. This revised form of the letter has generally been reproduced in *Letters on Yoga*. Thus, a number of letters are available both in their original form and their revised form.

As in previous collections of Sri Aurobindo's letters, the names of Ashram members and others have often been replaced by the letters X, Y, Z, etc. In any given letter, X stands for the first name replaced, Y for the second, Z for the third, A for the fourth, and so on. An X in a given letter has no necessary relation to an X in another letter. Names of Ashram members to whom Sri Aurobindo referred not as sadhaks but as holders of a certain position — notably Nolini Kanta Gupta in his position as Sri Aurobindo's secretary — are given in full. Sometimes the names of people who played a role in the history of the period are also given.

In his letters Sri Aurobindo sometimes wrote Sanskrit words in the devanagari script; these words have been transliterated into roman script in this edition. Words in Bengali script have likewise been transliterated. This policy is in accord with the practice followed in Sri Aurobindo's lifetime.

The reader may note that Sri Aurobindo almost always spelled the word "Asram" without an "h" in his manuscripts. Around 1945, due to failing eyesight, he began dictating most of his writings to his amanuensis Nirodbaran; Nirodbaran sometimes spelled the word without an "h", sometimes with one. In the present edition, the word is always spelled as it occurs in the manuscripts, both those of Sri

Aurobindo and of Nirodbaran. In headings and other editorial matter, the spelling "Ashram" has been used, since this is now the official spelling of the Sri Aurobindo Ashram.